# The University of Minnesota

## 1945–2000

*This history was sponsored by*

Office of the President
University of Minnesota Foundation
University of Minnesota Alumni Association
University of Minnesota Press

**History Advisory Committee**
Clarke Chambers, chair
David J. Berg
John Howe
Sally Gregory Kohlstedt
Paul G. Quie
Vernon W. Ruttan
Neil T. Storch

# The University of Minnesota 1945–2000

## STANFORD LEHMBERG
## ANN M. PFLAUM

MINNESOTA

University of Minnesota Press
Minneapolis • London

Published by the University of Minnesota Press
111 Third Avenue South, Suite 290
Minneapolis, MN 55401-2520
http://www.upress.umn.edu

Printed in the United States of America on acid-free paper

Library of Congress Cataloging-in-Publication Data

Lehmberg, Stanford E.
     The University of Minnesota, 1945–2000 / Stanford Lehmberg and Ann M.
  Pflaum.
         p.     cm.
     Includes bibliographical references and index.
     ISBN 0-8166-3255-3 (hard : alk. paper)
     1. University of Minnesota—History—20th century.   I. Pflaum, Ann M.
  II. Title.
  LD3350.L45 2001
  378.776'579—dc21                                            00-012206

To Professor Clarke Chambers, without whose
vision this volume would not have been
written and without whose interviews it would
lack freshness and vitality

# Contents

# Acknowledgments

THIS HISTORY OF THE UNIVERSITY owes its origins to the work of Clarke Chambers, a member of the history faculty since 1951. In the 1980s he and President Nils Hasselmo discussed the need for a study of the university covering the half-century from 1950 to 2000, picking up where James Gray left off in his history of the university from 1851 to 1951. Professor Chambers believed that the new history should be based in part on interviews with leading members of the faculty and others who had observed the institution at close hand, together with a wide range of primary written materials. By 1998 he had completed some 125 interviews—after his retirement in 1990 he devoted most of his time to the project—and it was clear that this oral history would form a major and unique part of the new volume. Most interviews lasted about two hours, although some were much longer and were conducted in several sessions. Their content is fascinating; the subjects generally described their own careers and analyzed changes in their departments and disciplines. All of these interviews were professionally transcribed by Beverly Hermes and Ann Westby. Both the tapes and the transcriptions have been deposited with the University Archives, where they are available to researchers. In 1998 and 1999, Ann Pflaum conducted additional interviews. We are grateful to those interviewed for granting permission to quote their comments. Quotations from interviews have been lightly edited; phrases or sentences occasionally have been deleted without indication. In general, however, we have not tried to smooth this material or make it conform to our own style. Its immediacy and freshness are part of its character and charm.

Although President Hasselmo hoped that Professor Chambers himself would write the history, he felt unable to do so. An advisory committee of senior faculty members was formed to consider the future of the project. The committee was chaired by Clarke Chambers, professor emeritus of history. Its members were David J. Berg, retired director of the Office of Management Planning and Information Services; John Howe, professor of history; Sally Gregory Kohlstedt, professor of the history of science and technology; Paul G. Quie, Regents Professor of Pediatrics; Vernon W. Ruttan, Regents Professor of Applied Economics; and Neil T. Storch, professor of history, University of Minnesota, Duluth. Their recommendation that Stanford Lehmberg and Ann Pflaum be asked to undertake the writing was approved by President Hasselmo in 1997. Lehmberg had been a member of the history department since 1969 and had served two terms as its chair, while Pflaum, then associate dean of the College of Continuing Education, had administrative experience in a variety of offices. Everyone agreed that the new volume should be a social and intellectual history, as well as an account of presidents and politics, and that it should be frank and honest, celebrating achievements but not glossing over difficulties that faced the institution. The authors were granted released time by the College of Liberal Arts, the provost for arts, science, and engineering, and the College of Continuing Education; they are grateful to Steven Rosenstone, W. Phillips Shively, Robert Bruininks, Harold Miller, and Gail Skinner-West for this support. Beverly Kaemmer, then acting director of the University of Minnesota Press, helped with contractual arrangements, as did the president's assistant Mario Bognanno. The president's office, the University of Minnesota Foundation, and the University of Minnesota Alumni Association made generous contributions toward the expenses of publication. In addition to those interviewed by Professor Chambers, a number of faculty members have contributed materials relating to their own fields of study, and some wrote short histories of their disciplines and departments for our use.

During the more than five decades encompassed by this history, the university grew greatly in size, welcomed a more diverse student body, and saw the number of women and men become approximately equal in almost all programs. University life in the 1940s and 1950s was shaped by the need to make space for returning veterans. In the late 1960s and early 1970s, Minnesota, like all institutions of higher education, faced the challenges of activism in civil rights, in anti–Vietnam War demonstrations, and in concern for the environment. Unlike what happened at a number of other public institutions, however, activism in Minnesota retained civility and a sense of dialogue, so that although the fabric of the community was strained, it was never rent. From the early 1970s through the end of the century, the university faced the challenge of economic setbacks, which led to a series of retrenchments and the resulting need to reallocate resources to programs and initiatives determined to have the highest priorities. Setting priorities is painful for any institution, but for Minnesota, because access to the university is held in extremely high regard, such choices were exceptionally difficult.

The picture that emerges from the interviews and other sources is remarkably consistent. We have found that in each of the decades, common themes were present. The first was the comprehensiveness of university programs. Ruth Eckert, professor of higher education and the first woman to be named a Regents Professor, had served as a senior staff member for the 1950 Minnesota Commission on Higher Education. As the author of the commission's report, she pointed out that a student might have entered the university nursery school at age three or four and continued on through graduate or professional studies three decades later.[1] Mechanical engineering professor Warren Ibele, who was dean of the Graduate School from 1975 to 1982, described another aspect of breadth:

> The range of scholarship that goes on at this place, all the way from A for agriculture to Z for zoology and everything in between, the Medical School and all the associated sciences, the College of Agriculture, the Institute of Technology, the College of Liberal Arts, the professional schools. Where else could you find that range of talent? Not that other institutions don't have spikes of excellence, but where do you get that comprehensiveness and breadth? Nowhere else in the world do you get that.[2]

The second theme was the role played by key academic leaders in building and maintaining excellence. In different disciplines and with different strategies, strong academic leaders fostered the growth of exceptional departments, balancing the multiple missions of teaching, research, and outreach. If there was a common approach, it was flexibility about boundaries and points of view.

The contribution of the university as generator of knowledge and economic development runs throughout as a third theme. The university's impact on the economy of the state has been based on agricultural research as well as innovations in technology, medical fields, and biotechnology. More than three thousand new companies have been created by university graduates. Minnesota alumni and faculty were responsible for inventions and discoveries such as Era wheat, the battery-powered pacemaker, taconite processing, the pressure-sensing device on jet engines, the "black box" flight recorder, and a retractable seat belt used in automobiles.

A fourth theme was size—the large number of students, faculty, and staff—and remarkable geographical outreach into all regions of the state. The university had just under 12,000 students in 1945, while in fall of 1999 systemwide enrollment was over 51,000, and there were about 370,000 living alumni. In 1945 the university had approximately 4,000 faculty and staff members; by 1998 there were over 17,000. In addition to its campuses—in the Twin Cities, Duluth, Crookston, Morris, and Rochester—the university had a presence in each of the counties of the state through its extension offices. Other university facilities included the Hormel Institute in Austin, the Lake Itasca Forestry and Biological Station, the Cloquet Forestry Station, Cedar Creek Natural History Center near Bethel, the Horticultural Research Center at Excelsior, the Minnesota Landscape Arboretum near Chanhassen, the Supercomputer Institute in Minneapolis, Sand Plain Research Farm at Becker, and the Soudan Underground Research Site. The university operated agricultural experimental stations (renamed Research and Outreach Centers in 1999) at Rosemount, Crookston, Grand Rapids, Morris, Lamberton, and Waseca.

The most pervasive theme that emerged was the impact of the university both as a symbol of educational opportunity and as a set of experiences that have transformed and enhanced the lives of students and faculty members. From students such as Garrison Keillor, Arvonne Fraser, Betty Ann Whitbeck, and Toja Okoh, from faculty members like John Wright, Sherwood Berg, and Sara Evans came varied accounts of the imprint of the university on their lives. No two stories were the same, but threading through each was a sense of gratitude and awe at the university's influence.

In a project of this magnitude, we have been assisted by many individuals in the colleges, departments, and administrative units on all the university's campuses. We regret that space considerations have made it impossible for us to include all the interesting information we have been given. Douglas Catterall, who completed his doctorate in history with Professor Lehmberg while the book was in progress, served effectively as a research assistant. Caitlin Fashbaugh and Tonya Cromey did fact-checking and proofreading. University archivist Penelope Krosch and her associates Lois Hendrickson and Karen Klinkenberg offered unfailing cooperation; Hendrickson's help in selecting illustrations was invaluable. Sharon Collison and Thomas Gilson of the Office of Institutional Research and Reporting provided crucial assistance and information for the appendixes. Our collaborators are too numerous to list here, but all deserve our gratitude. We offer special thanks to Clarke Chambers, David Berg, Andrea Hinding, Cherie Perlmutter, and Beverly Kaemmer, who reviewed the work as it was under way and offered valuable suggestions and corrections. They have been a continuing source of support and counsel.

*Acknowledgments*

We are conscious that this book touches only briefly on the topics addressed. For this reason, we seek to lead readers to additional sources through our notes. We end with particular thanks to the more than two hundred individuals who have shared with us their impressions and recollections of the university.

Stanford Lehmberg
Ann M. Pflaum

# Introduction

IN 1954, journalist Eric Sevareid, himself a graduate of the University of Minnesota, wrote this description of his alma mater:

> Even the citizens of the state think there are only three great cities in Minnesota—Minneapolis, St. Paul, and Duluth. But there are four, and the fourth is the University of Minnesota.... It is a miniature of American life, faithfully accommodating the taxpayers of the state in all their ideas of what their children and their civilization should grow up to be.... I know of no state university which belongs so unquestionably to the state, none which the people of the state so instinctively regard as part of their individual and corporate lives.... It feeds back into the state at least as much as it receives. From Lake of the Woods to Montevideo you will find its general extension courses, its branch schools of agriculture; you will find University staff working as county farm agents, home demonstration agents, consulting on local health and sanitation, organizing the techniques of community recreation.... No one will ever be able to calculate the number of state citizens...—as well as men and women everywhere—[who have] benefited by its fabulous range of research into cancer, polio, heart disease, into the secrets of iron ore or cheese, supersonics or atomic fission.[1]

The university had been founded in 1851, before the territory of Minnesota achieved statehood. The University of Minnesota shared such precedence with only a few other institutions, the University of Michigan among them. It is sometimes argued that this constitutional autonomy implied an unusual degree of independence for universities founded before the establishment of their respective state legislatures.

The university was not the only beneficiary of Minnesota's strong belief in the importance of higher learning. It is remarkable that in a state with fewer than two million people, five other public institutions—including the predecessors of Winona State University, Mankato State University, Moorhead State University, and St. Cloud State University—had been founded. The Duluth State Teachers College, which became part of the University of Minnesota in 1947, had been founded in 1896. Among private colleges founded during the nineteenth century were Hamline, St. John's, Gustavus Adolphus, Augsburg, St. Olaf, Carleton, Macalester, St. Thomas, and Concordia College in St. Paul and Moorhead.

The University of Minnesota was unusual in other ways as well. Among research institutions, it had remarkable breadth, offering programs in virtually all fields. The research tradition grew out of the vision of founding president William Watts Folwell (1869–84). Like his fellow New York State native Ezra Cornell, Folwell believed that a university should be "an institution in which any person can find instruction in any subject."[2] Folwell's successor, Cyrus Northrop (1884–1911), was able to implement this inspiration. By the end of Northrop's presidency, the university included the College of Science, Literature, and the Arts; the School of Engineering; the College of Agriculture, with experimental sites at Crookston and Grand Rapids; the schools of Law, Medicine, Dentistry, Nursing, and Pharmacy; and the College of Education. Research as well as instruction was pursued in all of these areas.

In addition to being a research university, Minnesota was a land-grant institution, benefiting from the genius of Justin Morrill, a congressman from Vermont who conceived the idea of setting aside public lands for the benefit of colleges dedicated to "such branches of learning as are related to agriculture and the mechanic arts."[3] Although Morrill's first bill was vetoed by President Buchanan in 1859, the congressman persisted; his measure finally passed in 1862. It gave Minnesota, like the other states, thirty thousand acres for each of its members of Congress: a total of one hundred twenty thousand acres, since Minnesota had two senators and two representatives. In most states, new "A & M" universities were established, thus creating such institutions as Iowa State, Kansas State, and Michigan State. Minnesota, however, was reluctant to create a second school. Largely through the influence of John Sargent Pillsbury, a regent and a state senator, the university added the land-grant mission to its responsibilities.

The land-grant tradition encouraged applied studies, outreach, and service to meet the state's needs, evoking strong citizen loyalty; in return, the land-grant institutions encouraged research and outreach programs to meet the needs of their states. During the post–World War II years, a number of the land-grant universities—and in this Minnesota was among the leaders—broadened their focus to include international exchanges and outreach. In a speech given shortly after he retired following fifteen years as president of the University of Minnesota, James Morrill noted that "more than any other group of American universities, the land-grant institutions have been present-day pioneers on the international frontier. They have sent more of their professors to underdeveloped countries than any other group."[4]

A third unique aspect lay in the university's urban setting, close to the heart of the Twin Cities of Minneapolis and St. Paul, the state's principal metropolitan area and the focus of its commerce and politics. By contrast, most other Big Ten universities were in communities like Ann Arbor or Madison or Champaign-Urbana, some distance from their state's largest cities. In an urban setting, students profited from the presence of orchestras, theaters, art galleries, and other cultural institutions; the Twin Cities, in turn, benefited from interaction with the academy. Many students had the advantages of being able to live at home while attending the university and to obtain part-time employment to finance their studies.

The university was well served by the presidents who followed Northrop. The six-year administration of the third president, George Edward Vincent (1911–17), brought enhanced academic strengths and more efficient administrative systems. A summer session regularized instruction for teachers; two extension divisions (agricultural extension, founded in 1909, and general extension, established in 1913) increased the university's outreach. Under Dean Guy Stanton Ford, a prominent historian who later became president of the university, the Graduate School reached a new level of distinction. By the end of the Vincent era, Minnesota's status as a leading research university was secure.

The next four presidents were Marion Le Roy Burton (1917–20), Lotus Delta Coffman (1920–38), Guy Stanton Ford (1938–41), and Walter C. Coffey (1941–45). Wartime conditions colored the terms of Burton, Ford, and Coffey. The 1920s and the Depression years of Coffman's presidency were noted for educational experiments combining (in Coffman's words) "social vision" and "effective individualism." "The University," he wrote, was "dedicated to the making of a better world to live in."[5] In the Coffman era, the university built Northrop Auditorium, established the Nolte Center for Continuation Study as the country's first campus-based conference center, and began a Minnesota tradition of student counseling developed by faculty members in educational psychology. The School of Business was established, and the university enjoyed a golden era of football under Coach Bernie Bierman. Coffman's name was given to the student union, the construction of which began shortly before his death. James Lewis Morrill, chosen to succeed Coffey in 1945, faced substantial challenges as he led the university into a new postwar era.

# Chapter 1

## The University at the End of World War II, 1945–1959

Research is the highest undeveloped potential of the University.

*—James L. Morrill, inaugural address, 1946*

ON NOVEMBER 13, 1944, the United States was still fighting in World War II. On that date, James Lewis Morrill, president of the University of Wyoming, sent a telegram to the chair of the University of Minnesota Board of Regents, Fred B. Snyder, accepting the office of president. Morrill was to assume his new duties as the eighth president on July 1, 1945. Ten weeks prior to Morrill's arrival to take up his office at Minnesota, Franklin Roosevelt died. Almost immediately, Roosevelt's successor, Harry Truman, was presented with perhaps the most critical decision any U.S. president ever faced—whether to authorize the use of the atomic bomb. Believing that the new weapon would hasten the end of the war in the Pacific, prevent an island-by-island assault, and save many lives, Truman gave his approval; atomic bombs were dropped on Hiroshima and Nagasaki on August 6 and 8.

American universities, including the University of Minnesota, had shared in the scientific breakthroughs that ushered in the atomic age. Four of the scientists prominent in the race to develop atomic weapons ahead of Germany—Ernest O. Lawrence, Merle Tuve, John H. Williams, and Alfred O. C. Nier—had Minnesota connections. Ernest Lawrence was the son of a superintendent of schools and teachers college president from South Dakota. He studied at the University of South Dakota and the University of Minnesota, and subsequently at Chicago and Yale. Lawrence had drawn his chief inspiration from William Francis Gray Swann, an Englishman with whom he studied at Minnesota. Working at Berkeley beginning in the late 1920s, Lawrence helped develop the high-energy accelerators necessary for nuclear studies; his thirty-seven-inch cyclotron, completed in 1937, won him a Nobel Prize. Lawrence's Minnesota classmate Merle Tuve, another protégé of Swann's, worked at the Carnegie Institution on similar problems.[1] John Williams, a member of the physics department at Minnesota, was one of the first scientists recruited to work in the top-secret national laboratories at Los Alamos, New Mexico.

Alfred Nier had earned B.S. and Ph.D. degrees at Minnesota. In 1942 he was an associate professor of physics and actively involved in government-sponsored research. Writer Stephane Groueff described him as "a kind of Stradivarius of scientific instruments":

> Al Nier had his fingers in nearly every pie of the Manhattan Project. Besides all the analyses and measurements, he was attempting isotope separation. . . . In his free moments he was also making trips to Berkeley to help Lawrence with his electromagnetic process. . . . When it came to building ultra-sensitive mass spectrometers and applying them to various analytical techniques, Nier was a true virtuoso. . . . Nier's most important contribution was the first separation of small amounts of Uranium-235 in 1940.[2]

Nier himself described the events surrounding his success in identifying uranium 235:

> A new instrument was built in about 10 days in February, 1940. Our glass blower built the horseshoe-shaped mass spectrometer tube for me. I made the metal parts myself. As a source of uranium, I used the less volatile uranium tetrachloride and tetrabromide left over from Harvard experiments. The first separation of U-235 and U-238 was actually accomplished on February 28 and 29, 1940. It was a leap year, and on Friday afternoon, February 29, I pasted the little samples on the margin of a handwritten letter and delivered them to the Minneapolis Post Office at about six o'clock. The letter was sent by airmail special delivery and arrived at Columbia University on Saturday. I was aroused early Sunday morning by a long-distance telephone call from John Dunning [who had worked through the night bombarding the samples with neutrons from the Columbia cyclotron]. The Columbia test of the samples clearly showed that U-235 was responsible for the slow neutron fission of uranium.[3]

Another physicist, John Tate, was recognized for his work on submarine detection. Bryce Crawford of the Department of Physical Chemistry was honored for research in the development of rocket fuels, carried out by a group of twenty scientists under his leadership.[4] In April 1948, I. M. Kolthoff and E. J. Meehan announced a new procedure for manufacturing synthetic rubber.[5] Kolthoff, internationally recognized for pioneering work in analytical chemistry and for wartime research with Meehan on methods of producing synthetic rubber, had come to the University of Minnesota in 1927 from the University of Utrecht.[6]

During the cold war, watching messages flashing from *Sputnik* to earth, university faculty members Dwain W. Warner of the Bell Museum of Natural History, Otto Schmitt of zoology, and Homer Mantis of physics, assisted by engineer Larry B. Kuechle of the Bell Museum, decided to see if they could develop a technology that would allow them to monitor animals in the wild. An electronic telemetry technology, initially developed at the university's Cedar Creek Natural History Center, located on five thousand acres in Anoka and Isanti Counties, was subsequently used throughout the world. Telemetry investigations were carried out subsequently under the direction of Dwain Warner and ecology professor John Tester.

More than eight hundred faculty members and civil service employees were granted leave from the university for military service.[7] A committee on medical research of the federal Office of Scientific Research and Development recognized the contributions of fourteen faculty and staff members in August 1946.[8] Plant pathologist Clyde Christensen was praised for creating a better strain of the penicillin fungus.[9] In June 1945, General Hospital 26, a military hospital staffed by University of Minnesota Hospitals personnel, received a Meritorious Unit Service award for its work in North Africa and Italy. The longest-serving general hospital in the Mediterranean, it had cared for some eight thousand patients.[10]

University women also contributed to the war effort. Through legislation advocated by Representative Frances Bolton of Ohio, a new branch of the armed services, the United States Cadet Nurse Corps, was established to make it possible for women "to serve at the sides of their brothers in the army and the navy." The University of Minnesota's Cadet Nurse program trained more nurses than any other program in the country. At the November 1943 football game between Minnesota and Iowa, President Walter Coffey (Morrill's predecessor) led the director of nursing, Katharine J. Densford, and nurse cadet Jeanne Larkin to the center of the field during halftime. Coffey then read a telegram from the United States surgeon general to the School of Nursing offering thanks "for the magnificent effort it is making toward winning the war." Fifty-five thousand fans present in Memorial Stadium as well as thousands listening to the game on national radio heard the tribute.[11]

The postwar years saw heady enrollments in collegiate programs in Minneapolis and St. Paul. Enrollment jumped in a single year from just under

12,000 in 1945 to more than 27,000 in 1946. More than twenty-eight buildings were built on the Twin Cities campus. Seventy-five hundred acres were acquired for the Rosemount Experiment and Research Station, the site of land appropriated by the federal government during the war for a munitions plant. Duluth State Teachers College became a part of the university in 1947 and was to take the first steps in its evolution to become a major regional university.[12]

As impressive as size and numbers was reputation. The College of Science, Literature, and the Arts was strong, with a number of faculty members of international repute. During the postwar years, the university maintained and built great departments. Although the circumstances and details differed from department to department, one common theme during these years was a transition from a pattern of reliance on a single powerful academic head or chair to broader participation in decision making.

University outreach was very much a fact of life in Minnesota. Students enrolled in four residential precollegiate schools of agriculture. The rigorous high school curricula of these schools were based on six months in residence at the schools and six months at home carrying out field and home projects. The schools, located in St. Paul, Crookston, Morris, and Grand Rapids, with a fifth added in Waseca in 1953, enrolled just under 2,000 students.[13] In addition, University High School had 356 students and the nursery school 157 students. Agricultural short courses were offered through extension agents in each of Minnesota's eighty-seven counties. Among the offerings were the dairy day conference, the farm help training session, swine feeders' day, and 4-H club activities. These programs and short courses reached close to 7,000 people in 1945. That same year, the General Extension Division had 21,000 registrations, about half in classes offered in the late afternoon or evening, taught predominantly by University faculty members, and in correspondence courses reaching students in every county. Over 3,000 professionals enrolled in courses offered through the Center for Continuation Study. Collectively, the noncollegiate programs reached more than 30,000 people.[14]

The postwar years were a time of increased research, helped in considerable measure by the availability of federal funds. In 1940–41, research expenditures were $485,000; by 1945–46, they had risen to $1.1 million, and by 1950–51 to just over $4 million. In 1940–41, the federal contribution was 30 percent of research expenditures; by 1950–51, federal dollars were funding 60 percent of research expenditures. By 1960, Morrill's last year as president, federal funding accounted for 71 percent of the total, just over

$15 million.[15] New fields of study were developed, and faculty members were called upon to advise in a range of research and public service projects: agricultural policies, the rebuilding of Seoul National University, social policy to rebuild Germany and Japan.

In some ways, Morrill was an unlikely person to have been president of the University of Minnesota: he was not a scientist at a time when science was emerging as a major international priority for research universities. He had studied classics at Ohio State, but did not have a Ph.D. His expertise was as an administrator rather than as a scholar. From 1913 to 1919 he was a journalist, becoming managing editor of the *Cleveland Press.* In 1919 he returned to Ohio State as alumni secretary and editor of the alumni magazine, and subsequently became one of its first vice presidents. Morrill was later named as president of the University of Wyoming.[16]

Despite his atypical credentials, Morrill served as president at Minnesota for fifteen years, longer than any other postwar president in the second half of the twentieth century. Moreover, he faced and surmounted with remarkable success a series of challenges. Some were simple and direct, requiring immediate action—finding space for returning veterans, for example. Others, such as maintaining and building great departments with their multiple missions of teaching, research, and outreach, were more indirect. He once observed that "it . . . takes some doing to maintain a great university."[17]

Morrill's inauguration, which occurred ten months after he took office, on April 25, 1946, represented a coming of age for the university. Never before had a University of Minnesota inauguration attracted as many delegates of national eminence. Never before had the themes of research and the national and international role of the university been presented so emphatically. Morrill was the first University of Minnesota president to explore the potential of research to change the world. The published proceedings of the conference held as part of the inaugural festivities, *The Crisis of Mankind: The Urgent Educational Tasks of the University in Our Time,* suggested that the major research universities were prepared to take on a larger role than had been the case previously.[18] Among the panelists were two university presidents, James Bryant Conant of Harvard and Fred Hovde of Purdue. Hovde was a University of Minnesota alumnus, an athlete, active as an early leader in the General College. Other presenters were scientists, ministers, and public officials.

Delegates from three hundred universities and ninety learned societies participated in the inauguration. Among the themes in his inaugural address, Morrill emphasized the importance of research, describing it as "the highest undeveloped potential of the University." His language reflected the influence of the atomic era: "Research is a chain reaction—releasing endless energy, cultural, social, and economic. . . . Research is the tested instrument of change and advance."[19]

During the postwar years, a number of Minnesota faculty members took on public service assignments, backing the idealism of the inauguration with action. A few examples illustrate Minnesota's impact in postwar rebuilding. Harold Deutsch (history) served as an adviser to the military in the Nuremberg Trials. Harold Quigley (political science) was director of research and analysis for the Civil Intelligence Section of the U.S. Department of State in Japan; his job was to develop background materials for General Douglas MacArthur, who was in charge of rebuilding the country.[20] In 1951, Gisela Konopka (social work) was designated by the U.S. State Department to serve as a consultant and lecturer on child welfare services for faculties of social work in Germany. Sherwood O. Berg, who was to be dean of the Institute of Agriculture, Forestry, and Home Economics from 1963 to 1973, worked as agricultural attaché in Yugoslavia (1951–54) and in Denmark and Norway (1954–57). Gerald McKay, College of Agriculture audiovisual specialist, spent a year and a half in Western Europe during the 1950s assisting agricultural colleges with information projects.[21]

## The Student Experience

Under President Morrill's leadership, the university faced a deluge of students who sought higher education after their war service. Enrollment had declined to just under 9,900 civilian students in 1943 (there were also about 1,200 in ROTC and other military training programs on the Twin Cities campus) but began to explode in 1945 with the return of veterans. The fall head count was 11,872 in 1945; it jumped to an amazing 27,982 in 1946, then fell back slightly to 22,637 in 1950.[22]

The G.I. Bill (technically the Servicemen's Readjustment Act of 1944) offered veterans five hundred dollars for tuition, free textbooks, and a living allowance of fifty dollars a month for single people and seventy-five dollars for married veterans. The G.I. Bill made college education possible for students from all walks of life, including students from poor families with no tradition of higher education. By 1965, throughout the United States, more than 2 million veterans of World War II and the Korean War had gained access to higher education.

The University of Minnesota had one of the largest veteran populations in the country. In all, it enrolled about 25,000 World War II veterans and, later, 10,000 veterans of the Korean War.[23] A number of persons who subsequently became members of the faculty were beneficiaries of the G.I. Bill; among them were Hyman Berman (history), Clarke Chambers (history), David "Dan" Cooperman (sociology), Walter Heller (economics), Warren MacKenzie (studio arts), Phillip Raup (agricultural economics), Maynard Reynolds (education), John Turner (political science), and Bernard Youngquist (experiment station).[24] Looking back over his long career as a University statistician and administrator, David Berg described the G.I. Bill as an outstanding example of a student aid program that "worked remarkably well."[25]

Of the more than 27,000 students enrolled at the university in the fall of 1946, 18,929 were veterans. Approximately 2,800 were graduate students. More than 90 percent of the students were Minnesotans. Data for 1947–48 showed that while most of the colleges reflected the heavy predominance of in-state students, the Graduate School was an exception. In the General College, 99 percent of the students were from Minnesota; in the Graduate School, the figure was 54 percent.[26]

A major concern during Morrill's early years as president was the increasing number of students. The university struggled to provide makeshift facilities for this throng. Minnesota was one of the first of the major public research universities to make plans to accommodate returning veterans. A Bureau of Veterans Affairs was established in the office of the dean of students to deal with books and supplies, records and reports, and advising and counseling.[27] Although classroom space was scarce, student housing was an even more critical issue. As early as 1945, President Morrill prepared a report on the problem of living accommodations, emphasizing "the distressing plight of the married veterans of the war just ended." Only emergency measures could prevent "hundreds, perhaps thousands, of Minnesota veterans [from being] driven outside the state to secure educational opportunity—although the educational facilities are here, generously provided by the state and never intended to be denied them." He added:

> Sometimes the statement is heard that "too many people are going to college." It is safe to say that those who so speak are always thinking of the children of someone else, never their own. Sometimes the remark is heard, "the University of Minnesota is already too large." . . . Too large for what? . . . Size is

a necessary measure of adequate library and laboratory facilities. Size does offer the guaranty of lower unit costs. Size, in a university, does provide a vastly wider range of professional training and opportunity. Size is one test of success. Size, in response to growing public need, is a proof of public service. It is a demonstration of democracy in education, and the proportion of high school graduates attending college in America will continue to increase.[28]

Evidence collected by E. G. Williamson, dean of students, included some heartrending stories. One student said, "I am badly in need of an apartment. I have been separated from my family for three years due to the war and want very much to live with my wife and child as soon as housing permits." Another veteran stated, "I went from apartment house to apartment house in search of a vacancy—without luck. I also put 'ads' in the paper and no results there. As a result, my wife and baby are living with my parents in South Dakota."[29]

Several emergency programs were put into effect. Barracks-style housing created in Memorial Stadium remained in use until 1949. Both men's and women's dormitories were "double-decked," so that Pioneer Hall accommodated 940 single men rather than the normal 536, while Comstock and Sanford Halls together housed 661 single women rather than 521. The most important project, University Village, began in 1946 as a row of trailers along Como Avenue. Intended to house the families of veterans, the trailers, Quonset huts, and metal barracks were originally owned by the federal government; title was transferred to the university in 1948. Hubert Humphrey, then mayor of Minneapolis, assisted in acquiring playground space donated by the manufacturer Minneapolis Moline. By 1950, the facility accommodated 674 families including 804 children—a population of more than 2,000. It was governed as a student cooperative, had a co-op grocery, a well-baby clinic, and a union (with a coffee shop, tot shop, library, game room, and study lounge, and a television set purchased in 1949). A play center was opened in 1948 to alleviate the problem of providing child care. Grove East, another student housing complex, was established next to campus in St. Paul in 1947; it housed 236 families.

Among those who found housing in University Village were James and Gladys Peterson. James, who had been a meteorologist in the Army Air Corps, entered the university in 1948, and received a Ph.D. in geology in 1952. Gladys recalled:

We arrived in Minneapolis in our 1938 Model A Ford with our three-month-old Jimmy and moved into the University Quonset hut section for non-resident and foreign graduate students. It was like living in the country because there actually were rabbits scurrying in the grassy areas between the huts. Our unit consisted of one room with basic furniture including a sleeper-sofa. A two- or three-burner hotplate was our stove. We had a small private bathroom without a shower. Showers were taken in a central building across the road, where there were also laundry facilities. Jim partitioned off one corner of our unit so the baby had a bedroom. Somehow we were able to fit an army cot in there for Jim's mother when she came from Illinois to visit us and her first post-war grandchild. After we were settled I used the trolley to get me to and from the Minneapolis campus, where I took an evening credit course, Introduction to Philosophy, which I loved.[30]

Even with the village, the university was able to provide housing for only about 3,000 students in fall quarter 1950. Three times that many lived with their parents while others lived in rooming houses. In some respects, living at home was not a bad thing; as the geographer John Borchert noted, "Our kids, in those days, would be home for dinner every night—two-thirds of them—having to talk to their parents around the dinner table about what they're doing and what their parents are doing. I probably over-estimate the amount of interaction that took place in these households, but maybe not by too much."[31] A study of student housing at the beginning of the 1957 academic year produced similar results. The chief difference was that considerably fewer students lived in rooming houses—a memorandum written in 1955 by Dean Williamson had complained of the deterioration of rooming houses—while correspondingly more lived in off-campus apartments.[32] A number of new dormitories were added in Minneapolis: Centennial Hall in 1951, Territorial Hall in 1958, and Frontier Hall in 1959. Bailey Hall in St. Paul opened in 1950. The staff of the Student Housing Bureau was doubled to provide additional assistance to students.[33]

Single men and women who lived in the dormitories were among the more fortunate students. The men in Pioneer and Centennial Halls had counselors, weekly maid service, laundry facilities, space for parking and washing cars, and a number of social organizations. "Smoking in your room is not objectionable," the residents' handbook said, but students were cautioned against smoking in bed because of the fire hazard. Centennial Hall remained open twenty-four hours a day, while the Pioneer lobby was closed

between midnight and 7:00 A.M.[34] The life of women was more fully regulated. Their dormitories closed at midnight on weekdays and at 2:00 A.M.
on weekends; all men were to be out by 11:00 P.M. on weeknights and
midnight during weekends. Study hours were from 7:30 until 10:30 every
school night. Rowdiness in the dining rooms was not permitted, nor were
the women allowed to come with their hair "up or uncombed."[35] Some of
these regulations reflect the concerns of Dean Williamson, who was the
last and most powerful proponent of the notion that the university stood
*in loco parentis* for its students. There were student governing boards in all
the dorms, and the Association of Rooming-House Students was established
to create a fraternal spirit among these students and to help integrate them
into campus functions.[36]

Students soon created nicknames for the temporary classroom buildings hurriedly erected to provide space for crowded classes. One of them
near the pharmacy was known as "the Pill Box," Temporary North of the
Library was "Booklet," and the temporary building near Murphy Hall was
called "Mrs. Murphy." Some of these buildings were removed in a few years
as permanent structures took their places, but others remained for decades.
The last of the temporary buildings to be removed, Temporary North of
Mines, was taken down in 1987 to make room for additional space for the
General College.[37]

Vernon Heath, later president of Rosemount Engineering (1968 to 1991),
entered as a freshman in 1947. He recalled living in quarters constructed
out of the squash courts underneath Memorial Stadium and paying eight
dollars a month for a bunk bed and a locker. "In that building," he said,
"you could, in any twenty-four hours, play cards or talk; there was always
somebody wandering around. The price was right and it was a great environment. Coming from a small town [Princeton, Minnesota], it was like
taking a step into a new world for me."[38]

The combination of more mature veterans with traditional undergraduates created an extremely diverse campus community. Al Sandvik, one of
the veterans, described his peers:

> Twenty-year-old men comported themselves as if in their thirties. They knew
> more about the world, themselves, death and survival than if they had been
> students who had stayed at home.... Common to all veterans was an abil-
> ity to sort quickly through what they had been hearing and dismiss the ir-
> relevant.... Veterans took on their education as a job, a tour of duty in ex-

change for a four-, six-, or eight-year degree allowing them to move up in career ranks.[39]

Anne Truax, who came to Minnesota as a transfer student from the University of Chicago, looked back on campus life from a woman's perspective:

> The veterans overwhelmed the university and the women who stayed at home. They were our chronological peers, but their experiences, I am convinced, made them insistent that we all return to normalcy as fast as possible. They wanted their education, their jobs, and their families as soon as they could get them. Everything was done with great intensity: play hard, work hard, get through quickly so they could begin real life.[40]

Reminiscences of some additional former students help capture the spirit of the time. Arvonne Skelton, later Arvonne Fraser, came from Lamberton, Minnesota, to attend the university's College of Science, Literature, and the Arts. Living first with relatives and later on campus, she expressed her view of her experience resolutely: "From the day I entered, I was in love with it." She reported her sense of excitement at the ideas of faculty members such as Henry Nash Smith, Theodore Hornberger, Tremaine McDowell, and Mary Turpie in American studies classes. After almost fifty years, she vividly remembered historian Alice Felt Tyler warning her class, "Your generation won't know the social and intellectual history of the times because nobody keeps journals." Fraser took these words to heart and kept carbon copies of nearly everything she wrote, materials she was later able to draw on for a memoir.[41]

Arvonne Skelton subsequently married Don Fraser (son of longtime Law School dean Everett Fraser), who would go on to represent Minnesota's Fifth District in the U.S. Congress and then become mayor of Minneapolis. Arvonne was active in national and international women's movements, leading the Women's Equity Action League and working with Anne Truax and with Phyllis Kahn, at one time a biological sciences faculty member and elected in 1972 to the Minnesota House of Representatives from a district that included parts of the Twin Cities campus. She was a close friend of Carolyn Rose of women's studies and knew Elizabeth Cless, founder of the first university-based continuing education program for women. Fraser said of this program that it was "another way the University of Minnesota was ahead of everybody else." She stressed the importance of women faculty as role models. She recalled, "I wouldn't be a feminist without Mary Turpie, Alice Felt Tyler, Carolyn Rose, and Mabel Powers."[42]

Judy Lebedoff, together with her brothers Jonathan and David—they were triplets—was an undergraduate in the late 1950s and was in some ways typical of those who lived at home: "I got a ride with a friend who drove quite recklessly. We learned never to schedule a fourth-hour class, as lunch at the Varsity Café was very social." Emly McDiarmid, daughter of the dean of the arts college, was one of her good friends. During Lebedoff's first two years she spent a good deal of time at Hillel House. "I was not interested in sororities or fraternities," she recalled. Commenting on the era, she described her contemporaries as "well-behaved, respectful, no drugs, none of us drank. Excitement for us was branching out and meeting people, particularly international students." She and her siblings were regulars at home football games: "We came from a Gopher football family. The Wisconsin game was always last—it was so cold I couldn't feel my feet."[43]

Emily Anne Mayer (later Emily Anne Staples Tuttle, a community leader, first DFL woman state senator, Hennepin County commissioner, and vice president of the University of Minnesota Alumni Association) did join a sorority. "Students interested in joining sororities signed up before school started," she said. "Rush began with open houses; invitations were issued to those the sorority wished to recruit." The challenge was to find students from outside the metropolitan area to live in the sorority houses; a typical house could accommodate six or eight pledges and about a dozen members. Mayer herself lived at home except for one quarter, "which was very social. My grades suffered." Like Judy Lebedoff, she occasionally ate lunch at the Varsity Café, only "sandwiches and cokes—I never touched coffee until I ran for public office." Mayer typically wore pleated skirts and a white blouse with a Peter Pan collar, or a sweater with pearls. She wore long hair in a page boy (she envied young women with curly hair who did not have to use curlers); she always wore saddle shoes or loafers, never overshoes, despite the winter snow.[44]

Mayer recalled hearing Hubert Humphrey speak to students and remembered Walter "Fritz" Mondale as a student. Mondale had transferred to the College of Science, Literature, and the Arts from Macalester College; he earned a B.A. degree in political science in 1951 and received a degree from the Law School in 1956. Minnesota was then a breeding ground for national politicians. Humphrey and Mondale both would be elected to the U.S. Senate—Humphrey served from 1949 to 1964 and again from 1971 to 1978, Mondale from 1964 to 1976—and both would be vice presidents of the United States, Humphrey under Lyndon Johnson and Mondale under Jimmy Carter. Orville Freeman, governor of Minnesota from 1955 to

1961 and U.S. secretary of agriculture from 1961 to 1969, received his undergraduate degree in 1940 and, following military service, his law degree in 1946. U.S. Senator Eugene McCarthy, though not a student or faculty member, was a familiar figure on campus, voicing his opposition to the Vietnam War. These political leaders exemplified the politics of conscience for which Minnesota was known.

At the end of the century, Mondale looked back on his university years:

> Dad died in 1948 and we had no money, so I had to go somewhere that I could afford, so I went to the university. I was happy to do it at the time, but the transfer [from Macalester] was basically the only option I had, which has made me a lifetime advocate of cheap tuition. It just clicked right away. I was interested in politics and had already connected a little bit with Humphrey, and I got right into that milieu in the political science department. It was wonderful right from the start. It was those professors that would somehow befriend you, sit down and talk with you, show some interest in your questions. People like Arnold Rose [sociology], Walter Heller [economics], and Michael Sovern [Law School] remained friends of mine for life.[45]

Harvey Mackay entered the university as a student athlete, playing on the golf team. Later the founder of an envelope company and a best-selling author of management books, Mackay credited golf coach Les Bolstad with teaching him to "visualize success." Like a number of other students, he remembered Harold Deutsch's lectures on the Second World War: "The rooms were just loaded, standing room only. People would hang on every single word he said."[46]

Betty Ann Whitman, a member of the Ojibwe tribe from Nett Lake, Minnesota, was attracted to the university because it was "the nearest best place" to learn about a world and a culture different from the one in which she had grown up. She commuted to the Minneapolis campus from the city's Kenwood neighborhood, where she boarded with a family. Whitman remembered the support of General College faculty members Tom Stovall, Dorothy Sheldon, and Gordon Kingsley. Fascinated by physics and English, she recalled murmuring "ah ha!" in a physics class: "I realized I had learned some of this already, not in school, but from my people." She also found out that what anthropologists taught about American Indians did not always square with what she herself knew. This realization led her to agitate for an American Indian studies program at the university.[47]

Beginning in 1949, the Minnesota Greek houses confronted the membership policies of their national affiliates. The Student-Faculty Senate required that Minnesota fraternities and sororities remove restrictive clauses from their charters to remain recognized as campus organizations. In 1953, the *Minnesota Daily* reported that the Minnesota Greek system had made this transition more successfully than its counterpart at New York University.[48] Although the University Senate resolution had eradicated policies that were restrictive as to race and religion, the reality was that membership in fraternities and sororities tended to be narrowly based. There were African-American fraternities and sororities, and also Greek houses with predominately Jewish members.[49]

In a large institution like Minnesota, far more students were not affiliated with the Greek system. Sverre Tinglum, a Naval Reserve Officer Training student who transferred from Miami University in Oxford, Ohio, to major in American studies at Minnesota, had doubts about whether to join a fraternity. His father, who had immigrated to the United States from Norway, disapproved of fraternities; he thought they were elitist. Thinking that pledging a fraternity might make him seem more American, Tinglum decided to participate in rush and accepted a bid. He observed three major groups of students on the campus in Minneapolis: the activists, the "socialite" Greeks in fraternities and sororities, and the more intellectual and artistic Dinkytown crowd.[50] Although he remained a member of the fraternity, Tinglum increasingly spent time with the Dinkytown crowd of intellectuals, philosophers, and musicians. He was impatient with university policies that seemed to regard students more as children than as adults: "I left home to get away from Mom and Dad. I didn't need another Mom and Dad from the dean's office. I wanted more respect, to be listened to."[51]

Dinkytown, the business center just north of the campus, "was part of our lives," Kate Schmidt said. "We never bothered with downtown. We had everything we needed right here."[52] Gray's Campus Drug was one of the last holdouts in this area, which changed dramatically in the 1990s; Gray's closed in 1998. Al's Breakfast kept on going, and its famous pancakes were featured in *Gourmet* magazine in 1994.

Another nostalgic reminiscence of student life in the 1950s was written forty years later by Minneapolis *Star Tribune* columnist Jim Klobuchar:

> I found a sleeping room on the second floor of Mrs. Perry's house at 1720 Como Ave. on the streetcar track. It was a mile and a half from Memorial Stadium and Gray Drug's meat loaf specials in Dinkytown. The sleeping room cost me $20 a month. Mrs. Perry was lenient with the date of payment, but not with tenants who invited female classmates for joint adventures into

academe at 11 P.M. Harold Deutsch taught me history, Mulford Sibley taught me Hegel and St. Augustine, and George Hage and Ed Gerald taught me how to avoid the traps of money and fame by going into journalism.

I rode the streetcar to and from campus for 10 cents a trip. I mailed my laundry to my mother every 10 days in a belted black box that took 45 cents in postage. I studied four hours a night, eating two summer sausage sandwiches and listening to Don Hawkins on KSTP radio when the night shrank towards midnight. On Thursdays I walked three miles round trip to take advantage of the six-White-Castles-for-50-cents offer available with a coupon from the *Minneapolis Tribune*. Fries were extra at 8 cents a bag.

Once a month I allowed myself the necessary recreation and debauchery by riding the streetcar downtown to Augie's Night Club. There I would stretch a beer through two hours in the hope of dazzling one of the older women from the nearby offices. None of them ever showed a symptom of being blinded. With luck, I could make the midnight streetcar lineup on Hennepin Ave. with enough change left for the morning paper. For all of these expenses, my parents allowed me $45 a month. It was a tight fit but I could make it by rationing myself to eight squares of saltines the last two days.[53]

Campus events followed a seasonal pattern: Welcome Week opened the academic year. Home football games drew campus and community to Memorial Stadium. Homecoming was in the fall. In the late fall and winter there were basketball and hockey games, and outdoor celebrations: Sno Days in Minneapolis and Foresters' Day in St. Paul. Spring brought Campus Carnival in the Field House, Ag Royal in St. Paul, Cap and Gown Day in May, and commencement in Memorial Stadium. In those days, there was a single ceremony for the whole university; separate commencements for individual colleges began in the 1970s. At Duluth, there were fall convocations, frosh hop, wood gathering for the homecoming bonfire, parades, and football games. The Yuletide Ball and Sno Week enlivened the winter, with ski jumping, cross-country slalom, and broomball. Three sororities and three fraternities helped lead the social events.[54]

St. Paul took pride in its campus traditions, particularly in being small enough for most in the campus community to know each other—if not by name, at least by sight. Gordon Schroeder, a senior in dairy husbandry, explained, "We're a different kind of people over here. We're less reserved, we aren't afraid to let our hair down. And you can't walk through the campus or the union without seeing someone you know."[55]

It was not always easy to enroll in the courses one wanted; closed classes and enormous sections were common during the postwar enrollment surge. Russell Bennett, Minneapolis attorney and longtime University of Minnesota Foundation board member (twice capital campaign chair), described his attempt to register:

> I was sixteen years old, right out of high school, and these lines went all the way around the mall up to the registration desk. Most of the students were veterans. I was so naive that when I got up to the window I said, "I want to take English Constitutional History," and they said, "That's filled." I went back and got in the back of the line again. It's a wonder I ever got registered. The veterans were smart. They got up there and they'd been used to standing in lines all during World War II, so they had a list of what they wanted to take and they were very willing to take anything else, just anything, and get started.[56]

Given the size of the university, students needed to work to develop a feeling of belonging. Bennett thought he was fortunate to have joined a fraternity; he lived at the Chi Psi lodge opposite Folwell Hall. "I don't care whether it's athletics or band or a fraternity, Greek system or whatever, you need something in a large university to make you feel you belong, and I did."[57]

Inevitably it was difficult to provide adequate advising services for all these students. Most entered the College of Science, Literature, and the Arts (SLA), predecessor of the College of Liberal Arts. Here students were classified as members of the Junior College for their first two years and were assigned to faculty members for advice. Roger Page, who was associate dean in charge of advising for many years, recalls that faculty members who had no other advising duties were expected to see twenty freshmen or sophomores, but many had more than that. Professor Clarke Chambers worked with thirty advisees immediately upon being hired in 1951 and within a few years had sixty or seventy. Dean Page regretted that even the "poor part-time instructors in English got ten. Chiefly, they got pre-business students, by the way. We tried to assign students in terms of their general interests, but we had all these pre-professional students, business having even then a very large number. We assigned them to the English instructors."[58] The Junior College Counseling Office in Folwell Hall was responsible for coordinating these efforts, but, as Dean Page admitted, it was unable to do much in the way of providing actual counsel. In a few years, the term was changed from *counseling* to *advising,* and the Bureau of Counseling and

Student Personnel Psychology was established in the College of Education to assist students with nonacademic matters.

One reason many students survived was that the college was willing to individualize requirements. Dean Page is again a source of collective memory:

> We were the largest liberal arts college in the United States. We had enormously large classes but our spirit, our intentions always were that we would individualize things. The name we put on the procedure in our college and our university was petitioning. The student would petition for an exemption to this, that, or the other, or when the student had some kind of problem that he or she wanted to explain, the student would fill out a petition. The Student Scholastic Standing Committee was the authority for acting on petitions. I suppose over the decades we acted favorably on thousands of them. . . . We had students working forty hours a week even in those days. Everybody thinks that's a new phenomenon. We had it then. We had older students, especially the veterans, with family responsibilities. . . . These people really can't attain their educational objectives following the usual rules and the usual procedures, and they don't always find it best to take the prescribed courses but some other courses that, one can make a judgment, are just as good.[59]

In 1944, anticipating future enrollment increases when World War II ended and influenced by Harvard's general education program, the University Senate recommended greater attention to general education and requested that SLA establish a Department of General Studies to carry this out. The Department of General Studies (renamed Interdisciplinary Studies in 1956) was established the following year and was headed by Russell Cooper, asssociate dean of Science, Literature, and Arts. It offered interdisciplinary courses through programs in the humanities, social sciences, natural sciences, and communication.[60]

The humanities program was created by two distinguished faculty members, Albury Castell (philosophy) and Joseph Warren Beach (English). They were joined by younger members from various departments, among them Herbert McClosky (political science) and Robert Ames (English). When Castell left for the University of Oregon in 1951, Ralph G. Ross of New York University was appointed to head the humanities program. Building on the Castell-Beach beginnings, Ross attracted an extraordinarily talented faculty that included novelist Saul Bellow, prize-winning poet John Berryman (later a Regents Professor), writers and essayists Isaac Rosenfeld, Jack Ludwig, William Phillips (then—and in 2000—editor of *Partisan Review*),

George Amberg (theater designer and scholar of ballet), Joseph Frank (comparative literature), Joseph Kwiat (English and American studies), and Philip Siegelman (political science).[61]

The social science program was headed by Arthur Naftalin. A political scientist, Naftalin left the program in 1954 to become commissioner of administration for the state of Minnesota and later mayor of Minneapolis. The core faculty, in addition to Naftalin, included Benjamin Nelson (historian and social theorist) and Andreas Papandreau. Papandreau subsequently headed the economics department at the University of California at Berkeley and still later became prime minister in his native Greece. Core faculty included Donald Calhoun (sociology) and Mulford Sibley (political science).

The faculty published *Personality, Work, and Community*, a three-volume introduction to the social sciences based on readings from seminal texts. The text provided an interdisciplinary framework for the study of human development, economic organization, and political and social life. In later years, senior faculty included Dan Cooperman (after leaving the program, he became the chair of sociology and of Scandinavian studies), social psychologist Fred Blum, political scientist Mordechai Roshwald, and historian Hyman Berman.

Natural science, headed by Mark Graubard (physics), and communications, headed first by Harold Allen (English) and later Daniel Bryan (English), rounded out the department's offerings. They offered lower-division courses that could be used to meet distribution requirements for graduation. Communications courses offered integrated forensic skills—speech, rhetoric, and writing, an alternative to conventional English composition courses.

The new courses proved popular with students; enrollment nearly tripled between 1944 and 1956. The Lebedoff triplets, Judith, David, and Jonathan, took a humanities course in 1956 from Joseph Kwiat, who had been Minnesota's first Ph.D. student in American studies. Jonathan Lebedoff recalled, "We met in small groups to discuss *War and Peace, The Brothers Karamazov,* and *Madame Bovary.* It was very different from freshman sociology with two thousand students and TV screens." Another perspective on the department can be seen in a eulogy at the time of Ross's death in April 2000. Former colleague Philip Siegelman recalled Ross's role as the chair and leader of the humanities program: "Like Saul Bellow and John Berryman or Allen Tate, he shaped our world by looking deeply into and understanding the nature of things.... They were what Saul [Bellow] has taken to calling 'profound noticers.' That they all should have been present on one campus in a single circle at the same time was miraculous. I've never experienced anything remotely like it since we left Minnesota thirty-four years ago, and Ralph Ross was the unwobbling pivot around which that vibrant constellation evolved."[62]

From the beginning, the department and its programs provoked debate within SLA. Some faculty questioned the premise of enduring ideas—a pivotal assumption in establishing the department. Another ongoing debate was whether general education is more effective offered through a single or an interdisciplinary perspective. Advocates for Interdisciplinary Studies argued that introductory courses offered by specialized departments sometimes failed to provide students with an integrated educational experience. Opponents argued that efforts at integration could be shallow and not fully representative of the intellectual content of established disciplines. There were also debates about what should be in the core of an undergraduate curriculum. Some faculty members in the interdisciplinary programs felt that, in comparison to colleagues in traditional disciplines, their teaching was not as highly regarded. As SLA became pressed for funds, economic factors came into play as the deans tried to address the financial needs of the entire college.

In 1958, the overarching structure, Interdisciplinary Studies, that combined the separate programs was dissolved, but the individual programs— humanities, comparative literature, linguistics, social science, natural science, and communications—continued, reporting to the dean. In 1964, following two studies of the programs and their curriculum, in a plenary session, the SLA faculty voted by a narrow margin not to replace faculty members in these programs when they left or retired. The action was seen as a de facto vote of no confidence. Consequently, programs gradually diminished as budgets were reduced and as faculty members obtained appointments elsewhere. (In 1966, Ross left the university to become Harley Burr Alexander Professor of Humanities at Scripps College and professor of philosophy in the Claremont Graduate School. Nelson left to join the faculty at Hofstra University, then later the Stony Brook faculty of the State University of New York, and still later, the graduate faculty of the New School for Social Research.)

David Cooperman and then Hyman Berman chaired the social science program following Arthur Naftalin. From 1968, following his defeat in his run for the presidency of the United States, to 1970, when he returned to the U.S. Senate, Hubert Humphrey taught interdisciplinary undergraduate seminars in the Department of Experimental Courses, which had emerged as a successor to the social science program. Experimental courses, in turn, led to the formation of new interdisciplinary studies such as women's, Afro-American, American Indian, and Chicano studies. Berman headed experimental studies from 1970 to 1976. Mark Graubard taught natural science until his retirement in 1972.

Humanities courses continued to be offered in considerable numbers, and the department continued into the 1990s. Faculty joining humanities in the 1970s, such as Richard Leppert, Pauline Yu, and Bruce Lincoln, welcomed the inclusion of non-Western material and works outside a narrowly defined canon. In the 1990s, humanities merged with comparative literature, forming the Department of Cultural Studies and Comparative Literature. At Minnesota as elsewhere, vigorous debates on the role of humanities in the curriculum continued.

Admission was relatively open; numbers and quality were controlled by scrutiny of a new student's record. A small arts college committee met until midnight several nights during the winter break to determine which students would not be permitted to return to school after their first quarter at the university. "Painful as that procedure was," Roger Page said, "we thought that the students were entitled to the information as soon as possible and not after the quarter began; so we always had the target of getting these horrible letters out to the students *after* Christmas but before the new quarter began."[63]

The university intensively studied the experience of students, noting their backgrounds, test scores, whether they lived on or off campus, and whether they had scholarships or loans. During the 1950–51 academic year, the Student Counseling Bureau had more than 8,000 interviews and administered more than 17,800 psychological tests. About a thousand students applied for scholarships (partly under a statewide freshman scholarship plan for able but needy students) and an additional thousand for loans; scholarship aid from university funds amounted to $97,937, with loans from university sources reaching $63,044. The 397 student organizations monitored by the Student Activities Bureau included fraternities and sororities, co-ops, religious groups, and special-interest clubs. Only 251 persons (almost all men) and twelve student organizations were involved in disciplinary action.[64]

In 1950, 560 international students from fifty-nine countries were registered through the Graduate School. The Office of the Foreign Students Advisor was established in 1946 and was part of the extensive network of student services and programs provided by the office of the dean of students. It was headed by Forrest Moore from 1946 to 1978. Josef Mesten-hauser, an émigré from Czechoslovakia, was hired to assist him. Making his way to the United States with the aid of an international student organization, Mestenhauser completed a bachelor's degree at Eastern Washington State College at Cheney and a doctorate in political science at the University of Minnesota. He was to serve international programs from 1951 to 1992, when he joined the College of Education and taught in its Comparative and International Development Education program. In 1952, the university initiated a reciprocal student exchange program, which would grow to include exchanges on nearly every continent.

The Student Project for Amity among Nations (SPAN) was formed by students at Minnesota in 1947 and was very active in succeeding decades. Among the earliest study abroad programs in the country, it drew participants not only from the university, but also from other colleges. By 1998, more than 2,500 students had participated in the program. Among SPAN alumni were Robert T. Holt, subsequently professor of political science and dean of the Graduate School at the University; national advocate for the arts Joan Adams Mondale (who participated in the program while she was a student at Macalester); and Diana Kuske Murphy, a graduate of the College of Liberal Arts and the Law School, and subsequently a member of the federal court of appeals in St. Louis.

Among faculty advisers to SPAN were author Saul Bellow, political scientist Werner Levi, and economics faculty member Francis M. Boddy. Journalism faculty member Mitchell Charnley was the first faculty adviser to the program, guiding it through its early years. Theofanis Stavrou, director of SPAN since 1964, observed that he believed that active leadership by students was a key factor in the program's continuing success:

> It is precisely because it is student managed. It was unique in that it required students who wished to study abroad to spend some time—often two years or more—studying the language, history, and culture of the area they hoped to visit. While abroad, they would undertake field research projects—they would visit the country and be exposed to its people, the culture, without being shut up in classrooms all day.[65]

Among those who have reminisced about the student experience during the 1950s are Douglas Wallace and Maynard Reynolds. Wallace, who was director of the University YMCA for a number of years, thought that "if there was ever a time of the golden era in the last fifty years for the University of Minnesota, it was in the late 1950s":

It was flush. I think there was less faculty tension and conflict during those years than what came afterwards, certainly less than in the 1960s and 1970s. There were lots of students then. It was the Eisenhower era. Students [generally] were not throwing stones or raising significant questions. There was no anxiety. We're talking about a period in which our economy was growing and flourishing off the restoration of Europe and some other parts [of the world] which had been war-ravaged. This was a time of recovery around the world during which many of the industries in this country were flourishing. In fact, it lulled them to sleep, as we discovered later on.[66]

Wallace's comments are strikingly similar to the view of American students as a whole expressed by the writer David Halberstam. Halberstam viewed the 1950s as an "era of general good will and expanding affluence [when] few Americans doubted the essential goodness of their society.... They were optimistic about the future.... For the young, eager veteran just out of college (which he had attended courtesy of the G.I. Bill), security meant finding a good white-collar job with a large, benevolent company, getting married, having children, and buying a house in the suburbs.... The traditional system of authority held."[67] As Wallace put it, paternalism was accepted until the end of the fifties, after which it was speedily rejected.[68]

Although he "thrashed around as many students did in the first couple of years trying to find a major," Wallace "wandered into a course on science and religion that was being taught by Paul Holmer of the philosophy department, one of the great lecturers at the university. I ended up majoring in philosophy. He was my adviser. I took seven courses just from him, some of them graduate courses when I was a senior."[69] Among his other philosophy teachers were May Brodbeck, later dean of the Graduate School, and Herbert Feigl, a leading figure in the philosophy of science. All in all, "it was an interesting time."[70]

The experience of a veteran graduate student is described by Maynard Reynolds, later a faculty member in the College of Education and a national figure in the field of special education. He came to the university in 1946 as a beneficiary of the G.I. Bill, having been in the Service Command of the 13th Air Force:

They had very interesting work there but did I build up a lot of motivation to do some other things. Take out four years and were we eager! When the professor made an assignment or suggestion to read something, I did it. I really don't think I had a terrible lot of awareness about the university as a whole. I knew a little bit about one corner of the university. The interplay or the availability of instruction across psychology, child development, education, and some other fields was much greater than it was later. I took a series of courses in philosophy with Feigl, and Alvin Sellers, and Mr. [Richard M.] Elliott, for whom the psychology building was named.

Reynolds regarded it as an honor that Elliott always said hello when they met on campus.[71]

## Intercollegiate Athletics and Intramural Sports

Athletics formed an important part of the student experience during the 1950s. As they had before the war, Big Ten athletics seemed almost larger than life, with precision marching bands, cheerleaders and dance teams, and wildly enthusiastic fans. The 1950 Golden Gopher football team had a roster of fifty-two players; it drew more than 50,000 fans. Although the capacity of Memorial Stadium was supposed to be just fewer than 53,000, crowds were in fact far larger; the highest attendance in the 1950s was 65,464.[72] On football Saturdays, University Avenue was crowded with cars, buses, and pedestrians making their way to the stadium.

Football tickets in those days cost three dollars and fifty cents, plus a quarter for a program. On home game days the dorms served lunch at 11:30 to allow students time to participate in pre-game festivities. Because the games were broadcast on the radio, timing was precise. Music on the public address system began at noon, at 12:50 the squads warmed up, 1:10 saw the entry of the marching band, and 1:15 the introduction of the cheerleaders. The flag ceremony followed a minute later with band music at 1:18 and announcement of the lineups at 1:25. The kickoff came exactly at 1:30. At halftime the 120 members of the marching band demonstrated their precision maneuvers, and spectators joined in singing the "Minnesota Rouser," the "Minnesota March," the "Minnesota Fight Song," "Hail! Minnesota," and "Our Minnesota." The band members—still all male—rehearsed twelve hours a week.[73] Growing attendance at major sports events during the 1950s helped the Department of Men's Intercollegiate Athletics clear a deficit that stood at nearly $1 million in 1950, expend just over $2 million on renovation of facilities, contribute approximately 85 percent of the budgets of intramural sports and physical education, and hold $750,000 in reserve for new programs.

Wendell R. Anderson, a history major, student athlete, and Olympic hockey player who graduated in 1954 and went on to become a legislator, Minnesota governor, a U.S. senator, and a member of the Board of Regents, remembered the broad impact of football: "You must understand that in those days, across the state if you walked into a food market, the radio was on. Everybody listened to the University of Minnesota football games. Gasoline stations, homes—if somebody was out on the lawn, they had a radio with them. It totally dominated Saturday afternoon."[74]

The 1950 football season was the last coached by Bernard "Bernie" Bierman. During his sixteen seasons, Bierman had 93 wins, 35 losses, and 6 ties and had led teams to six Big Ten titles and five national championships. But the 1950 season was disappointing. The Gophers won only one game and lost seven, with one tied. Bierman announced his resignation at the end of the November 11 defeat by Michigan State.[75] He was named to the College Football Hall of Fame in 1955. The 1950 football program (the *Gopher Goal Post*) said, "He is far more than one of the greatest football coaches of all time. Bernie Bierman is himself the essence of Minnesota."[76] In 1972, offices and facilities used by Men's—and later Women's—Intercollegiate Athletics were named the Bierman Field Athletic Building in his honor.

Bierman was succeeded by Wes Fesler, who had retired from Ohio State but was persuaded to return to coaching at Minnesota in 1951. The high point of his three seasons was undoubtedly the 22–0 victory over Michigan in 1953. The key to that success was senior Paul Giel, known to fans as "the Winona Phantom." Ross Bernstein, in an account of fifty years of athletics in Minnesota, described Giel's accomplishment:

> It was the greatest individual season any Gopher has ever had in Gold Country. . . . In what many have called the greatest-ever single performance in Gopher history, Giel single-handedly crushed the Wolverines, then ranked as one of the top teams in the country. Michigan came to Memorial Stadium to spoil the Gophers' homecoming festivities. That's when an absolutely possessed Paul Giel decided to take the game into his own hands. The Gopher captain rushed the ball 35 times for 112 yards, completed 13 of 18 passes for 169 yards as quarterback, returned a punt 41 yards, and even picked off two passes on defense.[77]

Giel was chosen Big Ten Most Valuable Player in 1952, and in 1953 was named United Press International Player of the Year and Associated Press Back of the Year. He was twice elected an All-American. In addition to playing football, Giel pitched for the Gopher baseball team. His strengths in both football and baseball, together with his academic record, brought him the Big Ten Medal of Honor in 1954. After several seasons in professional baseball, he came back to Minneapolis as manager of the Vikings football team and then sports director for WCCO radio. In 1971 he returned to the university as director of Men's Intercollegiate Athletics, a post he held until 1988.[78]

Murray Warmath was to serve as head football coach for the next eighteen seasons, from 1954 to 1971. Among the key players during Warmath's first years were Bob Hobart, Mike Wright, and Bob McNamara, who carried the ball on an 89-yard kickoff return against a great Iowa team in 1954, leading to a final score of Minnesota 22, Iowa 20.[79] Bob's brother Richard, known as "Pinky," also a member of the Minnesota team, described the impact that the opportunity to play football had on him and his brothers: "Being poor deprives you of a lot of things, but it doesn't deprive you of athletics." He remembered as a child listening to games on the radio with his brothers: "Your wildest dream was to be there some day."[80]

Basketball and hockey also drew large crowds. Basketball had two coaches during the 1950s, Ozzie Cowles and John Kundla. In 1955, guard Chuck Mencel became the first Minnesota player to be named Big Ten Most Valuable Player. His scoring record of 1,391 career points held until Mychal Thompson surpassed it at the end of the 1970s.[81] After 1952, John Mariucci coached the hockey team and player John Mayasich led the Gophers to a new level of success. Making a point of recruiting Minnesota players and serving as an unofficial godfather to newly developing hockey programs throughout the state, Mariucci simultaneously strengthened both high school and college hockey; the university's hockey arena was subsequently named in his honor. Dick Siebert's baseball team won the Big Ten title in 1956 and became the first Gopher baseball team to win the National Collegiate Athletic Association championship in the College World Series.[82] In 1952, Wally Johnson began what was to be a thirty-two-season career as head coach of the wrestling team; his athletes won Big Ten titles in 1959 and 1960. Coach Les Bolstad was highly regarded throughout the Minnesota golfing community.[83] Men's Intercollegiate Athletics also fielded teams in cross-country, gymnastics, swimming, tennis, and track and field.

During the summer of 1949, the field house was extensively remodeled, seating 18,025. The east end was dedicated to basketball; the west end, seating close to 7,000, to ice hockey. The building was named in honor of

Henry L. Williams, who had been head football coach from 1900 to 1921.[84] It was replaced by Mariucci Arena in 1993. During the spring, when the basketball season was finished, wrestling matches took place in Williams Arena and an indoor track was set up in its west end. Swimmers had the Cooke Hall pool, a facility the Gophers were to use until the completion of an Olympic-scale Aquatic Center in 1990. The university maintained a golf course near the campus in St. Paul, and there were tennis courts at several locations.

Intramural activities for men during the 1950s included football, basketball, baseball, bowling, hockey, softball, and volleyball teams as well as individual competition in golf, handball, horseshoes, boxing, swimming, and track. Bowling was particularly popular, partly because it was the only sport that took place throughout the school year. During the 1950–51 academic year, there were 231 bowling teams. Intramural competition took place in four categories: academic fraternities, professional fraternities, independents, and dormitories. Because the two men's dorms, Centennial and Territorial, competed against each other and the independents were poorly organized, the two fraternity groups had considerable influence over intramurals. Although there was as yet no intercollegiate athletic program for women, women did compete in intramural sports. In 1950–51, 6,500 women participated, as did 7,600 men; women competed through physical education and men through intramural sports.[85]

## Faculty

Although Twin Cities campus enrollment was among the largest in the country, its colleges and departments represented centers of interaction on a more personal scale. Departments, where teaching was organized and research agendas were set, were the basis for scholarly reputations; they served as the conduit through which graduate students were introduced to the culture of their discipline. Highly productive departments—in the arts college, the Institute of Technology, the Medical School, in St. Paul or Duluth— seemed to possess common elements. Many had a leader accorded considerable latitude in decision making, a practice that might later seem autocratic or authoritarian, but was mitigated by active engagement in research, openness to crossing boundaries, and dedication to the next generation of scholars.

Profiles of ten Twin Cities departments show how excellence was built and maintained. Five of these departments—American studies, economics, English, geography, and psychology—were in the College of Science, Literature, and the Arts. Two, chemical and electrical engineering, were part of the Institute of Technology. The remaining units considered here are surgery (from the College of Medical Sciences) and—from the Institute of Agriculture, Forestry, and Home Economics—the Department of Plant Pathology and the Department of Agricultural and Applied Economics.

## Economics

The economics department offers a fine example of effective leadership. Walter Heller came to the University in 1949 and proceeded to build up the department rapidly. N. James Simler, who served as chair for twenty-two years, from 1969 to 1991, recalled that "Heller hired people like Leo Hurwicz, Oz Brownlee, John Chipman, Jack Kareken, Ed Coen, and Harlan Smith. They formed a nucleus [that] we've built on ever since." Simler emphasized that Heller

> followed the same set of principles that we follow now and have followed ever since I can remember: we try to hire the best available people regardless of field and orientation. For example, if it should be judged a top priority this coming year to hire a labor economist, we would look very, very long and hard for such a person; but if we failed to find such a person, we would go after the best available person. What we would *not* do is hire a labor economist if that person was not judged up to our standards.[86]

At the end of the decade, Walter Heller left Minnesota to become chair of the U.S. Council of Economic Advisers. After five years in Washington, he returned to the university, and, as economics faculty member Craig Swan recalled, "he remained an active participant in public policy discussions." The essential core of the department in economic theory was in place, and there were strong faculty members in a number of other areas. Anne Krueger was a mainstay in both international trade and economic development. Herbert Mohring, John Hause, Jim Simler, and Ed Foster worked in applied microeconomics. As Swan said, "It was a department that was recognized."[87] Edward Foster, who joined the department in 1961, recalled its commitment to having upper-division courses taught by faculty members. As enrollment grew and faculty members took on additional research, graduate students began to do some upper-division teaching and became quite good at it, Foster noted. They were assisted, he recalled, by a teacher-training program that the department developed for them—a program that was still in existence at the end of the century.[88]

## Geography

Geography showed that great distinction could be built from a small base. At the end of the war, it had only two faculty members (Jan O. M. Broek, the head, and John Weaver). Within ten or fifteen years, it was on the way to becoming one of the most highly regarded geography departments in the country. It ranked tenth in a 1957 study, seventh in an American Council on Education rating in 1965, third in 1969, and first in 1993.[89] Because postwar enrollment was high, the department offered large lectures supplemented by laboratory and recitation sections staffed by graduate students. An important strategy in building the department was to retain funds that could be used to engage distinguished visiting faculty. Tenure-track appointments followed a strategy of "building teaching depth, strengthening cross-field research ties, and adding methodological competence in each new appointment."[90] John Borchert, who came from Wisconsin in 1949, led the way, and was soon joined by such scholars as John Webb, Fred Lukermann, Philip Porter, Joseph Schwartzberg, and Ward Barrett.[91]

In a self-study prepared in 1974, a number of faculty members described their views of the department's success. Porter noted that, in addition to being supportive of each other's work, faculty members also were respectful of differences in approach to the discipline: "There is no Minnesota School," he noted. John Rice suggested a connection between the department's high ranking and the high value it placed on individual freedom. Roderick Squires noted, "This department is quite the best I have encountered on two continents in terms of the intellectual ability and breadth of interest of the faculty." Lukermann pointed to the value of weekly staff meetings and coffee hours that included majors and graduate students, and visiting lecturers. Borchert, named a Regents Professor in 1981, cited contacts among departments within the College of Liberal Arts, ease of communication with public and private agencies in the Twin Cities and the region, and the interest of faculty members in comparative studies, resource management studies, and regional community studies.[92]

## American Studies

Minnesota was a national leader in establishing during the postwar period the new interdisciplinary field of American studies. A number of American studies faculty members were members of the English department faculty. Leo Marx, a major figure in American studies nationally and subsequently professor of American cultural history at the Massachusetts Institute of Technology, joined the Minnesota English department in 1949. An active participant in the new program, he recalled its early leaders:

> Tremaine McDowell was American Studies'... spiritual godfather, orga- nizer and enthusiastic administrator, but Henry Nash Smith was its intel- lectual light. Mary Turpie, its legendary godmother, was...devoted, con- scientious, and, from a student point of view, a consistently supportive presence.[93]

American studies programs were based on interdisciplinary methods and on their focus on American culture. The organizing committee that estab- lished American studies at Minnesota were chaired by Tremaine McDowell, a faculty member in English, and included Alice Tyler and Theodore Blegen from history (Blegen was also dean of the Graduate School), Ralph D. Nafziger from journalism, Asher Christenson from political science, Alburey Castell from philosophy, and a second faculty member from English, Theodore Hornberger. A number of the early faculty members who were active in American studies, including Henry Nash Smith, Theodore Hornberger, Bernard Bowron, Leo Marx, and Jacob Levenson, had come from Harvard's American civilization program. They had appointments in English, although they were recruited to Minnesota with the expectation that they would make American studies their central focus. In developing the curriculum, which was offered for the first time in 1945, the commit- tee sought a curriculum that achieved a balanced representation of history, literature, the social sciences, and fine arts.

Among highlights of the department during its early years was its role as the founder, in 1949, of *American Quarterly,* to become one of the pre- mier scholarly publications in the field, and hosting a national conference on civil rights in 1959, with Martin Luther King its keynote speaker. Dur- ing these years, Henry Nash Smith's nationally renowned *The Virgin Land* was published while he was at Minnesota. Leo Marx later wrote *The Machine in the Garden,* about the intersection during the nineteenth cen- tury of the prevailing pastoral worldview with the new realities of indus- trial America. These works represented what came to be known as the "myth and symbol" perspective in American studies scholarship and helped se- cure for Minnesota top rankings in the field.[94]

*English*

The postwar years were also a period of great productivity in the English department. Leo Marx identified three groups within the English department: mainstream literary scholars Joseph Warren Beach, John Clark, Samuel Holt Monk, and E. E. Stoll; New Critics Robert Penn Warren, William Van O'Connor, Leonard Unger, Allen Tate, and John Berryman; and Americanists Henry Nash Smith, Barney Bowron, and himself. Visiting scholars Saul Bellow, Isaac Rosenfeld, and Irving Howe, Marx thought, were closest to the New Critics.[95]

Despite the different groups, Marx recalled, "our friendships and social relations crossed ideological party lines, and we worked together in reasonable, if argumentative, harmony."[96] Upon reflection, however, he observed that collegiality may have been the result of external factors. "This tiptoeing around fundamental issues was facilitated by the presence of a common enemy: McCarthyism and other hyper-nationalistic expressions of paranoid anti-communism."[97] Undergraduate Sverre Tinglum remembered the excitement of Marx's teaching: "Everybody was standing in line to get into his courses because he was a radical; there was a glamour in being in a course taught by a radical wearing army fatigues."[98]

Asked what led to such an assembly of talent in the English department, faculty member Edward Savage credited Joseph Warren Beach, the nephew of President Cyrus Northrop, who had headed the department from 1939 to 1948 and was known for his writing on Henry James and an interest in Robert Frost, Sinclair Lewis, Edward Arlington Robinson, Carl Sandburg, and other contemporaries.[99]

James Shannon, later president of the University of St. Thomas, auxiliary bishop of the Archdiocese of St. Paul and Minneapolis, and, subsequently, head of the General Mills Foundation, described what it was like to be a graduate student at the university. He remembered particularly classes taught by novelist Robert Penn Warren, who had come to Minnesota in 1942. *All the King's Men,* a novel based on the life of Louisiana's governor Huey Long for which Warren received the Pulitzer Prize in 1947, was published during his time as a member of the English faculty. Shannon recalled Warren's Technique of the Novel course:

> He assigned us ten novels, one a week for ten weeks. He immediately disarmed everybody by his candor and his deep, deep courtesy. No student could ever ask a dumb question of Warren. He would take a poor question

and fashion it into a better question and give it a brilliant answer.... I've never met his match as a teacher.[100]

## Psychology

At the end of the war, the psychology department was already one of the most highly ranked departments within the university. Unlike a number of other nationally eminent psychology departments, it consciously embraced both pure science and practical application. Its first chair, Richard M. Elliott, had an amazingly long tenure, from 1919 to 1951. One of his most important appointments was D. G. Patterson, who entered the department after early experience in industrial consulting.

Minnesota was considered the leading university in the development of vocational psychology and related fields of student personnel work and guidance, as well as industrial and organizational psychology. During the 1950s, the department was also strong in social psychology as a result of the work of Leon Festinger, Stanley Schachter, and Benjamin Willerman. A related emphasis was testing. The Minnesota Multiphasic Personality Inventory was published in 1942 by one of Elliott's students, Starke R. Hathaway, working with neuropsychiatrist J. C. McKinley, head of medicine. The famous behaviorist B. F. Skinner had joined the department in 1936 and was at Minnesota when his groundbreaking study, *Behavior of Organisms,* was published two years later. Following Skinner's departure, Kenneth MacCorquodale led Minnesota's contributions to applied behavior modification. MacCorquodale helped develop faculty interests in psychopharmacology, research that combined faculty from psychology with faculty from the Medical School. In the 1940s psychology had added strength in personality theory and experimental social psychology. J. G. Darley's Laboratory for Research in Social Relations was an important initiative of the postwar period. Still another strength that emerged after the war was study of genetic elements in behavior.[101]

In attempting to explain the culture that led to this flowering of research, in a self-study done for a 1986 program review, members of the department referred to their collective belief in excellence and autonomy:

> The policy has been, roughly, to hire bright, high-drive people from top-flight Ph.D. programs and let them do their thing. If it is good, keep them on. The notion of a department chair or power elite pushing any substantive theoretical position, or a cross-domain methodology or a social, political, or economic common aim ideology is anathema. We have never needed it, don't want it, and have maintained a productive department without it.[102]

Psychology was also noteworthy for its collaboration with other parts of the university, including the Institute of Child Development, the Department of Communication Disorders, the Medical School, and the Student Counseling Bureau.

Although it is sometimes alleged that large enrollments diverted faculty from research, the psychology experience did not bear this out. Psychology enrollments were consistently among the highest in the university. The department taught 12,761 students during the 1947–48 academic year, at a time when the total fall head count was 25,856.[103]

## Chemical Engineering

The distinction of Minnesota's Department of Chemical Engineering derived to a considerable extent from the leadership of Neal Amundson, its head from 1949 to 1977. Originally a member of the mathematics faculty, Amundson moved to chemical engineering in 1947. He recalled:

> One of the things I decided when I became the department head was that I would not hire for the foreseeable future anyone trained as a chemical engineer. We hired one mathematician, five chemists, and one bacteriologist. At that time, it seemed to me that conventional chemical engineering research was extremely uninteresting. It was very empirical. There wasn't a lot of thought in it at all. It was just awful.
>
> I was probably the first mathematician in the United States to be appointed a chemical engineering department chairman. We had already shown what you could do by using highbrow techniques to solve problems. That was now an established step and, therefore, it was very easy to hire somebody else and say, "We want you to do the same thing but in your own field." So we hired [Rutherford] Aris and [L. E. "Skip"] Scriven and John Dahler and Ted Davis and Lanny Schmidt, and all those people were chemists, except for Rutherford "Gus" Aris, who was also a mathematician.[104]

Aris, a British scholar, was employed by Imperial Chemical Industries in London when Amundson met him. Amundson's description of how Aris was hired illustrates the informality of an era before formal search processes and committees were common. Aris had spent a year at Minnesota, then went to Edinburgh. Having liked Minnesota, Aris, as Amundson recalled events, "phoned me and asked whether there was a position he might fill. I said, 'We'd be delighted.'" Thus, Aris began a career of research and teaching in Minnesota. He was named a Regents Professor in 1978. In addition to his contributions to the department and the Institute of Technnology, Aris was an expert in Latin paleography.[105]

Scholarly linkages as well as chance were important in other cases. John Dahler was hired on the recommendation of a prominent chemist at Wisconsin. Dahler recommended Ted Davis, whom he had met at a seminar in Chicago; Davis was responsible for hiring Lanny Schmidt. Skip Scriven was working for Shell Development Company in 1955 but had an offer from Berkeley. "He called me up," Amundson recalled,

> and he said, "I have this offer and I'm probably going to accept it, but I think I ought to look at least at one other place just as a basis of comparison."
>
> I said, "Okay, that's fine. Why don't you come? We'll pick up all the expenses."
>
> He showed up, and we did everything that he liked. For example, he was a member of the YMCA there, and he swam, and that Sunday afternoon, my son and he and I swam at the YMCA here. And Shirley [Mrs. Amundson] made the kind of meal he thought was just out of this world, and he accepted our offer before he left town.[106]

## Electrical Engineering

Electrical engineering was shaped by William G. "Jerry" Shepherd, an electrical engineer who later served as vice president for academic administration (1963 to 1973). He had himself been a student at the university, entering in 1928. Staying on after his graduation, Shepherd for a time shared an office with Al Nier, the nuclear physics giant. After spending a few years at the Bell Laboratories working on vacuum tubes, Shepherd returned to Minnesota in 1947 and was immediately named a full professor. He remembered:

> When I first came back they were, figuratively, pulling people in off the streets to teach because they were so short of faculty. Most of those people were temporary. For the longer term, we began to recruit high-level scholars. Aldert Van der Ziel was one of the first ones that I recruited. He had been in Holland and he had quite a reputation. I was at a conference—I think it was at Princeton—in a dark auditorium for the slide show when somehow I heard his name and introduced myself to him, suggesting that he might come and visit. I had to leave before that particular talk was over. He sent me some of his papers. I got Henry Hartig [the head of electrical engineering] to extend him an invitation to come and visit, and we offered him a job. I wasn't there when he came for that visit, and it was later, when he finally joined the faculty, that we first saw each other in the daylight.[107]

## Surgery

The Department of Surgery may be singled out as an example of an outstanding component of the Medical School, perhaps the first among equals, as the Medical School had a number of exceptionally strong departments. Dr. Owen Wangensteen, who had earned M.D. and Ph.D. degrees at the university, was designated chair of surgery in 1930 but was given two years to study in Europe before taking up his new position. As he considered his duties, Wangensteen saw one of his key roles as creating "an atmosphere in which learning became an absorbing adventure."[108] One of his contributions as head of the department was his expectation that members of the surgical faculty should be involved in research, and that surgery residents should assist in research projects.[109] Richard Lillehei, speaking to the Wangensteen Foundation in 1977, described the surgery program as "a family, headed by a father figure with enough fallibilities to keep him human, but never enough to [let us] address him by any other terms but Dr., Sir, or the Chief."[110] A resident described accompanying Wangensteen on patient rounds: "If you follow him with a pencil, you can write down twenty original ideas each day."[111]

Bradley Aust, also a former surgical resident, attributed the strength of the surgery program to its strong connections to the basic sciences, noting particularly the ties with physiology.[112] Wangensteen himself had made the same point in 1961, noting that in addition to studying anatomy and pathology, surgeons needed to master the disciplines of physiology, immunology, microbiology, and biochemistry. The strongly collaborative relationship between Wangensteen and Maurice Visscher, head of physiology, was a pivotal factor in bridging the clinical and basic sciences. Recognized for his numerous research papers, Wangensteen is perhaps most widely known for creating a suction technique for dealing with bowel obstructions, credited with saving a hundred thousand lives. Another indicator of the success of the program he built was the distinction of the careers of those who studied under him as resident fellows. At the time of his retirement in 1967, thirty-five former fellows were full-time professors of surgery. The program at Minnesota had grown from 3 fellows when Wangensteen became chair to 180 when he retired in 1967.[113] Colleagues noted that Wangensteen's contributions could be measured not only through improvements in the practice of surgery but also "in the development of a cadre of academic progeny who spread out all over to perpetuate his concepts of surgical education."[114]

## Plant Pathology

Keith McFarland, later dean of the College of Home Economics but earlier director of resident instruction in the Institute of Agriculture, Forestry, and Home Economics, remembers a "benign dictatorship of department heads" in the mid-1940s and early 1950s. "Discussion at faculty meetings in the College of Agriculture was in large part the province of Elvin C. Stakman, H. K. Hayes, Ross Gortner, and O. B. Jesness. Heaven help the innocent who got in the way of their interactions."[115] E. C. Stakman, chair of plant pathology, was, like Wangensteen, referred to as "the Chief." He too had earned all of his degrees (B.A., M.A., and Ph.D.) at Minnesota; he was the leading figure in the department from 1913 until his retirement in 1953. Creating a cohesive connection between faculty and students, Stakman not only ensured the department's strength but also served as an ongoing mentor to his former students. During his career he advised 180 graduate students, one of whom, Norman Borlaug, received the Nobel Peace Prize in 1970 for work on increasing wheat production in Pakistan, India, and Latin America. Stakman was elected president of the American Association for the Advancement of Science in 1949 and served as a consultant to the U.S. Atomic Energy Commission's advisory committee on biology and medicine as well as a consultant to the Rockefeller Foundation. His work on the eradication of wheat rust was based on new understandings of physiological specialization in different species of rust, which translated practically into the introduction of strains of wheat not susceptible to blight. A sports enthusiast, Stakman was the driving force behind the plant pathology softball team, first as a player and later as coach. His team won the campus championship eighteen out of twenty years.[116]

## Agricultural and Applied Economics

Oscar Bernard Jesness had headed agricultural and applied economics since 1928. Born in Stevens County in western Minnesota, Jesness was fond of saying he was "weaned on a pitchfork." Early in life he came to the view that most personal problems could be solved by hard work. He earned all his degrees at Minnesota in a period before Minnesota had gained national prominence in economic analysis and theory.[117] During the Jesness era, research into farm management was derived from detailed accounting records kept by Minnesota farmers themselves: "The research approach of the department was in fact an intelligence-gathering activity. [The studies] were not aimed at discovering new relationships, or explaining the behavior of economic decision units, or pushing back the frontiers of knowledge. . . . Although many would not have won a prize for novelty, they were well received by many members of the farming community and by the agribusiness community in Minnesota." Willard Cochrane, a younger member of the faculty, believed that some work of this sort was appropriate but that "subject matter departments in a university must be concerned with problem-solving, exploring the unknown, and the idea of discovery."[118] After Jesness's retirement, this view came to prevail.

Jesness's successor, Sherwood O. "Woody" Berg, chaired the department from 1957 to 1963. Under Berg the department grew in national eminence.[119] Berg explained that he used four strategies in developing the department. He first took steps to increase the number of undergraduate majors to make more students aware of the field of agricultural economics. This was accomplished quite rapidly, relying on the leadership of Carroll Hess, whom Berg found expert at advising students. The result was that within three years the number of agricultural and applied economics undergraduate majors grew from twenty-seven to approximately three hundred. Next, Berg encouraged faculty members to become more global in their interests, noting that Minnesota was part of a world market. His third strategy was to strengthen economics courses, while his fourth was hiring and supporting new faculty members who were more interdisciplinary and placed greater emphasis on team research.[120] The department's name was later changed to applied economics.

It was Walter Heller who suggested the appointment of Philip Raup, one of the leaders in the new study of agricultural economics. Raup was at the University of Wisconsin following an unusually interesting career in the military and in the postwar rehabilitation of Europe. Jesness invited Raup to come to Minnesota as a full professor. Raup recalled,

> Marian and I drove to Minnesota in April 1953. The first thing that Jesness did was to take me to lunch at the Campus Club, which I thought was extremely significant. In my case, it was important because I didn't want to join a department that thought of itself as an enclave removed from and divorced from the mainstream of the general campus of the university. At Wisconsin, I had had a strong introduction to such a department; the agricultural economics department was a part of the university, on the same campus. At Minnesota I would be joining a university in which the agricultural economics department was three miles distant [in St. Paul, not Minneapolis].[121]

Jesness and Heller reassured him, and he moved. Heller also helped re-cruit Vernon Ruttan, who had worked with him at the Council of Eco-nomic Advisers. In 1965 Sherwood Berg hired Ruttan to be chairman of the Department of Agricultural Economics.[122] He was later appointed a Regents Professor.

Great departments could be assembled during these years in part because it was not generally difficult to obtain funding for the faculty. "Oh, it was so easy in those days," Neal Amundson reflected. State appropriations to the university nearly tripled between 1946 and 1950, rising from $5.3 million to $15 million. Federal involvement in research expanded enormously following the launching of the first Russian satellite, *Sputnik,* on October 4, 1957. Fellowships for graduate students and research grants for faculty were made available under the National Defense Education Act and by such agencies as the National Science Foundation, the National Aeronautics and Space Administration, and the Atomic Energy Commission. Each fellow-ship produced an augmentation given to the student's department. By the end of the decade, chemical engineering had a hundred graduate students, each of whom received $6,000 personally and brought another $6,000 to the department budget.[123]

## Administering a Public University

President Morrill, compared to the men who succeeded him, was quite formal. With his background in classics and journalism, he was an ardent believer in general and liberal education, especially the humanities. He was fond of quoting such diverse figures as John Ruskin and Socrates. He also was a believer in the university's land-grant and service missions. He allowed the deans considerable latitude and was not a strong advocate for central-ization. Shortly before his inauguration, he expressed his belief that land-grant institutions represented a useful model for the evolution of Ameri-can universities:

> No smug and too strictly planned reorganization of the American Univer-sity should be sought. . . . We can countenance a great deal of seeming aca-demic disorder if the state university will still cling with courage and reso-lution to the clear purpose which has made it useful: . . . to explore the contemporary social scene to discover new areas and activities which de-mand intellectual organization and creative treatment.[124]

He believed that the postwar university should meet "the new demands of an expanding economy and social order, [creating] new types of training, and answering the public commitment to the value of research."[125]

Morrill was popular with the faculty, partly because he usually ate lunch at the Campus Club and would "just go over and sit down at a table" of ordinary faculty members rather than being surrounded by other administrators.[126] One indicator of Morrill's style, which blended formality with collegiality, was that Theodore Blegen, who served as dean of the Graduate School throughout Morrill's fifteen years as president, did not call Morrill by his first name until they both retired.[127] Morrill always referred to his secretary, Peg Wipperman, as Miss Wipperman. "I don't think he even knew my first name," she recalled. Although such formality might seem forbidding, Wipperman found Morrill a kind and thoughtful employer.[128] To Ed Haislet, executive director of the Minnesota Alumni Association, Morrill "was the kind of person you would select as your father, if you could choose your own."[129] E. W. Ziebarth, later dean of liberal arts, thought that Morrill was more democratic than other presidents of research universities, interacting more frequently with deans and encouraging a more open approach to decision making.[130]

President Morrill and his wife, Freda, lived at 1105 Fifth Street Southeast, the former residence of Governor John S. Pillsbury, which had become the official president's house.[131] He estimated that his position as university president required him to be out six nights a week at speaking engagements and other university-related appearances.

Morrill had strong opinions about intercollegiate athletics. He had long been opposed to the idea of postseason games, believing that extending the season took too much time away from the classroom. In 1946, shortly before the National Collegiate Athletic Association voted to allow postseason play, Morrill wrote to Big Ten commissioner Kenneth "Tug" Wilson:

> I realize the plan is drawn so that no conference institution is required to send its team to the coast, even if it should be so designated. But any of us so designated would find it hard to live among the newspapermen and alumni if we declined to send a championship team to the coast.... I will frankly be sorry to see the change.... I wish that kind of hysteria and crazy thinking would crystallize around pro-football, thus giving it a more proper outlet.[132]

Among Morrill's associates in the central administration inherited from his predecessor, Walter Coffey, were Malcolm Willey, academic vice president, and William Middlebrook, business vice president. A sociologist with a doctorate from Columbia University, Willey had been at the university since arriving as an instructor in 1923. In 1934, he left sociology to enter administration, becoming vice president for academic administration in 1943. Active in both national and local civic affairs, Willey served on the board of the National Science Foundation. Locally, he was a member of the Walker Art Center board and the Minnesota Historical Society, of the Six O'Clock Club and the Skylight Club. Interested in liberal education, he in 1959 chaired the all-university advisory committee that planned the transformation of the West Central School of Agriculture into the University of Minnesota, Morris.[133] Inevitably, in a position as far-reaching as the academic vice presidency, Willey had some critics. E. W. Ziebarth defended Willey, believing that "he was more imaginative than much of the faculty felt, much more creative."[134]

David Berg, longtime director of the Office of Management Planning and Information Services and before that a staff member in the business office, thought that Willey "was more concerned with scholarly issues and was willing to let Bill Middlebrook run things—as long as his views were heard." Berg saw Middlebrook as "an extraordinary person, one of the more impressive people I've ever met. There was no question as to who was dominant in that pair. Middlebrook ran the university until he quit. In my experience, he was more powerful than the presidents he served."[135] Ziebarth put it slightly differently: "Malcolm Willey, it seemed to me, was always forceful enough, always a gentleman. It was Bill Middlebrook who came in carrying the big stick and flourishing it."[136]

Richard Caldecott, who later served as dean of the College of Biological Sciences, described Middlebrook's ability to cut through bureaucratic red tape:

> In June of 1955, after I had been on campus for two months, the State Department asked me to spend a month in Geneva, Switzerland, serving as one of the two U.S. geneticists at the Eisenhower Atoms for Peace Conference. They advised me that they would transfer the funds for travel and per diem into the AEC [Atomic Energy Commission] account. When I processed the application for travel, the dean called me to his office and advised me that it was college policy that no university funds could be expended for travel outside the state of Minnesota. The only exception was that adjacent states could be visited provided any overnight lodging that was necessary would take place in Minnesota. To make a long story short, I carried the

request to the academic vice president, who then sent me to Vice President Middlebrook. Within minutes, Mr. Middlebrook was on the phone to the dean and the problem was resolved. In those days, the power in the university rested in his hands. I found him to be a delightful but forceful individual who had the faculty's interests at heart.[137]

Middlebrook was largely responsible for the creation of University Grove, an area near the campus in St. Paul set aside for faculty homes; it was to become one of the principal attractions for senior faculty members.

Middlebrook served as Morrill's chief legislative liaison: "He would go over and testify in the legislature and refuse to tell them things. He'd keep a budget book in his lap, under the table. They'd ask him questions but he was able to say to legislators, 'I'm not going to tell you that' and they would take it."[138] Some thought that President Morrill left too much to Middlebrook, but Ziebarth found him to be "a man for whom I had enormous regard and high respect." It was Morrill who persuaded Ziebarth to take the office of director of the Summer School: "I came into his office, and he simply relaxed, and crossed his legs, and smoked a cigarette, and smiled. He always knew what was going on."[139]

Morrill was also assisted by some exceptional deans. One was E. G. Williamson, dean of students. Appointed in 1941, Williamson was an early believer in involving students in university affairs, not merely "keeping the lid on" their activities. James Mullin, then an undergraduate student, knew him well:

> Dean Williamson was a charismatic character, and he had a special way of relating to students. He talked me into becoming a freshman camp counselor for three years running, and I remember him very forcefully directing Mike Streitz and myself (both off the streets of North Minneapolis) and Mike's future wife, Patty Tierney, to come up with some plan that would take "Greek Week" out of the arena of frivolity, where it had wallowed since inception, specializing in toga parties, chariot races, and campus carnival, and harness the energy of the fraternities and sororities into something productive.[140]

Williamson introduced Mullin and other student leaders to Nathan Crabtree, the vice president for public affairs at General Mills, who was interested in Radio Free Europe. As a result of this meeting, the students undertook a fund-raising campaign for Radio Free Europe. Mullin recalled, "That was an accomplishment I had some pride in, though it was really Williamson steering the students in the direction he wanted us to go."[141]

Deeply committed to the interplay of research and practice, Williamson always emphasized the importance of undertaking serious studies of student life. He advocated four freedoms for students: freedom to discuss controversial issues and topics of their own choosing; freedom to hear speakers of their own choice; freedom of editorial comment in student journalism; and the right to participate in discussion of matters that affect students. This was not, he said, freedom without restraint, but freedom within the constraints of organized society. It was largely through Williamson's efforts that Minnesota achieved the student climate that made it possible to avert serious disturbances during the coming era of student protests. Although he was widely respected, students increasingly became restive under the paternalism that lay beneath the programs within the purview of the dean of students.[142]

From 1951 to 1963, Errett W. McDiarmid was dean of the College of Science, Literature, and the Arts. Earlier he had been head of the University Libraries, a position in which he established close contacts with many faculty members, especially those in the humanities. Search procedures were informal in those days, and McDiarmid had no idea he was being considered for the deanship "until President Morrill took me downtown for lunch and offered me the job." McDiarmid was well liked by faculty members because of his informal, personal style—he had photographs taken of many department faculties so that he could learn his colleagues' names—but in his later years some thought he was not forceful enough in dealing with disputes over general education and an early round of budget cuts. His greatest achievements were the creation of the Honors Division for students of outstanding abilities and his success in recruiting faculty of high quality.[143] After retiring as dean, he returned to teaching in the Library School and was active in gathering the works of Arthur Conan Doyle for the university's repository of Sherlock Holmes materials, the largest in the world.

Athelstan Spilhaus, dean of the Institute of Technology (IT) from 1949 through 1966, was a wunderkind with an astonishing range of interests extending from advanced geophysics to popular science as well as ancillary fields like urban design and mass transit. Born in South Africa, Spilhaus had studied geophysics at the Massachusetts Institute of Technology and had invented the bathythermograph, a device to plot seawater temperatures that was used in World War II to detect submarines in areas where sonar was not effective.[144] Never content to simply sit in the Dean's office, Spilhaus in 1951 was an adviser to the scientists testing atomic bombs in Nevada.

Three years later, President Eisenhower named him the first U.S. ambassador to the United Nations Educational, Scientific, and Cultural Organization (UNESCO).

The skyways that came to link buildings in downtown Minneapolis and on parts of the campus were Spilhaus's idea. A futurist, he dreamed of constructing domed cities and spent considerable time and energy arguing for worldwide birth control. In addition, he wrote a syndicated comic strip, "Our New Age," which popularized serious scientific knowledge. "Spilhaus was a great wanderer," Jerry Shepherd recalled. "He asked me to become associate dean and I then discovered I was really going to have to serve essentially as dean because he was gone so much.... I would have resigned after one year, but I agreed to stay for two and that was it." Spilhaus had a fine sense of public relations but, as Shepherd said, "there were some problems with him that became more and more apparent as time went on, and it got to the point where it became necessary to ask for his resignation." His aspiration to become president of the university was crushed, and as he went off in a fit of pique to work on the International Fair in Seattle, he was heard to refer to the institution as "that great gray mediocrity." But he was the longest-serving dean of IT, "really an innovator and in the best way, a fresh wind of change." Warren Ibele, professor of mechanical engineering and dean of the Graduate School from 1975 to 1982, spoke the mind of many when he credited Spilhaus with "bringing the Institute of Technology, the engineering departments, into the modern age." Spilhaus went on to hold a variety of government and academic posts; he died in 1998.[145]

The Institute of Technology was the second-largest college on the Twin Cities campus with 2,441 students in 1950, growing to 3,495 in 1960. Research expenditures grew from $850,000 in 1950 to $1.35 million just two years later. By the end of the 1960s, external research dollars had reached $6 million.[146] The institute had four major divisions: architecture, chemistry, engineering, and the School of Mines and Metallurgy with its Mines Experiment Station. E. W. Davis, director of the Mines Experiment Station from 1918 to 1951, played a pivotal role in mining through the development of equipment and processes that made the production of taconite economically viable. The Reserve Mining Company taconite plant at Silver Bay, Minnesota, was named in honor of Davis.[147] A second faculty member who had a major impact beyond the campus was James J. Ryan of mechanical engineering. Described by contemporaries as "one of those rare beings who never lost his sense of wonder," Ryan invented the retractable seat belt, explored other aspects of automobile safety, and served as a consultant on the development of the automatic flight data recorder—the "black box."[148]

The deans of the College of Education balanced their focus on teacher education in Minnesota with national research interests. Wesley E. Peik, recognized for his publications on social studies education and for his advocacy of higher standards for teacher education, had served since 1938. He died in 1951 and was succeeded by Marcia Edwards, who was named acting dean. Edwards had earned master's and Ph.D. degrees in educational psychology at Minnesota and subsequently joined the faculty. President Morrill attempted to persuade her to accept the deanship on a permanent basis, but, as Robert Beck recorded in his history of the College of Education, "she adamantly refused. Though she saw no problems . . . [in the College or the University], she felt that educators throughout Minnesota and other states were not yet ready to see a woman appointed dean of a major college of education."[149]

A search committee then chose Walter W. Cook, a professor of educational psychology who was respected for his research on spelling and on individual differences between students as well as his activities with the National Education Association. Under Cook, demonstration schools and student teaching expanded, a student placement office was created, and the Institute of Child Development and the School of Physical Education joined the college. The college's purview had always included higher education as well as elementary and secondary schooling. Cook was greatly concerned about the shortage of teachers as the number of children growing up in Minnesota increased, and he did what he could to train more. Beck commented that Cook was "kept from pomposity by his sense of humor; he refrained from calling attention to his own work but never hesitated to brag about that of his colleagues. Not long before his death in 1964 he unblushingly admitted that 'truthfully I don't know of another college which ranks above us.'"[150]

University College did not have a dean. J. W. Buchta had served as chairman of its curriculum committee since 1941, succeeding the physicist John Tate, who had led in the development of this intercollege program. Since it did not have its own faculty, University College drew on staff from various colleges; a committee of faculty members from other colleges also governed it. The college was established in 1930 to provide flexibility for students in shaping their own programs of study.[151] Prewar enrollment in the college was generally under 80 students. The influx of returning veterans found that the college suited their needs, and enrollment had increased to 298 in 1946.[152]

A second significant experiment, the General College, also dated from the 1930s. Horace T. Morse was its dean in 1950. Initially called "the Junior College of the University of Minnesota," it had started as an experimental program in 1932 with an emphasis on the average middle class of the population. Under its first director, Malcolm S. MacLean, the General College tried to address the fact that nearly half of the freshmen who entered the university failed to graduate. The original assistant director, Fred Hovde, was just back from study at Oxford. Later president of Purdue, Hovde taught chemistry and physics. MacLean and Dean Williamson offered a course called The World of Work.[153]

The General College was designed so that students would receive a coherent educational experience in their two-year program. The college was based on open admissions, research into student characteristics, and a student-centered approach to the curriculum. The movement from experimental unit to full collegiate status had come in stages: in 1940, the college was given its own budget; in 1946 (when Morse took charge), the director assumed the title of dean; and in 1951, the supervisory committee overseeing the experiment was discharged, having completed its work. The college had 1,488 students in 1950; ten years later the number was 2,497.[154] It is appropriate that the most prestigious all-university award recognizing outstanding undergraduate teaching was named for Horace T. Morse.[155]

Maynard Pirsig, dean of the Law School from 1948 to 1955, had been born in 1902 on an Iowa farm near the Minnesota border. His father, who had left school after the eighth grade, had hoped that Pirsig would become a lawyer and supported him through the Minnesota Law School. Pirsig was greatly influenced by Everett Fraser, his predecessor as dean. Like many other early leaders of the university, Fraser had run the Law School without much consultation. Under Pirsig there was increasing demand for faculty involvement, and his years proved to be a time of transition. A 1955 self-survey recommended that the faculty determine policy, with the dean as their leader and advocate of their views.[156] Pirsig stepped down as dean in 1955 and was followed by William B. Lockhart, who worked effectively in the more collegial practices of the period; both he and Pirsig did much to attract and retain high-quality faculty and students.[157]

Under Pirsig, the law faculty had reviewed the Minnesota Plan, an innovative approach to the structure and content of the curriculum initiated by Fraser in 1930. The major points at issue were how many years students should study as undergraduates before entering the Law School, and how many years the law degree should take. The faculty also considered how much of the course work should be offered by the law faculty and how much might be taken in other colleges. The faculty voted in 1957 to increase the time of prelaw studies and shorten and intensify the course work in the Law School itself, reducing the students' time from four years to three and a half. In fall quarter 1950, the Law School enrollment was 501, lower than the postwar height but well above the prewar range of 300 to 350.[158]

The university's first professional architecture degree had been awarded in 1877. In 1913 the Department of Architecture was organized and located within the renamed College of Engineering and Architecture; it was headed by Frederick Mann from 1913 to 1937 and by Roy Jones from 1937 to 1954. Led by Mann and Jones through the Beaux-Arts and modernist periods, the program was considered to be among the strongest in the country. In 1952, it had a faculty of thirteen and 180 students; practicing architects regarded it as being "twenty years ahead of the profession."[159]

Ralph Rapson, appointed head of architecture in 1954, continued the school's links to the modernist tradition. He had studied with Eliel Saarinen at Cranbrook Academy and immediately before coming to Minnesota had taught at the Massachusetts Institute of Technology, where he came into contact with modernists Walter Gropius, Marcel Breuer, and Alvar Aalto. During his thirty years as head of architecture, the school was recognized for strengths in architectural drawing and design as well as for its contributions to professional practice.[160]

The School of Social Work had close working relationships with both state and national social service agencies. By 1952, 1,200 students had completed baccalaureate-level study in social work, 318 had earned M.S.W. degrees, and 2 had received doctorates. Established in 1917, the school was one of the ten largest schools of social work in the country, offering specialized study in case work, group work, and community organization. One of the most illustrious graduates, Whitney Young, who received a master's degree in 1947, went on to become dean of the Atlanta School of Social Work and president of the Urban League. John Kidneigh served as the school's director for many years.[161]

The School of Journalism, like the School of Social Work, was part of the College of Liberal Arts. Funded with a bequest from the estate of William J. Murphy, publisher of the Minneapolis *Tribune,* the school, which had been founded in 1922, was headed by Ralph D. Casey from 1930 until 1958. Robert L. Jones served as director until 1967. It was ranked among the top programs in the country. In 1951, the regents approved a Ph.D. program in journalism, and in the 1960s the curriculum was expanded to include broadcast and magazine journalism, photojournalism, and public relations. Renamed the School of Journalism and Mass Communication in 1966, it was known for offering both liberal arts and professional education.

Faculty members Mitchell V. Charnley and George S. Hage were particularly remembered as mentors for their students. Other key faculty members during the postwar years included Roy E. Carter, Edwin Emery, J. Edward Gerald, Robert L. Jones, Raymond B. Nixon, and Harold Wilson. Alumni included well-known figures in the profession such as Hedley Donovan, Harry Reasoner, Carl Rowan, Harrison Salisbury, and Eric Sevareid.[162]

In the mid-1950s, the School of Business Administration occupied Vincent Hall. Richard L. Kozelka served as dean from 1945 to 1960. Postwar enrollment rose to more than 1,700 students in 1947 but by 1950 had fallen back to fewer than 1,000. A decade later it was 673. In 1948 the school received approval to offer a Ph.D.; in 1953 an M.A. in industrial relations was added; in 1960 an evening M.B.A. program was instituted, and entry-level programs in office and secretarial management were discontinued.[163]

Theodore C. Blegen had been dean of the Graduate School since 1940. A historian who received a doctorate from the university in 1925, he served for a time as head of the Minnesota Historical Society and wrote or was coauthor of more than twenty books. Most of these books, reflecting his Norwegian heritage, were on immigration or Minnesota history. One of the first scholars to use immigrant letters written home to Norway as a source, he anticipated the new social history, written "from the bottom up." Blegen was one of the candidates for president of the university in 1944 when Morrill was selected. He was (he wrote) "deeply disappointed" but came to appreciate Morrill's skill in dealing with people. Like Guy Stanton Ford, his predecessor as dean of the Graduate School, Blegen saw the recruitment of faculty and the building up of departments as a critically important responsibility.[164]

Under Blegen's leadership, the Graduate School grew significantly; more than 12,000 master's degrees and 3,000 doctorates were awarded while he was dean. Graduate enrollment in the fall of 1950 was 3,732, rising a decade later to 4,053 in the Twin Cities and Duluth and 627 at the Mayo Center in Rochester. As has been noted, research dollars expended for graduate programs grew dramatically, increasing from $1.5 million in 1946–47 to

$15.2 million in 1960–61.[165] Like McDiarmid, he was a Sherlock Holmes enthusiast and a member of the Baker Street Irregulars; in 1951 he wrote "The Crowded Box-Room," a study of the mind of Holmes.[166]

In 1948, the University Library had just over 1.4 million volumes, with close to 100,000 added the previous academic year. This placed it among the top three public academic libraries in the United States, behind the University of California and the University of Illinois. Priorities in addition to the collections were filling out periodical sets and acquiring materials related to Americana, English literature and history, and Swedish literature. Microfilm versions of newspapers became available, simplifying storage and making it easier for researchers to obtain information. Space issues in the postwar years were not limited to student housing and classrooms. University librarian Errett McDiarmid cautioned: "The storage of books represents a critical problem. Already the present capacity of the library building has been exceeded. Additional space must be found, either by way of departmental libraries or by semipermanent storage, or the library must face the alterative of discarding material from its collection." Despite this appeal, it would be two decades before a new library was constructed.[167]

## The Campus in St. Paul

In 1950, the St. Paul campus of the university consisted of Agriculture, Forestry, and Home Economics; the new school of Veterinary Medicine; the Minnesota Extension Service; and the Minnesota Experiment Station. Enrollment in these units totaled 1,854. The largest was agriculture, followed by home economics, forestry, and veterinary medicine. Home economics was predominantly female, the others predominantly male. Graduate programs, mainly in agriculture, attracted 399 students.[168]

The dean of agriculture was Clyde H. Bailey. A professor of agriculture biochemistry since 1921 and dean since 1942, he was known internationally for his research on the chemistry of wheat, optimum conditions for bread production, flour quality, and food technology. Bailey had worked with H. K. Hayes, who by "crossing and recrossing grain and corn varieties discovered the strains most likely to survive under exacting conditions of growth" like those in Minnesota.[169] When Bailey retired in 1952 he was succeeded by Harold Macy, a dairy bacteriologist.

Paul E. Miller headed agricultural extension from 1938 to 1954. Earlier he had been an agronomist at the West Central School and Experiment Station in Morris, the predecessor of the university campus there. His division included the 4-H program and extension home economics. Extension specialists advised farmers on agronomy, marketing commodities such as poultry, eggs, dairy products, and livestock, forestry, soils, vegetable gardening, and horticulture. Skuli Rutford, who followed Miller, served as director from 1954 to 1963. As was customary, extension agents helped to make available the findings of experiment station researchers in such areas as hybrid corn, new pesticides, weed control, and artificial breeding of dairy cattle.

Leon C. Snyder, who served for years as chief horticulturist, was well known for his newspaper columns on gardening. In 1956, he located land near Chanhassen that would become the Landscape Arboretum, expanding horticultural activities in the state. Another popular figure was Maynard Speece, an extension specialist who was often heard on WCCO radio before taking a post in the U.S. Department of Agriculture. In the years immediately following the war, it was hard to keep the county extension agent positions filled, partly because of inadequate salaries; in 1952 alone, there were forty-seven resignations and forty-five new appointments among the sixty agents.[170] Agricultural extension and the Agricultural Experiment Station remained important; in the eyes of many rural Minnesotans, they *were* the university.

Beginning in 1888, the St. Paul campus also housed the Central School of Agriculture, a three-year vocational program for young men and women offering introductory courses in agriculture as well as traditional high school subjects. It was one of five such residential schools in Minnesota; the others were at Morris, Crookston, Grand Rapids, and Waseca. J. O. Christianson, superintendent of the school between 1932 and 1960, traveled widely throughout the state, becoming well known as a public speaker. Ralph Miller, historian of the School of Agriculture, observed that "Christianson had a knack for being able to deliver the same speech to a group of farmers, bankers, businessmen, or educators and make it sound as if the speech had been written for them. In the 1950s period, he often used one of two titles, 'Our Part in These Times' and 'Rediscovering America.'" Christianson knew hundreds of farm families and seldom forgot a name or face. He recognized all the students and could tell where they were from, their family background, and if the bankers or some other group were giving them a scholarship. "His homey 'man of the soil' spirit won over every audience."[171] It was his vision of international agriculture education that established the student exchange program in 1948–49; now it is known as MAST (Minnesota Agricultural Student Trainee Program).

The Board of Regents approved several changes in terminology during the 1950s. The Department of Agriculture became the Institute of Agriculture, Forestry, and Home Economics; divisions became departments; and the Agricultural Extension Division was officially named a "service" to recognize its responsibilities at an administrative level higher than a department's. Today it is known as the University of Minnesota Extension Service.

In 1950, the School of Forestry primarily enrolled undergraduate students in programs that were heavily timber related. Over the next quarter century, research funding (mainly through the Agricultural Experiment Station) and the graduate program showed spectacular growth. During these years, the social and physical sciences joined the biological sciences with integrated programs focused on management and use of renewable forest resources. Under the leadership of Frank Kaufert, dean from 1947 until his retirement in 1974, the school gained collegiate status and was recognized as one of the top forestry programs in the nation.[172]

The University of Minnesota led the largest American university-building program in Japan and Korea. Professor Arthur Schneider, who had served as a forestry specialist with the American military government in Korea, was the in-country leader of an extensive University of Minnesota program to help rebuild Seoul National University. Professor Tracy F. Taylor of the College of Education served as administrative head of the program.

The program was initiated in 1955 under the auspices of the Foreign Operations Administration in Washington, which from 1952 to 1955 was headed by Harold Stassen, a university alumnus and former governor of Minnesota. A broad-scale operation, the Minnesota initiative included engineering and medicine as well as agriculture. Responsibilities of Minnesota faculty members and administrators in Korea included advice on curricula, reconstruction of buildings, acquisition of equipment and supplies, and renewal of libraries. In addition, on-site faculty members helped select individuals from Seoul University to undertake further study at the University of Minnesota. During this period, more than ninety faculty members from Seoul studied at Minnesota.[173]

Veterinary medicine, previously a department within agriculture, became an independent school in 1947. Before World War II, Minnesota veterinary students completed preveterinary requirements at the University of Minnesota and then transferred to a veterinary college in another state. One reason for the establishment of the College of Veterinary Medicine at Minnesota was that students were finding it increasingly difficult to gain admission to programs at other universities. Lobbying by seventy veterans of World War II was a crucial factor in the creation of the school. Dr. W. L. Boyd was the original director; in 1954, he was followed by Dr. W. T. S. Thorp. In 1947 twenty-four students were enrolled; remarkably, twenty-three of them completed the required courses and received their degrees in 1951.[174]

Facing a "mad scramble for space, supplies, faculty, and curriculum," veterinary medicine occupied army barracks as well as Temporary East of Haecker, conducted surgery classes in Old Anatomy, and held clinics in campus barns; its motto in those first years was "Make Do."[175] A veterinary clinic was constructed in 1950; funding was approved in 1952 for a veterinary science building, followed in 1957 by an appropriation for a diagnostic laboratory. The college served several constituencies: individual livestock and poultry producers, industrial producers, and—a relatively new constituency—the owners of companion animals.

In 1957 the regents granted the school collegiate status, and its director became a dean. The school had progressed from provisional accreditation in 1951 to full accreditation in 1957. Women accounted for 6 percent of the total enrollment in 1966, and the percentage increased thereafter. Responding to changes in demand, the college revised its priorities over the years; by the end of the century, it had deemphasized the study of beef cattle and become a world leader in swine, poultry, and dairy production services as well as preventive medicine for companion animals.[176]

Founded in 1900, home economics had more than five hundred students, all female, in 1950. Wylle B. McNeal served as chief of home economics from 1923 until her retirement in 1950. During her tenure, the introductory courses included Choice and Care of Clothing, Personal Relationships, Introduction to Nutrition, and Introduction to Related Art. McNeal was particularly interested in nutrition. The home economics building was named in her honor in 1960.[177]

One of McNeal's wisest actions was to support the work of two sisters, Harriet and Vetta Goldstein, who were energetically promoting study of the arts among home economics students. In their nationally recognized textbook, *Art in Everyday Life,* published in 1925, they set out their creed: "When beauty is expressed in our surroundings, it becomes a part of our life and our personality.... Good taste... is the application of the principles of design to the problems of life, where appearance as well as utility is a consideration."[178] During their long careers, the Goldsteins taught more than thirty thousand students. In 1943, they recruited Esther Dendel to help them. She has left a vivid description of her arrival in Minnesota:

The sisters met my train. I saw two smiling middle-aged women in dark cloth coats and sturdy, no-nonsense oxfords, both overwhelmed by large black hats. They were not handsome in a conventional way, but there was a distinguished air about them. It is something called presence. They wore no make-up, but their faces had that heightened aliveness which cosmetics are supposed to impart. It came, I think, from the interest and friendliness that shone in their eyes.... In the back seat of their immaculate black Chevrolet was a woolen lap robe that they had warmed in the oven and wrapped in paper to hold heat.... At the classroom next morning, I found there was no loom room, no pottery annex, no jewelry laboratory, no dyeing vats.... What I saw were some bare classrooms, a crowded office, and almost no equipment except a slide projector.[179]

These limitations are gone, in part because the Goldsteins willed their estate to the university to establish a design gallery. Named for the sisters, the Goldstein Gallery opened in 1976 with important collections of costumes, textiles, and decorative art; it contains illustrative materials for teaching about clothing and dress from 1760 to the present.[180]

Increasing professionalism and specialization, better equipment, and improved funding came to the St. Paul colleges in the 1950s. A new library was dedicated in 1953, and the student union was dedicated in 1959. International perspectives broadened the thinking of faculty and students, and the experimental work of the Minnesota Experiment Station was aided by the acquisition of the Rosemount site.

## College of Medical Sciences

The College of Medical Sciences at this time included the Medical School, public health, and nursing. With the end of the war, faculty members who had been in the military services returned to the university, and large numbers of young doctors who had gone directly from medical school to the army were able to begin residencies. Many departments were led by faculty members at the peak of their careers: Leo Rigler in X-ray diagnosis; Karl Wilhelm Stenstrom in radiation therapy; Wesley Spink, an expert on brucellosis who was studying sulfa drugs and penicillin; Cecil Watson in diseases of the liver; Wallace Armstrong on the use of fluoride in preventing tooth decay. Two major figures were Maurice Visscher, an acknowledged authority on the heart and circulation, and surgeon Owen Wangensteen, an ardent believer in the importance of a long-term commitment to research:

"Understanding the nature of a difficult problem comes rarely, if ever, all at once. Persistent fact-finding through research is the only instrument which can dispel the darkness which obscures our vision."[181] During the 1950s, Dr. B. J. Kennedy was widely recognized for his contributions to the development of the specialty of oncology and Dr. Robert Good for seminal findings about the immune system, a crucial prerequisite for transplant surgery.[182]

Dr. C. Walton Lillehei, appointed associate professor of surgery in 1951 devoted his career to heart surgery research. In 1952, Dr. F. John Lewis led a team of surgeons who performed the world's first direct vision open-heart surgery. In 1954, Lillehei and his associates began to use a cross-circulation technique for open-heart surgery. Blood from a donor was used to maintain circulation while the patient's own heart did not function. Early patients were children with symptoms so severe they were unlikely to live long unless their heart defects were corrected; the first successful operation was performed on a five-year-old girl. The Lillehei group had performed one hundred open-heart operations by the end of 1955. A bubble oxygenator developed by Dr. Richard A. De Wall made open-heart surgery practical.

Three years later, Lillehei began to use pacemakers—powered by electricty from wall sockets—to overcome heart rhythm problems. When the electricity went out, the pacemakers didn't work. Then Lillehei asked Earl Bakken, who was repairing medical equipment at the university, if he would make a device that would pulse electricity—give electric pulses—maybe seventy pulses per minute; it wasn't that difficult for an engineer.[183] They tried it out on a dog one day and put it in a human the next. In 1958, Bakken and his brother-in-law Palmer Hermundslie incorporated Medtronic Inc. to manufacture these portable pacemakers. By the end of the decade Lillehei and his coworkers had used them successfully on sixty-six patients.[184] The encounter between Lillehei and Bakken led to one of Minnesota's great medical technology success stories. By the end of the century, Medtronic had grown from its beginnings in a garage in northeast Minneapolis to a global medical technology company with annual sales of over $4 billion and more than 22,000 employees. Subsequently, St. Jude Medical, the world's premier heart valve manufacturer, developed from university-related connections. Over time, more than five hundred medical division companies were created. Informally referred to as "Medical Alley," these companies contributed significantly to Minnesota's economy.[185]

The University Hospitals, directed by Raymond Amberg, served the dual purpose of providing an educational setting for students and providing care for indigent patients. New buildings were needed to accommodate new procedures. The Variety Club Heart Hospital, completed in 1951, was the first hospital in the United States to be devoted entirely to heart patients. Originally many of the patients were suffering from rheumatic fever, a problem that became less common after Dr. Lewis Wannamaker promoted the use of penicillin to treat strep throat, the precursor of rheumatic fever.[186] University Hospitals, with the Elliott Memorial and Christian wings, were functioning with outmoded facilities built in 1911. A new hospital building opened in 1954, largely as the result of the work of Dr. Harold S. Diehl, who had been dean of the College of Medical Sciences since 1935.

Diehl campaigned to construct new facilities dedicated to the memory of Drs. Charles and William Mayo, both of whom had died in 1939. The plans had to be shelved during the war, but discussions with the legislature were reopened in 1945. Price increases, labor shortages, and complications during the Korean War delayed groundbreaking until 1950. When it was completed in 1954, Diehl commented, "I still feel like touching the walls to see whether they are real or whether they are a continuation of the dreams that we have had about this building for the past fifteen years." Further hospital construction began in 1957 with funds raised by Minnesota's Masons in support of a cancer hospital.[187]

A 1958 *Minneapolis Star* editorial described the Medical School as "one of the greatest in the world, if not the greatest." The editorial continued, "It is well known that the University medical school has less friction, less rivalry and less jealousy than any other similar organization in the country."[188]

Since 1915, the Mayo Foundation for Medical Education and Research at Rochester had been a part of the university's Graduate School. Mayo and the university created one of the first programs in the country to make it possible for M.D.s to study for a master's or doctoral degree while preparing for board certification in clinical specialties such as surgery, pediatrics, and obstetrics. In 1950–51, six hundred Mayo fellows were enrolled in graduate degree programs. Mayo was accorded four seats in the University Senate in 1957. The University of Minnesota faculty celebrated with their counterparts in Rochester in 1950 when Dr. Philip S. Hench, professor of medicine, and Dr. Edward Kendell, professor of physiological chemistry, were awarded the Nobel Prize for Medicine for their research on cortisone.[189]

## Dentistry

William H. Crawford, a specialist in prosthetic dentistry, served as dean of dentistry from 1945 to 1963. He had come to Minnesota from Indiana, where he had held a similar post. Dean Crawford strengthened the dental and dental hygiene curricula and was recognized for the development of programs in graduate and continuing education as well as the use of audiovisual systems for teaching. Crawford asked Leon Singer, who held an appointment in physiological chemistry, to teach in the dental school. Through many publications, Singer and Crawford were largely responsible for influencing public policy on water fluoridation. Despite some local opposition, fluoride was soon introduced into the water supply of most communities, and tooth decay was substantially reduced.

Another of Crawford's key appointments was Robert Gorlin. Originally assigned to engineering school as part of his military service, Gorlin was moved to dentistry. After earning a D.D.S degree and additional study at Columbia University, Gorlin was selected to be the dental adviser for a top-secret government project, Operation Blue Jay, involved in the construction of a line of radar bases to provide warning to the United States and Canada in the event of enemy attack. "The secretive nature of the project was dumbfounding," Gorlin recalled, "especially as intercontinental ballistic missiles were a reality, which made the bases obsolete before they were created." Gorlin came to Minnesota in 1951 to provide dental screening for the ten thousand construction workers before they were sent to northern Canada and Greenland to work on the radar bases. The screening took place out of the public eye, at the university's Rosemount Experiment Station, in facilities leased by the government. Gorlin enlisted Dental School faculty members to examine the recruits. This was mutually satisfactory, as it allowed the screenings to be done quickly and also gave the faculty members additional income.

Five years later, Gorlin joined the faculty as chair of the oral pathology division. He was happy that the university's structure allowed him to work with specialists in such fields as radiology, ophthalmology, and dermatology: "At the time I didn't see how remarkable this was," he recalled. He was particularly interested in research on aspects of the immune system being conducted by Robert Good of the Department of Pathology. Gorlin became recognized as an international expert in genetic malformations of the mouth, face, and head. In 1958 he was promoted to full professor, the youngest in the university, and in 1978 he was named a Regents Professor.[190]

The Dental School was the only one in Minnesota; it also had a strong regional presence. Most dentists in Minnesota and many in neighboring states were its graduates. In 1958, the school became affiliated with the University of Minnesota Alumni Association, offering that year the first annual Alumni Day. The dental clinics continued to offer a training site as well as an option for treating the public. In 1951, the clinic occupied space on the third floor of Owre Hall (named in honor of former dean Alfred Owre).[191]

## Nursing

The nursing school was a key component of the College of Medical Sciences. Katharine Densford had presided over the school since 1930 and was to remain dean until her retirement in 1959. One of the country's first nursing schools affiliated with a university, it had been established in 1909. An effective Densford regularly faced tight budgets, staff shortages, and a medical establishment slow to embrace change. She was highly regarded both at the university and nationally for her role in strengthening the nursing profession.

Densford's philosophy was that education should follow training and that the School of Nursing was "ready to do the work of a university." In 1946, with backing from President Morrill and financial support from the Kellogg Foundation, the school phased out its diploma program to concentrate on its bachelor's degree program. In addition, Densford added training opportunities for nurses in Minnesota's rural hospitals. Professionalism was taken further through the addition of professional master's degrees, established through collaboration with the College of Education in 1950 and 1951.

Densford's colleagues recall her national search for talented faculty members and her encouraging bachelor's degree holders to seek master's degrees, while those who held the master's degrees were encouraged to pursue doctoral study. In 1959—the year of the school's fiftieth anniversary—Densford was the speaker at the all-university Cap and Gown Day, an honor conferred each year on a respected faculty member or administrator. She was the first woman to give the address.[192] Densford retired that year, although she remained active in national and state nursing organizations. Weaver-Densford Hall, built in 1980, was named in 1997 in honor of Densford and longtime pharmacy dean Lawrence Weaver.

Densford's impact was as significant externally as it was within the university. From 1944 to 1948, she served as president of the American Nurses Association; she was a member of the National Commission on Hospital Care and chair of the Minnesota Nursing Council.[193] Acknowledged by her peers for her commitment to human rights, Densford personally reached out to Japanese American nurses who had been relocated from the West Coast to Minnesota during World War II. Through her efforts, African American graduate nurses became members of the American Nurses Association.

She lobbied for the creation of the Cadet Nurse Corps and helped ensure its success; nursing faculty member Lucile H. Petry became national director of the nurse cadet program. Cecilia H. Hauge, associate professor of nursing and director of nursing at the University Hospitals, became a lieutenant colonel in the Army Nursing Corps, serving as chief nurse of the 26th General Hospital, staffed predominantly by doctors and nurses from the University of Minnesota. Three other nursing graduates attained the rank of major; fifteen were colonels, and many more were first lieutenants.[194]

## Pharmacy

College of Pharmacy programs were strongly influenced by the vision of founding dean Frederick J. Wulling.[195] As dean of pharmacy from 1892 to 1936, Wulling helped shape the curriculum not only at Minnesota but also throughout the country. Students were expected to enter with appropriate high school studies as preparation for a three-year collegiate program. A fourth year, originally optional, later became mandatory. Wulling engaged in a lifelong campaign to ensure recognition of pharmacy as a health science profession comparable to the others, and he insisted that the education of pharmacists be equally well grounded.[196] In 1942, Wulling Hall was named in his honor.

Charles H. Rogers, the second dean of pharmacy, held the position from 1936 to 1957. Recruited by Wulling to the Department of Medicinal Chemistry, Rogers continued to emphasize the importance of a scientifically based curriculum and a research-oriented faculty. With faculty members like Rogers, Glenn Jenkins, Ole Gisvold, and Frank Di Gangi, the Department of Medicinal Chemistry was acknowledged to be one of the best in the country.[197]

In 1951, the only pharmacy college in the state received an A rating from the American Council on Pharmaceutical Education. Reviewers commended the curriculum, saying it was "substantial and well administered with a high standard."[198]

The field of pharmacy was affected both by wartime research and by a surge of discoveries made just prior to the war. This "golden age of drug discovery" prevailed from the 1930s through the 1960s, as antibiotics, antihistamines, steroids, and cardiovascular, antipsychotic, and anticancer agents were developed and marketed at a pace unmatched in history. Synthesizing new drugs was easier than extracting them from plants; it was also faster, and purity and potency were standardized more easily.[199]

## Public Health

The unit once known as the Department of Preventative Medicine and Public Health became the School of Public Health in 1944. Drs. Charles and William Mayo, in addition to their work in medicine, had long been active in the field of public health. Their interest led to funding for the new school at the university; one gift paid for facilities, and another endowed the Mayo Professorship of Public Health. The school was one of the first to be accredited by the American Public Health Association. Gaylord Anderson, an internationally known researcher in epidemiology—known as "Mr. Public Health"—became director of the school and filled the Mayo Professorship. Anderson replaced Ruth Boynton, who had served during the war years as head of both public health and the Student Health Service. Other faculty members with national reputations included Theodore Olson in sanitary biology, Marian Murphy in public health nursing, and Franklin Top in epidemiology.

In 1958, the school initiated the first Ph.D. program in epidemiology in the United States. Leonard M. Schuman, a specialist in cancer-related epidemiology and an author of the first Surgeon General's Report on Smoking, headed the program. The Laboratory of Physiological Hygiene, subsequently known throughout the world for its research on factors that contribute to cardiovascular disease, joined the school in 1949, as did programs in hospital administration, veterinary public health, maternal and child health, public health engineering (later known as environmental health and safety), and public health nursing. The school enjoyed substantial federal funding; its graduate enrollment grew from just under 100 in 1954 to 235 a decade later.[200]

Within this internationally recognized group of researchers, Ancel Keys probably had the highest public profile. During the war, working on diet for the military, he created the famous "K rations." In 1947, he led the first longitudinal study of risk factors in heart attacks.[201] He later studied health factors related to the diets of the English, Italians, and Japanese. An October 2, 1951, letter from Keys to his colleagues, subsequently published as "Notes from a Medical Journal," commented on King George VI's recent surgery for lung cancer: "A curious outcome of the King's illness is likely to be effective persuasion to cut down on smoking; the King was a very heavy smoker until two years ago."[202]

*Time* featured Keys's research in a January 13, 1961, cover story warning of the danger of diets with too much cholesterol—information widely accepted later but revolutionary at the time. Keys, who was "trying to find out why people got sick, before they got sick," was described as "a doggedly inquisitive scientist, as familiar a figure in the vineyards of Crete, the mountains of Dalmatia, and the forests of Finland as he is on the University of Minnesota campus."[203]

## The University Reaches Out

Outreach to the citizens of the state is a hallmark of land-grant universities, through both formally constituted and informally operating programs and services. In addition to the Agricultural Extension Service, the university had a second formally constituted outreach unit, the General Extension Division. Known as Continuing Education and Extension after 1972, the General Extension Division had been founded in 1913 to offer university courses in the evenings when working people would be able to take them. Those offerings soon became—and have remained among—the country's largest credit-based programs, offering citizens access to credit courses through the undergraduate colleges of the university.[204] Julius Nolte, trained as a lawyer and described by President Coffman as "a Renaissance man with a hat full of brains," had served as dean of the division since 1944.[205]

Nolte was influential in the establishment of a variety of new programs to meet the changing needs of the postwar era. He believed that, in addition to its traditional role of providing broad access to the university, the division should respond to the continuing education needs of those who already held degrees. Radio station KUOM broadcast more than 6,500 programs annually; over 40 percent of broadcast time was devoted to music, a like percentage to K–12 educational programs through Minnesota School of the Air, just under 10 percent for news, 5 percent for agriculture programming, and just over 2 percent for miscellaneous programs. Among the new initiatives begun under Nolte were the State Organization Service, formed in 1949 to provide information and training for nonprofit organizations; the World Affairs Center, begun in 1950; the first university telecourse in child psychology, offered in 1955; the Department of Radio and Television, established in 1957; and the Minnesota Plan, the first university-based continuing education program for women, established in 1960. In 1950–51, the extension division had just over 13,000 registered in its evening classes, 4,500 in correspondence study, and approximately 6,500 in conferences and institutes.[206]

Among the university-based museums were the Tweed Museum at Duluth, with its collection of Barbizon school paintings; the University Gallery, with holdings of American art of the 1930s; the Museum of Natural History (named the James Ford Bell Museum in 1967), with its "Touch and Feel Room," often the first museum experience of Minnesota schoolchildren; and the Goldstein Gallery, with collections of costumes, textiles, and decorative arts. University theater offerings in the Twin Cities and Duluth drew both community and university audiences.

The University of Minnesota was one of the few American colleges and universities to be home to a major orchestra. The Minneapolis Symphony Orchestra (later the Minnesota Orchestra) used Northrop Auditorium as its base of operations from 1930 to 1974. Richard Cisek, the orchestra's general manager from 1965 to 1977 and its president from 1978 to 1990, believed that it was mutually beneficial to community and university to have the symphony on campus; it "offered an easy way for all students, not simply music students, to attend concerts."[207]

The Department of Concerts and Lectures sponsored weekly convocations held each Thursday in Northrop Auditorium and summer concerts on the mall in front of Northrop. The University Artists Course, begun in 1919, made it possible for Minnesota audiences to hear serious classical music at an affordable price. In addition to its campus activities, Concerts and Lectures organized a roster of speakers for high school and college assemblies, civic and social organizations.

For forty-one years, from 1945 to 1986, New York's Metropolitan Opera made Northrop Auditorium a regular stop on its national tour; Minnesotans were among the most loyal audiences. As touring became more costly, the opera was forced to drop a number of cities from the tour, but performances at Northrop continued until touring was discontinued altogether.

One of the most important aspects of outreach for any college or university is connections with its alumni. During the post–World War II years, the Minnesota Alumni Association was an organization in transition: the greater part of its membership had attended the university prior to the war. Thousands of recent graduates, many of them veterans, sought membership in the association, and women began to join in larger numbers.

Alumni programs and activities became more professional. In the Twin Cities, the association developed programs of interest both to those who had attended the university before 1940 and to the smaller, younger cohort of the World War II generation. In 1947, at the annual Alumni Day, the association established the Greater University Fund with the stated purpose of becoming a conduit through which alumni and friends could make gifts to the university. The association also improved its business procedures, provided increased assistance to local alumni clubs, and expanded the alumni magazine.

In 1950–51 the alumni association had close to 13,000 members. The membership fee was four dollars annually; five-year memberships were available for sixteen dollars and life memberships for sixty-five dollars. Executive director Edwin Haislet worked with a volunteer board and a staff of seventeen full-time and three part-time members. There were six constituent societies: Law, Institute of Technology, Agriculture, Band, the all-women's Alumnae Club, and the all-male M Club (for sports fans). During the 1950–51 academic year, with $10,000 raised in alumni contributions, the association provided scholarships for thirty-eight students. There was record attendance at Alumni Reunion, University of Minnesota Week, and Homecoming. By 1960–61, membership had risen to just under 17,000 members.[208]

## The Duluth Campus

Duluth State Teachers College became a part of the University of Minnesota in 1947. The change had been under discussion since the 1920s, but the proposal was shelved during the war and was controversial with a number of politicians once it was resurrected. A. B. Anderson, who represented Duluth in the legislature, "doggedly fought off intense opposition until the closing moments of the 1947 session" and finally persuaded his colleagues to pass his bill unanimously.[209] Albert Tezla, a longtime professor of English, recalled that campus leaders were clear about their goals: "Having survived the Great Depression and World War II, we were service-oriented and hungry for creativity. Our primary task was to take the teachers college curriculum and develop it into a university curriculum."[210]

Raymond Gibson, the young president of Duluth State Teachers College, became the first provost of the University of Minnesota, Duluth (UMD), and bore the responsibility for overseeing the transition. During the early years, there were conflicts over funding. As a teachers college, Duluth State had been able to appeal to the Minnesota State Teachers College Board and compete for funds as an equal with other teachers colleges. This direct access disappeared when it became a part of the University of Minnesota. After 1947, the Duluth campus could not approach either the Board of Regents or the legislature without going through university administrative

channels. An additional challenge for the campus was the university's desire to re-rank members of the Duluth faculty so that their credentials would
more closely parallel those of faculty in the Twin Cities. In the end, after
this review was completed, most faculty members retained their former
rank.

Provost Gibson was largely responsible for UMD's acquisition of the
Alice Tweed collection of art. This large collection, particularly strong on
nineteenth-century French landscape paintings of the Barbizon school, had
been put together by Alice Tweed and her deceased husband, George Tweed,
a leading Duluth financier; she gave the collection and Tweed Hall, the
mansion in which it was housed, to the university. Perhaps Gibson's greatest achievement was the creation of a new campus, the Nortondale or upper campus that UMD occupied at the end of the century. This 160-acre
tract of land overlooking Lake Superior was purchased by Regent Richard
L. Griggs and a number of other Duluth residents and donated to the university. A plan for the new campus was adopted in 1948, and a science building was under construction by 1949.

Provost Gibson resigned in 1950.[211] Among the outstanding faculty members he had attracted to Duluth were three men destined to succeed him
as provost: John King, Raymond Darland, and Robert Heller. King's term
of office was short (1950–53), but it saw the adoption of a revised campus
plan in which all the major buildings would be connected, so that students
would not have to venture out into the severe Duluth winters. Winston
Close, then advisory architect for the university system, conceived this all-
weather scheme.

Under Provost Darland, UMD came of age, and most of the present
campus was constructed. Like King, Darland had been a naval officer in
the Pacific during World War II; he was a tall man, full of energy, who ra-
diated friendliness. He got on well with Alice Tweed and Regent Griggs,
who were among UMD's greatest supporters.[212] The Humanities Building
was completed in 1958. Among the other new buildings were the Health
and Physical Education Building (1953), the library (dedicated by Vice President Malcolm Willey in 1956), the Student Union, made possible by a
$400,000 gift from Stephen Kirby (1956), a Social Science building (1958;
renamed Cina Hall in 1985); and several student housing units. A sixteen-
acre tract of wooded land adjoining the campus, given to UMD by members of the William Bagley family in 1953, was designated a nature center.
Enrollment at Duluth in 1950 totaled 1,678 (1,165 men and 513 women).[213]
The degrees offered were the two-year associate in arts and four-year bachelor

of arts and bachelor of science; in 1950, 419 students completed B.A. or B.S. degrees while 2 received associate degrees. After 1953, master's degrees in some fields were offered through the Graduate School. Duluth had housed an Air Force ROTC since 1948. It joined the National Collegiate Athletic Association in 1956; the campus radio station was assigned the call letters KUMD in 1958.

## Legislative Relations and Political Issues

The university's successful expansion during the early 1950s was made possible by the privileged relationship it enjoyed with the state legislature. This was in large part a testimony to the influence of Gerald Mullin, a member of the state Senate. Elmer L. Andersen, a university graduate, later a regent, who had become president of the H. B. Fuller Company in 1941, was an acute observer of this period. He recalled:

> There was one member of the legislature whose sole and exclusive dedication was to the University of Minnesota. Gerald Mullin, senator from Minneapolis, devoted his entire Senate career to the university, and he was chairman of the university committee. He had a lot to do with nurturing the choice of regents. He had everything to do with the budget. I can still remember his plea to the Senate: "Please, let us go to the conference committee with the budget untouched. Don't reduce it. You know the House will be tough to deal with," and so on. I'm afraid it would be correct to say that Mullin was willing to trade a vote for almost anything in exchange for a vote supporting the university budget or university measures. No one since has fought for the university the way Gerry Mullin did. *That* made a success of the 1950s.[214]

Mullin had not attended the university; he was a graduate of St. Thomas, where he had received scholarship support.[215] Andersen described what he believed to be the sources of Mullin's loyalty to the university: "He just thought it was important for the state of Minnesota, that the university was the fountainhead of education and therefore the fountainhead of economic development. And then I think he loved the associations with the faculty, with the regents. He just loved the role and he was a lawyer, so it was almost as if the university was his client, and he just loved them."[216]

James Mullin, Gerald's son, added details.

> Once a month, if not more frequently, on Sunday evening there was a group of university administrators and educators at our home for dinner. It usu-

ally included Bill Middlebrook, Ray Amberg, and Dr. Morrill. Every once in a while they would let in a young guy by the name of Stanley Wenberg [later a vice president], but my mother wouldn't let him smoke cigars in our home, so I think he lost interest. Oftentimes Owen Wangensteen or Cecil Watson or Dean [Harold] Diehl from the Medical School would be there.

The younger Mullin went on to explain his father's commitment to the University:

My dad was an ardent believer in public education and was particularly committed to the land-grant institutions created under the Morrill Act. He felt that they had a special role to play in the education and cultural life of the states that spawned them, particularly in the Midwest, and he was convinced that our university could be an engine for economic expansion. The example he always used was Dr. [E. W.] Davis's pioneering work with the development of taconite in the '30s and '40s that spawned the great industry of the '50s and kept our iron mines working long beyond the time they might have.[217]

Observers noted that Morrill would wind up in a state of near physical exhaustion at the end of each legislative session, but that he seemed to enjoy the experience. On one occasion he said, "Every legislature is like every other one in the general nature of its people and the way they react. But every legislature also differs from every other in the particular content, political issues, and fiscal difficulties. . . . It's democracy at the operating end of a buzz saw."[218] Elmer L. Andersen remembered Morrill's appearances before the state finance committee: "He would take out a cigarette—smoking was pretty common at that time—and Morrill was something of a smoker, and he'd tap it, and he'd roll it, and he'd handle it, and he'd lay it down, and pick it up, and there used to be little games to see how much time would elapse before he would light it." President Morrill was a tremendously active lobbyist.[219]

Although few faculty members held radical views and the student left was all but nonexistent in the early 1950s, the University of Minnesota did not escape the attention of the anticommunist movement stirred up by Joseph R. McCarthy and promoted by the House Un-American Activities Committee (HUAC).[220] Incidents in the 1950s involved the dismissal of two physics department faculty members, Frank Oppenheimer and Joseph Weinberg. In 1947 the *Washington Times Herald* had accused Oppenheimer, the younger brother of J. Robert Oppenheimer, director of the Los Alamos laboratory that developed the atomic bomb, of having had communist affiliations in the late 1930s. The article made a number of other charges as well. Oppenheimer denied all the allegations in a letter to university administrators.

Two years later, however, when he was interrogated by the FBI and HUAC, he admitted that he had not been truthful and had in fact been a member of the Communist Party while studying at Cal Tech and Stanford. Before he left to testify in Washington, Oppenheimer sent President Morrill a letter of resignation, not expecting that it would be accepted. Following Oppenheimer's testimony, he met with Morrill, and Morrill accepted his resignation. Oppenheimer did not press for reinstatement. He left Minnesota in 1949, and his later efforts to find academic employment at the Massachusetts Institute of Technology, Cornell, and the University of Chicago were not successful; in 1959 he joined the physics department at the University of Colorado.[221]

Joseph Weinberg was suspended in 1951 after being indicted for perjury involving security issues in nuclear physics. In the end he was acquitted, but he left the academic world for private industry. Because neither Oppenheimer nor Weinberg was tenured, the university's actions were not questioned by the faculty or the American Association of University Professors (AAUP) as closely as they might have been had tenure rights been threatened.

A third case involved philosophy instructor Forrest Wiggins, one of the first African Americans to be employed at a major university. Not tenured, he was among thirty-eight instructors notified in December 1951 that their contracts would not be renewed. President Morrill defended the action, denying that it was motivated by racial discrimination or by legislative pressure due to Wiggins's alleged political views. Eleven days after Wiggins was sent his notification, Morrill received a petition signed by more than two thousand students requesting clarification of the decision.[222] In January 1952, Morrill defended the nonrenewal:

A few members of the legislature during the 1950 session did express to me and other members of the administrative staff, adverse comments and opinions regarding Dr. Wiggins as well as other members of the faculty. Every state university president in every legislature in the land hears this kind of comment and expects to hear it. But hearing it in legislative halls and yield-

ing to it are two very different things. Staff appointments are the responsibility of the President, Deans and department heads, subject to final confirmation by the Board of Regents, not the legislature. The legislative leaders
in this state fully understand this and have not sought to interfere in the
Wiggins case or any other.... Dr. Wiggins had no rights that have not been
fully protected by the tenure code.[223]

Faculty members involved with the AAUP acted less quickly than the
students did. A year later, seventy-five faculty members reexamined the issues, raising a number of the same points the students had raised. President Morrill stuck by his action, and Wiggins's affiliation with the university ended in June 1952.

Another test of academic freedom arose in the spring of 1952, when the
administration denied the request of a university student organization, the
Young Progressives of America, to host black singer Paul Robeson, known
for radical sympathies. President Morrill defended the decision, alleging
that Robeson was

> an embittered anti-American, anti-democratic propagandist. Ostensibly he
> would be brought to the campus as a singer; actually he would be regarded
> as the clearly identified symbol of Soviet sympathies in this country and
> abroad. I, for one, see no reason why the University should assist Mr.
> Robeson to raise money which, when he gets it, supports a program opposed
> to every democratic principle we are fighting as a country to preserve.[224]

It seems clear that the McCarthy influence affected the decisions in these
cases. Morrill's earlier record as a defender of academic freedom had been
stronger. In 1948, he had lent his authority to help defeat a Minnesota bill
that would have required faculty members to swear that they were not
members of any organization on the U.S. attorney general's subversive list.
The bill passed the House but was rejected by the Senate when President
Morrill and other leaders opposed it.

A year later, in a national speech in Williamsburg, Virginia, Morrill urged
alumni officers to defend academic freedom in their institutions and asked
that universities be given "the opportunity to face the issue of [academic
freedom] with good will and good faith, uncommitted and unpressured,
in the attitude of objective inquiry and in the climate of intellectual freedom."[225] Morrill's remarks were reported in the Minnesota Alumni Association's magazine; association president Arthur Hustad wrote, "Alumni

have a right to be proud of our President" and credited him with "enlightened leadership." Edwin Haislet, executive director of the association, also put his endorsement on record, calling Morrill "courageous."[226]

Several years later, in 1952, Morrill supported revised language in the tenure code affirming that "no person shall be removed from or denied reappointment to any faculty position because of beliefs in matters of religion, public policy, or in violation of the principles of academic freedom endorsed by the board of Regents."[227]

In retrospect, it appears that when professed principles of academic freedom came to a test, actions did not always match rhetoric. In this Minnesota mirrored other institutions. Historian Ellen W. Schrecker, in *No Ivory Tower: McCarthyism and Universities,* noted in 1986 that such uneven actions occurred frequently. She observed that in failing to fight McCarthyism vigorously, "the academic community behaved just like every other institution in American life. Such a discovery is demoralizing, for the nation's colleges and universities have traditionally encouraged higher expectations."[228]

Faculty governance changed significantly in 1954. Earlier, all professors and associate professors—the tenured faculty—were automatically members of the University Senate; assistant professors and instructors had no representation. The Senate met only once a quarter. A faculty committee headed by Horace T. Morse, dean of the General College, considered revision of the Senate constitution. "We felt that the Senate, as it was then organized, had several major defects," Morse said. "First, it allowed no representation of the assistant professors and instructors; second, it was too large to be truly effective; and third, seldom were matters of fundamental University policy brought to the Senate and discussed. Probably for these reasons, attendance was poor and there was little interest in Senate affairs."

The new constitution provided for elected representatives of all ranks of the faculty, although there was still some discrimination: there was to be one member of the Senate for every ten professors or associate professors, but only one for every forty of the lower ranks. Meetings would be held twice a quarter, still not very frequently. A valuable addition to the constitution was creation of the Faculty Consultative Committee, which would meet regularly with the president and chief administrators, but its members were to be elected only by full and associate professors. Inadequate as the reforms might seem in the coming years, they did, as Dean Morse said, "make the Senate a more representative and responsible body. [They were] supported wholeheartedly by President Morrill, [who] has cooperated splendidly, not only with the letter but [also with] the spirit of the

new constitution, and has earnestly tried to bring significant matters before the Senate."[229]

As the 1950s and Morrill's presidency drew to an end, the national pres-
tige of the University of Minnesota had never been higher. Federal support
for research had expanded fifteenfold, from just over $1 million in 1945 to
over $15 million in 1960.[230] Reentry programs for veterans and programs
for students were regarded as national models. Academic departments had
met the challenges of the postwar era and were productive in both teaching and research. Enrollment had grown from just under 12,000 students
when Morrill arrived in 1945 to more than 29,000 students in 1960.[231]

Outreach and service activities extended the university to include adult
and part-time students and to provide short courses and lectures throughout
the state. In 1945, enrollments in the General Extension Division, agricultural short courses, and the Center for Continuation Study reached 35,000;
by 1960, these programs enrolled more than 54,000.[232] Duluth had become
a part of the university system. Finally, and perhaps most important, there
was great optimism about the promise of research and the potential of the
university to aid in improving society, both in Minnesota and throughout
the world. Morrill could move on to a position with the Ford Foundation
with the sense of a job well done.

Inevitably, challenges remained. The university needed to plan for the
enrollment increases that would result from the postwar baby boom, recruit new faculty, fund new facilities, and improve faculty salaries and benefits.[233] There was concern about how to improve the standing of the football team. Gopher football fans who had grown up with the pre–World
War II record of Bernie Bierman's football teams (between 1932 and 1941,
the Gophers won seven Big Ten and five national championships and had
five undefeated seasons) were disappointed by the team's standing in 1950,
leading to Bierman's decision to retire from coaching. Under Coach Murray
Warmath, after a stronger showing between 1952 and 1958, the team ended
up ninth in the Big Ten in 1958.

In 1959, after a 33–0 loss to Iowa, someone put trash on Coach Warmath's
lawn, and comments were written anonymously on the blackboard at his
children's school. Team captain Mike Wright recalled that "we wanted especially to win because of all that [abuse of the coach] during the week."[234]
Despite a valiant effort, the team ended the 1959 season last in the Big Ten.
Sanford "Sandy" Stephens, recruited from Pennsylvania to play for the Gophers in 1958, recalled: "We all knew what a great coach and great man
Warmath was. . . . His wife couldn't go grocery shopping [without being

harassed] ... but he never mentioned this. If he could take all that and not complain, then we were going to go all out for him."[235]

These disappointing years at the bottom of the Big Ten were to be followed by two miracle seasons—with a storybook ending.

# Chapter 2
# Years of Growth and
# Years of Protest, 1960–1974

You got the feeling you could change things. I think we did.

*Steve Hammer, student participant in the 1972 demonstrations*

THE 1960S BEGAN in a mood of renewed vigor and optimism with the election of John F. Kennedy as president in 1960. During this period, increasing numbers of young scholars joined the University of Minnesota faculty and created challenging new programs. For most of the period, funding was ample. Federal support, especially under the National Defense Education Act and from the National Science Foundation, continued at a high level, and post-*Sputnik* funds for scientific research came from the Department of Defense as well as from a number of other federal agencies.[1]

The University continued to grow. In March 1961, *Time* magazine described the Minneapolis mall: "Khaki-clad boys and white-sneakered girls spew out of classrooms to the clang of bells at 20 minutes past every hour.... Since 1949, the sidewalks have been widened to keep people from butting each other into the shrubbery."[2]

By 1964, the children of World War II veterans, the "baby boom" generation, would begin entering the University, creating a secondary enrollment boom that was to last until the early 1980s. From preveteran days of just under 12,000 students in 1945, enrollments rose to almost 27,000 in 1960. Two presidents served the university during this period. A major challenge for O. Meredith Wilson, who served from 1960 to 1967, was to accommodate these burgeoning enrollments. For most of the Wilson years, the mood on the campus was much as it had been in the 1950s. By contrast, the greatest challenge for Wilson's successor, Malcolm Moos (1967 to 1974), was to lead the university through a time of increased activism in the civil rights, antiwar, environmental, and women's movements.

For Minnesota football fans, the early 1960s were a magical time. In a remarkable comeback, the team ended the 1960 season tied for first in the Big Ten.[3] The Gopher comeback had its origins not only in the tenacity of

Coach Murray Warmath, but also in the willingness of President Morrill to support him, and in national recruiting. In 1958, at the initiative of Coach Warmath and with assistance from university alumnus and Minneapolis journalist Carl Rowan, Minnesota was one of the first of the major universities in the country to seek out African American players; Judge Dickson and Sandy Stephens were recruited from Pennsylvania that year. Stephens recalled his and Dixon's first impressions of the Minnesotans:

> We felt they were interested in us as men and not just as football players, so Judge and I signed Minnesota tenders in my house. There were other reasons. . . . I wanted to measure how good I could be, playing in the best college conference in the country. . . . Also being Black, I knew there were other places where I couldn't play quarterback.[4]

Having played during the disappointing years, Stephens and his teammates could hardly believe their good fortune in the fall of 1960 when they defeated the opponents who had bested them the two previous seasons. The *Alumni News* reported public reaction to a Rose Bowl invitation:

> On the night of the announcement Gopher fans went wild. Students staged the sort of demonstrations that many people thought had gone out with the rah-rah and raccoon coat of the '20s and '30s. Streaming from sorority and fraternity rows, pouring out of dorms, the still growing crowd then swept into downtown Minneapolis, picking up a somewhat ragged but enthusiastic band along the way.[5]

The Rose Bowl provided publicity not only for the team, marching band, and cheerleaders, but also for the university itself. Special trains carried loyal fans to Pasadena. The dream ended when the Gophers lost 17–7 to the University of Washington Huskies.

At the start of the 1961 season, Warmath was understandably cautious about the team's performance: "Football's a lot like farming. Fellow has a fine crop one year. The next year he plants the same way, cares for his crops the same way—does everything he can to see that it comes up right. Maybe it does. Or maybe he gets hailed out or it gets too dry."[6]

In fact the results of the 1961 season were almost as good as those of the year before.[7] Quarterback Sandy Stephens was the first player since Paul Giel in the mid-1950s to gain 1,000 yards in a single season. Center Julian Hook and tackles Bobby Bell and Carl Eller also contributed significantly to the team's success. The team ended the season second in the Big Ten; when Ohio State turned down the invitation to the Rose Bowl, the Gophers went. They defeated UCLA 17 to 3, and Stephens was named the game's most valuable player (he was later elected to the Rose Bowl Hall of Fame). For Coach Warmath and those who had stood by him, the victory was gratifying. Stephens recalled that one of the most supportive fans was Hubert Humphrey:

> The thing I loved about Senator Humphrey was that he was with us when we lost. That year I was a sophomore, he was with us then. I didn't mind him coming into the locker room [during the 1960 and 1961 seasons] because he deserved it and was with us when we were losing.[8]

A fan in Pasadena observed that "when the gun sounded and Minnesota Coach Murray Warmath was lifted high and carried off the field, his smile could be seen all the way back to the Twin Cities."[9] O. Meredith Wilson attended the Rose Bowl three years in a row: as President of the University of Oregon in 1960, and as president of the University of Minnesota in 1961 and 1962.[10]

## President O. Meredith Wilson

Wilson succeeded Morrill as president of the university in July 1960. Wilson was born in Mexico, where his father had been head of an academy established by the Mormon Church. Having earned a Ph.D. in history from the University of California at Berkeley, Wilson taught at the Universities of Utah and Chicago before becoming president of the University of Oregon in 1954. Wilson recalled that before accepting Minnesota's offer, he asked University of Chicago president Robert Hutchins whether "it would be more important to become president of a great university [Minnesota] or to participate in the attempt to make a great one [Oregon]?" Hutchins advised Wilson to accept the Minnesota offer, noting that he thought Minnesota needed Wilson.[11]

For the first eight months they were in Minnesota, the Wilson family lived in the Pillsbury house. In March 1961, Wilson, his wife, Marian, and four of their six children moved to Eastcliff, the former home of the Edward Brooks family, which had been given to the university as an official residence for the president. There was considerable public interest both in the family and in their new home. An indication that times had not changed much in 1960 was the title of a *Minnesota Daily* article about the Wilsons: "Marian Wilson, A Wife's Smile Is Husband's Asset."[12]

*Minneapolis Tribune* columnist Barbara Flanagan described Eastcliff:

But for its eighteen rooms, the [residence] of the new presidential family at 176 North Mississippi River Boulevard might have been that of any Minnesota family with four children at home. Upstairs a radio was going with a nervous rock 'n' roll beat. Downstairs there was Big Ten basketball on television, loud and clear. At the side door, a small boy wondered, "Can Dave come out?" When the telephone rang, more than once, it was the president of the University of Minnesota who answered. It was never for him.[13]

Marian Wilson recalled an ongoing stream of visitors to the university. She was asked to host Sir Tyrone and Lady Guthrie as part of an effort to persuade the Irish director to locate his regional theater experiment in Minnesota. A mid-1960s visit by poet Robert Frost attracted so many students and faculty members to Northrop Auditorium that worried university officials suggested that students standing in the aisles and along the back walls be asked to leave. Not wanting to disappoint them, President Wilson let them remain. Marian Wilson noted that "one of our treasured family possessions is the book Frost marked in his own hand and from which he read 'Fences' and 'Death of the Hired Man.'"

The Wilsons regularly attended Minneapolis Symphony and Metropolitan Opera performances. Marian Wilson reported that she didn't miss a single Met performance during the seven years they were at Minnesota. Her husband attended almost as frequently, skipping only the Saturday matinee; he thought one opera a day was enough.[14]

A *Willmar Daily Tribune* article described Wilson as "a man of moderate views and temperament about most things. The one exception that burns through his unexcitable disposition is Wilson's desire that an institution of higher learning live up to its name."[15] Wilson faced a number of challenges: providing a quality education to a rapidly growing student body, constructing new buildings to accommodate these students, changing the collegiate structure, and improving relations with faculty, alumni, donors, and the legislature. Toward the end of his seven-year term, he would have to guide the university's response to changing societal mores.

In his February 1961 inaugural address, Wilson identified two early priorities: to increase efficiency to ensure high-quality education for the expected influx of new students, and to strengthen collegiality within departments and colleges.[16] The latter goal undoubtedly referred to tensions on the Twin Cities campus related to the physics department's move out of the College of Science, Literature, and the Arts and into the Institute of Technology. More moves were being suggested.

Understandably, the new president wanted to make changes in the senior administrative team. Errett McDiarmid was succeeded as dean of the arts college in 1963 by speech professor E. W. Ziebarth, widely known for his public affairs commentaries on radio and later on television. Ziebarth, who served as dean from 1963 to 1973, seemed a good choice to try to reunite the college. His nickname, "Easy," came not only from his initials, but also from his style: "If you ever played poker with me [and many did], you'd know precisely why I'm called 'Easy,'" he said.[17] Department chairs generally found him eager to listen to, if not always to support, their proposals for growth.

Wilson also made a change in the academic vice presidency. He viewed the situation dispassionately: "Malcolm Willey was already Vice President when I arrived. He was a better sociologist than the faculty thought he was, in my judgment, but he never really did have the full confidence of the faculty."[18] Wilson offered the position to Jerry Shepherd, whose background as chair of the Department of Electrical Engineering and associate dean of the Institute of Technology complemented Wilson's background in history. Shepherd accepted on condition that he be clearly recognized as the chief academic officer. He served as academic vice president from 1963 to 1973. Bryce Crawford, from the Department of Chemistry, served as dean of the Graduate School from 1960 to 1972. He was followed by philosophy professor May Brodbeck, who was dean until she went to the University of Iowa as vice president for academic affairs. Laurence Lundin was vice president for finance from 1959 to 1971.

Later in the decade, near the end of his term as president, Wilson guided another major administrative change. Athelstan Spilhaus had served as dean of the Institute of Technology since 1949. He was a brilliant scientist with broad learning and interests, and was credited with playing a major role in building and maintaining the Institute of Technology. Over time, however, it became apparent that he was perhaps too mercurial for the administration of an increasingly complex college. When Spilhaus departed in 1967, a *Minneapolis Tribune* editorial noted that he would be taking away "a pot full of ideas, an aura of excitement, and—often as not—uninhibited controversy."[19] Shortly after becoming dean, he had criticized American high schools for "tap dancing, typewriting, and tomfoolery."

In Wilson's biennial report to the regents for 1961–62, he reported on proposed collegiate reorganizations, describing the "guiding principle" of the reorganizations as "the concept of congenial academic neighborhoods." Changes during the biennium included moving economics from business administration to the arts college; astronomy, geology, mineralogy, and mathematics from the arts college to the Institute of Technology; and zoology and botany from the arts college to the newly forming College of Biological Sciences.[20]

Wilson later described the dilemma of where to place mathematics:

> The alternative was to maintain two departments at tremendous expense with a great deal of duplication and to allow the continued fostering of not only competition but also anger among scholars who ought to be friends. There was no conceivable way, given how I understood modern science to be developing, that I could take mathematics out of the Institute of Technology, and there was no comfortable way, given my doctrine of liberal education, that I could take it out of the College of Liberal Arts. But I did.[21]

As a result of these organizational changes, the College of Science, Literature, and the Arts in 1963 became the College of Liberal Arts, offering work in the humanities, social sciences, and fine arts, while theoretical science departments and applied scientific engineering joined the Institute of Technology. Warren Ibele, a faculty member in mechanical engineering and later dean of the Graduate School, reflected on the separation of sciences and mathematics from the arts and humanities:

> As I understand how liberal arts colleges operate or should operate, I think that they lost something when they lost the voice of science from their midst. I think it added a much-needed, valuable counterbalance, or governor, or stabilizing influence to offset those that are more given to excursions for one reason or another.[22]

Chemical engineering chair Neal Amundson, on the other hand, saw advantages in the new structure: "This system we have for science and engineering here is unique in the United States. Having all of the science and all of the engineering in the same college minimizes the standard fights that occur in all other universities between chemistry, physics, mathematics, and engineering."[23]

One concern about the new structure was that students in the sciences would lack background in the liberal arts. President Wilson worried about this, and before sanctioning the transfer of the biological sciences out of the arts college, he initiated discussions so that all concerned could "try to understand our mission better." He believed strongly that anyone who received a bachelor's degree should have a liberal education: "Being educated meant more than being a great chemist or computer specialist; it meant knowing something about our literary tradition and our historical tradition," said Wilson.[24] Initiated under Wilson and periodically revised, all-university liberal education requirements remained an important means to ensure that students fulfilled this ideal. The Council on Liberal Education and later the Senate Committee on Educational Policy contributed to the development of these policies.

The College of Biological Sciences, established in 1965, brought together the Department of Biochemistry (from the Institute of Agriculture, Forestry, and Home Economics) and the Departments of Botany and Zoology (from the College of Liberal Arts). There were soon two new departments: the Department of Genetics and Cell Biology, and the Department of Ecology and Behavioral Biology. The Medical School retained a separate biochemistry department, but the two departments offered a joint graduate program. President Wilson had advocated putting together departments in an area that was developing rapidly:

> We had very distinguished biologists in the Medical School, very distinguished biologists in the College of Liberal Arts, and very distinguished biologists in the agricultural college. When I would start discussions of how we could get a symbiotic relationship among them, I found it very hard to get any sort of serious conversation with the people in medicine who dealt in biochemistry and the people in agriculture who dealt with biochemistry. Maurice Visscher may really have been as wide-ranging a biologist as there was in America, and not to have the advantage of his leadership in other areas just because he was in medicine seemed a dreadful waste.[25]

Wilson persuaded Richard Caldecott to be dean of the newly created College of Biological Sciences. "He was the one that all three of the constituents admired. They could rally around him."[26] Caldecott had come to the university in 1955 as a geneticist for the U.S. Department of Agriculture working within the Department of Agronomy and Plant Genetics. The Atomic Energy Commission and the National Science Foundation had supported his research, and his projects had attracted a significant group of graduate students and postdoctoral fellows.

During Caldecott's deanship (1965–84), the College of Biological Sciences taught undergraduates from all parts of the university in its basic biology course. Within a decade, there would be more than six hundred biological sciences undergraduate majors and close to three hundred graduate students. The college also included the Bell Museum of Natural History, the Biological Process Technology Institute, the Gray Freshwater Biological Institute, and the Cedar Creek Natural History Area, where ecology professor John Tester conducted research on controlled burns as a forest management technique that would, decades later, lead to his assuming responsibility for creating a management plan for Lake Itasca Park in northern Minnesota. Contemporary accounts stressed its link to "the new biology," in which common scientific insights at the cellular and molecular level connected fields as diverse as kidney transplants and wheat rust. In one respect, however, President Wilson's dream for the biological sciences was deferred until the final year of the twentieth century, when greater integration was achieved during the administration of President Mark G. Yudof.[27]

Throughout the university, growth was almost taken for granted: enrollment grew, buildings and campuses rose, research dollars flowed in. There was growing recognition of the university's broad strengths in teaching, research, and outreach. Spurred on by *Sputnik* in 1957, federal dollars for research had also grown substantially. In fiscal year 1960–61, research expenditures from federal sources were just over $10 million; by 1969–70, they had grown nearly threefold.[28]

The Space Science Center was established during the 1964–66 biennium "to foster multidisciplinary approaches to the problems and challenges of space research and exploration." The center drew together representatives from the Institute of Technology (mechanical and electrical engineering), liberal arts, food science, the biological sciences, and the College of Medical Sciences. Faculty were drawn from astronomy, geochemistry, and microbiology. The center was successful in obtaining federal funds and represented an important focal point for interdisciplinary research, attracting more than $400,000 annually for space-related research.[29]

The University Computer Center, originally known as the Numerical Analysis Center, was established during the 1966–68 biennium.[30] In the liberal arts, the newly enlarged Institute of Technology, the health sciences, and the Institute of Agriculture, Forestry, and Home Economics, research productivity and rankings were high. The 1965 national Carter Report ranked Minnesota fourteenth overall; the 1969 Roose-Anderson report, a sequel to the Carter report, ranked it seventeenth.[31] During the first three months of 1961, two faculty members were on the cover of *Time* magazine: public health faculty member Ancel Keys was featured for his work on the connection between diet and cardiovascular health on January 13, and economist Walter Heller appeared on the March 3 cover for his role as chair of President Kennedy's Council of Economic Advisers.[32]

## The West Bank

The growth of the student body led to unprecedented building throughout the university. One of the most important changes of the 1960s was the development of the West Bank in Minneapolis. This had been a subject of debate ever since the influx of students at the end of the war created an obvious need for additional buildings. The basic decisions were made toward the end of the Morrill years. It was not easy to find space adjacent to the campus, which was hemmed in by railroad yards on the north and the Mississippi River to the west and south. To the east lay a residential area, Prospect Park, home of many faculty members—and Hubert Humphrey. It was, in the words of Warren Ibele, "a very vital and sophisticated community with significant political clout as the Second Ward, feisty and strongly DFL in complexion."[33] Expansion in that direction was not likely to be popular or feasible.

President Wilson, who was confronted by the campus expansion question immediately after his appointment, was concerned about the distance between different parts of the campus. He regarded Walter Library as its center:

> We spent a year, I guess, drawing concentric circles around the campus and then measuring distances that students would have to walk from the periphery to Walter Library. We could go out University Avenue, where the properties would be very expensive and the distance from Walter Library would become substantial. We could go out toward Prospect Park, and that would be an advantage geographically for the Medical School, but out there the distance to Walter Library would increase substantially."[34]

The West Bank was closer, and its heavy population of students and renters offered little resistance to developing a new campus there. Most administrators thought this was the only way they could go.[35]

Wilson recalled helpful advice from John Cowles Sr., publisher of the *Minneapolis Star* and *Tribune*:

> Cowles was the kind of journalistic statesman every community ought to have. He called me shortly after I came and said he would like to talk to me. "There's going to be a lot of discussion, argument, perhaps even angry

disagreement, about the West Bank. I know it's a decision that you and the faculty are going to have to make but I want to give you my judgment. I believe that the state legislature in acceding to the agreements about the West Bank and [providing] funds for its acquisition made a step they consider to be important. If you, after reviewing this, don't think it's wise, remember that changing will come at a price because the legislature will be so upset by the change in rules that you'll have a hard time getting other things that you need." I thanked him. I thought that he was being interested in the university. He was trying to tell me I could use my influence as I liked but that as a man on the scene, he felt he knew the price I'd have to pay if I changed.[36]

The plans for the West Bank were characteristic of the urban design of the period. In a 1949 *New York Times* article, architect Walter Gropius had urged "not Gothic but modern for our colleges."[37] Locally, both Winston Close, the University architect, and Ralph Rapson, best known as the architect of the Guthrie Theater and head of architecture at the university, were advocates of modernism. Minnesota's West Bank campus design resembled buildings constructed at about the same time at Yale, Brandeis, and Chicago Circle. As on other campuses in urban areas, planners had to deal with such issues as "high population densities, conflicting land-use patterns, and opposing interests in different segments of the population."[38]

On Wednesday, January 4, 1961, President Wilson turned the first shovelful of dirt in the West Bank groundbreaking ceremony. The first three buildings were to be a fourteen-story tower, at that time designated for both the humanities and social sciences; a twelve-story business administration building; and a four-story general classroom building (later Blegen Hall). President Wilson and Winston Close were enthusiastic about seminar rooms with a horseshoe seating arrangement on the top floor of the classroom building. "The idea is that, by special architectural design, you can establish conversation among as many as 100 persons," Wilson said. "There are exciting prospects here, in view of the great enrollment increases that lie ahead."[39] The buildings were connected by both tunnels and skyways (then called "glass breezeways").

Political scientist Mulford Sibley was one of the faculty members who deplored the sterile concrete environment of the West Bank. He particularly disliked the large paved area between the river and the Social Sciences Building. According to the political science departmental history, "One of his suggestions was suddenly and dramatically accepted. Workers with jackhammers carved diamond-shaped holes in the year-old solid concrete and planted saplings which now grace the area, and at least modify the harsh setting." The department proposed that the trees, which have now grown to a considerable height, be named Sibley Grove, but that did not occur.[40]

The old bridge on Washington Avenue was inadequate to link the West Bank to the rest of the campus. Wilson fought this battle too:

> All of our arguments for the West Bank were contingent on whether we could get [a new] bridge built. The bridge was identified as being a part of a highway system and the federal government was then absorbing, I think, 90 percent of construction costs if it were a highway. Then, as we went through the plans, we said, "There's no way we can settle for a bridge that's just one level. We've got to have a pedestrian walkway." They said, "Well, all right, we are willing to undertake to build the bridge so it can carry a pedestrian walkway, but the United States Highway Department doesn't build pedestrian walkways." So I finally decided to bull it out with them. I said, "You build that bridge without a pedestrian walkway and you'll have no highway for fifteen minutes every hour [the class change period]." After a long discussion, the highway department agreed that they would build both levels.[41]

By the end of the 1960s, the West Bank area retained a distinctive character. Cedar-Riverside Associates, which had acquired much of the land near the campus and had federal money for "new towns" (which included Jonathan, Minnesota; Columbia, Maryland; and Reston, Virginia, all on the edge of metropolitan areas), constructed several high-rise apartment buildings, ideally to accommodate a mix of income groups. The associates also owned many of the area's small older houses and rented them to students. The West Bank Tenants' Union, formed to protect the students' interests, organized a rent strike in 1974 and succeeded in negotiating lower rent.[42] A West Bank People's Center opened in a former Presbyterian church. On both the East Bank and the West Bank, progressive bookstores flourished, as did venues for singers and songwriters, among them Bob Dylan (known in his student days as Bob Zimmerman). Elements of the West Bank's countercultural ambience remained through the end of the century.

## Libraries

One of the most important buildings on the West Bank was a new library, originally planned as a small "library facility" for reserve reading. President

Wilson, convinced that "there was absolutely no sense in a library facility over there of the sort that they had in mind," decided to accept proposals for developing the West Bank only "if we could have a major library over there. We talked with the faculty about it. The faculty seemed to agree that that was an all right solution." University Librarian Edward B. Stanford (1951–71) and his predecessor, Errett McDiarmid (1943–51) concurred. As Wilson recalled, "The professional librarians all felt that we needed to abandon the idea of a little reading room on the West Bank and that we really had to have a major library facility. I think the library people might say it was their idea as much as it was my idea." The responsibility for carrying their views to the legislature fell to Wilson.[43]

Initially it was feared that funds would be inadequate to finish the entire building, so that the top floor would have to be left incomplete. Gerhard Weiss, a faculty member in German and a member of the Senate Library Committee, recalled that because the bids came in lower than the amount budgeted, the university was able to finish the entire building.[44] The design, as was common for the period, emphasized function; there was no soaring reading room or grand entrance typical of many libraries.[45] Completed in 1968, the library was named a year later in honor of President Wilson.

Wilson Library housed the humanities and social sciences collections and services. With space for more than 1.5 million volumes, the library had 2,200 study stations, which included 138 faculty studies and 65 graduate student carrels. Costing $10 million, this state-of-the-art facility was the first completely air-conditioned building on the Twin Cities campus. The new library had offices for library administration and support services, as well as special holdings such as the James Ford Bell collection of rare books, maps, and manuscripts; the Ames Library of South Asia; the East Asian Library; the Middle East Library; the map collections; the newspaper room; government documents; a record listening room; and the central catalog.[46]

Originally located in Walter Library, the James Ford Bell collection of maps and historic manuscripts relating to world trade was reinstalled on the fourth floor of Wilson Library. At first focused on French traders in North America, Bell later branched out with acquisitions documenting the origins and networks of international trade between 1400 and 1800. With guidance from curator John Parker, Bell made purchases related to Portuguese traders in India and China, as well as Jesuit contacts in China, India, and Ethiopia. Parker, curator of the collection from 1953 to 1991, observed of Bell, who in addition to being chair of the board of General Mills was a member of the university's Board of Regents (1939 to 1961), and the donor of the Bell Museum of Natural History: "If he had not been born into a milling family, he almost certainly would have been a professor of history or philosophy. He had a fantastic grasp of the past and its relationship to the present." Before his death in 1961, Bell had set up an endowment to ensure that his collection would remain intact and grow. It did so under the guidance of Parker and, after his retirement in 1991, curator Carol Urness.[47]

The libraries also housed other special collections. The immigration history collection, an international resource on immigration and ethnic history, was founded in 1965, organizationally a part of the College of Liberal Arts. The Charles Babbage Institute for the History of Information Processing was located in Walter Library. The Social Welfare History Archives and the Kautz Family YMCA Archives were located off campus. The Sherlock Holmes Collection began in 1971 with the purchase of a small library of first editions of Holmes stories by Sir Arthur Conan Doyle. With additional donations from Nobel prize-winning Mayo physician Philip S. Hench and California entrepreneur John Bennett Shaw, the holdings became one of the most comprehensive collections of materials related to the fictional detective and his creator.

In Walter Library on the East Bank, the Hess and Kerlan collections of children's literature were located in the Arthur Upson room on the first floor. Two collectors, University Medical School graduate Irvin Kerlan and George Hess, comptroller of the Burlington Northern Railroad, contributed gifts and bequests that made the libraries one of the nation's largest repositories of children's literature. In 1956, George Hess Jr. donated his collection of more than 60,000 dime novels, series books such as The Hardy Boys and Nancy Drew mysteries, and popular culture items. During his lifetime and following his death, Kerlan gave more than 66,000 volumes, including works by Marguerite Henry, Lois Lowry, Katherine Peterson, and Wanda Gág. The Hess and Kerlan collections formed the nucleus of the Children's Research Collection. In 1967, Karen Nelson Hoyle became full-time director of the Children's Literature Research Collection, serving through the end of the century. In 1974, a volunteer support group, the Kerlan Friends, was formed and made regular gifts for additions to the collections.[48]

## The Campus in St. Paul

For much of this period, the campus carried on as if the 1950s had never ended. The new St. Paul Student Center opened in 1960; students played a major role in its governance through the Board of Governors and of the campus as a whole through the St. Paul Campus Student Council. In addition to outreach statewide, the St. Paul campus colleges accelerated their international contacts. In 1960, J. O. Christianson, former head of the School of Agriculture long known for his interest in international exchanges, was named director of agriculture short courses and foreign contacts officer. With the closing of the residential School of Agriculture for high-school-aged students, Christianson turned his attention to international matters. In 1949, he had established the Minnesota Agricultural Student Trainee Program, which by its fiftieth anniversary year in 1999 had made it possible for more than 4,500 international trainees to participate in programs in the United States and Americans to study abroad. In 1998, the J. O. Christianson International Agriculture Award was created to celebrate the internationalism that Christianson had fostered.[49]

Sherwood O. Berg, dean of the Institute of Agriculture, Forestry, and Home Economics from 1963 to 1973, had a strong background in international agricultural policy and encouraged an increased emphasis on internationalism. In addition, he strongly endorsed interdisciplinary approaches in both basic and applied research, encouraging agronomists, soil scientists, animal nutritionists, and economists to see the points of connection in their research with the needs of agriculture and agribusiness. He also believed it was important to have an integrated view of community development, public affairs, youth development, taxation, zoning, and social issues.

Keith McFarland, assistant dean of agriculture, described the institute's new emphases in 1961: "Rather than a curriculum emphasizing the basic skills and practices of farming, the St. Paul colleges offered demanding, varied, highly professionalized courses of study. Forestry students, for example, were expected to handle inorganic and organic chemistry, biology, mathematics, physics, economics, and the professional subject matter that contributes to preparation of a professional forester."[50]

Frank Kaufert, director—and later dean—of the College of Forestry, was a national leader in obtaining passage of the McIntyre/Stennis Act of 1962, national legislation funding forestry research. Two years later the campus was selected as the location for the U.S. Forest Service North Central Experiment Station, which would facilitate the acquisition of research funds. Earth Day in 1970 and the active engagement of students in ecological issues influenced the movement away from a forest products orientation to a view of the role of forestry within the larger ecosystem. Women began to enroll in forestry programs in larger numbers.

Louise Stedman presided from 1951 to 1970 as chief—the term often used for heads of St. Paul colleges and major departments—of home economics. Stedman too had a particular interest in fostering international exchange opportunities. She was followed by Keith McFarland, who served from 1970 to 1987. By the late 1960s, in recognition that women's lives were changing substantially, family social science replaced home management and family living, and rotation in the home management laboratory was eliminated as a requirement for graduation. Faculty members assisted in various youth development projects initiated in the late 1960s through the Center for Urban and Regional Affairs and the Center for Youth Development.

Home economics student Linda Brekke liked the intimacy of the campus but also enjoyed the time she spent in Minneapolis. She noted that her generation of students—she entered the university as a freshman in 1963—"were on the cusp between the passive students who came before us and more militant students who came after. We were very idealistic, thought we could change the world. There was almost euphoria. It was the era of the Peace Corps, blacks getting the right to vote." As a student leader during her last two years at the university, she began to question dormitory regulations that specified how late women students could be out and who could be in their rooms.[51]

Before World War II, the veterinary medicine profession had been primarily concerned with large animals and with poultry raised for commercial purposes. A somewhat unexpected side effect of postwar suburban growth was an increase in family pets. A speaker at a national conference for veterinarians remarked that the suburbs had produced "two primary crops—babies and pets." This change in American culture led to a new emphasis on veterinary care for companion animals.[52] The entering class grew from twenty-four in 1947 to sixty-six in 1971. As of June 1972, the college had awarded 1,013 degrees and celebrated its twenty-fifth anniversary. In 1974, the Raptor Center, which has since attracted considerable public interest and support, was founded. Professor Ben Pomeroy, who had an international reputation for avian research, helped Minnesota retain its top-ranked position in turkey farming.[53]

The Agricultural Extension Service felt the impact of the New Frontier and Great Society programs of the Kennedy and Johnson administrations. While it continued to offer agriculture and home economics programs, and programs for youth, there was a new emphasis on science in the 4-H programs and broader outreach by extension home economists to senior citizens, disabled homemakers, and low-income families.[54] Other changes included increased emphasis on tourism and recreation. 4-H resources played a role in Minneapolis summer enrichment and Head Start programs in 1966. Extension educators expanded offerings related to the environment and the use of pesticides. International focus was present as the extension service played an active role in advising Chile on how to disseminate to farmers information developed in the country's agricultural research institutes. Charles Simpkins, soils specialist, and Roland Abraham, associate extension director, were part of the Minnesota research team that assisted Chile.[55]

Taken collectively, enrollment in agriculture, home economics, forestry, and veterinary medicine nearly doubled between 1960 and 1974, when it reached more than 3,500.[56] Research productivity had also risen, and outreach, both within the state and internationally, expanded.

## The Health Sciences

The 1960s and 1970s were marked by rapid increases in demand for health care services, driven largely by the 1966 passage of Medicare. Federal response to the "crisis in health" profoundly reshaped American health care delivery and professional education of doctors, nurses, dentists, pharmacists, and other health professionals. The Health Professions Educational Assistance Act encouraged states to start new schools and existing schools to increase enrollment by awarding grant funds for each additional student admitted.

Nationally, first-year enrollment in medical schools increased from 9,863 in 1968 to 17,186 in 1980. Federal funds were also awarded for new buildings for those schools adding to the supply of physicians, dentists, and others. Increased funding for the National Institutes of Health (NIH) supported the research agendas of an increased number of faculty members. Hill Burton provided funds for new hospitals and clinics.

In Minnesota, the Hill Family Foundation (later the Northwest Area Foundation) supported a study commission to determine the extent of the shortage of physicians in the state and the region. State legislators became partners in funding the expansion and were quick to assess their constituents' needs and responded with funding for new faculty, matching funds for buildings, and initiatives such as the development of the Family Practice, School of Medicine program on the Duluth campus and the Rural Physicians Associate Program, a successful model for recruiting Minnesota students who would likely return to rural areas upon graduation.

Enrollment in the health sciences nearly doubled during this period.[57] Planning for this expansion occupied the latter years of the 1960s. A new health sciences campus in the 1970s would be the result. Robert Howard was dean of the College of Medical Sciences from 1958 to 1970, followed by N. L. Gault, who served as dean from 1971 to 1983. A major step toward increased integration of the separate schools took place in 1971, when Lyle A. French, head of neurosurgery, was named the University's first vice president for health sciences.

Gault brought international experience to his role as dean of the Medical School, having spent time in Korea as part of the university's presence in the multiyear rebuilding of Seoul National University. He also had experience in Japan, earning him the Order of the Rising Sun, one of the country's most coveted honors. Before becoming dean, Gault had been active in the Minnesota Medical Foundation, serving as its secretary-treasurer when its assets were $60,000.[58]

Building on the tradition established under Owen Wangensteen, collaboration continued to be strong in the Medical School, with ongoing dialogue between the clinical and basic sciences departments. Shelley Chou, a neurosurgery faculty member and interim dean of the Medical School from 1993 to 1995, recalled these years:

> There were a lot of new ideas floating around and because the numbers were small in faculty and also in residents, it was almost like a family and everybody was interested in what everybody was doing in a most helpful way. It seemed to me then that we could move ahead without any limit. Money was available from the National Institutes of Health, Atomic Energy Commission, the National Science Foundation, and other federal and local sources. Research money was easier to get at that time.[59]

Surgeons continued their record-breaking research. The first organ transplant at the university, a kidney transplant performed by Dr. Richard Varco, took place in June 1963. Four years and eighty similar operations made it clear that doctors needed a better understanding of immunology and organ rejection. When Owen Wangensteen retired in 1967, Dr. John S. Najarian, a California native who had graduated with distinction from Berkeley and was then professor of surgery at the University of California medical school in San Francisco, was recruited to become chief of surgery. Dr. Najarian had been performing kidney transplants from related donors since the early 1960s. Also, Richard Lillehei, William Kelley, and David Sutherland, with immunologist Robert Good, became national leaders in transplant surgery—in kidney, pancreas, bone marrow, heart, and liver operations.[60]

Dental health improved as a result of fluoride, better nutrition, and better hygiene; thus researchers were able to focus as much on preventive as on corrective dentistry. They also began to take advantage of new compounds that could be used as bonding materials. Studies of the supply of dentists in the Upper Midwest carried out in 1965 showed that in proportion to the population, the number of practicing dentists had decreased. The demand for a larger class meant that the school would need new facilities.[61] Erwin Schaffer, dean from 1964 to 1977, was particularly successful in fund-raising and in working with legislators. Mellor Holland, an associate dean and historian of the dental school, judged Schaffer to have been one of the most effective deans in the school's history. Richard Oliver, who had been dean at the University of Southern California, succeeded Schaffer, serving from 1977 to 1986.[62]

Pharmacy also undertook new research and in consequence became, under the leadership of Dean Lawrence Weaver, more closely allied with the other health care professions. Weaver recalled that when he first came to the University of Minnesota in 1966 to become dean, he found "a College of Pharmacy in a large institution, isolated from the other health schools." He asked President Wilson, "Why don't you bring pharmacy into the world with the other health professions?" Wilson replied, "We need someone like you to do that."[63]

In 1967, the College of Pharmacy instituted a clinical education program, which created closer ties between the University Hospitals and other area hospitals. Within a few years, clinical education had become a part of every pharmacy student's training. The college continued to offer the bachelor of science degree in pharmacy, a five-year program established during the 1950s, and began its doctor of pharmacy degree program; the first Pharm.D. class graduated in 1973.[64]

New nursing degree requirements with majors in psychiatric and medical surgical nursing were developed and offered through the Graduate School. These changes occurred between 1959 to 1969, during the years that Edna Fritz was director, as part of the transition whereby nursing became a fully recognized profession encompassing clinical training as well as options for both undergraduate and graduate degrees. The discontinuation in 1965 of apprenticeship rotations—nurses served in the hospitals in exchange for room and board—represented a tangible indication of the new professionalism. Isabel Harris was named Fritz's successor in 1970, at the time the health sciences were reorganized, and Harris became the first head of nursing to hold the title dean. As a result of the health sciences reorganization, nursing became independent of the Medical School, moving to full collegiate status.[65]

Research continued to be a vital part of the School of Public Health. Dean Gaylord Anderson emphasized interdisciplinary cooperation among public health programs and encouraged an international perspective. In 1967, Ancel Keys and associated researchers published the landmark "Seven Countries Study," a study describing the relationship between diet and coronary disease. Henry Blackburn and his colleagues subsequently developed criteria for heart disease surveys to be used by the World Health Organization.[66] With students from forty-eight states and nearly fifty countries, the School of Public Health was "one of the most broadly cosmopolitan groups on the campus."[67] Among its programs during the 1960s and early 1970s was a Ph.D. degree in hospital administration, a program for training public health nursing educators, a hospital engineering program, a program in public health nutrition, an interdepartmental biology program offered in Duluth, and a dental public health program. Enrollment was the largest in any school of public health in the United States.[68]

Allied health programs in medical technology, occupational therapy, and physical therapy also experienced an increased demand for admission and for their graduates. The bachelor's degree program in mortuary science, one of few such programs in the country affiliated with a university, had a loyal following and was held in high regard nationally among accrediting organizations because of its university connection.

Health sciences students, like their peers in other schools and colleges, were affected by the social movements of the era. CHIP (the Council for Health Interdisciplinary Programs), established in 1970, was a new student group with representatives from each of the health sciences schools. For medical school student Thomas Kottke, one of CHIP's founders, leadership came naturally; his father was a faculty member in rehabilitation medicine and extremely active in politics. Kottke explained that he and nine other health sciences students founded CHIP because of their interest in increasing teamwork among health sciences professionals, a theme that was also evolving in the newly configured health sciences programs, and because it would give students a way of "getting down to a place at the table with the administration."[69] The innovation was a success, and CHIP remained one of the key health sciences student organizations for the rest of the century.

CHIP student volunteers offered free clinics, lectured in high schools, and informed contemporaries about drugs and their impact. In addition, CHIP served as the student liaison to the newly formed Health Sciences Deans and Directors Council. Kottke recalled the support that CHIP had received from Vice President Lyle French, Associate Dean Mead Cavert, and Assistant Dean Pearl Rosenberg. He remembered gentle prodding by Cavert, who asked, "How are you really going to do this?" He recalled Dean Rosenberg as "the mom of all medical students—you could talk to her." There was a wide range of opinion on social issues among medical students; a number of them were activists like Kottke, but "a lot were just trying to get through school" and espoused this point of view: "I just want to be a doctor, don't ask me to start a revolution."[70]

Nursing student Judy Larson Mogelson was an active member of Students for Integration. During the summer of 1965, after her graduation, she participated in a voter registration drive in Georgia. Twenty dental students wore white coats as they participated in a 1972 march to the Capitol to oppose the Vietnam War. Medical, dental, and pharmacy students sponsored a forum to express views for and against the war. College of Pharmacy students provided guidance on the impact of drugs in outreach programs.[71]

## Legislative Relations

Building and maintaining relations with the legislature claimed much of President Wilson's attention. Gerald Mullin had retired from the legislature in 1957; one figure who stood out now was Gordon Rosenmeier, an attorney from Little Falls. Wilson later observed:

> The legislature in the time I was there seemed to me to be of a superior character... [Gordon Rosenmeier] was often the most severe judge, but I think was always the most fair person you could get in the legislature when you finally came down to putting your case. I think that intellectually his stature and the stature of the chief committees that dealt with the university at the time would do honor to a state. I was proud of them and they were pleasant to work with.[72]

President Wilson spent a good deal of time at the legislature, although perhaps not as much as Morrill had spent. Wilson also developed connections in the business community and served on several corporate boards. The university received reasonable levels of financial support during these years owing to adequate revenues, support by key legislators, and the efforts of the university's chief lobbyist, Stanley Wenberg. Elmer Andersen remembered Wenberg as "a tremendous worker who had the grubby job of sitting in the Gopher Grille at the St. Paul Hotel till all hours of the night indulging with the senators who liked to do so. That was hard work, but he developed friendships and loyalties. His relationships were always very personal."[73] Political journalist D. J. Leary reminisced in the same vein: "So many things were done at the Gopher Grille. That was the second capitol."[74] Leary described Wenberg as "a huge guy with a huge cigar."[75] George Robb, who later became associate vice president for institutional relations, described Wenberg's impact:

> Stan Wenberg was easily one of the most intelligent people I've worked with. He had an extraordinary mind. He was an educational philosopher without the license. I remember very well a fishing expedition that we went on with faculty members from the College of Education. . . . The faculty members concluded, "That man knows more about John Dewey and educational philosophy than anybody around. Why isn't he writing?"[76]

## The Board of Regents

President Wilson also worked effectively with the regents. From 1945 to 1975, eighty people served as members of the Board of Regents, the policy-setting and governing body of the university.[77] An all-volunteer board, the twelve members were selected for six-year terms by the Minnesota Legislature. Eight seats were designated for representatives of the state's legislative districts. It had been customary for one of the four at-large seats to be held by a representative of organized labor, and, after 1977, one by a student. Another customary pattern was for the First District to select as its regent a representative from the Mayo Clinic. The functioning of the Regents' office was smoothed by continuity in its professional staff members. Duane Wilson, the board's first executive secretary, held that position from 1972 to 1985. His successor, Barbara Muesing, whose title was executive director and corporate secretary, held the position from 1985 to 1994; Steven Bosacker served from 1994 to 1999; Ann Cieslak was appointed in 1999. Muesing commented that she had once explained the role of the board to a puzzled citizen who asked what the regents do. "It's the Big School Board," she replied.[78]

The board had become more diverse as women, persons of color, and students became members. Regent Marjorie Howard, who had joined the board in 1953, served as the sole female regent until 1971. Josie R. Johnson, elected in 1971, was the first person of color to serve on the board. Between

1950 and 2000, fifteen women, five persons of color, and four students were members of the board. Regents who are persons of color were Josie R. Johnson, Hyon Kim, William E. Hogan II, Alan Page, and Wenda W. Moore. Regents who were students at the time of their election included Wally Hilke, Jessica J. Phillips, Darrin Rosha, and Michael W. Unger.[79]

Board membership carried heavy responsibilities and consumed a considerable amount of time, especially for the person serving as chair. Five chairs held office between 1945 and 1975, and eleven from 1975 to the end of the century. One obvious change in board practice was that both members and chairs had briefer terms of service after the 1960s. Fred B. Snyder retired in 1951 after thirty-seven years as chair and thirty-nine years as a board member. Ray Quinlivan, an attorney from St. Cloud, served six two-year terms from 1951 to 1963 as chair. Charles W. Mayo, the second generation of his family to serve on the board, was chair from 1963 to 1967. Lester Malkerson, representing the Fifth District, served from 1971 to 1975. After 1975, with the exception of Wenda W. Moore, who served three terms, the nine other board chairs through the end of the century served single two-year terms.[80]

William E. Hogan, chair between 1997 and 1999, observed that "as chair you are a point person for every issue. . . . It is a very delicate balancing act."[81] As will be seen, at particularly critical junctures such as selecting a new president, indicating to an incumbent president that it was time to move on, responding to crises in athletics, closing a campus, or selling a hospital, the board chair became more active. Elmer L. Andersen, who was chair from 1971 to 1975, reflected that "the board's job is to nurture, [to] generate public understanding and support, not to manage." He described colleges and universities as being composed of "fragile fabric that encases the love and transfer of learning. They operate by consensus, not fiat. They are imperfect institutions, but have worked remarkably well."[82]

Looking back at her sixteen years as a board member and three terms as chair, Wenda W. Moore thought that when she first joined the board, it functioned almost like a club. She recalled that "meetings were so formal and polite that if it had not been for guidance from Regents Loanne Thrane and 'the three wise men' [Elmer L. Andersen, Neil Sherburne, and Lester Malkerson], there were lots of things I would have missed."[83] Jean Keffeler was among the first regents, along with Mary Page, Alan Page, and Darrin Rosha, to go through a preselection screening process. Keffeler remembered being "struck by all the differing and tightly held views about what was or wasn't appropriate for a regent and by what was and wasn't seen as an appropriate way to engage in the necessarily political process of appointment."[84] Erwin Goldfine, a Duluth businessman who was a regent from 1975 to 1987, noted that serving on the board was time consuming: "I dedicated the first three hours of every day to university business," he said. "For every minute I put in, I got fifteen minutes reward."[85] Robert Bergland (U.S. secretary of agriculture under President Jimmy Carter), who joined the board in 1997, also commented on the workload: "It takes a lot of time, more time than I had really thought. I suppose I spend easily 100 hours a month on something related to the university, either at meetings in St. Paul or Minneapolis or out in the field."[86] David M. Lebedoff, who served on the board from 1977 to 1989, his last two years as chair, observed wryly, "When I ceased to be a regent, I thought my mailman was going to cry with relief because [no longer would] huge packages of material arrive daily." In a more serious vein, he noted, "There were regents with whom I agreed and some with whom I strongly disagreed. Virtually all of them, however, tried very hard to do a good job."[87]

Elmer L. Andersen was respected for the breadth of his knowledge about and dedication to the university. An alumnus, legislator, governor, journalist, and collector of books, he wisely guided presidents, fellow regents, and senior administrators. Patricia A. Spence, who joined the board in 1995 and became chair in 1999, said of Andersen, "He gave me advice before I joined, and he's given me advice many times during my tenure. I've visited with him at his home or communicated by phone or letter. It's so nice to have someone with his background and experience and wisdom to rely on."[88]

An important and lasting expression of President Wilson's interest in relations with the faculty was his work with the regents in establishing the Regents Professorships. The highest honor the university bestows, the award carries an annual stipend and a medallion to be worn with academic dress. The first Regents Professors were named at the June 1966 commencement: Ernst R. G. Eckert (mechanical engineering), E. Adamson Hoebel (anthropology), Alfred O. C. Nier (physics), Allen Tate (English), and Owen H. Wangensteen (surgery). Between 1966 and 2000, Regents Professorships were awarded to sixty-nine faculty members.[89]

## Intercollegiate Athletics—Twin Cities Campus

Intercollegiate teams during the 1960s and early 1970s experienced a range of successes and disappointments. It was nearly impossible to match the football team's glamorous Rose Bowl appearances, but for several years basketball came close. Throughout most of the 1960s, John Kundla was the coach, the first to recruit nationally for his team. Among the players he brought to Minnesota were three African American students, Archie Clark, Lou Hudson, and Don Yates. Bill Fitch and George Hanson followed Kundla as coach. Sheldon Goldstein, director of University Media Resources from 1978 to 1998 and a regular at basketball games, recalled coach Bill Fitch saying that "the arena was so empty and silent that while sitting inside you could hear the popcorn popping in machines located outside in the hall."[90] The basketball team was to have greater success during the four seasons (1971–72 through 1974–75) that Bill Musselman coached.

Musselman worked wonders with the team, which had a number of future National Basketball Association prospects: Jim Brewer, Ron Behagen, Clyde Turner, Keith Young, Bob Murphy, and Corky Taylor. With a flair for the dramatic, Musselman held pregame demonstrations of passing, dribbling, and finger-spinning. Dave Winfield, a star pitcher for the baseball team and a walk-on in basketball, recalled: "First thing I learned about Musselman was, while he let his teams *warm up* like the Harlem Globe Trotters, he never let them *play* like them. His players weren't loosey-goosey shootists and stylists. They were defensive specialists. Defensive with a capital D."[91]

In January 1972, there was a serious incident. Corky Taylor kneed and Ron Behagen stomped on an Ohio State player. The Gophers forfeited the game and Behagen and Taylor were suspended. Jim Brewer, Clyde Turner, Bob Nix, Keith Young, and Dave Winfield—who became known as the "Iron Five"—carried on for the rest of the season. Not expected to do well without Taylor and Behagen, the team won seven of its next nine games and ended the season with its first outright Big Ten title since 1919.[92] Winfield described his feelings:

> I knew I was going to play professional baseball, but that day I was part of the team that won its first Big Ten title in thirty-seven years—in a year we had barely made it out of some arenas alive. It felt great. More than great. Fantastic.[93]

John Mariucci, who coached the 1956 Olympic hockey team, continued as the Gopher hockey coach through the 1965–66 season. Noted for building hockey as a high school sport, Mariucci was described in a book on Minnesota sports heroes as "the godfather of American amateur hockey and the patriarch of puck in our state." Herb Brooks, Gopher and Olympic hockey coach, said of him, "Every kid that laces up his or her skates needs to give thanks to the man who started it all."[94] In recognition of his leadership and his eighteen years as Gopher hockey coach, the university's hockey arena was named in his honor in 1985.[95] Glen Sonmor coached the Gophers for six seasons, through 1971–72; his best season was 1969–70, when the team was first in the Western Collegiate Hockey Association. Gopher golfers won the Big Ten championship in 1963 and 1972. In 1983 the University golf course was named in honor of Les Bolstad, coach from 1947 to 1976.[96]

Dick Siebert's baseball team ended up first in the Big Ten Conference four times: 1960, 1964, 1968, and 1969. Except in 1962 and 1965, they were never lower than third. In 1960 and 1964, "Chief" Siebert's teams were both Big Ten and NCAA champions.[97] During the thirty-one seasons (1948–78) he coached Gopher baseball, Siebert won more than seven hundred games, eleven Big Ten titles, and three College World Series titles. He became a member of the College Baseball Hall of Fame, and in 1979 the university's baseball field was named in his honor.[98] Dave Winfield, who pitched 109 strikeouts in 1973, giving him second place in Minnesota records, said of Siebert, "He played no favorites and treated everyone alike. I learned a lot from him."[99]

It was not until the mid-1970s, during the administration of C. Peter Magrath, that the university, nudged by concerned activists, initiated steps to bring intercollegiate athletics into compliance with federal regulations mandating equal opportunity for women. Recreational sports continued to grow as students became more aware of the connection between physical and mental fitness. In 1972, the departments of intramural sports for women and men were merged under director C. E. Mueller.[100]

## Alumni and Donor Relations

Relations with alumni and donors claimed much of President Wilson's attention. In 1962, the alumni association was first among the Big Ten institutions to offer young alumni life insurance: $10,000 of insurance for an annual premium of twenty-six dollars. The association opened a dining and meeting facility for alumni in the Sheraton Ritz Hotel in downtown Minneapolis, and within a year the club had 1,800 members. Edwin Haislet served as executive director from 1948 to 1976. In 1969, the association undertook a survey of a cross-section of its members. Impressively, 67 percent of the 700 respondents indicated that they were involved in some form of continuing education. Over a quarter of them were employed in business or industry; just over 20 percent in education; 16 percent in medical fields; 13 percent in government. Over half were Republican; 23 percent were independents, and 21 percent were Democrats.[101] In 1960, there were close to 17,000 Alumni Association members; by 1973 the number had risen to just over 24,000. In 1973, following the announcement of Malcolm Moos's pending departure, alumni association president Harry E. Atwood chaired the Alumni Presidential Selection Committee, charged with developing and screening candidates. Atwood also represented the alumni association as a member of the Regents Selection Committee.[102]

At a December 1962 Sunday-evening meeting at the home of business-man Jay Phillips, President Wilson, Minneapolis attorney Henry C. Mackall, and Phillips made plans that were to revolutionize voluntary support of the University of Minnesota. Their plan was to establish a nonprofit foundation through which private donors could support the programs of the university. Their vision for the University of Minnesota Foundation was based on the successes of similar foundations at other Big Ten institutions. The three moved quickly, and in a matter of days trustees had been appointed and the board held its first meeting. Mackall was the first chair; Chicago businessman Carlyle E. Anderson was the first president. The board included fourteen alumni and five university administrators. Alumnus and board member Edgar Zelle's $1,000 contribution was the first gift.[103]

The foundation encouraged giving to the university not only by Minnesotans, but also throughout the United States. Arthur H. "Red" Motley (chair of the foundation from 1968 to 1971), who traveled nationally as president and publisher of *Parade Magazine,* made a point of looking up Minnesota graduates and seeking out potential donors of $10,000 or more. Other directors with national connections included alumnus Hedley Donovan, editor-in-chief of *Time* magazine; Frederick R. Kappel, chair of AT&T; Hubert Humphrey; George R. Russell, executive vice president of General Motors; and Carlyle Anderson, president of Wykoff-Anderson in Chicago. Two members of the founding board were women: alumna Isobel Gale and St. Paul community leader Charlotte Ordway. A majority of the founding directors were alumni.

Interviewed in 1992, foundation board chair Bernard Ridder recalled Motley as "a magnificent speaker, a great salesman."[104] From the beginning, Minnesota business and community leaders were willing to serve on the board. From its inception, the foundation emphasized the importance of the university as a resource for the state—an institution of equal importance

Soldiers in the Army Specialized Training Program were a familiar sight on campus during World War II. Here they march across the mall, with Coffman Memorial Union in the background. Photograph courtesy of the University of Minnesota Archives, Twin Cities.

During World War II, the university provided more cadet nurses than any other educational institution in the country. In the foreground of this gathering on the mall are (left to right) Patricia Grace, Elvira Spraitz, and Ruth Stryker. Photograph courtesy of the University of Minnesota Archives, Twin Cities.

Quonset huts, war-surplus buildings made available to colleges and universities by the federal government, were a distinctive feature of the postwar campus. Photograph courtesy of the University of Minnesota Archives, Twin Cities.

Registration in a precomputer era often took several hours and sometimes resulted in disappointment when courses were filled. Photograph courtesy of the University of Minnesota Archives, Twin Cities.

A Homecoming date at a Gopher football game held at Memorial Stadium, complete with a traditional corsage of chrysanthemums, was very special. Photograph courtesy of the University of Minnesota Archives, Twin Cities.

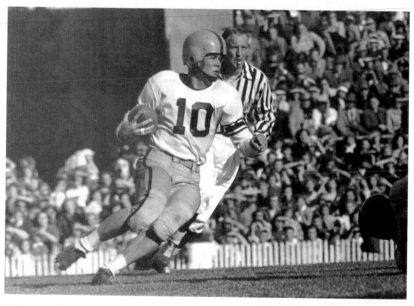

Twice an All-American, Paul Giel brought magic to Minnesota football during the early 1950s. Photograph courtesy of University of Minnesota Men's Intercollegiate Athletics, Twin Cities.

Alfred O. C. Nier, a faculty member in the Department of Physics, was one of the country's leading contributors to the Manhattan Project. He is pictured here in about 1940 with the mass spectrometer, an instrument used for sensitive isotropic measurements. Photograph courtesy of the University of Minnesota Archives, Twin Cities.

E. C. Stakman, chief of Plant Pathology and Botany, with Joseph M. Daley and Donald E. Munnicke in about 1945, examines organisms that cause disease in small grains. Stakman gained a worldwide reputation for his discoveries of disease-resistant varieties of grains. Photograph courtesy of the University of Minnesota Archives, Twin Cities.

In the late 1940s, Vetta Goldstein taught a short course on the proper care of furniture. Photograph courtesy of the University of Minnesota Archives, Twin Cities.

Robert Penn Warren teaches a course in the English department. Photograph courtesy of the University of Minnesota Archives, Twin Cities.

Edward W. Davis, head of the University's Mines Experiment Station from 1918 to 1951, discovered a profitable way to separate iron ore from taconite. Photograph courtesy of the University of Minnesota Archives, Twin Cities.

In 1971, former president J. L. Morrill (second from left), Raymond Darland (provost from 1953 to 1976; on Morrill's left), Richard Griggs (Regent from 1939 to 1963; on Morrill's right), and Robert Heller (provost from 1976 to 1987) view a model for future expansion of the UMD campus. Photograph courtesy of the University of Minnesota Archives, Twin Cities.

N. L. Gault, subsequently dean of the Medical School, and Katharine Densford, director of the School of Nursing, receive a gift from Il Sun Yun and Yeo Shin Hong, respectively president and dean of the School of Nursing at Seoul National University. The gift acknowledged the university's contribution to the rebuilding of Seoul University. Photograph courtesy of the University of Minnesota Archives, Twin Cities.

President James L. Morrill and his successor, O. Meredith Wilson, hold the presentation copy of *The University of Minnesota, 1851 to 1951,* by James Gray. Photograph courtesy of the University of Minnesota Archives, Twin Cities.

Quarterback Sandy Stephens led the Gophers to the top of the Big Ten conference and to two successive appearances at the Rose Bowl. Photograph courtesy of University of Minnesota Men's Intercollegiate Athletics, Twin Cities.

In 1959, Rodney Briggs, a faculty member in agronomy on the St. Paul campus, came to Morris as superintendent of the Experiment Station. He led the transition in 1960 from the precollegiate curriculum of the West Central School of Agriculture to the four-year liberal arts curriculum of the University of Minnesota Morris. Photograph courtesy of the University of Minnesota Archives, Twin Cities.

History faculty member John Q. Imholte was the second Morris provost, holding the position from 1969 to 1990 (after 1985 the provost was designated chancellor). Photograph courtesy of the University of Minnesota Archives, Twin Cities.

Stanley Sahlstrom was provost at the University of Minnesota Crookston from 1966 to 1985. He went on to serve as a regent from 1985 to 1997. Photograph courtesy of Berneil C. Nelson, University of Minnesota Crookston.

Home visits by faculty members were essential to the curriculum at the Southern School of Agriculture at Waseca. Student David Schroeder shows the account books documenting his home project to faculty member Boyd Fuller as his parents, Raymond and Evelyn Schroeder, look on. The Schroeder family still operated their farm near Jaynesville at the end of the century. Photograph courtesy of the University of Minnesota Archives, Twin Cities.

Edward C. Frederick (center), provost of Waseca, and Gary Sheldon, vice president for student affairs, accept the registration of Gary Mittelsteadt, the first student to enroll in the new college. Photograph courtesy of the University of Minnesota Archives, Twin Cities.

In the early 1960s the skeletal structures of the towers built to house the social sciences and business rose starkly on the West Bank of the Mississippi River. Photograph courtesy of the University of Minnesota Archives, Twin Cities.

Known as the "mentor of 1,000 surgeons," Owen H. Wangensteen served as chair of the Department of Surgery from 1932 until his retirement in 1967. He was one of the country's most respected leaders in academic medicine. Photograph courtesy of the University of Minnesota Archives, Twin Cities.

Surgeon C. Walton Lillehei was a faculty member in the Department of Surgery from 1951 to 1967. Lillehei's pioneering interest in biomedical engineering led him to commission the first wearable battery-powered pacemaker. He was also responsible for the first use of the bubble oxygenator. Photograph courtesy of the University of Minnesota Archives, Twin Cities.

John Najarian, who followed Owen Wangensteen as chief of surgery, is pictured with Jamie Fiske, whose life he saved through a liver transplant. Photograph courtesy of the University of Minnesota Archives, Twin Cities.

May Brodbeck, chair of the Department of Philosophy and of the university's Senate Committee on Educational Policy, became dean of the Graduate School in 1972. She was the first woman to hold this position at Minnesota. Photograph courtesy of the University of Minnesota Archives, Twin Cities.

Lillian H. Williams became director of the university's Office of Equal Opportunity and Affirmative Action in 1972. She was director until her death in 1984 and was one of the most effective and respected staff members at the university. Photograph courtesy of Marilyn Trettel, Office of Equal Opportunity and Affirmative Action.

Ruth E. Eckert was nationally recognized for her contributions to the establishment of higher education as a field of study. A faculty member in the College of Education, she was named Regents Professor in 1972, the first woman so honored. Photograph courtesy of the University of Minnesota Archives, Twin Cities.

In May 1972, violence erupted on the Twin Cities campus as Minneapolis police, armed with tear gas and mace, dispersed demonstrators in front of the Armory (the headquarters of the ROTC) and on the mall. The confrontation ended without loss of life or serious injury. Photograph by John Ryan.

Political scientist Malcolm Moos was the first alumnus to become president of the university. Shown here in Red Wing, he visited many communities in the state. Photograph courtesy of the University of Minnesota Archives, Twin Cities.

to alumni and nonalumni. Bernard Ridder, who joined the foundation board in 1967, recalled that when he was being recruited to join the board, Motley had told him: "If you have any interest in the state, you have an obligation to the university, because the university is the most important institution in the entire state. When you do something for the university, you're making an investment in yourself."[105] Donald Dayton, oldest of five Dayton brothers, recalled similar advice given him by his father, G. Nelson Dayton: "The university is the state's greatest asset, and anyone with the opportunity to be of service to the university should respond positively."[106] Dayton served as a trustee from 1969 to 1982 and as chair from 1973 to 1975.

Foundation gifts were intended to supplement, not replace, legislative support. The first named endowed chair, the Frederick R. Kappel Chair in Business and Government Relations, was created in 1967 through donations honoring founding trustee Frederick Kappel. Endowed chairs provided ongoing funding to recruit and retain top faculty; one of the foundation's earliest initiatives had been to raise funds to support the Regents Professorships. Founding trustee Jay Phillips made a key gift in 1967 to help launch the much needed health sciences teaching and laboratory facility, subsequently named the Phillips-Wangensteen Building. To recognize university donors, the board established the Governor John S. Pillsbury Fellowship (renamed the Presidents Club in 1977) for those making gifts of $10,000 or more.

In spite of its powerhouse board members, the foundation took some years to build up its fund-raising. Fred Lauerman and Roger Kennedy were the first two executive directors. Fund-raising increased when Robert Odegard became executive director in 1970. Odegard, a native of Princeton, Minnesota, graduated from the university in 1942 in agricultural economics. Following service in the U.S. Navy, he returned to his family farm and automobile dealership in Princeton. In the mid-1960s he joined the Minneapolis brokerage firm of Dain, Kalman and Quail (in 2000 called Dain Rauscher).

Odegard moved the foundation to much higher levels of giving. Asked how this had happened, Odegard in a self-effacing way said: "All of a sudden the thing began to take fire [and succeeded] beyond my wildest dreams."[107] In the early 1970s, soon after he became executive director, there were approximately 1,800 donors; annual gifts totaled approximately $4 million. By the mid-1980s, the donor base was close to 35,000 and annual gifts had more than tripled, to approximately $15 million. In February 2000, Odegard was awarded an honorary doctor of laws degree at the opening of the McNamara Alumni Center.[108]

One of the earliest examples of private fund-raising at the university had been the establishment in 1939 of the Minnesota Medical Foundation (MMF). Incorporated as a tax-exempt foundation, it focused on the Medical School. Its first volunteer president was Minneapolis pediatrician Dr. Erling Platou, who led the MMF from 1939 to 1949. He was followed by Dr. Owen H. Wangensteen, who headed the board from 1949 to 1954. Fund-raising momentum slowed during World War II, expanded after the war, and moved to much more ambitious levels in the 1960s.

By the late 1940s, the Minnesota Medical Foundation had expanded its philanthropic focus to include not only scholarships for medical students, but also research grants for faculty members, lectureships, awards, publication of the *University of Minnesota Medical Bulletin,* and support for student activities. After 1973, its scope included the School of Medicine at Duluth and subsequently the School of Public Health. Successive presidents, many of them physicians, held two-year terms of office. Among early lay board members were Donald J. Cowling, retired president of Carleton College; state senator Gerald T. Mullin; and business executives Malvin Herz, Lewis W. Lehr, and Terrance Hanold. Eivind Hoff was named executive secretary of the foundation in 1959, becoming its first paid employee. In 1961, the Minnesota Medical Foundation received one of its first major bequests: $200,000, which was applied to medical research. In 1967, it received a gift of $4 million from the estate of Royal and Olive Stone of St. Paul for research in cancer and heart disease.[109]

## Wilson and the Faculty

President Wilson made the welfare of the faculty a high priority. When he took office, faculty retirement arrangements were dismal:

> You didn't have a percentage of your salary set aside. You got a sort of arbitrary block of money funded for the future, and when I added up the amounts, they were blocks that were tied to expectations in the 1920s. There was no functional way to have the blocks modified by the changes in salary scales as society changed, or inflation developed, or as we got more distinguished faculty and had to pay higher salaries.[110]

Wilson, who had been a member of the board of TIAA (Teachers Insurance and Annuity Association), was persuaded that a percentage of each faculty member's annual salary should be put into a retirement account. He discussed this approach with the Faculty Consultative Committee, suggesting that the university should use "the sort of formula that the Carnegie people had developed when they set up TIAA and CREF [College Retirement Equity Fund]."[111]

Two local life insurance companies, Minnesota Mutual in St. Paul and Northwestern National in Minneapolis, had been managing faculty retirement funds. "My best judgment at the time was that I did not care whether it was TIAA or the two Minnesota insurance companies as long as the insurance companies would give the faculty an option to have a variable annuity if they wanted it," Wilson recalled. Another question was what percentage of a person's salary would be placed in the retirement account:

> Whether it was described as a percentage withdrawn from your check or whether it was an independent amount provided by the university was almost academic. Say we had $20,000 assigned for a professor of history. If we thought the proper amount to set aside for retirement was 15 percent, then we'd take 15 percent, $3,000, and set it aside for retirement, and you'd get a check for $17,000, or, since all the money appropriated for salary and retirement is part of the reward, we'd say, we will give you $17,000 salary, and we'll put $3,000 into retirement, and you pay no taxes on that.[112]

Wilson felt strongly that the university had a responsibility to guarantee adequate retirement benefits: "In the issue of retirement, the university has a stake of its own. It needs to be protected against any of its people being indigent or any wife being turned out in complete poverty. It has a problem of acquiring the best possible professors. In my judgment, a good fringe benefit was often more important than a contract."[113] In fact, a number of professors who retired before the new plan was implemented in 1964 did suffer financial distress; occasionally there were special allocations to assist them. Despite the advantages of the new plan, which was among the best in the country, benefits for those who retired for the next ten or twenty years continued to be inadequate because they had served so long under the previous system.

Like his predecessor, Wilson had to face challenges to academic freedom and, like Morrill, he made a major public statement endorsing the importance of this freedom to the university. He was convinced that "it would be a healthy advantage for the University of Minnesota if we faced the issue of academic freedom frontally and made a positive statement instead of always having to respond to some criticism."[114]

He and a committee of the Board of Regents prepared a statement defining the academic freedoms for which the university was responsible. Fred Hughes, a lawyer from St. Cloud, chaired the regents' committee and brought the statement to the board, which approved it in December 1963.[115] Wilson was pleased with the resulting statement, which he believed outlined for the regents the freedom they were responsible for protecting: "When the faculty came to their classrooms, they would know that there was a regents' policy that permitted them to speak their minds."[116]

Shortly before the statement was adopted, two incidents demonstrated how sensitive an issue academic freedom was. Benjamin Davis, vice president of the Communist Party in the United States, was invited to speak on campus in 1962. Wilson recalled:

> The position we took in the administration was that an audience of students who would listen to Ben Davis would find the answers themselves if Ben Davis weren't around. An audience of students denied the opportunity to hear Ben Davis would wonder what he had to say that would be so damaging. The best defense of a university community against a Ben Davis is to let him expose himself. The Board of Regents bought that. There were some who doubted, but it was not a difficult problem.[117]

Wilson also became involved in controversies surrounding political science faculty member Mulford Q. Sibley, a Quaker whose pacifist views were regarded as radical. Those who knew Sibley understood that he was a committed pacifist who often put forward arguments to generate discussion, even though he didn't necessarily believe them himself.[118] As academic vice president Jerry Shepherd put it, "There was nothing wrong with what Sibley was saying. . . . The public assumed he was advocating some of these things, when he really meant that they ought to be subjects you would discuss and examine on their merits."[119]

Milton Rosen, a St. Paul city council member, was disturbed by, among other things, a letter Sibley had written to the *Minnesota Daily* saying the university should allow communist teaching, a nudist club, and "free love"— all anathema to conservative Minnesotans. In January 1964, a debate between Sibley and Rosen took place in Coffman Union and was broadcast live throughout Minnesota. Shortly thereafter, another debate was announced: between Sibley and members of the John Birch Society. Wilson decided it would be "unwise" to allow the debate to take place and postponed it.

The John Birch Society debate was to have taken place prior to a legislative hearing to consider Sibley. President Wilson, realizing that postponement of the debate was controversial, offered the legislature an opportunity to relieve him of his position; the legislature did not take him up on the offer. In the end, the postponed debate never took place because a suitable alternative date could not be found. Both Wilson and Sibley survived, although Wilson was strongly criticized by the American Association of University Professors and student groups.[120] Looking back on issues of academic freedom, Wilson commented in 1967, "To try to prevent freedom is sort of like trying to put a cork in the spigot of a boiling tea kettle."[121]

Greatly admired as a teacher and scholar, Sibley served as adviser and mentor to hundreds of students and as the unofficial conscience of the university. He raised controversial issues and advised students who were interested, as he was, in peaceful forms of dissent. Political science/anthropology student Zev Aelony recalled that conversations with Sibley at Koinonia in Georgia influenced his participation in the nonviolent civil rights movement. He helped organize Students for Integration at the university, and was jailed in civil rights protests in Georgia in 1963 and 1964.[122] Sibley retired in 1982. An account by university staff writer Maureen Smith provides a sense of his role as "a Quaker saint":

> Not many faculty when they retire have such a crowd of people turn up for their last seminar. The crowd at Sibley's seminar included University President C. Peter Magrath, Dean of Liberal Arts Fred Lukermann, political science activist Marv Davidov, faculty colleagues, students, and former students wearing "Mulford" buttons. Not often are television cameras found on such an occasion.[123]

## The Morris Campus

The regents established the University of Minnesota, Morris (UMM), as an undergraduate liberal arts campus in 1960. From its founding as a four-year college, UMM served west central Minnesota and provided educational opportunities for capable students throughout the state seeking a University of Minnesota bachelor of arts degree in a small-college setting. Maintaining a focused liberal arts mission, academic excellence, selective admission, and controlled growth consistently guided the development of the college. The founders of Morris wanted to provide an affordable liberal arts education in a public, small-college setting.[124]

The original educational institution at Morris was a school for American Indians opened in the late 1880s by an order of Catholic nuns, the Sisters of Mercy. After a few years they abandoned their effort, but in 1897 the United States government purchased the property and began to operate a second Indian school. This too lasted only a short time; it closed because of the difficulty of attracting students from the reservations. Its facilities were then given to the state and converted into an agricultural high school, the West Central School of Agriculture, which began operations in 1910 with 103 students. There were a handful of buildings, including an agronomy hall, a home economics hall, a hospital, and a morgue, as well as a machine shed, ice house, barn, and silo. Nearly three hundred acres of land were included, originally rented but subsequently purchased by the university. Like similar institutions in Crookston, Waseca, and Grand Rapids, the school was associated with the university's College of Agriculture in St. Paul. It was intended "to give bright boys and girls who expect to become practical farmers and farmers' wives a thorough look at modern methods."[125]

Between 1910 and 1960, approximately 7,000 students attended the West Central School of Agriculture. Almost all of the students came from farms in the area; they had to be at least fourteen years old and had to have completed the eighth grade. Enrollment reached an all-time high of 455 students in 1947 but was down to 305 in 1958. By this time, most public high schools offered courses in home economics and farming, and agriculture itself was declining in relative importance, though still a vital part of the state's economy.[126]

As early as the 1930s, citizens from Morris and Crookston had proposed that the Board of Regents convert their agricultural schools into colleges. A more concerted effort was mounted in 1957 by a group that included state senator Fred W. Behmler and state representative Delbert F. Anderson, both from the Morris area. After Behmler suffered a stroke, the initiative rested with Anderson and a group of area leaders called the West Central Educational Development Association.[127] The president of the Minnesota Farm Bureau proposed in 1959 that a resolution be sent to the regents emphasizing the desire of the citizens of west central Minnesota to have a branch of the university established there. As one Morris resident commented, "It would seem logical for the university to expand at Morris, where it already has a fine campus, fourteen major buildings worth $5 million, and more than 800 acres of land, in preference to expanding in Minneapolis where site costs are so high."[128] President Morrill originally had doubts about proliferation of higher education institutions, and the mood of the legislature was cautious.[129] Morrill was reassured by a 1959 report of the Legislative Commission on Agricultural Schools. The authors of that report, who were studying possible uses of the university's four existing campuses housing the precollegiate schools of agriculture, recommended branches of the university at both Morris and Crookston. The report suggested that "the educational needs of western Minnesota beyond high school level are in the liberal arts fields"[130] and noted that while there were twenty-nine campuses in the eastern half of the state, there were only four postsecondary institutions in the western half.[131] An added factor in favor of supporting the proposed changes was that it might help reconcile legislators from Greater Minnesota to the university's proposed expansion to the West Bank.

After consideration of moving forward with both Crookston and Morris, it was decided to start with Morris. Vice President William Middlebrook wrote President Morrill that he "would favor Morris as having the best prospects. It does seem to me that this would be a desirable move in connection with legislative relationships."[132] In October 1959, the Board of Regents issued a statement that it was "desirable and feasible to begin the phasing out of high school instruction and to begin offering collegiate instruction at the West Central School and Station at Morris, Minnesota."[133] The experience at Morris would guide the regents in deciding whether to proceed at Crookston. Many legislators applauded the regents' action; legislator Peter Popovich acknowledged that it "was good on an experimental basis."[134]

Rodney Briggs, then associate professor and extension agronomist with the university's Institute of Agriculture, Forestry, and Home Economics, was asked to become superintendent of the West Central School of Agriculture and Experiment Station and to lead the transformation of the agricultural high school to collegiate instruction. He was a popular instructor with an entrepreneurial management style, an enthusiastic speaker, an activist faculty member, and a productive research scientist. His background in agriculture was ideal, both to work with the existing institution at Morris and to introduce the new college to regional audiences. Briggs described his new assignment: "It was my impression that if I were to go to Morris, I could supervise the development of a new collegiate enterprise which would surely be authorized by the . . . legislature and at the same time phase out the School of Agriculture."[135]

As he traveled around the region to develop support for the new institution, Briggs, initially dean and then provost, started wearing a Stetson hat, which became his trademark. A colorful, dynamic figure, already known on the speaking circuit for his extension and research work, Briggs accepted every speaking opportunity, and there were hundreds: Kiwanis, Lions, agricultural meetings, study clubs, high school graduations. It was said that he would speak to a kindergarten class if he was invited. He talked about the University of Minnesota, Morris, vision and reality, with anyone who would listen, and he successfully recruited students. After the campus was launched, Briggs remained visible and always accessible to students. He knew them all by name and knew many of their parents as well. Students were the most important asset, so, in spite of a small budget and the need to hire new faculty, he hired a full student services staff—in counseling, admissions, financial aid, housing, student activities, records, placement, and alumni affairs.[136]

The University of Minnesota, Morris, admitted its first students in the fall of 1960. That first year, 238 students came—good students, many of them leaders. Seventy-three percent were men, 27 percent women. Just over 90 percent of them came from within a thirty-five-mile area around Morris. The cost was $1,003 a year, including tuition, fees, books, and room and board. Forty-seven freshman courses were offered. Based on an agreement with the federal government at the time the Morris Indian School was closed in 1909, Native American students admitted to Morris were not charged tuition.[137]

Briggs, then acting dean, had attracted a talented thirteen-member faculty that included W. Donald Spring and James Gremmels in English; Jay Roshal in biology; James Olson, a science teacher from the former agricultural school, who stayed on to teach chemistry; and historian John Q. Imholte. Roshal, Spring, Imholte, and Olson all later served as division chairs. Imholte had been offered teaching positions at DePauw University in Indiana and at Morris. "I went to DePauw and was quite impressed," he said some years later. But he decided to go to Morris because "it was brand new and just getting off the ground and wouldn't that be fun? If you have any mark to leave, you're going to have a better opportunity to leave it at a new institution." During the first year, he taught American Government and Principles of Economics as well as courses in history.[138] Imholte would become dean and, subsequently, the college's second provost and chancellor. Imholte, Olson, and Gremmels were popular instructors at the end of the century.

The college had inherited a dozen major buildings, nine of them designed by Clarence H. Johnston Sr., one of the state's most prominent architects. The buildings ranged around a landscaped mall planned by the firm of Morrell and Nichols in 1911. Perhaps Minnesota's most prolific landscape architects, Morrell and Nichols provided site plans for many colleges, including Carleton, Macalester, Gustavus Adolphus, the University of North Dakota, Wartburg, and the university's campuses in Minneapolis, St. Paul, and Duluth.[139] A ten-year building plan anticipated facilities for 1,500 students at Morris. Intercollegiate athletics were introduced almost immediately, as were a fine arts film program and a series of concerts (arranged by J. S. Lombard, who managed Northrop Auditorium in Minneapolis).

A community symphony, organized by the first music faculty member, Ralph Williams, was one aspect of Rodney Briggs's attempt to foster local interest and participation. College spirit grew rapidly as Briggs and student leaders fashioned instant traditions. Beanies at freshman orientation, a reception at the dean's home, faculty-student retreats, a student newspaper, a yearbook, student government and other organizations, and a student hangout—Louie's Lower Level—soon created a sense of belonging. A men's basketball team was organized during the first year of the college's existence; two players later earned Ph.D.'s, one earned an M.D., and one received a law degree. English faculty member Gremmels was pressed into service as the first basketball coach. Imholte remembered a "homecoming" the first year, and particularly a faculty-student football game. In a key play, Imholte was supposed to be the ball carrier, but in the excitement of the moment, "Rod Briggs took the ball and made the touchdown himself."[140]

By the 1961–62 academic year, the Morris Cougars were competing in football, basketball, wrestling, and golf. Morris had originally joined with Bethel and Northwestern Colleges in Minnesota and Northland College in Wisconsin to form the Pioneer Conference, but by the end of the 1960s was a member of the Northern Intercollegiate Conference, composed primarily of Minnesota state colleges. Baseball, track, and tennis teams were formed, and the Cougars won their first conference championship in baseball. Women's volleyball, basketball, track, tennis, and softball teams began intercollegiate competition in the early 1970s; the women's basketball team was Minn-Kota champion twice during that decade.[141]

The Morris curriculum offered thirteen majors, seventeen minors, and a teacher education program leading to certification on the secondary level. The faculty was divided into four divisions: humanities, social sciences, science and mathematics, and education. The first formal graduation ceremony was held in June 1964 (one transfer student received his degree a year earlier).[142] Students from Morris often went on to graduate or professional schools in such areas as medicine and engineering. In the early years, some faculty members, notably Eric Klinger, who had an international reputation in psychology, advocated graduate programs at Morris, but they were never instituted. They would almost certainly have been opposed by the Twin Cities faculty, and, as Imholte observed, they would have weakened the Morris undergraduate program.[143]

President O. Meredith Wilson, who had become a strong advocate for the Morris campus, was pleased that it had maintained its liberal arts focus and grown in numbers. Support for the liberal arts mission from the president and the regents, as well as from campus faculty members and administrators, differentiated Morris from public liberal arts colleges in other states, where administrators bowed to pressures to add non–liberal arts offerings. Morris concentrated its resources and maintained its focus— and became one of the country's finest public liberal arts colleges.[144]

## The Crookston Campus

Crookston, the seat of Polk County, is located in the Red River Valley in the northwest corner of the state. Although the region's early history was based on lumber and fur, its economic growth has been linked to agriculture since the 1920s. The university's presence there consisted of the Northwest Experiment Station, established in 1895 on land donated by James J. Hill, and the Northwest School of Agriculture, which opened in 1905. Under Bernard Youngquist's leadership as superintendent from 1956 to 1984, the experiment station concentrated on swine, turkeys, sunflowers, sugar beets, vegetables, alfalfa, apples, crab apples, plums, drainage problems, and the effects of hail damage, coordinating this research with work being done in St. Paul.

Youngquist was also superintendent of the School of Agriculture. Like similar institutions in Morris, Waseca, Grand Rapids, and St. Paul, it offered residential high school work in agriculture, home management, and business—instruction that was no longer in demand by the 1960s. In his Ph.D. thesis, Youngquist had shown that schools of agriculture had outlived their usefulness and should be replaced by collegiate institutions. "You see," he recalled later, "I arrived at Crookston knowing that the end of the trail was in sight for the schools of agriculture." Stanley Wenberg, the university's liaison with the legislature, read Youngquist's thesis and "grabbed the ball. He went to the legislature and said, 'We've got to do something with these schools of agriculture and we've got to find a new role for them.'" The Regents agreed in 1965 to phase out the high school curriculum and introduce two-year college-level programs. In his final remarks to the last graduating class of the old school, the class of 1968, Youngquist observed, "While closing this school is saddening, it is necessary. Its closing is logical because the technical college concept makes it as old-fashioned as a butter churn."[145]

In addition to his responsibilities at the experiment station, as a way of being helpful to the new provost, Stanley Sahlstrom, Youngquist agreed to head the agriculture division of the new school. "I'll do this," he told Sahlstrom, "but I'll just get it rolling until you have a chance to get your feet on the ground. Then you'll need to bring on a qualified agricultural educator so I can give my full time to the research station." David Stoppel was brought from the General College in the Twin Cities to direct studies in general education, and Wayne Little came from the Wisconsin Technical Institute to head the business division.[146]

Since there were no support services—no University relations offices, no audiovisual or graphics services, no photographers—Provost Sahlstrom himself wrote the first catalog and designed the first brochure; he traveled throughout northwest Minnesota promoting the college. State senator Roger Moe of Ada said that "the Provost's gregarious grand style and ability to meet and greet people [were] almost a guarantee of success."[147] "I did not rest much many nights," Sahlstrom recalled. "The rule was three months on the job, three days in the hospital to recover."[148] Richard Christensen, who was hired to establish registration procedures, could not forget that the temperature was seventeen degrees below zero when he arrived. He found himself in a room equipped with only a desk, a chair, and a wastebasket.

Hershel Lysaker took charge of athletics, served as football coach, and assisted in recruiting students through area high school coaches, counselors, and superintendents. After thirty-two years as coach and athletic director, he retired in 1976; the gymnasium at Crookston was named for him in 1982. Over the years he had helped with janitorial duties, washed uniforms and handed them out at games, directed the band, and served as a counselor and mentor; he and his wife, Esther, became a surrogate family for players. His football and basketball teams won more than 70 percent of their games.[149]

The Crookston Technical Institute opened in fall 1966 with 184 students, more than had been anticipated. President Wilson and Sherwood Berg, dean of the Institute of Agriculture, Forestry, and Home Economics in St. Paul, spoke at the formal dedication several months later, and the seventy-voice St. Cloud State College choir added music. In a contest sponsored by KROX, the Crookston radio station, the sports teams were named the Trojans; the name was changed to the Golden Eagles in 1995.[150] In 1969 the name of the institution was changed from technical institute to technical college.

## The Waseca Campus

The Southern Experiment Station at Waseca, in south central Minnesota, was a meeting point of the dairy farms to the east and the cattle operations to the west—"all corn and hog land," a writer said, "but poultry and sheep are also important."[151] Its research was instrumental in developing new varieties of corn and soybeans and new breeds of shorthorn cattle, sheep, and swine. As early as 1919, residents had campaigned for a residential agricultural high school comparable to those at Morris and Crookston. They were not successful until 1947, when the legislature appropriated funds to establish the Southern School of Agriculture. Construction began in 1951, and Bernard Youngquist, then principal of the Northwest School, was brought in to oversee operations under the direction of R. E. Hodson, superintendent of the experiment station.

The first students had been admitted in 1953. The buildings included two dormitories, a kitchen and dining hall, classrooms, home economics laboratories, and facilities for training in business, science, and music, as well as a livestock pavilion and a meat-cutting laboratory. Like its sister institutions in Crookston, Morris, Grand Rapids, and St. Paul, Waseca worked on a six-month calendar, since many of its students were needed on family farms during the summer. One of the first students was Gary Sheldon, who later became a member of the Waseca faculty and administration. "It was an anxious experience at first but soon became enjoyable," he recalled. "Those students who were fortunate to spend four full years at the Southern School of Agriculture obviously developed many close friends for life because of the close living conditions." Dorm counselor Ted Nelson and his wife started their married life "with 28 girls and 32 boys in the dorm." Many school romances sprouted into families a year or two after graduation.[152]

The school was to operate for twenty years. Although the buildings were designed to accommodate as many as 450 students, the highest enrollment was 280, during the 1966–67 academic year. In 1968, shortly after Crookston had begun to offer college-level courses, the regents considered a similar transformation for Waseca, where there was felt to be a need to train "technical professionals" in agriculture. Edward C. Frederick, who was superintendent of the experiment station as well as head of the School of Agriculture, was asked to direct the transition from a high school to a collegiate curriculum.

The University of Minnesota Technical College at Waseca opened in the fall of 1971 with 131 students registered in programs in agricultural industries and services, agricultural production, agricultural business, animal health technology for veterinary assistants, horticulture, food industry and technology, and home and family services. Provost Frederick said, "We'll be turning out semi-professionals to help direct Minnesota's largest business. Between 30 percent and 40 percent of all jobs in Minnesota are related to agriculture."[153] Enrollment grew steadily during the 1970s, exceeding a thousand students by the end of the decade.

## The Duluth Campus

Provost Raymond Darland oversaw a period of notable growth at the University of Minnesota, Duluth (UMD): enrollment doubled, increasing from 2,668 in 1960 to just over 5,000 in fall 1973.[154] The campus had become more diverse; by 1975, it was drawing more than 40 percent of its students from outside northeastern Minnesota. Many came from the Twin Cities area, wishing to live away from home and be part of a small academic community. Student organizations increased from the fifty-one groups listed in the 1961 yearbook, the *Duluth Chronicle,* to ninety-five in 1970. By the 1970s, the faculty had quadrupled in size, and the campus had increased its acreage twentyfold.

The "shirtsleeve" design of connected buildings permitted movement between buildings that was "not only dry, but warm."[155] Thirteen major buildings—dormitories, apartment-style residences, laboratories, and athletic facilities—were completed between 1960 and the mid-1970s, made possible by legislative support and gifts from private donors. Among them were an addition to the Tweed Museum, Marshall Alworth Planetarium, the A. B. Anderson classroom building, Griggs Stadium, and the administration building, named in 1982 in honor of Provost Darland. Impressed with the design and utility of the Duluth campus, President Malcolm Moos called it "the campus of the future."[156]

On September 23, 1963, only two months before he was assassinated,

President John F. Kennedy visited the campus and addressed the "Land and Peoples" conference.[157] As was true elsewhere, student life began to change in the mid-1960s. Provost Darland upheld academic freedom by not interfering with the Student Association's desire to bring Nazi sympathizer George Lincoln Rockwell and American Communist Party head Gus Hall to the campus in 1965. English professor Wendell Glick, a nationally respected expert on Ralph Waldo Emerson, had been selected to introduce Rockwell. Glick recalled that Darland had been afraid that smooth rhetoric might convert students to Nazism. Glick had replied, "If they can be seduced by a man like that, we're not doing our job. . . . I bet he [Rockwell] did not convert a single student."[158] Later in the decade, Duluth students joined in the anti–Vietnam War protests. A moratorium on class attendance was observed on October 15, 1969. In April 1971, the campus celebrated Earth Days with a three-day conference on the environment; Stewart Udall, secretary of the interior under Presidents Kennedy and Johnson, was the keynote speaker. The following year, students heard from William Kunstler, who had defended the Chicago Seven in their trial related to demonstrations at the 1968 Democratic National Convention.[159]

Other prominent national figures who came to Duluth to give lectures included Arthur Schlesinger Jr., Arnold Toynbee, W. H. Auden, William O. Douglas, and Harry Reasoner. Armas W. Tamminen, who taught psychology from 1952 to 1981, was able to bring two of the greatest figures in his field, B. F. Skinner and Carl Rogers, to the campus in 1962. "The ballroom was jammed to overflowing," he recalled, as "psychologists came from all over the Midwest."[160] A bronze figure of Duluth's namesake, voyageur Daniel Greysolon, Sieur Du Lhut, was created in 1965 by the internationally known sculptor Jacques Lipschitz and installed in the courtyard entrance to the East Campus buildings and Marshall Performing Arts Center, where it became a signature landmark for the campus. The focus of student pranks, the explorer was occasionally to be seen with such additions as a cowboy hat or a yo-yo extending from a finger on his outstretched hand. On one occasion, students "painted yellow footprints leading down the pedestal, across the courtyard into the men's room, and back again to the top of the pedestal."[161]

UMD developed an important program in American Indian studies, linked to and serving the northeastern region of Minnesota. Robert E. Powless, a leading American Indian educator with a flair for public speaking who was hired in 1972 to direct the program, said: "I would like to think that I gave to the American Indian programs and particularly the Department of American Indian Studies some academic consistency and reliability and respect over the years because of the way that I've operated and the way that I teach my classes."[162]

Among the intercollegiate teams, hockey retained a special place for Duluth students and fans. Of the hundreds of athletes who put on skates, the best known was the All-American center Keith "Huffer" Christianson, who helped christen the new Duluth Arena in 1966 with a school-record six assists, leading the Bulldogs to victory over the Twin Cities campus Gophers. Ted McKnight, who was named an Associated Press All-American in 1976, finished his college football career with the highest rushing yardage total in UMD history and went on to play professional football with the Kansas City Chiefs and the Buffalo Bills.[163]

A number of new programs were developed on the Duluth campus during the Wilson and Moos administrations. A mobile laboratory on wheels, the biology bus, operated from 1971 to 1981; the UMD Air Force ROTC program began enrolling women in 1971. The first female second lieutenants, Bette MacTaggart and Patricia Mankowski, graduated in 1975. The Tweed Museum continued as an important regional resource for art. The Marshall Performing Arts Center, named for its benefactors, Julia and Caroline Marshall and Jessica Marshall Spencer, opened in 1974, providing a home for the Dudley Experimental Theater and for student performances of musical comedies. The Minnesota Repertory Theater also performed there.[164]

The University of Minnesota School of Medicine at Duluth opened in the fall of 1972; its special mission was to attract medical students who would go into practice in rural areas and small towns. Its students—about 80 percent of them drawn from small communities—spent two years in Duluth, then transferred to the Twin Cities campus for clinical training. Early in their two years, students spent time with community physicians in three-day community visits. James Boulger, then associate dean, noted that following this experience, "the students [came] back all fired up." A high percentage of graduates returned to rural communities to practice. "You see good medicine in Bigfork, Minnesota," Boulger said.[165]

In 1972, the Duluth campus celebrated its twenty-fifth anniversary as a part of the University of Minnesota. From a 10-acre site, the campus had grown to 244 acres. From a student body of 1,432 in 1947, enrollment had reached just over 5,200 undergraduates and close to 140 graduate students by the fall of 1971. In 1972, UMD offered five undergraduate and thirteen master's degrees. In 1947, there were 64 faculty members; in 1972, there were 281.[166]

## Wilson's Legacy

In 1967, O. Meredith Wilson resigned as president of the University of Minnesota and accepted the post of director of the Center for Advanced Studies in the Behavioral Sciences at Stanford University. A news release summarized Wilson's accomplishments: "President Wilson will not be remembered as a brick and mortar President." Rather, "the central feature of his administration has been the development of a very close relationship between the faculty and the administration, as well as between the faculty and the Regents. [His] emphasis has been on development and qualitative growth in academic programs."[167] Among Wilson's other accomplishments were the move to the West Bank, the development of international programs, academic reorganization within the Institute of Technology and the College of Liberal Arts, and formation of the College of Biological Sciences. Academic policy was improved through creation of the All-University Council on Liberal Education and the regents' academic freedom policy. The health sciences were to begin to take steps toward increased service to the state and a more integrated curriculum. Morris became a liberal arts college and Crookston a two-year college.[168] A "Presidential Extra" edition of the *Minnesota Daily* called Wilson "a rare man [who] tried to please everyone" and characterized his seven-year administration as "tranquil." He was quoted as telling the students, "I like you kids. I'm sure going to miss you when I go out to work with those old men in California."[169]

## President Malcolm Moos

Wilson's successor was Malcolm Moos. A native of St. Paul, Moos was the first University of Minnesota graduate to become president, and he brought to the position an understanding of the state and its politics that was to prove useful during one of the most tumultuous eras of the twentieth century. His father, Charles J. Moos, was a confirmed Republican who successfully managed nearly a dozen statewide political campaigns and served as postmaster of St. Paul from 1921 until 1933. Malcolm Moos was also a student of politics, earning a doctorate in political science in 1942 from the

University of California–Los Angeles (UCLA) after receiving bachelor's and master's degrees from the University of Minnesota.

Throughout his life and career, Moos had a foot in political, academic, and journalistic realms. Following his graduation from UCLA, Moos taught at the University of Wyoming, the University of Alabama, the University of Michigan, and finally Johns Hopkins University in Baltimore, where he also worked as associate editor of the *Baltimore Evening Sun*. A number of his books reflected his interest in the nexus between education and government. *The Campus and the State* was published in 1959 by the Committee on Government and Higher Education. His history of the Republican Party was published in 1956 and caught the attention of the president of the United States, Dwight Eisenhower. The following year, Moos joined the White House staff and subsequently became Eisenhower's chief speechwriter. Moos was the author of Eisenhower's famous valedictory warning about the growing influence of the "military-industrial complex." In 1964, Moos wrote a biography of President Eisenhower intended for children. Later, Moos wrote speeches for Republicans Nelson Rockefeller, John Lindsey, and William Scranton before joining the Ford Foundation in 1964 as director of policy and planning.

The social unrest of the late 1960s had an impact on Moos, his wife, Tracy, and their five children. For a brief time during the fall of 1967, when the family first came to the University of Minnesota, university police officers were assigned to protect the president and his family after an anonymous caller had threatened to kidnap the president. Simultaneously, dynamite was found on the West Bank, making more ominous the issue of campus security. Demonstrations became a regular feature of campus life. Tracy Moos described these years as "full of action, never dull." She credited her husband with "courage that was a model for other presidents."[170]

During the fall of 1967, Moos outlined key priorities. One of his major themes was the importance of a strong partnership between the university and the surrounding community. In his first major public address as president, part of the Communiversity Conference based on dialogue between twenty-five university students, twenty-five faculty members, and twenty-five community leaders, he explored ways to improve the links between the university and the community. Moos became a strong supporter of the Center for Urban and Regional Affairs (CURA), established the following year under the leadership of geography faculty members John Borchert and

Fred Lukermann. With its research and outreach initiatives, CURA exemplified the president's vision of an engaged university.[171]

A second priority related to meeting the needs of Minnesota's burgeoning higher education systems, swelled in numbers as the postwar baby boom generation reached college age in 1964. In a 1969 address on the "multiversity," Moos pointed out that enrollment in Minnesota's postsecondary systems had reached close to 150,000—far higher than the 95,000 prediction made by the Gale Commission on Minnesota Higher Education in 1956. His message was also directed to legislators, citing an urgent need for resources, with still more growth anticipated and enrollment not expected to level off until the early 1980s. He cautioned that planning for growth must be collaborative and should consider not only higher education, but also K–12: "We must not create a layer cake of institutions exclusively concerned with different segments of our population. Rather we must seek a marble cake—sharing missions and students. . . . permitting them to move in a mobile market of educational opportunities."[172]

Sociology faculty member David "Dan" Cooperman, who early on got to know Moos through the Communiversity Conference, described him as "a totally decent human being, a man of total sensitivity." Public policy and public relations were great strengths. Moos was elected chair of the Midwest Universities Consortium for International Activities, overseeing international research and assistance projects in Africa, South and Southeast Asia, and Latin America; was a board member of the American Council on Education; and was invited to give the commencement address at Notre Dame in 1973. David Berg, director of the office of Management Planning and Information Services, observed about Moos, "He was a good outside president. He was presidential. He made good speeches. He was quite insightful about politics and what was happening in the field of higher education. He was a good national statesman."[173]

A related strength was fund-raising. Moos, like his predecessor, O. Meredith Wilson, was very much aware of the pivotal importance of private support for the university and had become convinced that private funds would be needed to replace federal dollars diverted to the Vietnam War. During his term of office, the university established a Development Office. By the end of Moos's term of office as president in 1973, the university had risen in national rankings of private support from forty-ninth among all institutions to nineteenth. Another accomplishment during his administration was the completion in 1973 of the first of the new health sciences complex, which was to be named the Malcolm Moos Health Sciences Tower in 1983 to honor his role in support of the health sciences.[174]

As he built his team, Moos retained two key administrators who had served under his predecessor. William G. Shepherd, vice president for academic affairs, had been appointed in 1963 by O. Meredith Wilson. Donald K. Smith was made vice president for administration in April 1968. Smith, who had been at the university since 1963, had strong inside ties and balanced Moos's strengths in external relations. Hale Champion served as vice president for finance until 1971, when he left for a position at Harvard. Champion was replaced by James Brinkerhoff from the University of Michigan, who served as finance vice president from 1971 to 1980.

Other administrative appointments under Moos included the selection of Lyle A. French as the university's first vice president for the health sciences, Roy Richardson as director of personnel, Lillian H. Williams as director of equal opportunity, David J. Berg as director of the Office of Management Planning and Information, Clinton Hewitt as director of campus planning, and Robert Odegard as executive director of the University of Minnesota Foundation. Stan Wenberg remained the university's chief contact with the legislature through 1974. In 1968, a faculty member in the College of Education, Stanley B. Kegler, was made assistant vice president for educational relations and development and subsequently was to follow Wenberg with responsibility for guiding the university's relations with the legislature. Understandably, given the times, student issues assumed greater priority and, upon the retirement of longtime dean of students E. G. Williamson in 1969, the oversight of student matters was elevated to the vice presidential level and Paul H. Cashman, a faculty member in speech communication, became the university's first vice president for student affairs.[175]

In 1967, when Moos became president, campus unrest throughout the country was nearing its peak. Moos was widely credited with helping to keep the peace at the University of Minnesota through his willingness to listen to students and faculty and through the balanced way in which he handled the complex and volatile issues facing colleges and universities. He urged police restraint during demonstrations, and Minnesota came through these years far better than other large public universities. In his opening convocation as president, Moos showed that he was clearly aware of the challenges that he would face: "The towering issue today, at least for the student activist on the campus, is power." He pledged to continue

Minnesota's tradition of open communication between the administration and students. He indicated that he was supportive of activism, but also urged that it be exercised with "forbearance."[176]

## Campus Activism

During this period, the University of Minnesota, like most American colleges and universities, was feeling the impact of the civil rights movement, the women's movement, and the anti–Vietnam War movement. With larger numbers of students, greater diversity, and more strident demands for substantive change, retreat into scholarly seclusion was not possible. As an urban, land-grant institution, the university was a far from reluctant participant in the development of new academic programs, new forms of student support, and new outreach initiatives, bringing university-based expertise to bear on such issues as child development, delinquency, health, inner-city housing, and K–12 schools.

When Moos became president of the university in 1967, E. W. Ziebarth had been dean of the College of Liberal Arts for four years. He had known Moos previously and quickly became one of his chief advisers. Ziebarth saw Moos as "enormously interested in minorities and minority opinion. He was interested in American Indians. He was interested in the black movement. He tried to be helpful in the Eisenhower administration in converting the president of the United States to a more sympathetic view of black problems."[177]

In 1970, the editors of *Daedalus,* the journal of the American Academy of Arts and Sciences, looked back on the changes of the 1960s and their impact on higher education. The result was an entire issue devoted to "the embattled university." The editors observed that young adults "saw options for themselves and acted on those possibilities in a way their parents had never done." The authors noted, moreover, that "to live in the University today is to be aware of subtle changes that have taken place." They observed "an erosion of authority and the setting aside of precedents once thought to be inviolable."[178]

At Minnesota, activism did not lead to the same level of violence, loss of community, or loss of hope for institutional change that occurred at other universities. Arguably, this was not because Minnesota activists were less passionate and energetic than their counterparts on other campuses, but, rather, because they met with greater sympathy from faculty members and administrators, from public officials, and from corporate leaders. The social fabric may have been more resilient in Minnesota because students and activists knew, or knew of, both local and national political leaders. These leaders, moreover, were themselves noted reformers. During the years when Hubert Humphrey was mayor of Minneapolis (1945 to 1948), the city enacted the country's first Fair Employment Practices Act. Humphrey had helped stir the national conscience with his speech on civil rights at the 1948 Democratic National Convention.[179] In 1963, Congressman Donald Fraser personally made inquiries for university student Zev Aelony, who had been imprisoned in Georgia in a civil rights demonstration. In the summer of 1968, University alumna Gladys Brooks was sent by the governor of Minnesota to the Mississippi state prison, Parchman Farm, to check out allegations of improper treatment of jailed Minnesota civil rights demonstrators, most of whom were University of Minnesota students. Dean of students E. G. Williamson, although he was personally somewhat conservative, in 1963 created one of the first human relations positions in an American university. For the position he selected Matthew Stark, who had been coordinator of counseling for university residence halls from 1954 to 1960. Stark, then dean of students at Moorhead State University, had been active in a variety of organizations such as the Minnesota Civil Liberties Union and the Governor's Commission on Human Rights.[180]

## Civil Rights

Civil rights was one of the arenas in which the new activism first became apparent. In speaking of his own career of public service, Walter Mondale indicated that civil rights was the issue that ignited his interest in public affairs. This was reinforced by his student years at the university under sociology professor Arnold Rose, who had worked with Gunnar Myrdal on *The American Dilemma,* an epic study of race. Mondale observed: "Faculty came off the campus totally committed to reform, internationalism, and civil rights. They did more per capita than any state in the union on civil rights." Mondale noted the strong national record of black Minnesota alumni: Roy Wilkins as head of the NAACP (the National Association for the Advancement of Colored People), Whitney Young as head of the Urban League, and Carl Rowan in the U.S. State Department.[181]

Campus activist Marv Davidov, who had been jailed for breach of the peace in the Jackson, Mississippi, freedom rides, recalled being met by six hundred people in Minneapolis after his release from the Jackson jail; he subsequently gave talks at the university. He encouraged football player Carl Eller to attend a performance at the university of the National Student Nonviolent Coordinating Committee freedom singers.[182]

The human relations programs established in the 1960s encouraged students to learn about and participate in the civil rights movement. Student body president Jim Johnson drove with Matthew Stark to participate in Martin Luther King's march from Selma to Montgomery in March 1965. Johnson, later chief of staff for Walter Mondale and chair of the federal lending program Fannie Mae, observed, "While I am convinced we did some good on the project, I think the benefit was certainly matched by the benefit each of us received through the project."[183] Matthew Stark observed, "We not only didn't avoid King's Civil Rights Movement, we had a busload of our students in that march."[184] Jack Mogelson and Judy Larson were among the twenty-four Minnesotans who participated in the 1965 voter registration and accommodation-testing program sponsored in a number of Southern towns by Martin Luther King Jr.'s Southern Christian Leadership Council.[185] Mogelson recalled: "We were almost run off the road by people who didn't like the fact that there were college students in a car from Minnesota. We had problems with some of our people involved in public accommodation testing in a restaurant that was owned by one of the people on the sheriff's staff introducing some gas into the air-conditioning system, which was meant to get our people sick. There were some episodes that were less than pleasant."[186]

## Founding Afro-American Studies

On the Twin Cities campus, the demonstration that created the strongest legacy and clearest outcome was the January 14–15, 1969, occupation of Morrill Hall—the administration building—by African American students who had formed, with community representatives, the Afro-American Action Committee (AAAC). That demonstration led directly to the creation of the Department of Afro-American and African Studies and, indirectly, to American Indian studies and Chicano studies.

Black leaders, including Horace Huntley, Rose Mary Freeman, and Mahmoud El-Kati, were eager to discuss the recruitment of black students and the establishment of programs for them with Moos and members of his administration. In the summer of 1968, John Wright and several other black students undertook a recruiting initiative. Wright later noted: "It was a very limited operation. We went door to door canvassing in communities in Minneapolis and St. Paul, handing out application forms, talking about university missions, about financial aid."[187] At about the same time, the history department sent one of its younger faculty members, Al Jones, to several Southern universities to recruit black graduate students. The pressure to inaugurate an academic program in black studies came more from the outside than from within the university.

As associate dean of the College of Liberal Arts, Lloyd Lofquist was involved in plans for the new department. Although there had been a number of meetings, it appeared to observers, including John Wright, who was later to become a faculty member in Afro-American studies, that little was happening. Moos met regularly with black leaders, and it was generally felt that he was sympathetic to their concerns. To the black students, however, he did not seem to be particularly effective in marshaling resources and getting broader support for these initiatives.[188]

In retrospect, Wright saw that the decision to escalate negotiations and initiate a confrontation with the administration was shaped, in part, by developments elsewhere:

> Our basic plans, and the list of demands and requirements, were in part patterned on those stratagems and ideas that were fairly consistently being presented to universities and colleges around the country. Black student unions were meeting in national gatherings then. There was an agenda being pushed at large. The request for a formal program of recruitment, for the creation of a student support services program—the program that would become the Martin Luther King Program—the creation of a department of Afro-American and African Studies, the recruitment of black faculty, those were all essential parts of our plan.[189]

The twenty-four-hour occupation of Morrill Hall was a joint effort involving activists from the campus as well as community groups. Seven black students led by Horace Huntley and Rose Mary Freeman had asked for an appointment with President Moos on Monday, January 13. Because Moos was out of town, they met with Vice President Paul Cashman, giving him a set of demands and setting a deadline of one o'clock the next day for the university to respond. Moos met with fifty or sixty black students on Tuesday afternoon, saying that actions already under way would deal with their concerns. This did not satisfy the protesters, who went to the bursar's office and the Office of Records on the first floor of Morrill Hall, permitting no one to enter those offices but allowing students and civil service personnel to leave. The blockade, which continued the rest of the day and all night, was generally peaceful.[190] Josie Johnson, then a community organizer for the Urban League and subsequently a member of the Board of Regents (1971–73), a policy fellow in the College of Education, and ultimately associate vice president for minority affairs, was one of the people from the community who became involved: "I can't remember exactly who asked me to come. I came to bring food to the students. Somebody got in touch with me late one night."[191]

President Moos did not call the police or attempt to have the building cleared. Instead, he authorized negotiations. Academic vice president Jerry Shepherd admitted that "the occupation was quite a kick in the pants, and we got down to serious discussions."[192] In addition to Shepherd, the chief negotiators for the university were Vice President Paul Cashman and Assistant Vice Presidents Fred Lukermann and James Reeves, who was black. "I was the one from central administration who was there all night negotiating with people," Lukermann said. "Jim Reeves and I were actually accused at one time of organizing the occupation of Morrill Hall, because we were supposedly sympathetic." Lukermann asked Harry Davis, a prominent black civic leader, to help with the discussions.[193]

Accords were announced shortly after noon on Wednesday. The Afro-American Action Committee approved the university's ongoing plans for establishment of a program in ethnic and racial studies, which would include black studies and involve members of the local black community, although decisions about curriculum and faculty would be left in the hands of the faculty. With this understanding, and with the university's agreement to create the Martin Luther King Program to assist and advise black students (in fact, the program assisted low-income students regardless of race), the black students withdrew and the occupation of Morrill Hall ended. Commenting on the occupation, former president O. Meredith Wilson said that there had been "some rudeness" but none of the "blood-letting" that had occurred at other universities.[194]

There were other demonstrations as well. On January 22, 1969, student demonstrators, this time predominantly white, demanded abolition of the Reserve Officers Training Corps and the Department of Criminal Justice Studies, and urged that university scholarships be substituted for ROTC scholarships. On March 9, 1970, demonstrators, allegedly looking for secret files, ransacked the office of the Department of Criminal Justice Studies.

*Antiwar Demonstrations*

On April 30, 1970, the Nixon administration announced the U.S. invasion of Cambodia. The following weekend, National Guard troops opened fire on student protestors at Kent State University in Ohio, killing four students. Ten days later, a similar episode took place at Jackson State, a predominantly black college in Mississippi; two students died and a dozen were wounded. Closer to home, fatal violence occurred at Madison, Wisconsin, where a university building alleged to house defense research was wrecked by a bomb explosion; there was one death.

The day after Nixon's televised speech, a group of University of Minnesota students and faculty met to plan a campuswide protest. On Monday, May 4, 1970, five thousand students and faculty members voted to strike the university in opposition to the United States offensive in Cambodia and possible resumption of bombing in North Vietnam. They demanded complete and immediate withdrawal of all U.S. troops from Southeast Asia and asked the University Senate to endorse the strike as "a necessary and legitimate" means of protest.

At noon the next day, about forty-five hundred people attended a memorial service for the slain Kent State students. Several hundred strikers then occupied Morrill Hall but relinquished it when President Moos agreed to speak to the crowd outside. He denied that a civil service worker had been dismissed because of support for the strike, and he indirectly spoke in favor of the protest. That evening he issued a statement proposing the following Friday as "a day of reflection and contemplation for our campus— I would urge and encourage all members of the university community to use the day in accord with their own conscientious assessment of their country's situation and their personal responsibilities."[195] Classes could be held, but neither students nor faculty members would be required to attend them.

Teach-ins on U.S. foreign policy, the military and the war, and corporate responsibility were held on Wednesday. On Thursday, mass picketing was conducted at most campus buildings, but Bill Tilton, student coordinator of the strike, warned that it must not be coercive. The Twin Cities Campus Assembly, acting for the Senate, approved the proposal to suspend classes on Friday and, if faculty and students desired, on one day each week for the remainder of the academic year. Several hundred faculty members agreed to wear white armbands as a sign of their desire to help maintain order. The demonstration reached its climax on Friday and Saturday. On Friday, May 8, about six thousand persons joined a rally held on the steps of Northrop Auditorium. Speakers included Roger Jones, an associate professor of physics, and a DFL candidate for governor, Nicholas Coleman. Resolutions passed by the faculty of the Colleges of Business and Education were read; food donated by several large food companies was distributed.

The strike, supported by a cross-section of students and faculty members, encompassed radicals, liberals, and moderates. The Board of Regents passed resolutions congratulating Moos and his associates for "leadership exercised in attempting to keep peace and intelligent purpose highlighted at this university" and commending students for "their responsible behavior and respect for people and property." Regent Lyman Brink commented how "politely [he] was greeted by pickets in front of Morrill Hall." On Saturday, May 9, a large crowd of students, faculty members, citizens, veterans, and clergymen marched from the university to the state capitol. Student groups from Augsburg, Macalester, St. Thomas, Hamline, St. Catherine's, and Concordia joined as the throng passed their campuses. Estimates of the size of the crowd at the capitol varied from twenty thousand to fifty thousand. Follow-up efforts included a program in which students went in pairs on a door-to-door campaign to engage residents in their movement.

A separate protest occurred just north of the campus, in Dinkytown. On April 1, a group of students had occupied a site where the Red Barn chain planned to build a fast-food restaurant. About fifty Minneapolis police officers and an equal number of Hennepin County sheriff's deputies, armed with rifles and shotguns, took up their positions as a helicopter circled overhead. After a brief scuffle, the demonstrators were cleared away and bulldozers moved in to demolish the four storefront buildings the protesters had occupied. By six o'clock the next morning, they were a pile of rubble. There were no serious injuries. Three university administrators, Paul Cashman, Donald Zander, and James Reeves, had worked in the streets to try to contain confrontation between the protesters and the police. The protesters had the last word, a pacific one: by midafternoon, the site had been converted into a "people's park" by a group of seventy-five young people who planted daisies, chrysanthemums, and bachelor's buttons, all to the sound of rock music.

On May 16, 1970, during the student strike, protesters presented five demands to President Moos: remove ROTC from campus, stop war-related research, sell stock in companies providing munitions, commit to a no-reprisal policy, and close down the university as a protest against the war. May 20, May 26, and June 3, 1970, were designated "days of reflection" on the "national crisis." Significantly, there was no violence. At the high point of the strike, informal counts showed that class attendance had declined by 10 percent and close to six thousand students had accepted the special grading arrangement that allowed them to be evaluated on a pass/fail basis rather than through letter grades.[196]

Not all parts of the campus or all the campuses reacted to the war in similar ways. There was a "sleep-in" antiwar protest in Coffey Hall in St. Paul, but the St. Paul students generally were less inclined to activism. Sherwood Berg, at the time Dean of the Institute of Agriculture, Forestry, and Home Economics, recalled an offer of assistance from forestry students: "We understand there's a little trouble on the other campus. We're here to tell you that if you need any help, just let us know and we'll go right over there and clean them out." Berg replied, "I think we'll handle it in a little different manner, but I am sure the president will appreciate knowing that he has this support."[197]

Shortly after these displays of activism, the Office of Student Affairs conducted a survey of student opinion and involvement. More than two-thirds of those interviewed (67.8 percent) expressed strong or moderate disapproval of the U.S. military action in Cambodia. Most identified their own involvement as moderate or slight. Many had attended campus rallies (57.7 percent) or taken part in teach-ins (37.6 percent), but only 13.4 percent had participated in campus picketing, and only 11.4 percent marched to the capitol. About a third had contributed money to the strike effort or written letters to senators, congressmen, or the president.[198]

Student dissatisfaction with the war did not necessarily mean dissatisfaction with the university. A survey of a random sample of students during the boycott revealed that 21 percent of the students were "extremely satisfied" and 57 percent were "moderately satisfied" with the university. On the more negative end of the scale, 10 percent said they were slightly satisfied, 1 percent were neutral, and 5 percent were "slightly dissatisfied." Despite their efforts, the students doubted that their protests would change national policies: 61 percent said they probably would not and 25 percent believed they definitely would not. The survey showed that participation in strike-related activities varied greatly in nature and extent but that large numbers of students did become involved. Darwin Hendel, the author of the survey, concluded that the student activities were primarily issue-oriented acts of conscience and not a "protest for protest's sake."[199]

The year before the student strike of 1970, a number of students and faculty members had been active in a series of antiwar demonstrations carried out against Honeywell, one of Minnesota's largest companies. Originating as a manufacturer of heating controls, Honeywell had applied automation to industrial controls, aerospace and defense, and computers. Honeywell's defense contracts—in particular, the production of cluster bombs—led to demonstrations. There were similar demonstrations against other companies with military contracts, but the dialogue between protesters and Honeywell executives had a particularly Minnesota dimension.

In 1969 four Institute of Technology faculty members—Ed Anderson (mechanical engineering), Woods Haley and Roger Jones (physics), and Val Woodward (genetics)—had become concerned by Honeywell's manufacture of cluster bombs for the government and its use of university research in the bomb design. Activist Marv Davidov, who was then teaching in the Experimental College, spearheaded the protest. Davidov later recalled:

> Ed Anderson had worked in [the Honeywell] missile program and quit in disgust. Ed calls [James] Binger [head of Honeywell] and says, "There's a group called Honeywell Project."
>
> Binger says, "Yes, I know. They caught one of our guys at a forum at Coffman. I know about them."
>
> "They want a meeting with you."
>
> Binger said, "Bring three of them up immediately."
>
> Ed, Woods, and I met for two hours with him. I said, "Jim, you guys have been making cluster bombs and other hideous weapons for a long time now...."
>
> I said, "Jim, we have a plan. We'll bring in experts to help you convert to peace programs with no loss of jobs. But we're also going to come to your homes, your country clubs, your businesses, and we're going to demonstrate."
>
> "You have every right to do that," he said.[200]

Several hundred students from the university and colleges all over the state were involved in the Honeywell protest at its height. So were members of the community, including Erica Bouza, wife of Minneapolis police chief Anthony Bouza. Honeywell's position was that the company was working for a democratically chosen government and was "proud to provide our troops with the necessary weapons"; opponents of this position should vote for leaders who would alter the nation's military policy. In fact, the company was already reducing its defense contracts, laying off some employees, and considering ways of converting to other projects. By 1973 most of the activists had lost interest and the protest faded. "Peo-

ple got tired of struggling," said Davidov, noting an observation by activist Philip Berrigan that "the average life of a movement activist is six
months."[201]

## New Departments and Programs

Meanwhile, within the university, new departments and programs were introduced in response to student demands. Fred Lukermann was instrumental in supporting the new Department of Afro-American and African
Studies, which was approved by the regents in June 1969 and began to offer
courses in 1970. The logical place for it was in the social sciences division
of the College of Liberal Arts. The first faculty members were Josie Johnson, Lillian Anthony, Earl Craig, and Milt Williams (Mahmoud El-Kati).
"You can see," Lukermann commented, "that this was not really a discipline,
but a cross-disciplinary department; there were sociologists, political scientists, history people involved."[202]

Josie Johnson said later that "the town-gown nexus was a strong one.
So Anna [Stanley], Rose, Huntley, that group of students, became sort of
the connection between the university and the community. We worked with
Mahmoud El-Kati, Earl Craig, John Wright—John was a younger person
but a student of ours—John Taborn, Reginald Buckner, and Anita Tucker.
I trained Anita, who was also a Fiskite [Johnson was an alumna of Fisk Uni-
versity], to take my job when I went to the Board of Regents."[203]

John Wright moved from demonstrator to professor. Initially as a graduate student and later, after a decade at Carleton College, Wright returned
to the university, where he became affiliated with Afro-American studies,
English, and American studies, ultimately becoming a full professor. In 1999,
he was among one of the first groups of faculty members selected for the
university's Academy of Distinguished Teachers. Wright's research focused
on the Black Arts movement and on Ralph Ellison and other African American writers affiliated with the Harlem Renaissance. Looking back on the
department at a thirtieth anniversary symposium in 1999, Wright noted
that it, like American studies twenty years earlier, was based on a strong
commitment to interdisciplinary work and that in the early years it tended
to be descriptive. Faculty members with diverse interests were recruited:
Reginald Buckner as a scholar of jazz; Anita Brooks, a researcher on the
black family; and Geneva Southall, a scholar in music literature and piano
performance. Wright noted that "the courses were rigorous, established academic credibility, not a place where black students could walk through."

The department, Wright believed, was "more solidly based financially than others in the Big Ten."[204]

A degree program in American Indian studies was established in 1969 and one in Chicano studies in 1972. History professor Clarke Chambers observed that the new departments of Afro-American studies, Chicano studies, and American Indian studies served two audiences: "They had to create an academic viability on their own. They had to relate also to the larger community of citizens in the metropolitan area and in the state." Lukermann credited the departments with helping the university broaden its enrollment of students of color: "I believe they were absolutely necessary and did work well in changing the enrollment characteristics of the university; that is, they were the reason we could recruit the number of blacks, the number of American Indians, and the number of Chicanos that are now [in 1984] present here."[205]

President Moos had been interested for a number of years in the role of the university in the community. Sociologist David "Dan" Cooperman believed that in comparison to his predecessors, "Moos was far less conservative and far less wary about the university's contact with the community." To carry out his vision of an engaged university, Moos asked Fred Lukermann to undertake several pilot projects. One was a summer program in which high school minority students undertook intensive college preparatory studies. Another, supervised by Cooperman, involved the establishment of "storefront universities."

"This meant," Cooperman said, "that I made contact with community leaders, largely again minority, in some—I suppose you might loosely call it a ghetto area. I would try to get faculty to teach, on a voluntary basis for a period of five to ten weeks, a course that they felt would legitimately attract college-level students but to teach it in a slightly different way. Students who had never taken college credits before could sign up for such courses. They could get college credit without paying tuition."[206]

Such efforts were centralized under the new Center for Urban and Regional Affairs (CURA). Lukermann served briefly as acting head, followed by his fellow geographer John Borchert. CURA was intimately involved in the Martin Luther King and HELP (Higher Education for Low-Income Persons) centers set up after the Morrill Hall agreement. Later it sponsored a number of scholarly studies of urban issues as well as community outreach programs. Lukermann regarded it as "an enormous success. I attribute it to the original intent not to make it permanent in the sense of the projects. They were experimental and we killed a lot."[207] After the Vietnam

War, CURA established a clearinghouse for information on refugee issues, bringing university expertise to bear on resettlement needs of Southeast Asian refugees.

## Feminism at the University

The 1960s and 1970s were also a time of feminist activism. In 1960, the university had created the Minnesota Plan for Continuing Education for Women, one of the first university-based programs for women returning to higher education. Edith Mucke, who would become its director in 1974, recalled reading a newspaper article about a liberal arts seminar, New Worlds of Knowledge, designed as an open door for women who would like to come back to the university. "I had reached a point in my life where I didn't know what was ahead," Mucke said:

> One of my children was married. The other daughter was getting ready to go off to college, and life looked pretty bleak to me. I came over to the campus and had an interview with Dr. Vera Schletzer, who was just getting started in the program at that time. After I had talked with her for about an hour, I came out of there feeling like I was walking on a cloud—just wonderful. I felt I had a whole new life ahead of me.[208]

Mucke took classes from a number of the university's best-known teachers, including John Berryman (English), Herbert Feigl (philosophy), Mulford Sibley (political science), and Leonard Unger (English). After she completed her bachelor's degree, Mucke was offered a position in the program. Mary Turpie, "one of the great pillars of the American studies department," advised her to accept the position. "From the very beginning we had a glorious team."[209] The program was copied throughout the country and cited as a model by Betty Friedan in her pathbreaking book, *The Feminine Mystique,* published in 1963. Friedan urged that more institutions copy the Minnesota program: "Education and re-education of American women for a serious purpose cannot be effective by one or two far-sighted institutions, it must be accomplished on a far wider scale."[210]

Sara Evans, who joined the history faculty in 1976, recalled the impact of *The Feminine Mystique* on her life when she was a student at Duke University:

> Reading Betty Friedan's *Feminine Mystique* made it clear to me that I was not going to just get a teaching certificate and teach secondary school, but I wanted to go on and be able to teach in college. . . . As an undergraduate I had been very active in civil rights and the anti–Vietnam War movement. . . .

I also had a new sense of why I wanted to pursue scholarship in American history and, specifically, in women's history. I felt we had to know our history if we wanted to make history.[211]

The University Women's Center was established in 1965 as an outgrowth of the Minnesota Plan. Kathryn Scott Randolph served as director of the program, which became known as the Minnesota Planning and Counseling Center for Women, for three years; she was succeded by Anne Thorsen Truax, who held the position until 1991. While Continuing Education for Women retained its emphasis on mature women, the Women's Center concentrated on traditional-aged students, offering a seminar titled Lifestyles of the Educated American Woman and creating a library and seminar room in the center's Walter Library offices. Truax was part of a committee that convinced the marching band to accept women and helped create the Carol E. MacPherson Scholarship for women returning to the university. In 1973, she was one of the founders of the women's studies department.[212]

Other manifestations of feminism included Minnesota's pioneering role in 1969 in establishing the Council for University Women's Progress, one of the first university-based women's action groups in the United States. The council played a role in passage by the University Senate and the regents of the university's first affirmative action plan for women faculty, a new civil service grievance procedure, and the abolition of nepotism policies. The group published statistics in 1971 showing that only 125 of the 1,400 nontemporary faculty were women and that anthropology, history, music, psychology, and other departments had no women. The group also raised the issue of salary equity.

In 1970, Marjorie Howard, the only woman on the Board of Regents, called the administration's attention to the salaries offered to three new deans. The men, Jack Merwin of the College of Education and Lee D. Stauffer of the School of Public Health, were being appointed at salaries of $31,500 and $27,000 respectively. Isabel Harris, appointed at the same time to be dean of nursing, was to receive a salary of $20,500. Following Regent Howard's inquiry, Harris's salary was raised to $25,500; university officials explained that the earlier salary had been the result of "a mistake in the personnel forms."[213] Among the leaders of the Twin Cities group were Joan Aldous, professor of sociology; Shirley Clark, a faculty member in education; Carolyn Rose, professor of sociology; and Anne Truax.[214] In 1971, Eugene Eidenberg, assistant vice president for administration, was appointed equal opportunity officer, and Lillian H. Williams was appointed deputy equal opportunity officer.

Federal regulations (Title IX of the Education Amendments of 1972) were to have significant implications for gender equity and led to the creation in 1975 of women's intercollegiate athletics programs. In 1973, Shyamala Rajender filed a lawsuit when the chemistry department refused to consider her for a tenure track position; the suit would have a significant impact at Minnesota and elsewhere throughout the remainder of the twentieth century.

## International Students and International Studies

In 1960, there were 1,101 international students at the university. The university continued to add to the programs and services available to visiting students and scholars. Historians Clarke Chambers and Harold Deutsch offered "American life" seminars in their homes, and faculty members in St. Paul often had international students for meals so they could spend time with American families. The World Affairs Center, begun in 1950 and located within the General Extension Division (later the College of Continuing Education), brought together all of the principal organizations in Minnesota concerned with foreign policy. Its university anchors were William Rogers and Barbara Stuhler (later executive associate dean of the College of Continuing Education), who were guided by an advisory council representing those organizations. The World Affairs Center served for nearly thirty years as a community and university forum for the discussion of global issues. It was disbanded for budgetary reasons in 1984. The Minnesota International Center, located on the campus, although not officially a part of the university, was an important asset, useful to both the university and the broader community. It identified American host families and also sponsored lectures and programs to introduce Minnesotans to international visitors as well as international guests to Minnesota residents.[215]

International and area studies programs increased, a number of them supported with funding from the National Defense Education Act and foundation grants. Built on the interdisciplinary model of American studies, the new centers included Scandinavian, Russian, Southeast Asian, and Latin American studies. Although at Minnesota, as elsewhere, there were differences in perspective between faculty members whose orientation was primarily discipline-based (economics, political science, history, and so on) versus faculty members whose interests focused on a particular geographic area, the programs continued to grow and flourish as more students and faculty members became interested in international study.[216]

The Office of International Programs had been established in 1963 with a $1.25 million grant from the Ford Foundation. These funds were used to create a small grants research fund, to offer faculty seminars and workshops, and to add positions in selected departments. One such grant was to university faculty members Robert H. Beck (education), Harold C. Deutsch (history), Philip M. Raup (agricultural economics), Arnold M. Rose (sociology), and John G. Turnbull (economics) to analyze contemporary Western European social, economic, political, and military institutions. With Ford Foundation funding, Minnesota faculty members advised the University of Concepción in Chile in developing institutes of biology, chemistry, physics, and mathematics. A second initiative in Chile was to aid in agricultural production and the establishment of agricultural extension services. A third initiative provided advice to the Federal University of Paraná in Brazil on improving agricultural production and better education of farmers on new agricultural techniques.[217]

International programs were guided by an all-university council and by committees on Asia, Latin America, Western Europe, Russia and Eastern Europe, economic and social development, and international relations. Although there were federal funds for a wide variety of initiatives, there was special emphasis on initiatives that would help developing countries establish programs in agriculture, engineering, economics, and public health. In one such initiative, university advisers assisted Tunisia in developing an economic research office to advise the government on public policy issues related to the production and marketing of field crops, olive oil, and cattle.

In 1963, the Institute of Agriculture, Forestry, and Home Economics established the Office of International Agricultural Programs (OIAP). Headed by John Blackmore, it played a national role helping the United States respond to increased demand for technical assistance abroad. Over the next three decades, OIAP helped to develop a series of USAID-funded institutional building projects in Morocco. The Morocco project, considered one of the most successful of all the USAID projects, laid the groundwork for strong connections between University of Minnesota faculty members and their peers in Morocco, continuing through the end of the century. In 1998, the College of Agricultural, Food, and Environmental Sciences, in collaboration with Moroccan institutions, embarked upon a program with Senegal, similar to the one with Morocco. Between the 1960s and the end of the 1990s, the Office of International Agricultural Programs helped link University of Minnesota faculty members in the College of Agricultural, Food, and Environmental Sciences, the College of Natural Resources, and the College of Veterinary Medicine to projects in more than twenty-five countries. Among them were faculty initiatives in the Caribbean, Burundi, Chile, Malawi, Russia, and Tunisia.[218]

William Wright, director of international programs, observed of the late 1960s and 1970s that "this was the heyday of U.S. involvement in international affairs and development, and education; the foundations were caught up in it, and they were putting money in universities to encourage international programs. It was high, wide, and handsome for a few years."[219]

The awarding of the Nobel Peace Prize in 1970 to Norman Borlaug, who served as an adviser to the International Maize and Wheat Improvement Center established by the Mexican and the United States governments, was an indication of the high profile of international economic initiatives during these years. Borlaug, who received bachelor's, master's, and Ph.D. degrees from the University of Minnesota, was a student of Minnesota plant pathologist E. C. Stakman. Borlaug had lived in Mexico since 1944, serving as an adviser with funding from the Ford and Rockefeller Foundations. Borlaug, whose research expertise related to the development of high yield varieties of grain, received the Nobel prize in recognition of his contributions to the "green revolution." His research had worldwide implications but was of particular importance for Latin America, India, and Pakistan.[220]

Other international study, travel, and work programs included the Peace Corps, established in the 1960s during the administration of President John F. Kennedy; the University of Minnesota consistently was among the largest sources of Peace Corps volunteers. On the Twin Cities campus, the International Study and Travel Center, a student-run and student-fee-supported program, helped arrange economical travel and lodging for students abroad.

International and area studies programs were also offered. As early as the 1950s, foundation money was available for area studies programs. The first of them, Scandinavian, brought in a specialist in Scandinavian government from North Carolina.

The Russian area studies program was led by history faculty member Theofanis Stavrou, who acknowledged later that "area studies received a lot of criticism, especially at Minnesota, where they were more theoretically oriented and where they believed in what they called problem solving instead of concentrating on an area."[221] Stavrou noted that, at Minnesota, attention to international topics developed on an institutional level rather than on the basis of a series of departments devoted to particular geographic areas. National Defense Education Act funding helped the university create a program in South Asian studies.

## A Change of Administration

About halfway through his term, faculty leaders began to question President Moos about his decisions.[222] Later, in May 1973, Vice President Shepherd and his two chief associates, Lloyd Lofquist and Fred Lukermann, announced that they intended to resign before the beginning of the next academic year. Their reasons were various, but the resignations deepened concerns about Moos's leadership.[223] Faculty members in the University Senate, among them economist Walter Heller, publicly declared that there was "a leadership crisis" in the university.[224]

Moos and the university had faced an economic crisis in 1971: significant retrenchments in the university's budget. Some cuts had been anticipated, but the actual figures were distressing—one hundred faculty positions were lost—and it appeared that central administration was not making adequate plans to meet the situation. The 1973 legislative appropriation led to a hiring freeze. Retrenchments were all the less palatable because of revelations that the president had overspent his entertainment and travel allowance by $18,000 during 1969 and 1970, and had paid a quarter of a million dollars for a prop-jet airplane.[225]

Early in May 1972, Moos was in Canada at a meeting. His absence could not have come at a worse time: he was not present when the most serious disturbance in the history of the university began.[226] Twenty years later, the *Minnesota Daily* looked back:

> National Guardsmen patrolled the campus and students sang atop barricades thrown across Washington Ave. Protesters had been throwing rocks, running through tear gas and howling for peace for two days during the wildest unrest in University history.[227]

The demonstration was a response to President Nixon's escalation of the Vietnam War and his May 8 order that North Vietnam ports be blockaded and mined. A May 10 antiwar rally on Northrop plaza drew two thousand students. By early afternoon, the protesters had moved to the university Armory.[228] Eugene Eidenberg believed that the students intended to set fire to the Armory; unable to reach Moos by telephone, he asked Charles Stenvig, the former police chief who had been elected mayor of Minneapolis, to bring in the city police to protect the building. Demonstrators blocked traffic on Washington Avenue and a riot developed. Police chased students with tear gas and arrested thirty-two. Later that day, Governor Wendell Anderson was persuaded to activate the National Guard. On May 11, Eugene McCarthy addressed a crowd estimated at six thousand. On May 12, the police finally gave students the street; regarding this as a sign of victory, they soon dispersed.[229] This demonstration was the closest that Minnesota came to the violence that erupted at Columbia, the University of Wisconsin, and the University of California.

A panel appointed to review the events reported that there was "no one to blame and few to praise," although it criticized the Minneapolis police. Steve Hammer, one of the demonstrators, looked back with some optimism: "There was a good spirit about it. . . . You sort of got the feeling you could change things, and I think we did."[230]

A year later, in the summer of 1973, the regents decided that a change had to be made at the top. Among the issues said to have coalesced the regents' thinking were the misgivings of the faculty senate; the resignations of Shepherd, Lofquist, and Lukermann; and the president's increasing remoteness, including his absence during the May 1972 protest.[231]

Regent Elmer L. Andersen linked his concerns about Moos in part to the discrimination lawsuit brought by faculty member Shyamala Rajender alleging discrimination in hiring by the Department of Chemistry on the basis of gender and national origin.[232] Andersen later recalled:

> It was perfectly clear to the Board of Regents that there was discrimination, that this woman was very well qualified and should have been appointed, and it would seem pretty clear that a department that was all male just didn't want a woman. The regents argued with the president about that incident, not wanting to confirm [his action]. The president was pleading that he'd lose stature with the faculty [if he backed down]. I remember telling him at the time, "This is too much to expect a Board of Regents to do." That led to the board's feeling there had to be a change.[233]

Andersen and others also acknowledged the considerable contributions that Moos had made as president, in particular his handling of demonstrations. Regent Lester A. Malkerson observed that "Moos would listen, he would talk to people. He would bend, but he didn't break—I think that during those very severe times he lent a lot of stability to the university by being able to do this." Lyle French, who had been appointed vice president for health sciences by Moos, recalled the effectiveness of his role as an advocate on behalf of the health sciences. Robert Odegard, who had been executive director of the University of Minnesota Foundation during the Moos administration, looked back on Moos's significant contributions as a fund raiser. In reflecting in 1976 on his legacy as the tenth president of the University of Minnesota, Moos indicated that he wished to be remembered for his handling of social unrest, management through times of retrenchment, support for improving access to the university for women and minorities, the increase in private support for the university, and advocacy for a university involved in the affairs of the community and the world.[234]

The *Minnesota Daily* offered its assessment of the Moos presidency, noting that he had faced twin crises: the crisis of student activism and the crisis of economic contraction. The *Daily* suggested that he handled the student crisis better than the economic crisis. Overall, his was judged a successful presidency:

> Moos came to the University at perhaps the most difficult time in history for college presidents.... Moos will be remembered by the communiversity as the University's first homegrown president and as such one who had an intense pride in the institution. He will also be remembered as the man who tried to keep the University from flying apart as it was subjected to the most intense pressures in its history; we feel the legacy of his tenure will guide the University in surmounting these pressures.[235]

In July 1974, Moos became chief executive officer of the Center for the Study of Democratic Institutions in Santa Barbara, California. He died on January 28, 1982.

# Chapter 3
# Planning in a Time of Austerity,
# 1974–1984

Planning will be one of the magic words of the 1980s. If educators do not plan, then someone else will surely do it for them.

*C. Peter Magrath*

THE DECADE BETWEEN 1974 AND 1984 was a time of marked contrasts. On one hand, there was a strong sense of pride in the accomplishments of the region and of the university. On the other hand, it was an anxious period unsettled by an increasingly uncertain economy. During this time, University of Minnesota administrators, like their counterparts at other universities, turned to long-range planning to help them deal with fiscal problems. Although a number of programs and initiatives were phased out, reallocation made it possible to start others. Faculty, staff, and students were all affected by the new economic realities. Concerns about careers and earnings became as prominent as political and social activism had been earlier.

*Time* magazine featured Minnesota in an August 1973 article titled "Minnesota: A State that Works"; Governor Wendell Anderson was on the cover. At a time when Washington was preoccupied with the unfolding Watergate scandals, Minnesota looked like paradise. *Time* praised Minnesota's honest politics, support for education, low crime rate, quality of life, balanced economy, and civic activism by business leaders. The article referred to the leadership of Senators Hubert Humphrey and Walter Mondale as well as to a group of "citizen politicians" that included, in addition to Wendell Anderson, Arthur Naftalin, Martin Olav Sabo, Al Hofstede, and Douglas Head. *Time* characterized the University of Minnesota as "probably the dominant and most prestigious institution in the state," describing it in a phrase attributed to Malcolm Moos, as "a felicitous mixture of New England influence and the spirit of the frontier."[1] Minnesota's Walter Mondale was vice president of the United States from 1977 to 1981 under President Jimmy Carter. And Minnesotans were proud that eleven of the twenty members of the 1980 Miracle on Ice Olympic Hockey Team and Coach Herb Brooks had connections with the Gophers and the UMD Bulldogs.

When C. Peter Magrath arrived in 1974 to assume his duties as the eleventh president of the university, Minnesota seemed calm in comparison to the turbulent national scene. There were still demonstrations, but they were fewer and in a lower key. Just three weeks earlier, Richard Nixon had resigned as president of the United States, thereby bringing to a close the political turmoil that had followed the discovery of a break-in at Democratic Party headquarters. Washington's problems seemed remote from the campus. Although there were demonstrations about boycotting lettuce and grapes produced by nonunion labor and rent increases in Cedar Riverside, the situation was not as tense as it had been during Nixon's escalation of the Vietnam War. Concern about the economy led to an emphasis on planning and reallocation rather than revolution. By the time of Malcolm Moos's resignation, the university had begun to experience a series of retrenchments necessitating staff cutbacks and program curtailments. In addition, Minnesota—like colleges and universities all over the country—was beginning to realize that higher education faced a future of probable enrollment declines. The first of the baby-boom generation had entered college in 1964; the last would matriculate in 1978, when they turned eighteen.

The mid-1970s to the mid-1980s was an important decade for women and gender equity: the Twin Cities campus women's studies department was formed in 1972–73; the Center for Advanced Feminist Studies a decade later. Women's studies was added in Duluth in 1981 and in Morris in 1982. The Rajender case—a lawsuit over gender equality in faculty appointments—left an imprint not only in Minnesota but also nationally, as colleges and universities struggled to create gender equity. The visit of an official University of Minnesota delegation to China in 1979 was a highlight among various international initiatives. New facilities for the health sciences were constructed in the Twin Cities. A two-year medical program was created in Duluth, and UMD consolidated its collegiate structure. Investments were made in Morris, Crookston, and Waseca as well as in experiment stations and extension facilities. During the 1970s, for the first time, the university was to have a physical presence in Rochester.

Long-range planning was seen as a guide to the tough choices these years required. Political science faculty member Samuel Krislov looked back wistfully to earlier times: "Gone are the days," he said, "when planning at the university was a matter of waiting your turn. . . . If your department didn't get a position one year, you figured they owed you one and they would give it to you the next year."[2] Planning and reallocation became a fact of life on each of the campuses. Joseph Kauffman of the University of Wisconsin, an expert on the American college presidency, observed that presidents during the 1960s and early 1970s needed to be "cool under fire" and skilled in "crisis management"; subsequently, they needed to be "diplomat-healers" and "tight-fisted money managers."[3] Student life was different too: activism was less common. This was the economic and social climate that awaited the university's eleventh president, C. Peter Magrath.

## President C. Peter Magrath

Following President Moos's departure in June 1974, the regents asked E. W. Ziebarth to serve as interim president. Ziebarth, who had just resigned as dean of the College of Liberal Arts, was respected by many regents, legislators, and faculty members. More than four hundred candidates emerged in the search for Moos's successor, which ultimately was narrowed to three: David Saxon of UCLA, Richard Cyert of Carnegie Mellon, and C. Peter Magrath of the State University of New York at Binghamton. Cyert withdrew. Saxon's candidacy stumbled. He had spoken at a luncheon meeting and said, "One thing is clear to me, you can't afford to have two Universities of Minnesota."[4]

This statement alienated supporters of the university from outside the metropolitan area, who thought these comments had negative implications for the coordinate campuses. On April 5, in a straw vote, the board had voted along urban–Greater Minnesota lines, seven to five in favor of Saxon. Later regents agreed they would not offer the position to a candidate without a two-thirds majority. A number of regents reconsidered their votes and by April 8, they voted unanimously to offer the presidency to C. Peter Magrath.

On August 30, it became public that another factor, anti-Semitism, may have affected the search process. This revelation led to newspaper articles and legislative hearings. It was alleged that on a number of occasions during the selection process, several regents, most notably Regent L. J. Lee, had questioned Saxon, who is Jewish, about his religion. Although they admitted that religion was discussed, the regents unanimously denied that it had led to the selection of Magrath. Minnesota Senate Majority Leader Nick Coleman was not as sanguine as the regents. He observed, "If not the only factor, religion was one of the factors that went into the decision."[5]

The legislative committee appointed to look into the allegation of anti-Semitism in the presidential selection process held hearings during the fall of 1974 and adopted findings in January 1975. Although the committee, chaired by Senator B. Robert Lewis of St. Louis Park, found "that anti-Semitism was not involved in the final selection," it did conclude that "the inappropriate topic of religion was raised repeatedly during the selection process." The legislative report also noted that concerns about anti-Semitism raised by the university search committee members (Warren Ibele and Samuel Krislov) and the University Senate Consultative Committee expressed to Regent Sherburne were not relayed to Regents Lee and Krenick. The legislative subcommittee recommended that in the future there be more careful scrutiny of candidates for the Board of Regents, that the Board of Regents adhere to principles of equal opportunity in employment, and that the regents should adopt written procedures for future selection processes.[6]

C. Peter Magrath was not aware of this issue as he participated in the search process. One of his major dilemmas was that at the time he was initially approached about considering the Minnesota presidency, he had been president of the State University of New York at Binghamton for less than two full years, making the consideration of another position inopportune.

Magrath recalled his interview with Regent Elmer L. Andersen, who had visited him in Binghamton to talk about the Minnesota presidency:

> I was asked by Elmer Andersen, What did I want to do with the rest of my life? I said, "Elmer, I really would like to be the president of a great big Midwestern land-grant university, but I don't think this is the right time. I am literally only in my second year at Binghamton and I like it there. Things are going well and I've got some things on the way. It's a wonderful faculty. It's a great place." Andersen cleared his throat. "Peter, let me tell you something. There are only so many land-grant universities in the United States. There are a smaller number that are Midwestern land-grant universities. Right now, there's only one that I know of that's looking for a president. This doesn't happen every other moment." And he smiled. Of course, that was very persuasive.[7]

The president-designate was forty years old, younger than any other newly appointed president except the first, William Watts Folwell, who was only thirty-six in 1869. Magrath was born in Brooklyn but spent his high school days in occupied Germany, where his father worked with a shipping line. He graduated summa cum laude from the University of New Hampshire in 1955, received a doctorate from Cornell in 1962, and taught at Brown from 1961 to 1968. He left Brown to become dean of the College of Arts and Sciences at the University of Nebraska, so he was knowledgeable about

Midwestern institutions.[8] "In Nebraska," he recalled, "I fell in love with the sprawling, complex. . . . usually wonderful big, public universities. That's . . . the kind of institution . . . I wanted to be active in."[9]

Magrath came to Minnesota in the fall of 1974, bringing Mitchell Pearlstein with him from Binghamton as his assistant and speechwriter. Pearlstein found Magrath clear regarding his priorities: "The Regents, the legislature, and journalists were at the top of the list, but faculty members would be hard pressed to argue that they weren't sufficiently attended to during that period." Pearlstein also commended Magrath for his vision: "He always had a sense of the whole, and a sense of history, and a sense of what needed to be done over a longer period, a sense of strategy. At the same time, if there was one aspect of his style that would stand out, it would be his correspondence. He corresponded feverishly. If someone would burp in his direction, he would write him a thank-you note. That is an example, it seems to me, not only of grace and just being politically smart but it's having a sense of the trees, of the individuals involved—a great compassion, great empathy, great attention to detail."[10]

One of the first issues Magrath faced was whether the university should boycott lettuce and grapes produced by nonunion labor and serve produce picked by Cesar Chavez's United Farm Workers. The debate lasted most of fall quarter. Demonstrators picketed Eastcliff, and in early October, Roberto Acosta, a General College student, fasted for twelve days while occupying President Magrath's outer office. At night he slept in the Newman Center, returning to Morrill Hall by day. The occupation was congenial.

On October 3, the president issued a public statement: "I think he [Acosta] is a sincere young man. I just hope he doesn't hurt himself."[11] Subsequently, Magrath ordered a survey of student opinion at the university's residence halls and then instituted the "two bowl" policy, in which students could choose between union-grown lettuce and produce from other sources. "It may be that the two-bowl plan will keep the issue before the community," he said.[12]

In fall 1974, the campus was more peaceful than in the late 1960s and early 1970s. Although students were more skeptical than in the 1950s, neither were they activists. A study by Arthur Levine of Columbia found that

students are optimistic for their own futures, yet pessimistic about the future of their country. They are idealistic about the kind of country they would like to live in but pragmatic about making it in the world they have to live in. They are liberal about social trends and life styles, but more conservative than they once were about political issues. . . . For the student generation of the 1970s, the bright illusions about American society were lost. They were tarnished by the misdeeds and duplicity of the nation's leadership . . . and darkened by the loss of heroes.[13]

*Minnesota Daily* editor Brian Howell observed in 1978 that "if the campus gets any quieter, we're all going to sleep."[14] The following year, however, Howell's successor found her time as editor of the *Daily* far from quiet. In April of 1979 when Kate Stanley, a journalism major, was elected editor, she could not have anticipated the controversy in which she would soon be embroiled. The finals-week humor issue of the *Daily,* published on June 4, was a takeoff on the *National Enquirer*; a picture of Christ on the mall in front of Northrop Auditorium was accompanied by an interview Stanley described as "exceedingly irreverent." Other parts of the issue parodied *Playboy* and the *Minneapolis Star*.[15]

Although Stanley was not editor of the *Daily* when the humor issue was published and indicated that she would not have approved it, when she became editor on June 13, 1979, she found herself at the center of what would become a three-year legal battle involving freedom of the press. The first thing she faced was the question of what to do next. Legislative hearings were held in the fall. In April 1980, the administration recommended to the regents that students offended by *Daily* content be allowed to request a refund of the portion of their student services fee that funded the *Daily.* The regents backed Magrath. The *Daily* editors then sued the regents, arguing that making student fee support refundable violated the newspaper's right of free speech. Attorney Marshall Tanick took the case pro bono. Stanley and the *Daily* lost in District Court, but on appeal before the Eighth Circuit Court, they won.[16] Magrath considered the position he took in the *Daily* case one of the mistakes he made as president: "I think I was wrong. . . . If I had to call that one again, I'd call it the other way. I feel badly about that because I feel so strongly about the First Amendment."[17]

The humor issue was an anomaly. For many years, the *Minnesota Daily* had been among the most respected student newspapers in the United States. Stanley noted that it frequently received awards from the National Collegiate Press Association and the Society of Professional Journalists.[18]

Governor Anderson introduced Magrath at his inauguration on November 26, 1974, saying that he rejected the notion that the state should reduce its commitment to the university, even in a time of fiscal austerity.

Magrath's address introduced four key themes: making a great university better, embarking on a planning process, seeking increased state support, and renewing commitments to minorities and women. Central to his message was the strong relationship between the health and prosperity of the university and that of the state: "The future of Minnesota and its capacity for continuing national leadership . . . is profoundly bound up with the role it enables its university to perform." He also urged expansion of graduate and professional programs as well as increased emphasis on recruiting and scholarships for minority students.[19]

Magrath appointed a number of new administrators, including Walter H. Bruning, a former assistant of Magrath's at Nebraska, who became vice president for administrative operations; William H. Hueg Jr., deputy vice president for agriculture, forestry, and home economics; and Stanley B. Kegler, vice president for institutional planning and relations. Lyle French continued as vice president for health sciences, serving from 1970 until 1982, when he was followed by Neal A. Vanselow. James Brinkerhoff was vice president for finance from 1971 to 1980. Frank B. Wilderson Jr. was vice president for student affairs. The most important appointment for any new president is that of the vice president for academic affairs. For this key position, Magrath and the search committee advising him selected Henry Koffler, who had held the Frederick Hovde Distinguished Professorship and Chair of Biological Sciences at Purdue University.[20] Serving under Koffler were Albert Linck, associate vice president for academic affairs, and Shirley M. Clark, assistant vice president for academic affairs.

Magrath faced several personal challenges during his presidency. He was hospitalized for four weeks in early 1976 with Guillain-Barré syndrome, a rare viral infection causing weakness in the arms and legs. Magrath worked from his hospital bed and later from his home at Eastcliff. Aides reported that the pace of his work hardly faltered.[21] In 1977, Magrath and his wife, Sandra, were divorced. In 1978, Magrath married Diane Skomars, whom he met following his separation. Skomars, who had been director of the university's Student Activities Bureau, resigned from this position following their marriage. In recognition of the fact that she helped host receptions, traveled, and served on committees on behalf of the university, the president chose to give her a portion of his salary. She was the coauthor of *The President's Spouse: Volunteer or Volunteered*, based on accounts of the experience of other presidential partners.[22]

Establishing working relations with the legislature was a major priority for Magrath, and it came to be regarded as one of his strengths. Warren

M. Anderson, majority leader in the New York state legislature, described Magrath as having been "as effective a spokesman for university programs as anyone the state of New York has ever seen."[23] In looking back on his years as president of the University of Minnesota, Magrath commented on the importance of legislative relations:

> There had been erosion of public support, and particularly legislative and political support, for the university when I went there. That was certainly the message I got from people like Elmer Andersen and others. I worked very hard, obviously with a lot of help from other people, to try to open up a more open and direct relationship with the Minnesota Legislature.[24]

George Robb, assistant vice president for institutional relations and planning, confirmed that Magrath made improving legislative relations a high priority.[25] Political scientist Charles Backstrom, in assessing university legislative relations, described the approaches of earlier presidents:

> Morrill would go over [to the legislature], and he would have a phalanx of vice presidents sitting behind him, and [the legislators] would raise a question, and he would turn to vice president so-and-so. He would never answer a question himself. They had a kind of contempt for him because he wasn't in charge of his show; they saw that he wasn't the master of the U. Meredith Wilson was different. He talked to the vice presidents, and everybody else, and tried to find out everything about the U, and then *he* answered all the questions. [The legislators] said, "By gosh! This guy really knows and is in charge of that place."[26]

As he attempted to gain the respect of the legislature, Magrath had to make the case for university needs in the context of more than sixty Minnesota public institutions of higher education; the largest number of them were the community colleges. With all these institutions requiring funding and with competing priorities in other sectors, Magrath had to state the university's legislative request forcefully and at the same time show an awareness of other needs.

One of the first things Magrath did was to reorder the priorities in the pending biennial request, substituting faculty salary increases for most of the new positions that had been proposed before he became president. The change had a triple benefit: it demonstrated that the Magrath administration had its own priorities and was willing to assert them, it won support from the faculty, and it demonstrated that the president was fiscally responsible and sensitive to state resource limitations. The *Minnesota Daily* praised this move, saying the President had shown "political savvy."[27] As a further indication of his commitment to planning, Magrath undertook personally to update the university's mission statement.[28]

In an informal review near the end of Magrath's first year as president, faculty members offered, on the whole, favorable reactions. They found Magrath more available to faculty groups and more active in chairing University Senate meetings than Moos had been. History professor Paul Murphy, at the time a member of the Senate Consultative Committee, encouraged Magrath to consult with the committee more frequently and at early stages as issues or problems developed. Rutherford Aris, a chemical engineering faculty member, praised Magrath's work on revising the mission statement.[29]

Given the state's economy, Magrath was not optimistic about increased funding. In February 1976, he wrote, in what had become a periodic letter to members of the university community:

> Certainly we need to ask for what we need, and I do not propose to shy away from such requests. At the same time we must be realistic in realizing that austerity is with us in terms of financing higher education, and that we will face some difficult moments in justifying even a stripped down request.[30]

His misgivings continued into the fall:

> We are fortunate in living and working in a state where education, at all levels, has always been highly valued and supported. This is perhaps our greatest asset in Minnesota. Nevertheless, the blunt fact is that throughout the United States higher education no longer enjoys the high priority of a few years ago; we are in a different environment.[31]

Under the circumstances, it was necessary for the university to develop policies and procedures for reallocation of resources. In February 1979, President Magrath wrote that "we must develop a mechanism and strategy for reallocation; if we do not, then it will be done by the pressure of events, or by legislative committees and similar external forces."[32]

In this uncertain financial situation, the question of whether the faculty wished to adopt collective bargaining arose. Some argued that unionization was necessary in times of financial stress, so that the faculty could present its case more forcibly to the regents and the legislature. Others were reluctant to replace existing structures of faculty governance, including the Senate and its committees, with union leaders. A petition requesting an election on the issue had been submitted in 1973, but there were questions about the composition of the bargaining unit, and state labor officials allowed the Law School, the health sciences, and the coordinate campuses to vote separately.[33]

Another question was whether department heads would be allowed to vote; it was not clear whether they were still faculty (and so eligible) or administrators (hence ineligible). Stanford Lehmberg, who was then chairman of the history department, still has vivid memories of being interviewed in a state office building. When he was asked what he did, he said that he did not hire faculty members, or fire them, or grant promotion and tenure, or inflict disciplinary action, or determine salaries, or assign teaching duties. All of these things were done by committees or by the dean. His chief function was pastoral: he tried to hold the department together and prevent difficulties from arising. The bemused examiners concluded that he was indeed not an administrator.

While arrangements for elections were under way, the university was subject to a "cease and desist" order imposed by the Minnesota Bureau of Mediation Services that prohibited any changes in the terms and conditions of employment until the elections had been held. In April 1978, the bargaining unit in the Twin Cities voted against collective representation, but the cease and desist order was not lifted pending votes by the other units.[34] The regents supported modifications recommended by the Senate in tenure criteria, grievance procedures, and policies on private consulting by individual faculty members, so they appealed to the Hennepin County District Court to have the restrictions lifted.[35] Eventually the restrictions expired; the issue of collective bargaining went dormant but rose again before the end of the century.

The University was larger, more diverse, and more technologically complex in the 1970s and 1980s than it had been in the 1950s and 1960s. Minority enrollment was counted for the first time in the early 1970s; students of color were 4.6 percent of the student body. By 1970, women represented 40 percent of the student body. The curriculum changed both through the formation of new departments such as Afro-American studies, American Indian studies, Chicano studies, and women's studies, and through changes in existing departments. The information revolution left its imprint broadly as students and faculty members had access to increasingly faster computers. The libraries moved from a card catalog to an electronic catalog system. During an exciting time of innovation, one major negative was that there were not sufficient resources for all programs to grow and develop simultaneously. Choices had to be made as colleges and departments struggled to define how their resources would be deployed. New facilities were needed for the health sciences, including a new Medical School at Duluth; agriculture was to struggle in 1984 with one of the most serious recessions since the 1930s.

## The Chambers Report

As the largest college in the university, the College of Liberal Arts (CLA) was dramatically affected by the changes during these years. They were dealt with by political science faculty member Frank Sorauf, who served as dean from 1973 to 1978, and by Fred Lukermann of geography, dean from 1978 to 1989.

In 1979, Lukermann appointed a committee to study undergraduate education. It had been eleven years, he noted, since the college had reviewed its curriculum, and a number of major changes had taken place. Historian Clarke Chambers was named chair of the committee, which came to be known by his name.

After many hours of discussion, the committee issued an interim document in May 1979 and a final report in January 1980. Both reaffirmed the college's commitment to undergraduate education and recommended changes that would demand more from both students and faculty members. Among other things, the committee had considered the changing characteristics of CLA students, noting that more of them were older, that a number of them transferred to the university after completing one or two years at a community college, and that many of them would "stop out" at some point in their academic careers in order to work, travel, or pursue other interests. It had also taken note of the fact that declining enrollment might offer opportunities for increased individual instruction and for a greater sense of community. The goals were "to sharpen critical thinking, to enlarge esthetic appreciation, and to promote learning experiences that transcend the mere learning of facts, methods, and theories."

Perhaps the most significant aspect of the Chambers Report lay in its recommendation of two new graduation requirements. The first had to do with the study of world cultures; understanding them had become increasingly important in the modern world. Students could now be expected to confront cultural traditions different from their own and should include in their degree plan at least two courses dealing with cultures other than those dominant in North America and Europe. The committee specifically singled out courses dealing with the societies of East, Southeast, and South Asia, the Middle East, Africa, and Latin America, as well as the American Indians.[36] In addition, the committee strongly recommended the requirement of a major project. The committee advocated improved advising, in which faculty members themselves needed to be involved, and reconsideration of each department's requirements for the major. It addressed the issue of integrative study. Both faculty and students had expressed uneasiness that the opportunity to synthesize work done in different courses was generally missing. The committee reluctantly concluded that the college probably did not have the resources it would need to introduce an integrative study requirement—an interdisciplinary senior seminar, for example— but it urged that the exploration of initiatives in this area be assigned a high priority in college deliberations.[37] The report was adopted and a number of its recommendations were phased in during the next few years. In fact, the college went beyond the committee's recommendations so far as foreign languages were concerned, by adding one quarter to the existing requirement in 1983.

## New Programs on the Twin Cities Campus

Despite fiscal problems, there were some new programs on the Twin Cities campus. The Center for Austrian Studies was founded in 1977; most (70 percent) of its $1 million endowment was a bicentennial gift to the American people, raised through the sale of U.S. bicentennial decals in Austria.[38] The opening of Rarig Center on the West Bank in 1972 provided a new home for the theater department, which was able to expand its offerings.

One of the changes with far-reaching impact was the establishment of women's studies. In 1972, faculty members Joanne Arnaud (political science), Carolyn Rose (sociology), and Toni McNaron (English), along with graduate students Andrea Hinding, Elsa Greene, and Susan Phipps-Sanger, framed a statement documenting the case for establishing a women's studies program at Minnesota. Its first courses were taught in 1972–73 under the auspices of American studies, whose head, Mary Turpie, was enthusiastic and helpful; McNaron was the first director of the women's studies program, assisted by a twenty-one-member governing committee chaired by Andrea Hinding. The committee included faculty members and students, mainly women, but also physicist James Werntz, director of the Center for Educational Development, and Harlan Smith, a faculty member in the economics department.[39] Janet Spector, who came to women's studies from anthropology, found involvement with the new department energizing: "It was the most exciting work I've ever been involved in, I think, beside my feminist archaeology, which was also creating a field."[40] Within several years Sara Evans,

Naomi Scheman, Gayle Graham Yates, and Cheri Register had joined the faculty. Despite university budgetary problems, the program grew. Spector noted that the founding faculty encouraged a research emphasis. She also cited contributions to the new program made by Shirley Clark, a College of Education faculty member, then serving as assistant vice president for academic affairs. Spector referred to women's studies as "a university within a university." Graham Yates succeeded in shepherding the proposal to establish a permanent women's studies department through the College Council, serving as its first permanent chair. One of the key challenges was finding a workable balance between functioning as an academic unit, engaging in teaching and research, and functioning more broadly as an advocate for women's issues.

Anne Truax, director of the Women's Center, observed that the existence of several venues for women's programs, such as the Women's Center and Continuing Education for Women, in addition to women's studies, allowed women's studies to ease through some of the tensions over what was academic and what was not. Truax also believed that women on the campus were "very successful" in avoiding gay-straight divisions.[41] By the mid-1980s, women's studies at Minnesota had become one of the most highly regarded programs in the country.

The Center for Advanced Feminist Studies (CAFS) was established in 1983 to serve as a base for research and scholarly activity for feminist scholars from across the university and to create an interdisciplinary minor in feminist studies. One of the center's early initiatives was a personal narratives project and national conference; some of the narratives were published by Indiana University Press. The Center funded a 1984 research project titled "Comparable Worth and the Political Process: The Consequences of Implementation." Sara Evans (history) and Barbara Nelson (of the Humphrey Institute of Public Affairs) served as project directors. The resulting analysis was based on comparable worth legislation passed in Minnesota in 1982. Directors of the center through 1987 were Janet Spector (anthropology), Toni McNaron (English), and Ruth Ellen Boetcher Joeres (German, Scandinavian, and Dutch).[42] As Janet Spector said, "We probably had more feminist scholars at this university than anywhere else in the country. We had some key people, and Minnesota became a very attractive place for people doing feminist work, and many students came here."[43]

Before he became dean of CLA in 1978, Lukermann encouraged the university to join the Union of Experimenting Colleges and Universities, established in the late 1960s with funding from the Ford Foundation. When funds were available to begin pilot programs at about twelve campuses, Lukermann asked Barbara Knudson of Continuing Education and Extension (CEE) to draft a proposal for a "university without walls" to serve people "who had some kind of formal barrier which prevented their participation in the university. That could be disablement of some sort, or physical distance—we took in people who didn't live here, some who were in prison," Knudson recalled.[44] When the application was successful, the new program was housed first in CEE; it was transferred in 1972 into an expanded University College, of which Knudson became dean.

Other experiments associated with the College of Liberal Arts were the Office for Special Learning Opportunities (OSLO), active in arranging internships and independent study; the Living Learning Center, which began in the YMCA before it moved into CLA; and the Inter-College Program, which made possible intercollegiate majors. The Educational Development Fund was made available to evaluate proposed innovations.

Cross-disciplinary studies was proposed by a small committee including Wallace Russell (an associate dean of CLA), May Brodbeck (a philosopher who served as dean of the Graduate School), Ted Wright (chairman of the English department), and two students. Marcia Eaton, a new faculty member in philosophy, headed the unit. Her special interest was aesthetics, which she thought of as being inherently cross-disciplinary, so she knew "what many of the problems are that people confront when they take on an interdisciplinary study." The program offered courses in language and art, law and society, multiculturalism, medical sciences, and the environment.[45] As recurring retrenchments made it increasingly difficult to maintain both the new programs and the older, ongoing programs and majors, cross-disciplinary studies was ended. Roger Page, associate dean of CLA, noted that although the cross-disciplinary program was a "very, very good program," it attracted only a small number of students, and it became increasingly difficult for faculty to justify the considerable preparation that the courses required. The bachelor of elected studies program, which had been developed to experiment with freeing students from meeting major requirements, also was discontinued after a few years.[46]

A new college was created on the Twin Cities campus: the Hubert Humphrey Institute of Public Affairs, named in honor of one of Minnesota's most distinguished public officials, offered master's degrees in public policy as well as a number of noncredit programs and services. Its mission was "to combine graduate education for careers in all aspects of public affairs with functions of a policy 'think tank' and a public service program in the land-grant tradition."[47] The institute (previously called the School of Public Affairs) moved in 1982 to a new building (designed by Leonard Parker and Associates) that also housed a permanent exhibition of memorabilia from Humphrey's public service career: he was mayor of Minneapolis, a U.S. Senator, and vice president of the United States. With an indoor atrium adjoining the museum and the John and Elizabeth Bates Cowles auditorium, the center offered a site for conferences and seminars. Policy fellows carried out a range of research projects, and the institute hosted a group of visiting international fellows each year. Harlan Cleveland, formerly president of the University of Hawaii, served as the first dean, from 1980 to 1986.

The economic challenges of these years were hard on the newly formed ethnic studies programs. Like other departments, they operated with extremely tight budgets; they also faced the challenge of balancing the academic expectations of the university with the service expectations of communities of color. In 1975, American Indian studies, headed by Roger Buffalohead, had 200 undergraduate students and 25 graduate students; Chicano studies, directed by Manuel Guerrerro, had 100 students; Afro-American studies, chaired by music faculty member Geneva Southall, had 1,800 students. Among the courses offered were Afro-American History and Culture, Music of Black Americans, and Black Participation in American Politics.[48]

Although some programs and innovations were short-lived, a number became permanent: Afro-American studies, Chicano studies, American Indian studies (at both Duluth and the Twin Cities), and women's studies (at Duluth, Morris, and the Twin Cities). The Center for Urban and Regional Affairs remained a point of contact for innovation and service, linking university researchers and external organizations. The two extension services, Continuing Education and Extension and the Minnesota Extension Service, routinely experimented with programs. Continuing Education and Extension's Neighborhood Programs began in 1969 with state funding to allow the university to offer classes in inner-city Twin Cities neighborhoods at substantially reduced tuition; at the end of the century, Neighborhood Programs still was a point of entry to the university, having served more than sixteen thousand persons.

## Changes in Established Departments and Disciplines

During the 1960s and 1970s, as a result of financial pressure and new disciplinary outlooks, core colleges, departments, and programs underwent major changes. Given the tumultuous changes in the United States during the

1960s and 1970s, it is understandable that American studies at Minnesota would be affected. Tremaine McDowell retired as chair of American studies in 1960 and was followed for eight years by faculty member Bernard Bowron. Mary Turpie, who had been with the program since its founding, advising undergraduates and, later, master's degree students, became chair in 1969, a position she was to hold until 1975. American studies experienced a time of considerable change as a new generation of scholars with new perspectives became a part of the department. Edward Griffin, a faculty member in English who taught in American studies, recalled that in addition to preparation for scholarly careers, the program was considered excellent background for museum work, the business world, government service, the foreign service, and historical societies.[49]

In 1973, Roland Delattre, a specialist in American religion and philosophy, became the first person appointed directly to the American studies faculty. Delattre's writings addressed the role of philosophy and religion in American life. He was cofounder of the *Journal of Religious Ethics*. Historian David Noble, who specialized in the history of American historiography, was regarded as one of the giants of American studies. John Wright, an American studies Ph.D., went on to become a member of the English and Afro-American studies departments. Mulford Q. Sibley, whose appointment was in political science, studied American politics. Edward Griffin, who chaired the department in the 1980s, like Delattre wrote on the American colonial period—Delattre on Jonathan Edwards and Griffin on an opponent of Edwards, Charles Chauncy.

Subsequent-generation scholars Elaine and Lary May made major contributions to the reputation of the department. The department benefited also from the addition of Carol Miller, whose research focused on contemporary American Indian literatures; Riv-Ellen Prell, whose interests included history and cultural anthropology with an emphasis on religion, ritual, ethnicity, and gender; and Gayle Graham Yates, who concentrated on the American South and women's spirituality. George Lipsitz, who left for the University of California at San Diego in the 1990s, added expertise in ethnic studies and popular culture. Lary May's research and writing focused on the American film industry and Elaine Tyler May's on women's history and the history of the family. In 1995–96, Elaine Tyler May served as president of the American Studies Association. David Roediger produced pathbreaking scholarship on labor history and racial formation. Others on the faculty in 2000 showed a breadth of scholarly perspective. Brenda Child wrote about American Indian history; Catherine Cenzia Choy addressed contemporary Asian American issues and Philippine and Filipino American studies; Roderick Ferguson explored the intersection between sociological theory and African American literature; and Jennifer Pierce documented workplace gender and racial inequalities.

At the end of the century, the curriculum became more diverse with the addition of feminist studies, media studies, popular culture, and anthropology to the study of history, literature, political science, and sociology of its founding years. The term *American studies* came to include African American, Chicano/Hispanic, Native American, and Asian American perspectives. During this period and beyond, the department continued to be one of the top three to five American studies programs in the country. Its chairs in the 1980s and 1990s included Edward Griffin, David Noble, Elaine May, and David Roediger, and in 2000 historian Jean O'Brien, a scholar of American Indian history. George S. Hage from journalism and John Howe of history served as interim chairs.[50]

The English department also changed during the 1960s and 1970s. It had come to be the smallest in the Big Ten because it did not receive as many new positions as did its peer departments. In addition to large classes and heavy teaching loads, English faculty members faced major intellectual and social shifts. Speaking of the United States generally, Margery Sabin of Wellesley noted the presence of radical social protest in the late 1960s, deconstruction in the 1970s, and ethnic, feminist, and Marxist cultural studies of the 1980s. These trends had an impact in Minnesota in English and a number of other fields.[51]

During this time, a number of faculty members looked at their research and teaching differently: doing less lecturing, holding more discussions, and being more open to student concerns. Some members of the department had been involved in antiwar movements in the 1970s. Faculty member Toni McNaron described how the war in Vietnam had led her to rethink her approach to teaching:

> I realized one day that there was a way in which lecturing for ten weeks, testing, and grading was not unrelated in my sphere of influence to what the country was doing in the colony of Vietnam. I understood something about academic colonization. In that scheme I was not on the right side. That was very hard for me, because I thought of myself as this forward-looking open-minded person.[52]

There were new courses in African American literature on the Harlem Renaissance, courses on American women writers, courses that explored the theories of deconstructionist authors. Faculty members Toni McNaron, Shirley Nelson Garner, and Madelon Sprengnether introduced feminist perspectives in their courses. In 1980, they described these approaches in a paper titled "Feminist Studies in Literature." A course in modern and contemporary literary theory allowed students to discuss deconstructionist, postmodern, or poststructural theories of writers such as Jacques Derrida, Michel Foucault, Roland Barthes, and Jacques-Marie Lacan.

Multicultural studies had an impact, resulting in such courses as American Literacy and Cultural Diversity and in courses that introduced students to literature from third world countries such as Nigeria, Zimbabwe, India, and Jamaica. Creative writing came to be a more important component of the department's offerings; among those teaching in this area and publishing significant work of their own were Patricia Hampl (made a Regents Professor in 1997) and Michael Dennis Browne.

Until the 1980s, the composition program had been part of the English department. Under the leadership of Donald Ross, Robin Brown, Julie Ann Carson, and Martin Steinman, it became a separate unit, with Lillian Bridwell-Bowles as its head. Policies for the program were established by a board made up of faculty from several College of Liberal Arts departments. Bridwell-Bowles and CLA dean Fred Lukermann envisioned a department as an interdisciplinary enterprise, with upper-division courses focused on writing for specific disciplines, such as writing for the social sciences. Teaching assistants were drawn from a variety of departments, handling the advanced courses related to their own fields. In the 1990s, the Task Force on Liberal Education decreed that the teaching of writing be undertaken by departments across the university and no longer centralized in the composition program. The new structure and a new plan for Writing Across the Curriculum went into effect in fall 1999. At that time, Joel Weinsheimer was director of the composition program.

Finding cost-effective ways to manage smaller departments was one of the planning issues facing virtually all colleges and universities. In a number of instances, combining departments offered an effective option. This strategy led to the formation of the Department of Classical and Near Eastern Studies. Created in 1987, the department brought together faculty from classics, art history, Ancient Near Eastern and Jewish studies, and South and Southeast Asian studies. The new department formed a home for disciplinary specialists in areas such as Greek and Latin philology; biblical, rabbinic, and New Testament studies; ancient Mediterranean art and ar-chaeology; and Sanskrit.

Three Regents Professors were affiliated with the department. William McDonald, a specialist in Greek Aegean archaeology, Rutherford Aris, and Thomas Clayton. Aris, whose primary reputation lay in chemical engi-neering, had scholarly interests in classical paleography. Clayton, a Renais-sance scholar, studied the influence of the classical world on Shakespeare. Others in the department included Thomas Kelly, a historian of ancient Greece; Sandra Peterson, a specialist in Greek philosophy; and Theofanis Stavrou, a historian of Greece and Russia, who had founded the univer-sity's Modern Greek Studies Center. When the Department of Art History refocused its programs on modern art, two specialists in ancient art, Sheila McNally and Fred Cooper, transferred to the new department. With its expanded scope, the Department of Classical and Near Eastern Studies ex-perienced substantial increases in both the quality and the number of grad-uate students, who came to Minnesota from such places as Stanford, Michi-gan, and the University of Chicago.

Department chair William Malandra noted that the addition in the 1990s of two endowed chairs, the Berman Family Chair in Jewish Studies and Hebrew Bible and the Sudnet Family Chair in New Testament and Chris-tian Studies, filled respectively by Bernard Levinson and Richard Pervo, expanded the department's capabilities in the study of religion in antiquity. Andea Berlin created an archaeology program focusing on the Greco-Roman period in the eastern Mediterranean, with special emphasis on biblical ar-chaeology in Israel. Two shared positions were created at the beginning of the twenty-first century. The first of these, addressing the history of the ancient Near East, with shared teaching with the history department, be-gan in 2000; the second, in Greek history, with shared teaching with the Center for Near Eastern Studies (CNES), began in 2001. Added strength was also anticipated through Dr. Abraham Franck's commitment to a planned gift to endow a faculty position in Hebrew language and literature. Through the maintenance of a strong faculty in classics and the strengthening of the ancient Near East faculty, the department became a leader in North America in bringing together in one interdisciplinary program the study of the civilizations that form the foundations of Western culture.[53]

In the history department, the traditional dominance of European, British, and American perspectives was supplanted by a broader vision in which the department sought to cover virtually the entire world. New fac-ulty members hired to teach courses in Asian, African, and Latin American history included Ted Farmer and Ann Waltner (China), Byron Marshall (Japan), David Lelyveld and David Kopf (India), Allen Isaacman and Lansine Kaba (Africa), and Stuart Schwartz and Robert McCaa (Latin America). There were changes in approach and methodology as well. Political history declined in popularity as the emphasis on social history grew. Historical demography gained importance with Steven Ruggles's analysis of U.S. census data, a project that attracted substantial outside founding and interest.

Feminism had a great impact; there were new courses dealing exclusively with women, and the role of women came to be a topic in virtually all offerings. The department led the way in the hiring of women and was exceptionally successful in attracting such leading exponents of women's history as Sara Evans and Mary Jo Maynes. The infusion of new faculty members quickly began to foster dialogues across time, geography, and methodology. During this time, the Center for Early Modern History and the Workshop on Comparative Women's History were established. In the 1990s, an unprecedented number of faculty retirements brought challenges and opportunities. To meet them, the department adopted a strategy of hiring colleagues who would enhance traditionally strong fields such as medieval history and also be willing to engage in cross-field dialogues, anchoring its intellectual foundations. Having hired fourteen new faculty members in the four years ending in 2000, the department was in the middle of this major faculty transition. Like English, history had a small staff compared to other Big Ten departments. With about forty faculty members, the history department was about half the size of that at Michigan and about two-thirds the size of Wisconsin's, the two Big Ten departments it regarded as peers.[54]

The School of Music underwent significant changes. One of its major challenges was to grow in order to remain nationally competitive.

Longevity of leadership was an early strength. Two chairs led the department of music for more than sixty years after its founding in 1902 by Emil Oberhoffer; Carlyle Scott from 1905 to 1942, and Paul Oberg from 1942 to 1965. After such long and distinguished leadership, the department faced a critical need for growth and diversity in its degree programs. Roy Schuessler, an internationally respected opera and oratorio singer who headed the department from 1965 to 1975, took the important step of strengthening the department's academic mission by gaining approval from the College of Liberal Arts for four new degrees: the B.F.A., the Ph.D. in music education, a D.M.A. in performance, and the B.S. in music therapy. Schuessler also supervised the merger of the MacPhail School of Music into the university, initially as a part of the School of Music and subsequently part of Continuing Education and Extension, until it again became independent in 1993. Schuessler also started the call for a new music building to replace the aging Scott Hall.

Composer Lloyd Ultan, chair of the department of music at Washington University, came to Minnesota as department chair in 1975. Because of the increasing number of degree programs, faculty members, and students, the department became the School of Music in 1980, and Ultan became director. During Ultan's tenure it became evident that future growth and achievement would be limited if a new building was not constructed. Ultan began the development of a grassroots effort, engaging alumni, students (who staged a sit-in demonstration), the state's music educators, and civic leaders like Judson Bemis and Elinor Bell to win university and legislative support for a new building. Their efforts were successful, and Ferguson Hall, named after longtime faculty member Donald Ferguson, was completed in fall 1985. Ferguson himself, then 100 years old, helped break ground for the state-of-the-art facility that he did not live to see completed. Architects Winston and Elizabeth Close, both musicians themselves, utilized a site on the edge of the Mississippi River that helped complete the West Bank by forming a courtyard between Ferguson Hall and Wilson Library. Under that courtyard, Ultan was able to locate the part of the new facility that was dearest to him: a dedicated music library within the School of Music.

The university's musical traditions have enriched both university and community life since the early 1900s. Perhaps one of the most memorable Minnesota traditions that has extended deep into the fabric of the university and the state was the growth of the university band program under Frank Bencriscutto, known affectionately as "Dr. Ben," who served as director of bands from 1960 to 1992. During his tenure the program grew from one concert band and a small marching band to five concert bands, a 200-plus piece marching band, and a rapidly growing jazz program. Highlights of these years included trips to the Rose Bowl in 1961 and 1962; concert tours of Russia, Mexico, China, and Scandinavia; and frequent appearances in Washington, D.C., at the White House, Kennedy Center, and inaugural events.

While these were good years for the School of Music, change was again in the air. Ultan stepped down as director in 1986, and CLA dean Fred Lukermann named a search committee of music faculty and civic leaders, chaired by historian Stanford Lehmberg, to find a new director. Their work brought Karen Wolff, acting dean of the Cincinnati Conservatory, to Minnesota to assume the directorship in 1987. With a vision to enhance the reputation and the quality of the school, Wolff received strong support from Dean Lukermann and from President Hasselmo to build on Minnesota's enviable international reputation in composition by focusing on expanding the performance faculty.

The Wolff years were full of excitement. Richard Cisek, then president of the Minnesota Orchestra, said that with Wolff "came a burst of energy, imagination, and creative enterprise. It was obvious good things were beginning to happen."[55] New programs included the establishment of the endowment for the Ethel Hitchcock Chair for Collaborative Piano, abounded. The faculty grew with the addition of outstanding musicians and scholars, and the music education program, which comprises half of the school's enrollment, was transferred from the College of Education to the School of Music. Additionally, Wolff advocated building a new and acoustically superior concert hall on the West Bank as a performance option to the aging Northrop Auditorium. Wolff worked closely with civic leader Judson "Sandy" Bemis, donor Ted Mann, university administration, and the Minnesota Legislature to bring this critically needed facility to reality.

Wolff also campaigned for the School of Music to become a freestanding conservatory, independent of the College of Liberal Arts. As economic and political problems faced the university in the early 1990s, Wolff saw the handwriting on the wall and left in 1991 to become dean of the Oberlin Conservatory.

Wolff's unexpected departure paved the way for Vern Sutton, longtime director of the university's Opera Theater and associate director of the school under Wolff, to become acting director in 1991; ultimately he was named director by Dean Julia Davis in 1993. Sutton's visibility in the metropolitan community was well known, first in his many performances with the Center Opera (which became the Minnesota Opera), and on Garrison Keillor's "A Prairie Home Companion" radio show. Under Sutton's leadership, Ted Mann Concert Hall was designed and built, and the school's endowment was substantially increased with major gifts for scholarhips and opera program support. Sutton may be best known for creating and directing the Opera on the Farm program, in which operas were performed on farms for regional audiences around the state. Eventually, three tours in eight years, including two tours of Aaron Copland's *The Tender Land,* drew tens of thousands of people who crowded farmyards to see this powerful program.

University finances and changing CLA administration during Sutton's tenure affected the resources of the school, which caused the faculty to begin to rethink its mission and direction. A new strategic plan, "Music for the New Millennium," emphasized, in addition to the continued priority given instructional and degree programs, community partnerships and internships, revisions of the curriculum to reflect changes in technology, and a greater emphasis on world music and new music.

When Sutton announced his retirement as director in fall 1998, new CLA dean Steven Rosenstone formed a search committee of faculty members, alumni, and community musical leaders to conduct a national search for a replacement. Rosenstone, a passionate advocate for the arts, saw the possibilities in the arts as a revitalized part of the mission of CLA. In spring 1999, Jeffrey Kimpton, a director at the Annenberg Institute at Brown University, was named the seventh director of the school. Kimpton was no stranger to the Twin Cities, for he had been the founding director of the instrumental music program in Apple Valley High School from 1976 to 1982; he also had led music programs in the public schools of Wichita, Kansas, and at Yamaha Corporation. Kimpton began his work by listening to hundreds of students, faculty members, alumni, friends, music educators, university officials, and metropolitan musical leaders in order to create a vision for what music at Minnesota could be in the school's second century.

Those conversations led to dramatic results indicating the future direction of the school. Resources from CLA increased, as Dean Rosenstone fulfilled his pledge to invigorate the music and arts environment on the West Bank. Key new faculty members and staff were hired; new programs were initiated in public relations, admissions, and student services; the curriculum was strengthened to add increased academic and musical rigor; and parts of Ferguson Hall were remodeled and new instructional technology was added. Important partnerships and collaborations with area musical organizations were rekindled, and the school launched an aggressive capital campaign to help grow the endowment that would keep it nationally competitive in the years ahead. The school was poised for a new generation of leadership and innovation.[56]

For the College of Education, the 1960s through the 1980s brought three major challenges. The first was to maintain academic and research excellence (the college was considered among the top ten nationally) despite repeated retrenchments. The second was to accomplish a shift in mission with less emphasis on teacher training and more on postbaccalaureate education. A third challenge was to protect the college's initiatives for teachers and administrators, its educational enrichment offerings, its programs for at-risk populations, and its role in educational policy making. College leaders faced this challenge through rigorous economizing and priority setting. During these years, decision making, as was frequently the case elsewhere, became more democratic as departments and faculty members played a more active part in college planning.

The deans who faced these challenges included Robert J. Keller, who had been director of University High School from 1956 to 1964 and helped steer its merger with Marshall High School in 1968; he served as dean from 1964 to 1970. Educational psychologist Jack C. Merwin was dean from 1970 to 1976. William E. Gardner, first as acting dean and then as dean, headed the college from 1976 through 1991. By 1976, the increase in postbaccalaureate enrollments, part of careful college planning, had risen to 57 percent of the college's enrollment, up from 37 percent in 1969 and 29 percent in 1950. The college's seven departments (curriculum and instruction; psychological and philosophical foundations of education; Psychoeducational Studies; vocational and technical education; the School of Physical Education, Recreation, and School Health Education; educational administration; and the Institute of Child Development) were highly ranked nationally.[57]

Faculty research was varied. Faculty members carried national reputations for research that addressed the standardization of a widely used intelligence test for young children; studies of infant development, children's emotional development, and foster children's development; creation of a standard test measuring intellectual progress in students with developmental disabilities; and cooperative, competitive, and individualistic learning. The College of Education had three Regents Professors: Ruth Eckert, a faculty member in higher education who received this honor in 1973; Robert Beck, a faculty member in the history and philosophy of education and author of *Beyond Pedagogy: A History of the College of Education,* who was named Regents Professor in 1976; and Willard Hartup, director of the Institute of Child Development and a faculty member in child psychology, who was similarly honored in 1993.

In an interview for this book, Robert Bruininks, who was to succeed Gardner as dean in 1991, commented on the centrality of research and graduate education:

We had always been an experimental college in teacher education. We had always had postbaccalaureate models here. We were one of the first universities to develop an alternative career track for people who were coming out of other fields—business, sciences—and wanted to enter the world of teaching. The conversion, while dramatic, was made in light of these long-standing exemplars that had been around for nearly twenty years.... It builds very strongly on the liberal arts tradition, which I think is terribly important to people, if they are going to be good, creative, resourceful teachers.[58]

Bruininks noted that the curricular changes were also influenced by national concern about the quality of teaching and learning in the nation's schools. If there were going to be a major improvement in the schools, he recalled, leadership would need to come from institutions such as Minnesota. The resulting changes, he pointed out, "grew mostly out of the school reform agenda of the 1980s, [from] the feeling that if we are going to fix education and fix the practice of education, we had to really reform the preparation of teachers. We had to deepen their roots in the liberal arts and strengthen their clinical practice, that is, give them more field-based experience."[59]

If one part of the College of Education were singled out as an example of the exceptional research and instruction for which the college is known, the Institute of Child Development would be an obvious choice. Founded in 1925 aided by funding from the Laura Spellman Rockefeller Memorial, it celebrated its seventy-fifth anniversary during the 2000–01 academic year. Originally a freestanding unit within the university, since 1957 it has been a part of the College of Education. Consistently recognized nationally as one of the top institutions in the field of child psychology, it was ranked for most of the 1990s by *U.S. News & World Report* as the number one child psychology graduate program in the country. Its first director, Yale Ph.D. John E. Anderson, headed the institute for more than a quarter of a century, from 1925 to 1951. He was followed by Dale B. Harris and, from 1959 to 1971, by Harold W. Stevenson, who reinvigorated the institute, confirming its strong empirical research base in child psychology.

More than three hundred students had received Ph.D.'s by the end of the century; they moved on to research and teaching positions throughout the world. In addition to its doctoral program, the institute has approximately three hundred undergraduate majors each year in a program offered cooperatively with the College of Liberal Arts. Other collaborative relationships link the institute with other parts of the University of Minnesota, such as the Department of Pediatrics in the Medical School, psychology in the College of Liberal Arts, and family social science in the College of Human Ecology. The institute also operates the Shirley G. Moore Laboratory Nursery School for research and training purposes.

Regents Professor Willard W. Hartup, the third director, who held that position from 1971 to 1982, described the institute as a good fit in the Midwest: "Children as an object of scientific study haven't always appealed to some of the older, more conservative institutions in the country. But it fits with the Midwest's ideas that we human beings can change the way we live. We can study values and behavior because they're important if we want to change the way we live."[60]

Subsequent directors—W. Andrew Collins (1982–89), Richard W. Weinberg (1989–99), and Ann Masten, appointed in 1999—continued the active emphasis on research. The research for which the Institute of Child Development is known included social development and interpersonal relationships, cognitive and perceptual development, and the relationship between the brain and cognitive functioning.[61]

In addition to research and instruction, outreach and public service were priorities in the College of Education, continuing even during the lean retrenchment periods of the 1970s and 1980s. A 1993 compilation of university-wide K–12 outreach programs listed more than 268 university programs, 96 of them in the College of Education, followed by the College of Biological Sciences with 25, the Institute of Technology with 21, and the College of Liberal Arts with 19.[62] Among the College of Education programs were the Elementary Science Assessment Project, working with school districts to evaluate the teaching of science in grades one to eight, and U-Teach, developing strategies to encourage students of color to enter the field of special education. The Minnesota Symposium on Child Psychology was offered annually for professionals in child and family services by the Institute of Child Development.

Faculty members were active in university administration and governance, and in public service, both within the university and beyond. During World War II, Dean Walter Cook provided advice for J. Robert Oppenheimer on the design of the school being built at the Los Alamos atomic research facility. Tracy F. Tyler was the senior University of Minnesota official involved in the rebuilding of Seoul National University in the 1950s, and Robert Keller, subsequently to be dean from 1964 to 1970, had served as an adviser to the Korean Ministry of Education. Ruth Eckert, head of the higher education program, was the college's first Regents Professor and the first woman so honored. Eckert was a major contributor to the Bureau of Educational Research within the College of Education and to the Bureau of Institutional Research, responsible for university-wide research on students, faculty members, and staff.

Frank B. Wilderson Jr., a professor in educational psychology, served in the central administration as vice president for student affairs from 1975 to 1989. Shirley M. Clark, chair of educational policy and administration, became acting vice president for academic affairs for the university system and provost of the Twin Cities campus in 1988 and 1989, filling in at a critical time following the resignation of President Kenneth H. Keller. Educational psychologist Robert Bruininks, holder of the Emma M. Birkmaier Professorship in Educational Leadership, became dean of the college in 1991, holding that position until 1997, when he was selected by President Mark Yudof to assume the position of executive vice president and provost.

It was no minor accomplishment that graduate programs grew and were innovative, despite the challenges of periodic economic downturns and retrenchments. Rather than issuing centralized mandates, deans of the Graduate School encouraged innovation by individual departments. Chemical engineering faculty member Kenneth Keller served as acting dean of the Graduate School in 1974, taking the position after May Brodbeck left for the University of Iowa. Mechanical engineering professor Warren Ibele was dean from 1975 to 1982 and political scientist Robert T. Holt from 1982 to 1991.

Margaret Davis (named a Regents Professor in 1982), having taught at Michigan and Yale and done her doctoral work at Harvard, had a comparative perspective on graduate work in research universities. She came to the university as professor of ecology and head of ecology and behavioral biology. She viewed the Graduate School positively:

> One of the assets of this university is the Graduate School and the way graduate programs are organized. We have graduate programs that are free-standing. They're often strongly associated with a department . . . but actually answer directly to the dean of the Graduate School. . . . When a new field comes into existence, a committee of faculty can get together and petition . . . to start a program that encompasses the field. . . . Most universities can't do this because their graduate programs are tied to departments.[63]

Ronald Phillips, a faculty member in agronomy and plant genetics and also a Regents Professor and member of the National Academy of Sciences, agreed with Davis about the potential for innovation in Minnesota graduate programs. He observed that with programs in both the agricultural and the biological sciences, "essentially any idea you have you can institute here because there's expertise, equipment, and facilities to do it."[64]

All colleges and campuses of the university were affected by developments in information technology and computation that escalated dramatically during the 1970s and 1980s. In 1980, the Institute of Technology established the Microelectronics and Information Science Center, with assistance from Control Data, Honeywell, and Sperry Univac. In another innovative partnership, Research Equipment Incorporated (REI) was founded, soon doing business as the Minnesota Supercomputer Center, Inc. It acquired supercomputers and sold time on them to both the university and businesses. The time purchased by the university was made available to the university research community through the Minnesota Supercomputer Institute.[65]

The 1960s through the 1980s were years of continued growth for University Libraries. During these years, the libraries maintained their position among the top academic libraries in terms of interlibrary lending. Walter Library housed the Science and Engineering Library, University Archives, and Special Collections as well as the education and psychology and science and engineering reference libraries. Wilson Library housed the humanities and social sciences collections and services. The Bio-Medical Library in Diehl Hall served as a resource for the health sciences. The St. Paul Campus Central Library, which had been constructed in 1953, met the needs of faculty and students in agriculture, the biological sciences, natural resources, home economics, and veterinary medicine. The Law Library was respected for the breadth of its holdings and as a resource for students and faculty as well as for the profession.

Among other branch libraries were entomology, fisheries, and wildlife; forestry (natural resources); plant pathology; veterinary medicine; and music. Endowed by former governor Elmer L. Andersen and Eleanor R. Andersen, the Andersen Horticultural Library opened in 1974 at the University of Minnesota Landscape Arboretum in Chanhassen, housing botany, ornithology, and natural history materials. The Architecture Library served faculty members and students in the College of Architecture and Landscape Architecture. The Waite Library in Agricultural Economics, the Eric Sevareid Journalism Library, and the Mathematics Library were some of the libraries associated with departments and colleges.

The Givens Collection of more than six thousand books, pamphlets, and manuscripts related to African American literature was donated to the university to honor Minneapolis business leader Archie Givens Sr. Based on a collection gathered by Richard Lee Hoffman, professor and playwright at New York City Technical College, it is one of the country's most comprehensive assemblages of African American literature. The oldest piece is a 1773 first edition of Phyllis Wheatley's poems, the first book published by an African American. The Givens Collection has special strengths in the Harlem Renaissance.

During these years, the libraries met the challenges associated with moving into the digital era while at the same time responding to increased demand on instruction and reference services. The establishment of MINI-TEX (the Minnesota Library and Information Network) in 1969 made it possible to share the University Libraries collections with other libraries and to encourage statewide sharing of library resources, making the University Libraries among the top interlibrary lending institutions in the United States. The libraries moved from the Dewey decimal classification system to the Library of Congress classification system to conform to the practice of many research libraries and became a member of two national electronic networks, the Online Computer Library Center and the Research Libraries Group. In 1987, University Libraries launched LUMINA (Libraries of the University of Minnesota Integrated Network Access) on its online catalog. A grant from the Bush Foundation assisted the libraries in 1989 to become the first academic library in the United States to make a full conversion of the card catalog to machine-readable format.

Following Ralph Hopp, who served as university librarian from 1971 to 1975, Raymond Bohling was interim librarian during 1976. Eldred R. Smith then became the seventh university librarian, holding that position until 1987. The latter part of Smith's term was a time of some administrative difficulty. History professor John Howe became interim university librarian following Smith's departure in 1987. In 1989, Thomas A. Shaughnessy became the eighth university librarian.[66]

## The Campus in St. Paul

The Institute of Agriculture, Forestry, and Home Economics had been reorganized in 1970 into three colleges, each with its own dean. In 1973, influenced by the creation of the health sciences vice presidency and to accord comparable status to the programs of the Institute of Agriculture, Forestry, and Home Economics, the university appointed H. J. Sloan acting deputy vice president for agriculture. In 1974, William F. Hueg assumed the position following Sloan's resignation for health reasons. Soon after his appointment, he identified three immediate priorities: university-sponsored international programs, new research facilities in St. Paul, and better communication with Minnesota citizens about the benefits they received from the state's investment in agriculture.

Known for his candor, Hueg put a mounted butterfly on his desk when he assumed his new position, "to remind me of the metamorphosis I am going through.... I was told my directness might be a liability, but I am learning to count to twenty and I believe I have mellowed a little in the last few years."[67] Hueg was once described as "a cross between Billy Graham and Johnny Carson."[68] He was also an effective advocate for the institute and its programs: during his time as director of the experiment station (1966–75) and as deputy vice president and dean of the institute (1974–83), funding for experiment station programs increased from $3.2 million a year to $34 million. Hueg was followed by Keith A. Huston, experiment station director from 1975 to 1979, by Richard Sauer, 1980 to 1986, and C. Eugene Allen, 1987 to 1996.

The Colleges of Agriculture, Forestry, and Home Economics continued to participate in a variety of international activities, including programs in China, Russia, Argentina, Korea, East Africa, and Morocco. The Office of International Agricultural Programs, which dated from the 1960s, helped the College of Agriculture with various international projects. One of the longest-lasting international partnerships was with the Institut agronomique et vétérinaire Hassan II in Morocco in which the University of Minnesota was the lead American training institution. Between 1969 and 1993, more than 130 Moroccans received doctoral degrees and over 200 received master's degrees in the United States. Hassan University became one of the most respected agricultural universities in Africa.[69]

Richard Skok became dean of the College of Forestry in 1974, serving in that position until 1993. The college was recognized as one of the top forestry programs in the United States: its undergraduate program was ranked third in the Gourman report of 1980, and the college received an overall ranking of fourth from *Change* magazine in 1975. In 1988, in recognition of its broader scope, the College of Forestry was renamed the College of Natural Resources. Skok observed that "many of the youth inspired by the environmental movement saw university forestry programs as one of the few available academic opportunities to express their concerns."[70]

The environmental movement also had a major impact on the College of Biological Sciences' Cedar Creek Natural History Area, which in 1982 was chosen one of the first eighteen sites for the National Science Foundation's Long-Term Ecological Research Network. Also during the 1980s, the Department of Ecology and Behavioral Biology expanded into population and evolutionary genetics, leading to a change in name to the Department of Ecology, Evolution, and Behavior (EEB). EEB was further strengthened by the addition of faculty from the Department of Zoology when that department was disbanded in 1976.

Changing women's roles continued to have an impact on the College of Home Economics. One of Keith McFarland's early challenges when he became dean in 1973 was obtaining a suitable building for the college, which had never had adequate facilities. He was able to generate statewide support, working primarily through county extension home agents. Organizational changes within the university also reshaped the college. Family life instruction (from the Department of Sociology), the Center for Youth Development and Research (from the Center for Urban and Regional Affairs), and the School of Social Work (from the College of Liberal Arts) became a part of the college, adding important research perspectives. McFarland served as dean until 1987.[71]

Societal changes also affected the College of Veterinary Medicine. The college was an early leader in accepting women into the profession and called upon the resources of the university's institutional researchers to survey women students on their experience in the college. Students reported that acceptance was easier with increased numbers. In 1975, veterinary student Jan Best noted that she did not see the field as an appropriate choice for everyone:

> If students say they are interested in veterinary medicine, you can talk for ten minutes and tell if they are going to make it. You have to like chemistry and biology, not just animals.... I don't want people in Veterinary Medicine who shouldn't be there.[72]

Sidney Ewing became dean of veterinary medicine in 1972, following W. T. S. Thorp. He served in that position until 1978. Robert Dunlop, previously dean of Murdock University in Australia, was dean from 1980 to 1988; faculty member Ben Pomeroy filled in as interim dean between 1978 and 1980. The college's graduate programs continued to be ranked among the country's top three programs. In fall 1973, 220 of the 270 students enrolled in the college were male and 50 were female. The gender ratio was to change dramatically over the next three decades as more women chose to enter veterinary medicine. In fall 1998, there were 221 women and 76 men.

Veterinary medicine reflected the greater informality of the late 1960s and early 1970s: "Students vociferously voiced opinions on everything from the relevance of biochemistry to whether the notorious histopathology 'black box' exam ought to be graded pass/fail. And decorum gave way to such shenanigans as the senior class's annual water fight—an event that disappeared . . . after it accidentally turned into a police cruiser car wash."[73]

The experiment station was both a mechanism for funding with dollars contributed by the state and federal governments and an integrated network of locations where research was carried out by faculty members and researchers affiliated with the Colleges of Agriculture, Biological Sciences, Forestry, Home Economics, Veterinary Medicine, and the University of Minnesota Extension Service. In addition to facilities on or immediately adjacent to the St. Paul campus, experiment station research was carried out at six branch sites. The Northwest Agricultural Station in Crookston was established in 1895 with land donated by railroad magnate James J. Hill. The North Central Experiment Station in Grand Rapids was formed in 1896, the West Central Experiment Station in Morris in 1910, and the Southern Experiment Station in Waseca in 1912.

In 1947 the Rosemount Experiment Station was created when the university acquired 7,500 acres in Dakota County that had been taken over by the federal government during World War II to create a munitions factory. Approximately 3,000 of the 7,500 acres were used for experiment station purposes. Twelve years later, in 1959, the Southwest Experiment Station at Lamberton was established, completing the network of six branch experiment stations. The multiple sites made it possible to test animals (dairy, beef, swine, sheep, and poultry), plants, grasses, trees, shrubs, fruits in the different Minnesota soils and climates. (The Northeast Experiment Station at Duluth closed in 1967 and its experiments were transferred to other sites.)

Other outreach facilities used for basic and applied research included the Horticultural Research Center in Excelsior, founded in 1907 as the Fruit Breeding Farm; the Lake Itasca Forestry and Biological Station and the 3,700 acre Cloquet Forestry Station, both established in 1909; and the Cedar Creek Natural History Center, a 5,000 acre site north of the Twin Cities. The Sand Plain Experimental Farm at Becker, located on land owned by Northern States Power, was the site of research on crop irrigation systems, greenhouses, and fish culture facilities drawing on waste heat from the power generation plants. The Minnesota Landscape Arboretum in Chaska, created in 1958, specialized in horticultural and landscape varieties suitable to the Minnesota climate. The Hormel Institute in Austin provided research relevant to the meatpacking industry. Collectively, these sites, along with the extension offices in each of the counties and the Soudan underground research site near Tower, represented the broad geographic reach and diverse areas of research expected of a public land grant university.[74]

Among the major accomplishments of the experiment station was the development of a new strain of short-stemmed hard red spring wheat, released in 1970 and known as Era wheat. The station helped develop crops new to Minnesota, especially sunflowers and soybeans, and was involved in the introduction of new varieties of barley, oats, hybrid corn, apples, grapes, blueberries, and bluegrass suitable for the Minnesota climate. There was research on growing wild rice in cultivated paddies, on genetic and nutritional changes in pigs, on ways to produce leaner meat, and on water quality.

In 1984, because of record production of corn, soybeans, and wheat in the United States, Japan, and Europe, world prices plummeted, causing one of the worst slumps since the Great Depression. Patrick Borich had very recently been appointed permanent dean and director of the Minnesota Extension Service, following Norm Brown, who became director of the Kellogg Foundation. Borich recalled assembling his administrative staff as soon as he was informed of the severity of the financial crisis and telling them: "You all have a plan of work for the year. I would like you to throw it away! We are going to embark on a major response to this crisis."[75] Within a week, the extension service initiated a comprehensive series of programs, Project Support, to assist rural families. Among them were a lender mediation program, stress education, and FINPACK—a computer-based economic modeling system that could be tailored to the financial situation of an individual farmer. These programs proved to be so successful that they became permanent.

Minnesota 4-H leader Leonard Harkness retired in 1980. At the time, he was the longest-serving 4-H director in the country, having held that position for more than three decades. County fairs and the Minnesota State Fair offered venues where livestock, agricultural produce, homemaking, and crafts of the 4-H Club members were judged by experts. For many 4-H members, the Minnesota State Fair was a high point in the year and, for those who stayed at the fair, the week frequently represented their first time away from home. Adapting to the changing expectations and experiences of young people, 4-H began to offer a greater range of programs, made them more flexible, and paid increased attention to the needs and interests of urban and suburban youth as well as to those of the traditional members in Greater Minnesota. Young people developed increased self-confidence through 4-H training in group activities and leadership.

A hands-on leader, Borich emphasized the importance of serving the public. He recalled guidance he got from Richard Sauer, at the time head of the experiment station, when he became director:

> My boss, Dick Sauer, and I decided to drive to each of the legislative districts and meet with the local senator and two representatives from the district and meet, then, with three or four other local leaders that our local staff had pulled together.... We spent an entire summer doing that.... It was great learning about how legislators thought about the university and how they thought about the extension service and the experiment station. By the way, none of them knew the difference between the experiment station and the extension service. That's when we decided we couldn't talk about two separate [legislative] items.[76]

## New Curricula and New Facilities in the Health Sciences

Vice President Lyle French described the health sciences commitment to meeting the state's evolving health care needs:

> We realized there was going to be more community care.... There was going to be more ambulatory care. We also [saw] that there was going to be more coordinated care of patients—between the physician and the dentist and the nurse and the pharmacist.... We decided to develop a curriculum that was entirely different. It was to get a team effort in training our students to practice together when they finished.... We decided to go to the legislature, through the regents, and build some buildings to carry out the new curriculum.[77]

This revolution in thinking about health care influenced the curricula in the health sciences schools and also had a significant effect on the design of the four new health sciences buildings that were constructed between 1973 and 1986. A number of health sciences centers in other states moved to new locations as they expanded to meet the burgeoning demands for health care professionals. At Minnesota, it was decided that the health sciences would remain on the site between Washington Avenue and the Mississippi River, which almost inevitably meant expansion upward. The first of the health sciences buildings (later named Malcolm Moos Health Sciences Tower) was nineteen stories tall; it housed the dental school and provided teaching and laboratory facilities for the Medical School and the School of Public Health.[78]

The Phillips-Wangensteen Building was designed to house faculty offices, research labs, and outpatient clinics; with health care patterns moving away from long-term hospital stays, clinic space was needed for both teaching and patient care. Finished and ready for occupancy in 1976, the building was named in honor of a major donor, Jay Phillips, and surgery chief Dr. Owen Wangensteen. Weaver-Densford Hall was constructed between 1977 and 1981 for use by pharmacy and nursing. This eleven-story tower was named in 1997, in honor of Katharine Densford, director of Nursing, and Larry Weaver, dean of Pharmacy, each of whom had been an exceptional leader. Funding had come from the state, the federal government, professional pharmacy and nursing groups, and private individuals.[79]

The fourth new building in the health sciences complex was a new hospital. As plans began to take shape, it was difficult to know how many patients the hospital should be designed to accommodate. Planners anticipated that the new health care environment would increasingly encourage ambulatory care in clinics and other outpatient settings; the length of hospital stays was declining precipitously, and Medicare and private insurers were searching for the most cost-effective treatment sites. This put a teaching hospital at a competitive disadvantage. An oversupply of hospital beds in the Twin Cities made things even more challenging.

The debate over the number of beds aside, university administrators were convinced that it was imperative to replace the outdated hospital. Most of the patient rooms were in buildings erected between 1911 and 1929. Laboratories and operating rooms were poorly equipped and inconvenient, and the hospital was inadequate for clinical teaching. To provide leadership and governance focused directly on the hospital, the Board of Regents in 1974 established a separate board of governors for the hospital. The board considered the needs of the hospital and concluded that a new building was the most viable option. In 1980, hospital board chair Harry Atwood, a Minneapolis business executive, announced plans to construct an eleven-story hospital on the site of Powell Hall, a dormitory formerly occupied by nursing students.

As construction began, President Magrath had doubts about the planned number of beds. Influenced by the concerns of other hospitals and a Minneapolis *Star Tribune* article, Magrath called an urgent meeting to reexamine the plan. In 1982, hospital administrators presented a revised plan for a smaller hospital with eight floors and 432 beds. Magrath later described the decision to scale back:

> What we did, after a very open discussion with the Board of Regents, was to pull the plug. The hole had been dug! I drove by it every day on the way to work. We pulled the plug on the larger hospital.... A more moderate, but still very substantial, hospital was built. Now, I feel pretty good about that decision.[80]

As Leonard Wilson, the historian of the Medical School, wrote, "The opening of the new hospital in 1986 marked the first time in its seventy-seven-year history that the hospital possessed a thoroughly modern building of adequate size in which it could provide a completely integrated hospital service."[81]

N. L. Gault, dean of the Medical School, cited the Rural Physician Associates Program (established in 1971) as well as the initiation of family practice as a medical specialty (in 1969) as evidence that the school took seriously its land-grant mandate to reach out to citizens throughout the state. The Rural Physician Associates Program established a one-year option that allowed students to gain experience in smaller communities. The Duluth School of Medicine emphasized rural medicine, another university response to the health care needs of Greater Minnesota.

In 1982, Charles and Marilyn Fiske made a national plea for a donated liver to save the life of their young daughter, Jamie. The University received calls from five hundred potential donors, "including some, who in their earnest desire to help, confused their kidneys with their liver and, thinking they had two livers, offered to donate one."[82] The story of the successful liver transplant, accompanied by photos of Jamie and Dr. John Najarian, captured national attention.

When Lyle French left the health sciences vice presidency to return to neurosurgery in 1982, he was praised for his leadership in creating the new health sciences curriculum and campus. Minnesota Senate majority leader Roger Moe said at the time: "Dr. French has represented the University very successfully.... He laid out the details of a particular project in a clear and concise manner.... His knowledge and poise at times of legislative setback bodes well for people like me who support a strong University and research arm."[83]

French's successor as vice president, Neal Vanselow, along with Dean Gault, supported a student-led initiative to devote more attention to medical ethics. Vanselow and Medical School faculty members sought advice from sociology, dentistry, philosophy, and other departments. With a grant from the Northwest Area Foundation, Paul Quie, subsequently a Regents Professor, became interim director of the new Biomedical Ethics Program. The first permanent director was Arthur Caplan.

As Quie later recalled, Caplan immediately created a sensation: "He came in like a whirlwind. He had his Ph.D. in philosophy and was an enormously bright person and capable of expanded activities in the academy. . . . He had an amazing ability to discuss highly charged, sensitive subjects without polarizing."[84]

The Center for Bioethics was popular both on campus and off: Caplan and his successor, Jeffrey Kahn, were regularly called upon to advise journalists, public officials, and members of the medical community on biomedical issues. At the end of the century, Kahn was a regular columnist on the Cable News Network Web page. The center offered bioethics courses, including a graduate minor and a joint degree program in law, health, and life sciences.[85]

## International Programs

In 1973–74, 2,115 international students from ninety countries were enrolled, more than three times the number who had enrolled in 1950. During the 1970s, Continuing Education and Extension established an international study program, making study abroad with university faculty members available to students and the community. Subsequently renamed the Global Campus, the program concentrated on providing study-abroad opportunities for students—both from the University of Minnesota and other institutions. By the 1990s, Global Campus, by then a part of the Office of International Programs, was finding places for more than a thousand students to study abroad. Another international program, Minnesota Studies in International Development, offered internships in developing countries, drawing strong students from the university and from other colleges and universities in the United States.

Administratively, during the 1980s, the university began to centralize many of its international offices, beginning with the International Student Office and the Office of International Programs. The College of Liberal Arts had created an international center related to its language and area studies programs, evolving into the Institute for International Studies, in 1999 re-named the Institute for Global Studies.

The first Chinese students attended the university in 1914. For the next thirty-five years, many students from China came to the university to pursue degrees in agricultural sciences and engineering. In 1949, when the relationship between mainland China and the United States ended, so did the student exchanges. In 1979, following President Richard Nixon's reopening of relations with China, the arrival of students from China resumed. In the two decades after the reopening of China, the University of Minnesota hosted more than three thousand students and scholars from the People's Republic of China, Hong Kong, and Taiwan. Exchange of faculty members and collaborative research had resumed in the early 1970s.

In 1979, Wenda W. Moore, chair of the Board of Regents, led a delegation of University of Minnesota faculty members and administrators to China. The symbol and ceremony of that visit laid the groundwork for restored connections with University of Minnesota alumni in China and for new opportunities for study and research. Devotion to the university was tangibly evident as dozens of former university students, at considerable hardship, traveled many miles to be with the visiting delegation and to signal their loyalty to the university. Moore and other delegates reported that joining with these alumni in singing the "Minnesota Rouser" brought home to them the meaning of a global university.

Following this visit, the university created the China Center on the Twin Cities campus to offer cultural programs and serve as a clearinghouse for students and faculty. By the mid-1990s, more than a hundred delegations from China had visited the university and, with more than 1,200 Chinese students and scholars enrolled in programs such as agriculture, engineering, and the health sciences, the university was one of the largest host schools for Chinese students in the United States.[86]

International students appreciated the friendliness of classmates and the assistance they received from advisors. Exchange scholar Zhai Qihui (Qi-Hui Zhai) worked with Richard Jones in the Department of Entomology, Fisheries, and Wildlife between 1979 and 1981. Upon her return to China, she became professor and head of the Department of Insect Physiology and Biochemistry at the Institute of Zoology in the Chinese Academy of Sciences. She recalled her Minnesota years:

> I not only gained advanced knowledge and learned about modern technol-
> ogy, but deepened my knowledge of the United States, a great Western na-

tion, and enhanced my friendship with its great people.... My research on the ladybug made me the "ladybug lady" of the Twin Cities.... I was featured in the first *Matrix* television series about the university. I was then invited by schools and organizations to give talks about China.... The days I spent at the University of Minnesota impressed me so deeply, I can never forget them.[87]

The renewal of connections to China not only brought a new stream of students to the University of Minnesota, but also made it possible for delegations visiting China to renew connections with alumni. Tang Peisong received his B.A. degree in botany magna cum laude before moving on to Johns Hopkins for a Ph.D. in plant physiology. Tang was the author of more than two hundred journal articles and books. He and two colleagues became known as the fathers of plant physiology in China. Attracted to the university because of its reputation in agriculture, he gravitated to the College of Science, Literature, and the Arts "because I discovered I needed a solid general foundation in science and liberal arts before specialization." A person of broad interests, Tang graduated with a major in botany and a minor in chemistry and physics. He has become a respected authority on plant physiology, praised both for his theoretical research and for his contributions to field training and applied research, and is credited with enhancing scientific knowledge for farmers.[88]

Yien-si Tsiang earned M.A. and Ph.D. degrees at Minnesota in three years and stayed on to carry out corn experiments under Professor H. K. Hayes. Tsiang returned to China in 1947. After serving on the Chinese American Joint Commission on Rural Reconstruction in Nanking and later Taiwan, he was named to a ministerial-level position in which he was involved in creating Taiwan's economic policy; he is credited with the "Taiwan economic miracle" that lifted the per-capita income from $200 in the 1950s to over $12,000 in the early 1990s.[89]

## Intercollegiate Athletics

The University of Minnesota took the first steps toward creating an intercollegiate athletics program for women in 1971. Earlier, women had been able to participate in intramural sports, and Norris Gymnasium, named in 1975 in honor of Anna Norris, a pioneering advocate of the importance of physical activity for women, was built in 1914 for women. A major impetus for women's intercollegiate athletics came with passage of Title IX of the Education Amendments of 1972. Although Title IX regulations dealt broadly with equal opportunity for women in all aspects of college and university life, they were known best for the mandate to eliminate inequity in athletics. On the Twin Cities campus, the eleven men's intercollegiate sports had a budget of $1.2 million in 1971–72, while Women's Intercollegiate Athletics received $7,336.

What the discrepancies meant in practical terms can be seen in the experience of swimmer Terry Ganley, who in 1974 became the first woman at the University of Minnesota to achieve All-American status. She and her teammates had to raise the money for her and swimming coach Jean Freeman to travel to the national competition at Penn State. The Minneapolis *Star Tribune* described the situation: "Resisting [the temptation] to draw analogies if a similar trip were earned by a male athlete, Terry and Jean Freeman decided to hustle T-shirts. They raised $550 selling T-shirts in the lobby of Cooke Hall. Terry couldn't even watch the action of the state high school swim meet at Cooke Hall in early March. She was busy hustling T-shirts in the lobby."[90]

The official history of Women's Intercollegiate Athletics recorded that "the budget had little or no money for meals, so Gopher coaches and athletes had to improvise. How do you feed a swimming squad of 25 on $30? Lots of white bread and bologna sandwiches made the rounds on swimming teams' road trips."[91] In July 1972, Eloise Jaeger of the Department of Physical Education wrote to Vice President Stanley Wenberg that "the demand by women students to be accorded the same privilege as men to compete at a varsity level presents us with a situation which we can no longer (nor should we) ignore."[92] The *Minnesota Daily* described differences in expenditures between men's and women's intercollegiate athletics in the Twin Cities as "mountainous": just over $27,000 for the women and $2.2 million for the men in 1973–74.[93] Jaeger was pleased with the changes made by the new administration: "It's fantastic. It seems more was accomplished in three weeks last summer under [President] Magrath and Stan Kegler than in the previous six years."[94] Andrea Hinding, who served as the first faculty representative for women's athletics, believed that the administration's efforts had been in good faith. She thought that "they probably saw themselves caught between the new mandates of the law, feminism, and equal opportunity on one side, and athletic interests that were rich, powerful, and historic on the other."[95]

The Department of Women's Intercollegiate Athletics was separated from the Department of Women's Physical Education and given independent status in 1975. Minnesota was unusual among Big Ten schools in not combining men's and women's athletics in the same department. Belmar Gunderson, a member of the physical education faculty and a former amateur tennis player who had competed at Wimbledon, served as interim director of the new program, succeeded in 1976 by Vivian Barfield, who left a position as assistant athletic director at the University of Massachusetts. In 1976, the university carried out a systemwide self-study of compliance with the gender equity implications of Title IX regulations.[96] Partly as a result of this study, the university administration asked the legislature to add $1.7 million to the $200,000 that had already been allocated to Women's Intercollegiate Athletics. Another sign of change was the decision to allocate $20,000 for need-based scholarships for women athletes. "You can change attitudes about women's sports," Barfield said, "or you can change by legislation and then attitudes will slowly change as people are conditioned. It has been left to women all along just to make do. Well, we can't just make do any more. That's why we have Title IX."[97]

Women's Intercollegiate Athletics offered competition in ten sports: basketball, cross-country, field hockey, golf, gymnastics, softball, tennis, swimming and diving, track and field, and volleyball. From 1972 through 1982, Minnesota teams competed within the Association for Women's Intercollegiate Athletics, then moved in 1982 to the National Collegiate Athletic Association (NCAA), which had begun to offer women's programs. One of the high points of women's activities came in 1978, when the volleyball team won a Big Ten championship, a state title, and a third-place finish in regional competition. Laura Coenen, who played in the early 1980s, was chosen for the Hall of Fame, and her number (44) was retired in 1983.[98]

Vivian Barfield left in 1981 and she was succeeded by Merrily Dean Baker, who came to Minnesota from Princeton University. Baker served until 1988, when she was followed by Chris Voelz. Barfield, said Voelz, "did battle and left it a better world for Merrily Baker and eventually for me."[99]

The 1970s had brought different faces to Men's Intercollegiate Athletics: a new athletic director and new football, basketball, and hockey coaches. Former Gopher football star Paul Giel became director of men's athletics in 1971, following Marsh Ryman, who had held the position since 1963. Bill Musselman became basketball coach in 1971; in 1972, Cal Stoll became head football coach and Herb Brooks was hired as hockey coach. The new athletic director faced serious financial problems. With a deficit of half a million dollars and declining public support, Giel developed a promotional campaign, "Return to Gold Country," to increase interest, attendance, and contributions. Giel, the coaches, and other staff members made more than eight hundred public appearances, often presenting film highlights of the teams in action. These sessions proved to be so popular that reservations had to be made up to three months in advance.[100]

The Gopher hockey team enjoyed exceptional success under Herb Brooks, a St. Paul native who had played for the Gophers between 1955 and 1959 and gone on to Olympic teams in 1964 and 1968. The high point of Brooks's seven seasons was winning the Western Collegiate Hockey Association (WCHA) title at the end of the 1975–76 season. Brooks was to leave the Gophers to coach the 1980 Olympic team; since eleven of the team's twenty members were either Gophers or Duluth Bulldogs, Minnesota could claim a considerable contribution to the American gold medal subsequently known as "the Miracle on Ice."[101] Returning to the Gophers in 1981 following his Olympic year, Neal Broten received the Hobey Baker Award, the hockey counterpart to football's Heisman Trophy, given each year based on a vote of more than fifty NCAA coaches. Three years later, UMD Bulldog Tom Kurvers also received this award.[102] Brad Buetow's six seasons as head Gopher hockey coach included two WCHA titles, in 1980–81 and 1982–83.[103]

During the 1974–75 basketball season, two Minnesota basketball players attacked an Ohio State player, the Gophers' second-highest scorer, Mark Landsberger, decided to transfer to another school, and Coach Bill Musselman decided to leave his basketball coaching position at Minnesota.[104] Jim Dutcher coached for the next eleven seasons, leading the team to a Big Ten title in 1981–82. Among the starting players during this era were Dave Winey, Philip "Flip" Saunders, Mark Hall, Mychal Thompson, Randy Breuer, and Kevin McHale, who was subsequently named to the National Basketball Hall of Fame.[105] The Gophers ended the 1976–77 season second in the Big Ten; by the end of the 1977–78 season, Mychal Thompson was to win a place in basketball records as the second-highest scorer in the twentieth century.[106]

With Memorial Stadium needing repairs, supporters of a new downtown Minneapolis sports facility proposed that Gopher football move to the new stadium. Although some student leaders protested, arguing that the team would lose its university identity if it did not retain its own stadium, both athletic director Paul Giel and football coach Joe Salem supported the move. Playing in the dome, they said, would boost attendance and help in recruiting. The first Gopher home football game in the Humphrey Metrodome was played on September 11, 1982. The change of venue did not produce positive results on the scoreboard. After the Gophers lost six straight games, Salem resigned, and University of Arkansas coach Lou Holtz was designated his successor.

Between 1976 and 1978, the university was involved in a dispute, leading to litigation, with the National Collegiate Athletic Association over allegations that the basketball team had violated several NCAA rules. One student had visited the Wisconsin cabin of a Gopher fan, another had borrowed a car from an assistant coach's mother-in-law, and a third had sold his complimentary tickets.[107] The NCAA placed the basketball program on probation for a year and told the university to proceed with disciplinary measures against the athletes. In accordance with Big Ten procedures, the Twin Cities Assembly Committee on Intercollegiate Athletics held hearings and determined that the violations were not of sufficient magnitude to warrant suspension.

This did not satisfy the NCAA, which proceeded to place all of the Minnesota men's athletic programs on indefinite probation. Convinced that the NCAA decision was unjust, President Magrath and athletic director Paul Giel decided to appeal; they established a "Fairness Fund" to cover the legal costs.[108] Magrath had believed that it was appropriate for the university's committee to decide the issue. A further point was that the athletes were entitled to due process, and one student had obtained a state court order requiring it. The NCAA suggested that the president might have overruled the committee, but Magrath said that would have been in direct contradiction to the principle of faculty control that governed the Big Ten universities. "After all of Minnesota's teams were put on probation," Magrath said, "I decided that there was no alternative but legal action against the NCAA."[109]

In October the president again described "the NCAA Saga," noting that the Circuit Court had ruled against the university. In subsequent litigation, the Eighth Circuit ruled that the university was required to declare the students ineligible. The ruling established as a matter of law that the university and other NCAA members should abide by the rules of the NCAA—an organization they had chosen to join.[110]

## Growth in Private Support

Private fund-raising, which had been growing since the establishment of the University of Minnesota Foundation in 1962, provided a lifeline for the university at this troubling time. Foundation executive director Robert Odegard explained that the university's outreach and economic impact gave it a considerable advantage in fund-raising:

> The University enjoys an advantage in seeking corporate donations because it has directly generated a huge amount of economic activity. Agribusiness, the mining industry (which was literally saved when Professor E. W. Davis invented the taconite process) and the computer industry are indebted to the University for providing both technological advances and skilled employees.[111]

The foundation raised $13 million in 1983, a 300 percent increase over 1974, when Magrath arrived in Minnesota; the university had moved into seventh position in private support among both public and private universities.[112] Foundation chairs between 1975 and 1985 were Curtis L. Carlson, John G. Ordway Jr., Elmer L. Andersen, Raymond Plank, and George T. Piercy.[113] Private giving to the Medical School also grew as the Minnesota Medical Foundation (MMF) continued its successful efforts. When the School of Medicine opened in Duluth in 1972, MMF included it within its purview. Eivind Hoff continued as executive director through 1985.[114]

## Alumni Association

The mid-1970s through the end of the 1980s was a time of change for the Minnesota Alumni Association (MAA). Ed Haislet retired in 1976 after twenty-eight years as executive director. Those years had shaped a tradition of a strong, no-nonsense partnership between the association and the university. This relationship, which successors were to continue, combined loyal support with thoughtful commentary by an alumni group not shy about addressing important public questions related to the university.

In 1979, following three years under the leadership of Vincent Bilotta, who had come to Minnesota from the University of Kansas, Steven Roszell became executive director. That year the association offices returned to Morrill Hall from an off-campus site on University Avenue. Given the high cost of renovating Memorial Stadium and the view that the university should help support a downtown sports facility to be used by the Gophers and the Vikings, the MAA supported moving Gopher football to the Hubert H. Humphrey Metrodome.

In January 1983, more than three hundred alumni came together as a "presidential network" to help lobby for the university's needs with the legislature. Two years later, Margaret Sughrue Carlson became executive director when Roszell was selected to serve as associate vice president for alumni relations and development, overseeing both the two foundations and the alumni association. Carlson, along with MAA volunteers Sarah R. "Penny" Winton, Harvey Mackay, and Fred Friswold, continued and strengthened the legislative advocacy. Although university administrators initially worried about the possibility of "amateur night at the state capitol," they came to appreciate the MAA volunteers as they prepared position papers and researched the issues responsibly and thoroughly.

In 1985, Minnesota Alumni Association national president Penny Winton made the selection of members of the University Board of Regents a top priority. A blue ribbon committee chaired by former Regent Neil C. Sherburne studied ways to broaden and strengthen the pool of candidates to be voted on by the Legislature. The work of this twenty-three member committee encouraged the Legislature to create the Regent Candidate Advisory Council to recruit, screen, and recommend regent candidates. Activism in legislative advocacy and regent selection gave the Alumni Association a higher public profile. Added visibility proved helpful in boosting membership numbers. There were 16,000 members when Ed Haislet retired in 1976; by 1988, the number had risen to 35,000.[115]

# The Duluth Campus

The mid-1970s to the late 1980s was a challenging time on the Duluth campus too. Robert Heller, who had been a faculty member and department head in geology, served as provost from 1976 to 1987; his title was changed to chancellor in 1985. His goal was to keep the campus on course toward its goal of becoming a comprehensive university. Neil Storch, who wrote a history of the campus, explained:

> Heller knew the faculty, community, and the political realities of UMD's situation. His interest in creating new programs was one of his many strengths. Given his passion for new programs, it is not surprising that the chancellor frequently found himself in difficult situations. Heller pushed for rapid expansion of the Duluth campus, but he had to contend with the president of the University of Minnesota and other central administrators in Minneapolis who envisioned a far more modest role for UMD. The chancellor's drive for new programs was based on his vision for the campus. UMD was to be

a comprehensive university offering liberal arts, graduate, and professional programs. To realize this vision, Heller needed a talented faculty, interested in both teaching and research, and state-of-the-art physical facilities.[116]

When Heller became acting provost in 1976, a major restructuring of the campus had been in place for two years. Enrollment in fall 1976 was 6,561; it was to rise above 7,000 in 1980 and be close to 7,500 for the rest of the century.[117] As it grew, the campus began to attract students from a broader geographic region. In 1965, 13 percent of the student body came from outside the Arrowhead region, where the campus was located. By the mid-1970s, that figure had risen to just over 40 percent.[118]

From a single collegiate structure, the campus had reorganized into two colleges and four schools by 1974. The largest was the College of Letters and Science, followed by the School of Business and Economics and the College of Education. The graduate program, the School of Medicine, and the School of Fine Arts were much smaller. In the early 1980s, Duluth added a bachelor of computer science degree program and a new women's studies program.[119] Among the leading women's studies scholars and teachers on the campus were Jane E. Maddy (psychology), Edith J. Hols (English), Judith A. Trolander (history), Belin Tsai (chemistry), and Mary Zimmerman (behavioral sciences). Susan Coultrap-McQuin was selected to head the program, which offered approximately twenty courses.[120]

Relations with legislators and private donors were important in building the campus. Among strong supporters were Erwin L. Goldfine, a member of the Board of Regents from 1975 to 1987; Gerald Heaney, a former regent who became judge of the Eighth District Court of Appeals in 1966; and George "Rip" Rapp, the first dean of Duluth's College of Letters and Science and founding dean of its College of Science and Engineering.[121] One of the initiatives proposed during the 1980s was an institute dedicated to research on minerals, alternative energy, forest products, and water. Governor Rudy Perpich, a native of the Iron Range, appointed a committee to study the feasibility of such an institute. Subsequently, the Natural Resources Research Institute (NRRI) was established. Under the leadership of its first director, Michael Lalich, the institute began operating in facilities on the former Duluth Air Force Base.[122]

In addition to legislative support, private philanthropy contributed to UMD's growth. A four-year campaign completed in 1984 raised nearly $13 million for endowed faculty positions, scholarships, academic programs, and research. Private giving had an impact on many programs of the campus, including the Sax fund created through gifts from the estates of Jonathan, Simon, and Milton Sax and used for purchasing art and construction of the Sax Sculpture Gallery at the Tweed Museum. In 1979, Glensheen, the former Congdon family mansion, was opened for public tours under the auspices of the campus.[123]

Heller was particularly pleased by the 1980 creation of a study-abroad program, the first year-long program in the university system. (Heller himself had participated in an international education symposium in Bulgaria in 1968, and his daughter had a positive experience with a study-abroad program.) After negotiating with several British universities, the Duluth program found a home at the University of Birmingham. Despite some complaints about housing arrangements in the late 1990s, the Study in England Program continued to offer a valuable experience to about fifty undergraduates a year. UMD also developed opportunities for study and travel in Sweden, Finland, and France.[124]

In 1980, UMD faculty voted by a large margin to unionize and chose the UMD Education Association, rather than the Association of American University Professors, as their agent. Here the margin was much narrower: UMDEA received 57 percent of the votes cast, AAUP 43 percent. In 1984, UMDEA issued a position statement, "The Need for Campus Autonomy within the University of Minnesota System," which argued that the regents should appoint a provost for each campus, including the campus in Minneapolis and St. Paul. Although the resolution was not adopted, decision making inevitably became more decentralized as the campus and academic programs grew.

During this period, Duluth emerged as a powerhouse in the Western Collegiate Hockey Association. Coach Mike Sertich led the Bulldogs to their first championship in 1984, and the team won league titles again in 1985 and 1993. Sertich became the first individual to be named WCHA's Coach of the Year in three consecutive years (1983–85); he received the award again in 1993. In 1984, senior Bulldogs defenseman Tom Kurvers won the Hobey Baker Memorial Award, given to the outstanding U.S. collegiate hockey player. His teammate Bill Watson received the honor in 1985, as did Chris Mariucci in 1994. Neil Storch explained that hockey has given UMD visibility that has put the school on the map: "There is a David-and-Goliath appeal in competing against teams from institutions such as Wisconsin, Colorado, and the Twin Cities."[125]

In addition to hockey, there were ten varsity sports for men: football, basketball, swimming, wrestling, skiing, track, cross-country, baseball, golf, and tennis. Varsity competition for women was offered in basketball, softball, swimming, tennis, and volleyball. Competition in all sports, except hockey, was within the Northern Sun Athletic League and represented Division II competition within the National Collegiate Athletic Association. Marsha Bevard Kulick proved herself a record-setting wheelchair athlete, winning seven gold medals at the International Wheelchair Olympic Games in 1981, six gold medals in swimming at the Olympic Games for the Disabled in 1984, and a leadership award from the President's Council on Physical Fitness and Sports.[126]

The new School of Medicine soon made its presence felt, both within the state and nationally, as it came to be recognized as one of the country's most successful programs in family practice and rural medicine. Michael Heck entered the UMD School of Medicine in fall 1977. Following two years at UMD, he completed his M.D. on the Twin Cities campus and did his residency training in family practice in La Crosse, Wisconsin, before ending up in Chisholm, Minnesota. Heck selected UMD because he was interested in small-town practice: "It is really a great heritage, a part of the land-grant tradition, to have trained people willing to go to the four corners of the state to be teachers, lawyers, historians, accountants, and doctors." Dr. Jim Boulger at UMD was a mentor who, Heck recalled, "always helped you through self-doubt, assured you that you would survive." To return the support he received, Heck hosts Rural Physician Associate Program students in Chisholm. Heck's wife, Karen, a graduate of the University's dental school, is also an advocate for small-town practice.[127]

Psychiatrist Mary Vomacka, who also spent two years at the UMD School of Medicine and then completed her medical training in the Twin Cities, practices at an outpatient mental health clinic near Willmar. She has chosen to work three days a week, using the remaining time to be with her family and pursue her interest in music. "You can have balance if you work hard to structure your career to allow for it," she observed.[128]

In 1984, the school initiated a program called Native Americans into Medicine. By 1996, the program had trained 10 percent of the country's American Indian doctors.[129]

Because of funding shortages, the College of Social Development became a department in the College of Education in 1984. That fall, science and mathematics departments were shifted from the College of Letters and Science to a new college, the College of Science and Engineering, established in part to create new programs in chemical engineering, industrial engineering, and electrical and computer engineering. George R. Rapp, formerly dean of the College of Letters and Science, became dean of the new college, a position he was to hold until 1989. Sabra Anderson became dean in 1990, one of a small number of female deans in the country heading science and engineering programs. She served until June 2000.[130]

Having served as provost and chancellor for more than a decade, Robert Heller retired in 1987. The following year, the Mathematics-Geology Building was renamed Heller Hall.

## The Morris Campus

The 1970s and early 1980s witnessed the maturation of the Morris campus. John "Jack" Imholte had become the second provost in 1969. Imholte, like his predecessor, Rodney Briggs, made his highest priority the development of the core faculty. Imholte noted that both of them believed that "whatever resources we had, the best way they could be spent was in the process of acquiring faculty. If you can't be first class in some other ways, be first class in faculty recruitment.... We hired, almost without exception, young faculty with a great deal of potential."[131]

Imholte knew the campus well, having taught history and been a division chair and dean. He was modest, where Briggs had been effusive. Friendly in demeanor, Imholte proved a forceful leader. Elizabeth "Bettina" Blake, who came to UMM in 1979 as dean, credited Imholte with courage and steadfastness as he held to the liberal arts focus of the campus in the face of threats of closing and repeated budget retrenchments: "He was obliged to say no more than yes because funds were so scarce, yet he kept morale up and costs down, while inspiring people to surpass themselves and their expectations."[132]

By 1975, there were ninety-three faculty members, greatly expanded from the original thirteen. Enrollment had increased at a controlled rate of 150 students a year, reaching a high point of 1,763 in 1972. In the mid-1970s, the number of students declined, largely because of demographic changes that affected higher education generally.[133] Heightened recruiting efforts were effective and by 1980 enrollment began rising again, reaching 2,000 students in 1988. Continuing Education in the Twin Cities supported the expansion of its programs at Morris; led by Roger McCannon, this became the primary link between the liberal arts campus and the surrounding region.

New buildings were low-lying, more reminiscent of the campus in St. Paul than of the urban modernism of the West Bank. They included a science complex (1968), a library named for Briggs (1973), a fine arts center

(1973), a physical education building (also 1973), three residence halls, a food service center, and a heating plant. The older humanities and social sciences buildings were renovated during the 1970s. Imholte gave much credit for the new buildings to Delbert Anderson, the state representative from nearby Starbuck, who, by good fortune for the campus, was then chair of the Legislative Building Commission. The construction took place at a good time; Imholte estimated that the fine arts building, which was put up for between $4 million and $5 million, would have cost $12 million to $14 million by 1984, or (one may guess) $20 million by the end of the century.[134] The building boom came to an end in the mid-1970s. Subsequent long-range plans identified five major buildings that were still needed: a university center, a classroom-office building, a large auditorium suitable for convocations as well as theatrical and musical performance, a field house, and an addition to the science building.[135]

Imholte led the college's first significant fund-raising campaign. At a regents' dinner in May 1981, he surprised those present by announcing twenty-three gifts of $10,000 or more, most of them from regional friends of the campus. The college gained experience in fund-raising in the 1980s, which it drew on in the university-wide Campaign Minnesota that was launched at the end of the century.

The Morris campus was changed by the student activism of the Vietnam War era. After contentious debate that saw the faculty divide into liberal and conservative factions, students were successful in gaining seats on the campus governing body.[136] Later, the campus instituted major educational reforms, dropping a number of general education and graduation requirements and emphasizing students' freedom to plan—with faculty advice—their own education. In student affairs, assistant provost (later vice chancellor for student affairs) Steve Granger encouraged policies that put responsibility on the students. An honors program was instituted, allowing freshmen to meet in small seminars with a faculty member to study intellectually challenging topics. Freshman seminars created a more informal relationship between faculty and students. Students began addressing faculty members by their first names. The formal and sometimes authoritarian teacher-student relationship evolved into a more egalitarian approach to teaching and learning that remained in evidence at UMM at the end of the century.

The composition of the student body changed as well. Challenged by a group of student leaders and socially conscious faculty members to seek a more diverse student body, UMM established a minority student program.

Over the next three decades, under the direction of William Stewart, the program became a model of recruiting and student support services. As Native Americans, African Americans, Latinos, Asian Americans, and others came to Morris, the campus worked hard to create acceptance and understanding. Students often led the way in making both campus and community more open and diverse. Without fanfare, the campus became more welcoming for women, using inclusive language, expanding women's studies courses under the leadership of several members of the social sciences faculty, and offering continuing education programs for area residents, primarily women.[137]

Bettina Blake, a professor of French, was the first female senior officer at UMM. Her title initially was academic dean; she subsequently became vice chancellor for academic affairs and dean. Blake, who had held administrative positions at both Barnard and Wellesley Colleges, brought with her from those prestigious liberal arts institutions the concept of the "teacher scholar." If faculty members could provide personalized undergraduate teaching and advising and still meet the expectations for distinguished scholarship of the Columbia University Graduate School, the faculty at Morris could do the same in relation to the Graduate School in the Twin Cities. The already excellent faculty at Morris rose to the challenge; the campus became increasingly a place where serious, highly motivated students were matched with a university-level faculty from whom distinction in both teaching and scholarship was expected. Under Blake's leadership as academic vice chancellor, Morris became better known in the national higher education community. In her early years on the campus, she recalled, people were "so low key about the institution and its true value that 1980 came and went without any celebration of the twentieth anniversary of the beginning of the college." The oversight was corrected the following year when students organized a twenty-first birthday "Coming of Age Party."[138]

The campus came of age in other ways, too. Five years of federal grants during the 1980s helped fund long-range planning, improve academic services, and develop new upper-division courses. Other accomplishments of the 1980s included redesign of the general education program, new computers and computer training, and the establishment of a development office. As a result of increased national exposure, Morris was written up in *Kiplinger Newsletter* and *Money Magazine* as a "best buy" in American higher education. From that time on, Morris was regularly lauded in national publications for offering a high-quality liberal arts education at modest cost.[139]

## The Crookston Campus

At a fall 1984 meeting of the Board of Regents held in Crookston, Stanley Sahlstrom, founding provost, announced that he would retire the following June. By this time the campus had more than a thousand students and offered nineteen options for majors in agriculture, sixteen in business, four in hotel, restaurant, and institutional management, and one in home and family services. Courses in communications, psychology, science, and the humanities were provided. In addition, the campus housed a number of outreach programs, including an Elderhostel, introduced in 1978, which offered courses on such topics as quilting, detective fiction, and Minnesota wildlife.

Sahlstrom soon joined the Board of Regents, where his knowledge of higher education proved invaluable. He was succeeded in Crookston by Donald Sargeant, who had been head of the agriculture division from 1970 and then associate provost for academic affairs from 1973 until he became chancellor in 1985. Under Sargeant, the college continued "hands-on learning" as a hallmark while taking steps to reposition itself as a four-year institution in the 1990s.[140] Crookston collaborated with neighboring East Grand Forks Technical Institute in offering a two-year associate in applied science degree; technical courses were taught in East Grand Forks and general education courses in Crookston. Satellite teleconference offerings began the next year, and soon two-way interactive instructional television was established in cooperation with Continuing Education and Extension on the Twin Cities campus, so that students in Crookston could ask questions of instructors in the Twin Cities.

Larry Smith replaced Bernie Youngquist as director of the Northwest Experiment Station in 1984. Research on sugar beets and sunflowers was given a high priority, as was the development of the new "Wheaton" variety of wheat and "Robust" strain of barley. The dairy herd was increased in size and a new wing was added to the dairy barns, equipped with automatic milking, computerized systems to identify each cow, improved ventilation, and above-ground tanks in which to store manure. Feeding systems were also automated and the diet of each cow precisely determined.[141]

## The Waseca Campus

Within two years after it was transformed from a school of agriculture to a school of technology, in 1973, the campus's survival was threatened by a legislative finance committee's recommendation that the new college program be phased out. Objection to the program was based on Waseca's proximity to Mankato State University. Provost Edward Frederick defended the new college and its role; he said it "fill[ed] the gap between the skilled and the professional worker in agriculture and agribusiness," arguing that the workplace would need "three semiprofessionals for each professional." Advocates noted that "UMW is not a textbook college. The emphasis is hands-on, laboratory-oriented learning by doing."[142] The animal health program, designed as a training program for students who wanted to assist veterinarians, provided internship experience, offering students a quarter on the campus in St. Paul in cooperation with the College of Veterinary Medicine and field trips to the Minnesota and Chicago zoos.[143]

Each of the seven program areas—agricultural business, agricultural industries and services, agriculture production, animal health technology, food industry and technology, home and family services, and horticultural technology—combined theory and practice. In addition, students took one-third of their course work in the arts and sciences division. The college awarded the associate in applied science degree. The spring quarter 1975 Pre-Occupational Placements (POP) give a good sense of the diverse interests—of seventy-five placements, the three largest were at florists and nurseries, farm implement retailers, and horse farms.[144] In addition to the traditional small-college sports including football, basketball, and wrestling, UMW offered students the opportunity to compete in programs sponsored by the National Association of Colleges of Teachers of Agriculture. Teams and individuals competed in four areas: soils, livestock evaluation, dairy, and general livestock. The Drama Club produced *Barefoot in the Park* in 1975.[145] By the mid-1980s, enrollment had stabilized at just over a thousand students.[146]

## University Planning and Equal Opportunity

Tight budgets intensified planning initiatives in colleges and universities all over the country. The All-University Planning Council had been created in 1979 to advise President Magrath on long-range planning and to suggest the process and criteria for evaluating results. Decisions would be made by the vice presidents and the deans. As vice president for administration and planning, Robert Stein was the original leader of this effort, but in September 1979 he left that position to become dean of the Law School. Nils Hasselmo, an associate dean of the College of Liberal Arts, became vice president for administration and planning in January 1980 and served until

September 1983, when he accepted the position of academic vice president at the University of Arizona. Carl Adams, a faculty member in the School of Management, was called on to help develop the planning process and the university mission statement. Others who were active in planning included David Lilly (dean of the School of Business), Robert Holt (dean of the Graduate School), Cherie Perlmutter (representing the health sciences), John Wallace (a philosopher particularly interested in undergraduate education), Jack Merwin (dean of the College of Education), and John Turner (professor of political science).

Although the planning process was helpful, it did not take the sting out of retrenchment. In October 1981, President Magrath addressed a special meeting of the Board of Regents. All state agencies had been asked to show how they would operate if their appropriations were reduced by 8, 10, or 12 percent. At the university, this would mean reductions of $37 million to $57 million. At Magrath's urging, the regents passed a resolution stating that the proposed reductions would make it impossible for the university "to continue serving the state as a major contributor to its economy and to its cultural and intellectual vitality."[147] Magrath and the regents offered to return $10 million to the state. In the end, Governor Al Quie and the legislature cut the university's funding by $25.6 million. By the spring of 1982, Magrath thought that the worst of the retrenchments were over and that the university "was unlikely... to face budget cuts like this again."[148] The University of Minnesota had avoided declaring financial exigency, as the University of Washington had done. On the other hand, retrenchments had seriously affected morale and placed a significant burden on department administrators. It was difficult for the liberal arts faculty to feel comfortable about the Institute of Technology's getting a $650,000 increase, based on doubled enrollments, when liberal arts had been cut $1.5 million. Still, history faculty member John Howe viewed planning as essential:

> My ox has been gored like hell. I believe there's some danger of distorting the mission of the University. I worry about the core areas of liberal arts. At the same time, I believe the planning work is absolutely essential.[149]

Management faculty member Bruce Erickson observed that planning had shifted university decision making: "The University used to be run by deans running independent units. Now the locus of power is the vice presidents."[150]

Gender equity was an increasingly major concern. The differences in salary between the deans of nursing, education, and public health put pay equity before the regents and the public.[151] Shyamala Rajender's allegation that the refusal of the chemistry department to consider her for a tenure-track position was discriminatory ultimately led to a class action suit filed on behalf of women in faculty or professional and administrative positions. In 1980, after seven years of litigation, Rajender and the university reached a court-approved settlement awarding Rajender $100,000. A panel of special masters was appointed by Judge Miles Lord to hear the claims of other women who believed they had been discriminated against. In their national study of academic litigation, authors George R. La Noue and Barbara A. Lee commented on the impact of the Rajender decision:

> It is unprecedented to have three special masters reviewing every policy and every personnel decision affecting faculty women on the campus for ten years. . . . The irony is that all this should have happened at the University of Minnesota. . . . The University has had a special liberal tradition in a state that has been a national leader in civil rights litigation. Indeed, in 1976, the University of Minnesota was the first university in the country to have its affirmative action plan accepted by HEW [the U.S. Department of Health, Education, and Welfare]. Perhaps that the suit did happen at UM is a sign of how deep and how complicated is the problem of sex discrimination in American universities.[152]

Magrath later commented:

> I have some regret about the Rajender case. Early on, Elmer L. Andersen told me, "You ought to really look into this. I'm not sure it was handled the right way." What happened in her case had occurred before I went there. I listened—I'm not blaming them—to the attorneys and to the position of leading representatives of the Department of Chemistry, but in this case particularly with regard to attorneys. I wish that I had looked into it and intervened and maybe made a decision that would have been unpopular with some faculty but might have spared the university—promoting affirmative action and equal opportunity, which I strongly support, without qualification. I don't like universities being run by legal decrees.[153]

Charlotte Striebel, a professor of mathematics and chair of the Committee on Equal Employment Opportunity for Women, commenting on how the Rajender case was handled, said that "it was nothing but the administration putting its head into the sand."[154] There were rumors that the university could have settled Rajender's initial complaint for $50,000 but was persuaded by chemistry faculty members not to do so.[155]

One result of the case was to establish a new position, that of general counsel. Stephen Dunham was recruited for the position. Another change was an increased role for the Office of Equal Opportunity and Affirmative Action, which not only played a role in helping monitor Rajender compliance, but also oversaw university compliance with federal and state equal opportunity policies. Director Lillian Williams, a strong advocate for women and minorities, won the respect of the faculty and administration. Within the Institute of Technology (home of the chemistry department) as well as elsewhere in the university, there were a number of initiatives to improve gender balance. Institute of Technology faculty member and associate dean Sally Gregory Kohlstedt helped design new approaches to recruiting that almost doubled the number of women faculty and increased retention of women graduate students. Similar efforts were undertaken in other colleges and departments. Women were half of the student body in the university system by 1999. The number of women faculty members increased between 1980 and 1997: from 27 percent to 39 percent of the assistant professors, from 16 percent to 32 percent of associate professors, and from 6 percent to 15 percent of full professors.[156]

## Magrath's Resignation

Before the 1981 budget crisis, Peter Magrath had asked the regents for a brief sabbatical during the summer of 1982. By that time he would have completed eight years of service (longer than he had originally thought likely) and wanted time to study public policy issues in higher education. Kenneth Keller, the academic vice president, assumed his responsibilities during his absence.

In spring 1984, as Magrath approached the tenth anniversary of his appointment, the Board of Regents conducted a second review of his performance. Like the first review in 1979, it was directed by Joseph Kauffman, a professor of educational administration at the University of Wisconsin. Kauffman interviewed about a hundred people, including regents, deans, faculty and staff members, and students. A subcommittee of the Board of Regents, composed of Erwin Goldfine, Wenda Moore, and Wally Hilke, coordinated the evaluation. Its text was not released to the public. Regent Goldfine had doubts about the review's fairness. "It got to be one of the dumbest processes in America," he said. "It opens every can of worms for those antagonists that want to take on a witch hunt."[157] Others pointed out that given the serious fiscal problems facing the university and the stresses of running such a large and complex institution, a decade was about as long as any president could endure.

Whether there was a connection with the review or not, President Magrath announced in June 1984 that he was resigning and had accepted a position as president of the University of Missouri system. In his farewell address to the regents, he observed that a presidency is made effective through the work of others:

> When the undergraduate program on the Twin Cities campus is listed as the third best offered by any university, it is the undergraduate faculty who deserve credit. When Morris is cited as one of the "fifty colleges that offer high academic standards and below average prices," it is the UMM campus leadership that merits applause. When a national report on graduate schools includes eighteen of our programs in the top ten and thirty-eight in the top twenty, it is the graduate faculty and deans who deserve recognition.[158]

Magrath urged the board to continue its commitment to planning and setting priorities. He thanked its members for their contributions to the university. Speaking of his duties as president, he noted that he had "survived 113 regents meetings, twenty regents, fourteen vice presidents, five provosts, countless deans, and three football coaches." More seriously, he observed that "the presidency of this or any major university is not an easy assignment. It is a complex leadership position."[159]

Jeanne Lupton, who had served as Magrath's assistant before becoming dean of the General College, reflected on Magrath's contributions as president. She believed that the planning process he established provided a stable framework for setting priorities in a time of unprecedented economic difficulty; his successors used it to guide planning. Magrath had been supportive of diversity and change, encouraging greater diversity in the faculty and student body, helping to present the university to international constituencies, advocating more equal athletic opportunity for women, and supporting new thinking about the role of the General College.[160] Others praised Magrath for his practice of consulting widely prior to making a decision. Fred Lukermann, dean of the College of Liberal Arts, observed that "his success in being here ten years is really a job of balancing trends and forces. You've got to be a consummate politician to land on your feet after ten years."[161]

In 1998, the library on the campus in St. Paul was renamed the Magrath Library in recognition of the university's eleventh president.

# Chapter 4
# Finding Focus, 1985–1997

B Y THE MIDDLE OF THE 1980s, it appeared that constrained resources had become a permanent feature of university life. Although the university had considerable experience in setting priorities and making choices through the planning process set in motion by President Magrath, even more difficult decisions had to be made during the next twelve years. The role of the General College was reconfigured, resources were reduced for some colleges, and additional resources were made available for others. Between 1986 and 1996, more than $100 million was reallocated within the university. Two of the more difficult decisions were closing the Waseca campus and the sale of University Hospitals to the Fairview Health Care System.

In addition to setting academic priorities, the university, like all major organizations, was expected to upgrade its management systems. This meant replacing aging central computer systems, creating new accounting and registration systems, installing a new telephone system, and providing campuswide Internet access. Stanford University administrator Raymond Bacchetti, speaking to faculty and administrators at the University of Minnesota, had cautioned that managerial systems needed to be carefully planned in order not to destroy the essence of an academic community. A university, he observed, is "both a tight ship and a loosely guided tour."[1]

While colleges and universities were adopting managerial practices from the private sector, American businesses were adopting policies and practices from higher education. As businesses became increasingly aware of the importance of knowledge as the source of innovation and productivity, they began to modify their personnel policies to offer the kind of independence found in universities. Some corporations began calling their facilities campuses.

Increased interaction between institutions of higher education and businesses went smoothly for the most part. Minnesota businesses enthusiastically hired university graduates, encouraged employees to serve on univer-

The East Bank (background) and West Bank (foreground) of the Minneapolis campus are connected by the Washington Avenue bridge spanning the Mississippi River. Located on the eastern perimeter of Minneapolis and within a ten-minute drive of downtown St. Paul, the campus offers easy access to the resources of both cities. Photograph by Bordner Aerials.

Following forty-three years of effort by alumni and friends of the university to create the first alumni and visitors' center on the Twin Cities campus, the McNamara Alumni Center, University of Minnesota Gateway, was dedicated in February 2000. Designed by Antoine Predock with KKE Architects, the dramatic granite and copper-faced structure houses public meeting spaces, the heritage gallery, and offices for university organizations. Photograph by Timothy Hursley.

The Frederick R. Weisman Art Museum, at the eastern foot of the Washington Avenue bridge, is the work of world-renowned architect Frank O. Gehry. Completed in 1993, the building presents a color and light show as the stainless-steel facade reflects brilliant sunlight and the vivid oranges and purples of sunset. Photograph by Tom Foley.

The "V" formed by sidewalks on the St. Paul campus mall leads to the Student Center and Coffey Hall (the administration building). To the north and east are the barns, greenhouses, and plots devoted to research and instruction. Photograph by Tom Foley.

Designed by RSP Architects Limited and dedicated in 1993, the Ecology Building on the St. Paul campus houses two units in the College of Biological Sciences, the Department of Ecology, Evolution, and Behavior, and the research facilities and stored collections of the James Ford Bell Museum of Natural History. It contains classrooms, research laboratories, and greenhouses as well as faculty and graduate student offices. Photograph by Tom Foley.

University of Minnesota Duluth has a sweeping view of Lake Superior and overlooks Minnesota's fourth largest city. Photograph courtesy of the University of Minnesota Archives, Duluth.

The library of the University of Minnesota Duluth is one of the most technologically advanced in the state. It opened in fall 2000, serving the campus and the region. Photograph by Brett Groehler, University Relations and Development, Duluth.

Located in west central Minnesota, the University of Minnesota Morris is recognized as one of the nation's outstanding public liberal arts colleges. Adjacent to the campus is the West Central Research and Outreach Center, one of six research experiment stations in Minnesota. Photograph by Steffen Photo.

Morris students on the steps of Camden Hall, which houses the Division of Social Sciences. Photograph by Stephen Woit; courtesy of University Relations, University of Minnesota Morris.

The University of Minnesota Crookston, recognized for its innovative leadership in polytechnic education, is located on the northern edge of the city of Crookston in the Red River Valley. The Northwest Research and Outreach Center is near the campus. Photograph courtesy of Media Services, University of Minnesota Crookston.

A faculty member at Crookston works with students using personal computers. Since 1993, when it became the first college to give all full-time students a laptop computer, Crookston has been known informally as the "laptop" university. Photograph courtesy of Media Services, University of Minnesota Crookston.

Waseca was the home of the Southern School of Agriculture from 1953 to 1973 and of the University of Minnesota Technical College from 1971 to 1992. Waseca remains the site of the Southern Research and Outreach Center. Photograph by Steffen Photo.

Waseca students participate in orientation in 1979. Photograph courtesy of the University of Minnesota Archives, Twin Cities.

In 1993, the University of Minnesota joined Rochester Community College, Riverland Technical College, and Winona State University at the University Center Rochester to better serve the educational needs of the southeastern area of the state. Photograph courtesy of the University Center Rochester.

sity advisory committees, and made generous contributions to university fund-raising campaigns. Corporate-university perspectives clashed briefly in 1996 during deliberations over the university's tenure code; resolution of the differences led to a revised tenure code that recognized the role of faculty members as independent professionals.

Three presidents led the university during these challenging years: Kenneth H. Keller (1985–88), Richard Sauer (interim president, 1988), and Nils Hasselmo (1989–97).

Some of their more controversial decisions stemmed from actions or proposals that impinged on the public's expectation of the openness of the university. Even though there had long been admissions requirements, the view persisted that the university belonged to everyone in the state. To Minnesotans, education represented a pathway and an opportunity. Any proposal that might limit access, however rational, was felt viscerally as a potential loss or threat.

## The Keller Years

Because President Magrath's resignation came rather suddenly in 1984, an interim president was to be named to serve until a permanent successor was found. The obvious candidate was Kenneth Keller, who as vice president for academic affairs had been the chief academic officer and formal second-in-command. A regents' policy stated that interim appointees should not be excluded from consideration for permanent posts, but in this instance a majority of the regents voted that the acting president should not be considered for the permanent position.[2] Keller faced a dilemma. He was arguably a strong candidate to be the new president and, if he chose to be a candidate, it was understood that he would not accept the position of acting president. Keller decided that he wished to continue as academic vice president and, as a service to the university, accept the role of interim president until a new president was appointed.[3]

Soon after Keller became interim president, Governor Rudy Perpich asked to address the regents. As Keller recalled, the governor "was very critical of the university" and accused it of being "incapable of making decisions, incapable of planning."[4] Perpich had appointed a task force to advise him about changes needed in Minnesota's postsecondary systems. When the task force failed to recommend bold actions, Perpich decided to go to the regents and subsequently to the heads of the other postsecondary systems. David Lebedoff, who was a regent at the time, described the meeting:

The governor came over to a luncheon meeting we were having in Coffman Union. He asked each university to do unilaterally what the commission [he had appointed] had not done and to focus its mission—I think he used the words "focus its mission"—and to do what it did best and stop doing the other things so there wasn't all this duplication of mission throughout the state. He said, "If you do that, if you have a commitment to doing what you do best and you focus on what you do best, I'll just throw so much money at the university that you'll be very pleased." That was the impetus [for the Commitment to Focus plan].[5]

Keller recounted the meeting:

I remember the governor saying that the university was running amok. "It makes no decisions. It only grows. It has no idea of what it ought to do." I, having little to lose, said to the governor that I thought he was wrong on the basic point, that in fact the university more than most had been involved in planning. We'd done lots of planning. We did know what all the issues were. There was [just] a need to put it together, and in fact I could put together a plan in a month.[6]

This was the impetus for Keller's "Commitment to Focus" document, written in February 1985. In nine pages, Keller summarized the planning that had taken place over the previous five years. Among the principal elements in Commitment to Focus were strengthening graduate education and research, reducing undergraduate enrollments to improve the undergraduate experience, strengthening preparation requirements, and transforming the General College from a degree-granting program to one that would offer developmental and enrichment skills. Each of the colleges was to focus on areas of unique strength, particularly research. Undergraduate enrollment reductions would occur naturally as a result of demographics and also through encouraging more students to attend community colleges before transferring to the university. Implicit in the plan was that through focus, the university could move up from the top ten into the top five among public research universities. In return, the state was asked to continue to fund the university at current levels despite pending enrollment declines.[7]

All of the discussion in the first month, Keller recalled, was positive: "There were certainly concerns about access, concerns about this and that, but not a lot of argument. In other words, it wasn't 'We accept it' or 'We reject it.'" The regents' view was that "this is really good food for thought as we think about a new president and as we think about what we need to do." There was no direct response from the governor, but a number of newspapers ran editorials saying, "This is terrific! This is exactly what the university should be doing."[8]

Regent David Lebedoff confirmed this account:

> I cannot begin to tell you what a stirring response that document caused. We got hundreds of letters and phone calls. So many wise and good people, respected people in their own communities and throughout the state, wrote to say, "This is it! This is what hasn't been done and what needs to be done. Go for this!" There was a huge amount of sentiment for Commitment to Focus, and it became well known around the country.[9]

All the regents but one voted to adopt Commitment to Focus as the university's long-range planning document.[10] Meanwhile, the presidential search had been going forward. The regents turned to the Presidential Search Advisory Service of the National Association of State Universities and Land-Grant Colleges for advice and assistance. The Faculty Advisory Committee, headed by John Howe, was charged with undertaking the screening process. Howe noted that the initial list of names didn't impress the committee. "Before the search was over, we asked directly, 'Should Vice President Keller be considered as a candidate?'" Yes, they were told.[11]

The leading outside candidate was Lattie Coor, president of the University of Vermont.[12] When it became known that there was growing sentiment to include Keller among the candidates, Coor withdrew. After some debate, the regents voted nine to three to change their earlier position and allow Keller's candidacy to go forward. Keller, who had been present throughout the meeting, was then asked to be interviewed. He recalled the sequence of events:

> We had the public interview... with the only candidate. The vote was eleven to one, and I was declared president. It was not a particularly good start on the presidency and probably had an effect on some bad decisions that I made.[13]

The new president was fifty years old. He had been born in Brooklyn and, like many gifted students, had attended Stuyvesant High School. Excelling in science and mathematics, he had a broad range of interests and was editor of the school newspaper. He entered Columbia University in 1952 on a Navy ROTC scholarship. Although he was keenly interested in English literature, he ultimately majored in chemical engineering; he rowed in the crew and was one of the leaders of the Inter-Fraternity Council. After graduating, he joined the navy and was assigned to Admiral Hyman Rickover, helping to design nuclear submarines. After his naval service, his interests turned to the promising new applications of chemical engineering to medical science; he returned to graduate school at Johns Hopkins University, earning a Ph.D. in 1964, the year he was recruited by Neal Amundson to come to Minnesota. He later served as head of the Department of Chemical Engineering, as associate and then acting dean of the Graduate School, and as chair of the Faculty Consultative Committee. In 1980, when Henry Koffler left Minnesota, Keller was named vice president for academic affairs, the position he later identified as the most rewarding of his career, in 1980.[14]

History professor Ted Farmer describes the effect of Keller's assuming the presidency: "There was a tremendous surge of energy. I've likened it to a ship dead in the water in which somebody started the engine suddenly. The whole thing began to shudder, and roll, and churn, and surge. Things began to happen in every facet of the university. Perhaps it was inevitable that not everyone would be pleased."[15]

Contentiousness surfaced almost immediately over the selection of a new Board of Regents chair. David Lebedoff was the choice of the majority of the board members; some of the regents who opposed him were also less supportive of Keller. Charles McGuiggan of Marshall wished to be chairman. In the interest of harmony, Keller indicated his willingness to work with McGuiggan and asked Lebedoff to withdraw his candidacy. Over time, it became apparent that the all-important relationship between board chair and president was not good. A 1993 magazine article described communication between the two as "minimal and laced with distrust."[16] Keller later said that he had misjudged his ability to work with McGuiggan and he noted that he did not cultivate close personal ties with the regents as Magrath had done: "My predecessor spoke to them every day. I thought that was excessive. If I erred, it was on the other side, in not spending enough time with them."[17]

Keller realized that he needed to present Commitment to Focus to the people of the state. During his three years as president, he gave an average of two hundred talks a year outside the university; he estimated that he may have reached as many as sixty thousand people directly, and they seemed to favor the plan: "Wherever I spoke, whether it was the Kiwanis Club in Redwood Falls or whatever, that group always gave me the feeling that they agreed." Unfortunately, most of Minnesota's 4 million people got second-hand information on Commitment to Focus.[18]

Political commentator D. J. Leary, who also traveled around the state, saw the public reception of Commitment to Focus differently. Where Keller had seen acceptance, Leary saw doubt and anxiety: "It was *the* major blow to grassroots feeling. It was palpable." He recalled hearing an outraged citizen verbally attack the chancellor of the state university system under the mistaken impression that he was the author of Commitment to Focus. The angry parent had exclaimed, "You're saying that our kids have got to go all the way to Montana to get a Ph.D.! We won't stand for that!" Leary also noted that a state official took speaking engagements around the state just to attack Commitment to Focus, saying, "They're going to close down education, and they're going to close down agriculture, and try to run everything."[19]

Leary also sensed that the citizens' view of the university was changing:

> Prior to 1980, there was a sense in Minnesota that it was the birthright of the sons and daughters of farmers and miners and engineers and working people to go to the university. But more and more, fewer were even applying. Instead they were going to the state universities, to Mankato and St. Cloud, and the university lost their ongoing affection and loyalty.[20]

Making Commitment to Focus understandable was not an easy matter. History professor Hyman Berman, who had close ties to the governor, remembered advising Keller that "because legislators are nodding does not necessarily mean they agree with you; it just means they hear what you are saying."[21]

In the colleges and on the campuses, the task was to transform a fairly general planning document into specific proposals. Early on, General College was required to drop its two- and four-year degree programs, offering instead a place for students to enter the university before transferring to upper-division majors in other colleges. The undergraduate liberal arts mission of Morris was confirmed, and it restructured its liberal arts offerings around core courses and provided support for speech communication and geology, added a major in computer sciences, and provided new funding for freshmen orientation. Duluth reemphasized its role as a regional university, building strengths particularly at the upper division and master's levels. It reduced the number of places in its supportive services division for students from outside its region, took steps to eliminate two-year degree programs, and created new faculty strength in management information systems computer applications. Crookston and Waseca gave the highest priority to their two-year degree programs in agriculture and related fields. Waseca added new strength in business affairs and computer technology, and Crookston in instructional computing and health, physical education, and recreation. The legislature also agreed that funding would not be cut when enrollment declined.[22]

Roger Benjamin, named academic vice president and provost of the Twin Cities campus in September 1986, oversaw a second stage of implementing Commitment to Focus. Benjamin, formerly a professor of political science and associate dean of the College of Liberal Arts, had been involved in the studies that led to Commitment to Focus but had left Minnesota in 1983 to become provost of the University of Pittsburgh, where much of his time was spent in planning. Edward Foster, who had earlier helped implement a transformation of the School of Management, served as an associate vice president for academic affairs, working closely with a faculty advisory task force chaired by Charles Campbell, professor of physics. Foster described the committee's work:

> As individuals, they were not people who were in general deeply committed to undergraduate education, but they came to the overall conclusion that the arts and science floor of the university was at serious risk, and undergraduate education was at serious risk. Given that this was their conclusion, and given the committee's instruction to "balance the budget," it wasn't just a matter of tinkering with $50,000 here and $100,000 there. They said, "We need millions. The only way that we can do that is to cut off some of the periphery of the university, some of the things that aren't part of the core." They came up with a recommendation for closing veterinary medicine and dentistry, in part with an eye on national supply and demand in those areas, and the availability of alternative places to get the education.[23]

When Foster presented the Campbell report to Keller in June 1987, "he paled and said, 'You killed me.'"[24] Keller immediately understood the firestorm the report would create. Furthermore, he thought the recommendations to close the dental school and the College of Veterinary Medicine were inappropriate because they were the only such schools in Minnesota and met the criterion of "uniqueness" established in several planning documents. Board chair David Lebedoff was equally aghast. Over lunch with Benjamin, he asked that the report be sent back to the committee for reconsideration of the proposed closings, but he was informed that it had already been sent to the faculty.[25]

Finance vice president David Lilly likewise was struck by the potential impact of the recommendations and called the Campbell report "the end of the world." The report "created the raison d'être for the people on the Board of Regents who were against Keller in the first place to begin to go after him."[26] As Keller himself put it, "The problem I faced was that there wasn't anybody in the world who would believe this was the Campbell committee recommendation and not a Keller plan being run up the flagpole."[27]

In the end, the committee's recommendations were not implemented. The administration and the regents rejected them, particularly the recommendations regarding dentistry and veterinary medicine. Both schools mobilized their alumni and supporters and mounted such effective campaigns that their budgets were actually increased and their programs strengthened.[28] The report also advocated closing the mortuary science program, but the program had influential alumni throughout Minnesota who were effective advocates on its behalf.[29] The planning that followed during the fall of 1987 stemmed more from Keller's original Commitment to Focus document than from the committee's suggestions. A few small units judged to be not central to the university's primary mission were spun off or restructured. The MacPhail Center, which continued to provide musical instruction for pre-collegiate-age students, became an independent institution. KUOM, the university's radio station, which had broadcast a broad mix of public programming, was transformed over time into Radio K, a student-run station focusing on popular music and programs appealing to students.

It is difficult to make a final or balanced judgment about Commitment to Focus. As a broad profile for reorganization and change, it met the challenges of its time and awakened the university community to the need to rethink its programs. In retrospect, John Howe, a member of the Campbell committee, commented that "the final outcome of all this planning was not very inspiring and illustrated the extraordinary difficulty—perhaps even the impossibility, given the size, complexity, and participatory governance of the University—of significant redirection."[30]

## The Minnesota Campaign

One of Keller's greatest successes as president was the Minnesota Campaign, which sought to raise $300 million in private gifts, at the time the largest sum ever sought by a public university. Public universities could no longer depend on public funding to meet their needs; private gifts supplemented public support and helped the university maintain a margin of excellence.

The major thrust of the campaign was to raise funds to endow 100 faculty chairs. While the public at large was unsure about Commitment to Focus, the community of donors reacted favorably. Keller said that he often heard comments to this effect: "This is a university that is now moving in a direction it should. We want to support the university."[31]

Keller, Lilly, and Steve Roszell, executive director of the University of Minnesota Foundation, planned the campaign. Lilly, who had left his position as dean of the School of Management to join central administration as vice president for finance in the last year of Magrath's presidency, found an innovative way to create a match for contributions: persuade the state to release the Permanent University Fund to the university. (The fund was created by the Morrill Act of 1862 authorizing the sale of public lands to benefit designated universities.) Through this release, and by agreeing to forgo the annual income from the fund, the state conveyed to the university $65 million, which could be used to match donors' gifts for endowed chairs.

Foundation board members Russell Bennett, Curtis Carlson, and Elmer L. Andersen chaired the campaign. Bennett recruited Carlson:

> Curt, you went to West High School. I went to West High School. You went to the University of Minnesota. I went to the University of Minnesota. But then our career paths drifted apart. He laughed. We've got to have a campaign to raise some capital funds, and the foundation has to do that. That's why we are a foundation, and you're the logical person to head it up.[32]

Carlson stepped forward generously with a gift of $25 million—the lead gift in the campaign and the largest single private gift to the university in the twentieth century. The $300 million goal was exceeded by $65 million. When the campaign began, the university had 17 endowed chairs or professorships; when it ended three years later, there were 144. The momentum of support for faculty continued after the campaign ended, and by the close of the century, the university had more than 295 endowed faculty postions, helping to attract and retain exceptional faculty members. In addition to their contributions to research and scholarship, the chair holders brought in awards and research funds and attracted talented graduate students.[33]

Bennett recalled the active role played by Carlson—who "would make any call we asked him to. We could take his airplane and fly out to California"—and Keller: "Every place Ken and I went," Bennett said, "we found that the corporations and civic leaders were prepared to commit themselves to the campaign. We got more than $4 million from 3M and more than $3 million from Honeywell." Bennett believed that "we'd have hit $400 million if the Eastcliff situation hadn't come along. We hadn't even started the public campaign."[34] Keller's wife, Bonita Sindelir, was also helpful in the campaign, joining him in several meetings with members of the Binger family to make the case for a McKnight Foundation contribution. The Bingers subsequently sent Keller a two-paragraph letter. As Keller recalled it, the first paragraph read, "Dear Ken, We like very much what you're doing with Commitment to Focus." The second said, "Here's $10 million in unrestricted funds."[35]

Keller estimated that during his years as president, he spent a third of his time on the campaign: "When I went to talk to a donor, it wasn't passive. I spent a lot of time at it. You had to entertain people, to get to know them. It never happened in one meeting."[36] He was also quick to acknowledge campaign co-chair Bennett's help: "He is just a wonderful guy and put in extraordinary time in the most selfless way imaginable. His involvement in the campaign was much, much deeper than you can imagine."[37]

Recalling Sage and John Cowles's satisfaction in establishing a chair in dance, Keller said: "They were very devoted to dance; the idea that there would be a dance program at the university that they were able to make happen was enormously valuable to them."[38] John Cowles Jr. was publisher of the Minneapolis *Star Tribune*; Sage Fuller Cowles was a dance performance artist. Funding for the liberal and performing arts was particularly welcome because a number of donors who had both liberal arts and professional degrees tended to favor endowments for the professional schools that were most directly linked to their success. As Bennett said, "Poetry, and the arts, and history, and a lot of things that are just as important were harder to raise money for."[39] The campaign led to the Edelstein-Keller Chair in Creative Writing, the Union Pacific endowment for the Center for Early Modern History, and $5 million from a McKnight Foundation gift used to strengthen the arts and humanities. The campaign was a great success. A poll conducted in summer 1987 showed that more Minnesotans had "favorable" or "very favorable" impressions of the university than at any time since 1964. Positive responses added up to 84 percent.[40]

## Eastcliff

Remodeling of Eastcliff, the President's official residence, led to trouble. Eastcliff had been in poor physical condition for years; repairs had been postponed because of the retrenchments of the 1970s and 1980s. Elmer L. Andersen, who was well acquainted with the issue from his years as a regent (1967–75), noted that although the board had urged both Malcolm Moos and Peter Magrath to attend to Eastcliff, both demurred.[41] Andersen's memory was acute and painful:

> The Board of Regents [told] Malcolm Moos that something needed to be done at Eastcliff, that it was a ceremonial center and it wasn't properly equipped for what it was supposed to do. It was deteriorating physically; it needed attention. We needed to have a committee to set up a program and finance a proper rehabilitation of Eastcliff. So he agreed to the committee, and we set it up, and we got an appraisal and an estimate. It was going to cost quite a bit of money, and I remember Mac saying, "Elmer, we can't. I can't in good conscience with all the disturbance there is and the concern of the students and the general social instability. I can't go to the legislature with an item for Eastcliff, so please forget it." So we forgot it.
>
> Then along came Peter Magrath, and we went through the same thing with him. He said, "Elmer, we can't [provide] adequate salaries for the faculty, so their real income is actually going down. I can't see us spending a lot of money on Eastcliff when I haven't the money for salaries, so please forget it." So we forgot it.
>
> Then Ken Keller came along. We said, "We just have to do something about this. It just cannot go on any longer. The place is beginning to crumble." So Ken Keller bit the bullet and, of course, it became a big fracas.[42]

Keller actually contemplated not living at Eastcliff, but everyone told him he had to. Russell Bennett confirmed Andersen's account of "twenty-five years of regents and presidents ignoring the upkeep of Eastcliff. Nobody had the guts to say, 'That white building needs to be painted'; it just kept getting worse and worse."[43]

By fall 1987, the costs of repairing and reconstructing the fence around the property, remodeling the kitchen, and enlarging the dining room came to approximately $600,000. Keller recalled, "Newspaper columnists went around and talked to Twin Cities contractors and said, 'Can you imagine a kitchen for $600,000?' They said, 'No, you don't have to spend that on a kitchen. You could do that for $200,000.' When we corrected the columnists and said, 'The kitchen actually cost under $200,000,' they said, 'If you think the number means anything you don't understand what the issue is about.'" The entire project took three years; because the workmen kept discovering additional problems, it cost about $1 million, including routine maintenance.[44]

At the same time, Minneapolis's *Star Tribune* and the *St. Paul Pioneer Press* were engaged in a circulation war. Although both frequently supported the university, they now outdid each other in criticizing it. For about forty days in a row, Keller noted, "there was a story about what was going on with Eastcliff, and then [the issue] became my suite of offices at the university. At one point, evening television actually had a picture of my office with a price tag on every item in it." Keller's desk became the most controversial object.

## Keller's Resignation

Early in 1988, relationships within the Board of Regents and between the president and some of the regents grew increasingly strained. On the one hand, a number of the regents and some legislators seemed to have come to terms with the adjustments in university planning that had been evolving during the previous year. On February 7, the *Star Tribune* carried an article titled "Legislators, Regents Respond Favorably to Focus Plan." Representative Ben Boo of Duluth was quoted as saying that the plan "doesn't have nearly the nags, explosions, and barrages of some of the earlier recommendations." Senator Gene Waldorf of St. Paul found the request for added funds "right in line with what we expected." Representative Lyndon Carlson of Crystal applauded what he saw as a good fit between support for the Institute of Technology and the need for new jobs in industry and the high technology field. Regents Wally Hilke and Elizabeth Craig also commented favorably on the plan.

Despite greater acceptance of Commitment to Focus, other issues divided the board. Newspaper articles now pointed out that the university had a $50 million contingency fund composed of unexpended balances in a number of smaller accounts. Lilly thought it appropriate to centralize these funds and make their expenditure a matter for deliberate decisions by the president and the regents.[45] This was intended as an act of prudence in a time of uncertain resources—and the reserve was in fact only 5 percent of the overall budget—but it was interpreted as an act of deception, raising the issue of accountability and suggesting to some state officials that the university had substantial resources and could make do with smaller appropriations. The regents said that they were unaware of the reserve fund;

the administration believed it had identified the reserves in various reports to the regents.

Unraveling of support for the president came as a result of a series of financial issues unrelated to Commitment to Focus. On February 3, there was a report that the remodeling costs for Eastcliff were more than twice the budgeted amount and that $200,000 had been spent remodeling the offices of the president and his staff. The following day, the legislative auditor was asked to examine the university's physical plant costs. On February 10, the legislative auditor was ordered to undertake a study of costs at Eastcliff. On February 25, a new university telephone system was shown to be $9 million over budget. On March 2, following a one-and-a-half-year investigation, the men's basketball program was placed on probation for rule violations during the years the team was coached by Bill Musselman. On March 9, a report suggested that Keller had approved the cost overruns at Eastcliff. The following day, the legislative audit revealed the existence of the $50 million reserve fund. On March 13, three years to the day after he was appointed as president, Keller resigned.[46]

George Robb, associate vice president for institutional relations, observed:

> This may be controversial, but I think [Keller's] primary supporters on the board were not willing to step up to the plate when it really got threatening. Some of his strongest supporters got quiet in a hurry. Some of those that he had alienated by not paying a lot of attention to them just gained strength through all that. Everything that Keller was doing was one more example why they shouldn't support him."[47]

Richard Sauer, who was soon to be appointed interim president, commented:

> I had enough exposure to [the situation] to know that several board members had their own political agendas and that there had been a culture of expecting the president to do what they wanted done to satisfy whatever political pressure was brought on them. Ken was not going to cave in to that, so I think they were very angry with him.[48]

David Lebedoff, who had succeeded McGuiggan as board chair in 1987, commented that Keller "mobilized constituencies that had not been strongly supportive of the university and he reinvigorated the faculty, all toward the end of a greater university. I think Keller's political judgment in terms of winning popular support for the program was not always the equal of his managerial skills or his visionary genius." Lebedoff also pointed out that Keller did not convey clearly the fact that the enrollment declines that were part of the Commitment to Focus plan were in large part going to occur naturally as a result of the demographic reduction in the number of college-age students. This downsizing was misconstrued as a plan to reduce access. "I think a perception grew," Lebedoff said, "that we were going to be a small elite school and no one was going to get in." Fears about access had accelerated over time and were not helped by the Campbell report. Lebedoff believed that some of the regents should have done more to advocate Keller's plan: "There was a fault line. On one side of the fault line were the access people and on the other side, the excellence people. There was a growing suspicion of elitism, I think completely unfounded, but growing nevertheless." Lebedoff noted also the impact of the remodeling of Eastcliff and the perception of excessive expenditures for a kitchen, which "ran against the culture of Minnesota." Summarizing the situation, Lebedoff said:

> I think he [Keller] came to share the perception that he had become so controversial that, rightly or wrongly, he could no longer effectively lead the university. The legislature was contemplating putting on the ballot an initiative to take away the autonomy of the university. I think Keller saw the necessity of resignation. The choice was his. It was a tragic time. It was very difficult for all of us, and painful, and it still is. And much misunderstood.[49]

Keller described the last days of his administration and reflected on his own mistakes and those of others:

> The weekend before I resigned, I had a Friday-morning meeting with the Board of Regents, which I read as only weakly supportive. I met over the weekend with a number of people. I mentioned earlier how much I depended on Steve Dunham [the university attorney]. I met with Steve, and with Richard Heydinger [vice president for institutional relations], and with Stan Kegler [immediate past vice president for institutional relations], and with D. J. Leary [political commentator and analyst]. We met and we talked, and talked, and talked. I decided—that was on a Sunday afternoon—that it was time, that I had to step aside, and so I did. By the way, the day before I resigned or maybe the day I resigned, there was a paid advertisement in one of the papers with several hundred signatures of University faculty, asking me not to do it. Other people called. George Latimer [mayor of St. Paul] called about that time and said, "Don't do it. I know what you're thinking about. Don't do it. This will pass."[50]

Some observers thought that Governor Perpich had joined the attack on Keller, but as Keller recalled, "He was actually quite supportive, not publicly, but in his own interesting and bizarre way, he was supportive. His answer was, 'Move out of Eastcliff. That will really show them.' The governor's other suggestion was that I 'throw a hand grenade somewhere else, by closing either the Morris or the Crookston campus, which would draw a lot of attention away.'" Keller refused.[51]

Keller continued:

Naturally, I've thought about my own role in all of this. The first thing that I would accuse myself of is that I hadn't paid sufficient attention to the Board of Regents, so that I didn't have a depth of support that would have carried me through this. I don't think I ignored the board. I think I tried very hard to teach the board, but teaching the board is a little bit different from nurturing and taking care of it. I think that was the first thing.[52]

The second thing is that I didn't properly read the need for handling this as a public relations issue. I made the assumption that it would be seen for what I think it was: a minor, trivial issue that ought to be viewed in the light of a lot of other things that I was doing. For too long, I did not organize a public relations response. I responded. I apologized, or I explained, or I did these things, but it was not the kind of effort that I think would be mounted at the university today under such a threat.

That leads to what is probably the thing that I most strongly accuse myself of, and that is a certain degree of hubris. There are two ways of looking at the role of public relations. One is to say that it's a kind of self-serving, crafted nonresponse that lacks integrity. But the other way is to say that it's a necessary response and you cannot assume that your magnetism and personal worth are so obvious to everybody that you needn't engage in that sort of thing. That's the sense in which I would accuse myself of some hubris, of thinking that the very quality of my role spoke for itself. Today, as I look back on it, I see that at least part of that has elements that could reasonably be identified as hubris, not arrogance and not elitism—I choose the word carefully—but hubris in the sense of giving more to your credibility, to your capacity than you warrant, of taking on a role that isn't necessarily yours.[53]

The events had elements of an ancient Greek tragedy set in a twentieth-century American university. After resigning, Keller went to Princeton University, where he taught in the Woodrow Wilson School. In 1990, he became a consultant on science and technology for the Council on Foreign Relations, where he ultimately held a council chair and commuted from Princeton to New York; he traveled in Latin America, Asia, and Europe.

While he was still at the council, Keller began coming back to Minnesota once a year to teach a chemical engineering course. In 1992, G. Edward Schuh, Dean of the Humphrey Institute of Public Affairs, persuaded Keller to teach about science, technology, and international affairs in the institute and asked him to return to the university full time. Keller recalled:

> We [Keller and his family] came back with a proper sense of both caution and possibility; we were coming back to a place we loved and to a huge circle of friends that we'd made, and we were now older and wiser and knew enough to hold off negative publicity and not get badly affected by it if it were to occur. I took a blood vow that I would not get involved in university politics or do anything else that might threaten the continuation of my marriage, if not my life.[54]

## Interim President Richard Sauer

Following Keller's resignation, the regents named Richard Sauer interim president. Sauer, who was forty-eight, had been vice president for agriculture, forestry, and home economics since 1983; a native of Walker, Minnesota, he had taught at St. Cloud (Minnesota) State, Michigan State, and Kansas State before coming to the university as director of the Agricultural Experiment Station in 1980. He met with the legislature immediately after assuming office, intent on restoring the university's credibility, and received a standing ovation when he was introduced at the House of Representatives. "It was incredible," he said. "It must have lasted a minute."[55] He also undertook visits to communities outside the metropolitan area; one stop was St. James, where he addressed the chamber of commerce and a high school assembly.[56] The new administration brought several changes in personnel. David Lilly, vice president for finance, and Roger Benjamin, vice president for academic affairs, left the University. The University's basic policies, however, remained unchanged. Sauer praised Keller's plans and said that he would follow them while he was interim president.[57]

Several important issues came up during Sauer's tenure. Learning that the legislature intended to cut the university's budget by the amount in the reserve fund, Sauer decided that the university should withdraw its request for new funding (technically a supplementary budget bill). He met with the House Subcommittee on Appropriations, formally rescinding the request but saying that the university needed to retain its flexible financial reserves. "I took the university's request off the table so it was no longer an issue, and they left us alone," he said. "They appreciated my openness and direct approach. I nipped it in the bud."[58]

Sauer subsequently appointed a financial review committee whose members included Lyndon Carlson and Gene Waldorf, chairs, respectively, of the House and Senate committees on university appropriations; state auditor Arne Carlson; James Noble, head of the legislative auditor's office; state finance commissioner Tom Triplett; Warren Ibele, former dean of the Graduate School; and Regent Elton Kuderer. Sauer addressed citizens' views and concerns in a number of speeches.[59] He noted that despite recent events "I was encouraged by the unmistakable sense that Minnesotans care very much about their university." Furthermore, he noted:

> The real work of the university never faltered. Classes went on. More than 10,500 students received degrees. Faculty were awarded research grants totaling $180 million. . . . Researchers developed a potential drug treatment for AIDS and a vaccine that might protect animals and humans from Lyme disease. The Minnesota Extension Service went all out to help both urban and rural Minnesotans cope with the summer's drought. Completion of a record $365 million fund-raising campaign affirmed the commitment of private donors. Faculty, regents, and administrators kept academic planning on track.[60]

Following his interim presidency, Sauer became head of the National 4-H Council, a post in which he combined his administrative abilities with his interest in agriculture. He later expressed gratitude that he once again had a private life; he was glad to be away from the pressures of heading a large university.[61]

## President Nils Hasselmo

The faculty advisory committee, headed by biochemist Victor Bloomfield, assisted the regents in the search for a new president. Although a number of candidates were suggested, the slate was soon narrowed to two contenders: Robert Stein, dean of the Law School, and Nils Hasselmo, academic vice president at the University of Arizona.[62] The final vote, as Hasselmo put it, "was not a landslide":

> It was rather contentious, although when it came out seven to five for me, then of course they converted it into a unanimous vote. Some of the peo-

ple who voted against me became some of my staunchest supporters later on, so there was not a lingering problem. The board was in one sense, I think, shell-shocked by what had happened to Ken.[63]

On January 1, 1989, Nils Hasselmo officially became president of the University of Minnesota. He said that he regarded Sauer's work as very important, because Sauer "had begun to reestablish whatever had been lost in the turmoil of [Keller's] resignation; he was beginning to clear the agenda and reconnect with the legislature." One of Sauer's symbolic changes had been the removal of Keller's controversial desk from the president's office; he replaced it with "one of those little scribe's old-fashioned desks that looked like something Cratchit in Dickens's *Christmas Carol* would sit at and write," Hasselmo said. Actually it was a secondhand bookkeeper's desk that had been used by the Dayton Company.[64] Hasselmo brought in a small desk made by his grandfather: "I thought that in Minnesota, nobody's going to get after me for having a desk made by my Swedish carpenter grandfather."

"My entire administration," Hasselmo said, "drew very, very heavily on what had gone before, partly going back to the strategic planning process of the late 1970s and the work that Peter Magrath and people like John Turner did in analyzing the university's situation." He was determined that the idea of Commitment to Focus would not die, although the word *focus* might be in ill repute: "I was asked about this when I was interviewed by the Board of Regents, and I told them that I subscribed to Commitment to Focus because I didn't want to imply that I was repudiating what I thought was a splendid idea and a splendid achievement on the part of Ken Keller. The fact that he had to leave under miserable circumstances had nothing to do with the soundness of the ideas that he had put on the table."[65]

Hasselmo was born in a village in western Sweden, six miles from the Norwegian border. His father, a schoolteacher and church organist, came from southern Sweden, his mother from Lapland. He attended high school in a nearby town of 11,000, studying mathematics and science as well as languages—English, German, French, and Latin. Before going on to the university, he served (as was usual) in the Swedish military, receiving officers' training in the Royal Signal Corps in Stockholm. During this period, he later recalled, he used to open the gate for Princess Christina and her nurse when they went for walks. The military training "took us out of our childhoods and brought us into an adult world."[66]

The Swedish equivalent of the G.I. Bill helped finance Hasselmo's higher education at Uppsala University, where he realized that his first love was linguistics: "It was the study of the Indo-European languages and their fascinating family relationships; I learned how you could study the historical development and actually make deductions concerning what historical stages of languages looked like on the basis of comparative evidence and historical trends." The French structural linguist Ferdinand de Saussure especially influenced him.[67]

Hasselmo came to the United States in 1956 to accept a scholarship from Augustana College in Rock Island, Illinois, where he would meet the woman who was to become his wife, Patricia Tillberg of Moline, Illinois. In 1959, he moved to Harvard, where he had received a scholarship and where he was eager to work with Einar Haugen, who had recently published a study titled *The Norwegian Language in America*. His first visit to Minnesota was in 1962, when he did linguistic reconnaissance work in Swedish communities—Lindstrom, Almelund, Center City, Litchfield, Dassel—for the dialect archives at Uppsala. "That's when I really fell in love with Minnesota," he said, "when I saw that marvelous grassroots culture of Minnesota."[68]

After teaching for a year at the University of Wisconsin, Hasselmo accepted a position in the Scandinavian department at Minnesota in 1965. Subsequently, he became chair of the department, associate dean and budget officer of the College of Liberal Arts, and vice president for administration and planning under President Magrath. As vice president he dealt with the Rajender consent decree as well as personnel, the university police, and intercollegiate athletics. He made his most important contributions in strategic planning. After three years (1980–83) as vice president, he left for the University of Arizona, where, as provost, he was executive officer, with twelve deans reporting to him. "I found the change of scenery, intellectual and in other respects, interesting and stimulating," Hasselmo commented. He helped transform Arizona into an outstanding research university where strategic decision making was used to foster intellectual excellence in the biological sciences, archaeology, astronomy, and physics; Arizona built excellence "one scholar at a time, giving them the opportunity to exercise intellectual leadership and literally build the department," much as Morrill and Wilson had done at Minnesota thirty years earlier. This experience was to prove useful to Hasselmo when he returned to Minnesota.[69]

One of Hasselmo's first actions as president was to hire Gordon "Gus" Donhowe as vice president for finance. Following David Lilly's departure, there had been a search for his successor, but Hasselmo was not satisfied with any of the finalists. He turned to Donhowe, who had been a member of the search committee: "Gus, I'll give you a job where you'll have twice as much to do and half the salary you now have. I want you to come and be finance vice president." Donhowe accepted. Since Hasselmo had made the appointment without a search, he appointed Donhowe on an interim basis, subsequently conducting a national search for the position.[70] Donhowe, clearly the top candidate, was ultimately confirmed through the search. He had been a vice president at Pillsbury, president of the Fairview Health System, and Minnesota finance commissioner under Governor Rudy Perpich; he had accompanied Perpich to his famous meeting with Keller and the regents. "He had technical competence but also an awful lot of political savvy," Hasselmo said. "It was just a delight to send Gus over to the legislature to talk to them."[71] It was obvious that many of the legislators agreed. Donhowe rapidly became popular with faculty members as well. Other senior appointments included Leonard Kuhi, who came from the University of California to be vice president for academic affairs, and Richard Heydinger, who continued to head institutional relations.

At the time of Keller's resignation, Governor Perpich had appointed a committee to review the financial administration of the university. Edson Spencer, a former chief executive officer of Honeywell who had been chairman of the board of the Ford Foundation and was active in a number of corporate and civic organizations, chaired the committee. Among its members were Donhowe, who was not yet a university employee, and Jean Keffeler, who was to serve as a member of the Board of Regents from 1989 to 1996 and as chair from 1993 to 1995. Keffeler recalled that service on the Spencer committee reactivated her involvement with the university; she was a 1967 graduate of the College of Liberal Arts and subsequently earned dual master's degrees in public administration and social work from the university.[72]

The Spencer committee's report was made public on November 30, 1988, the same day on which Hasselmo was appointed. Spencer praised the president-elect, saying, "We have a marvelous new president who can carry the university forward,"[73] but the report itself was (in Hasselmo's words) "pretty hard-hitting when it came to the changes in financial management that needed to be undertaken. The first time I met with Governor Perpich, he practically beat me over the head with the report. So it became my bible for infrastructure reform."[74] Hasselmo had a number of conversations with Spencer, who was "extremely critical of the management of the university but also very supportive of the university in terms of its importance to society."[75]

A second report, prepared by legislative auditors, criticized the university's management of its physical facilities. Donhowe hired Sue Markham to oversee the physical plant including space management, construction, and janitorial services. History professor Clarke Chambers reminded Hasselmo of President O. Meredith Wilson's dictum: "If you're a smart president, there's one thing you won't do, and that's touch physical facilities." Markham, Donhowe, and Hasselmo introduced major reforms and cut the facilities management budget by some $13 million. Hasselmo was gratified to see the changes, which continued under his successor, Mark G. Yudof.[76]

As part of an attempt to reestablish confidence in the university and reconnect with constituencies across the state, Hasselmo and his aides instituted what they called the "grade report," a list of problems and what had been done to deal with them. The Board of Regents heard about progress with the grade report at every meeting, and it was also used for public relations.[77] There were also changes in financial management. The central reserves were transformed into a smaller strategic investment pool, which included interest accrued through more aggressive investment of university resources. The university and its foundation both changed their investment strategy from playing it absolutely safe at minimum interest rates to a mixed strategy of taking some risks while the investments generally were quite secure.[78] One result of the new strategy—and a booming stock market—was that the endowed chairs established by the Minnesota Campaign enjoyed greater income.

In his inaugural address, delivered on October 20, 1989, President Hasselmo said that "access to excellence" would be the goal of his administration: "Ensuring that the university provides access to excellence is the most fundamental issue we face." Limited resources meant making choices. In teaching, the university should concentrate on the special kind of undergraduate education that is set in the environment of graduate and professional instruction and research. In research, the state needed to invest in the intellectual talent for scientific work, humanistic scholarship, and artistic activity: "The state needs a capability in the study of the universe and the atom, the human mind and the human body, Shakespeare and the gene, Bach and superconductivity." In public service, access to excellence meant that the university had to be a statewide resource for problem solving and provide access to all the expertise available on its campuses. "There is nothing that is more important for the state of Minnesota at this time," the president concluded.[79]

## Times of Retrenchment

The early months of 1991 were a difficult time on a number of counts. In January, there was the untimely death of finance vice president Gus Donhowe. In March, the administration presented a five-year plan to restructure programs and reallocate approximately 10 percent of the university's state funds, close to $58 million. The university had already been through extensive retrenchments, with more than $30 million in net reductions in the past twenty years and over $30 million in reallocation across units. The rationale for continued retrenchment and reallocation was that it appeared to be the only way of "improving quality within limited resources."[80] The most drastic change, closing the Waseca campus, was expected to yield $6.4 million.

The decision to close Waseca had been made by Hasselmo and Vice Presidents Gus Donhowe and Leonard Kuhi, and approved by a 10–2 vote of the Board of Regents. Ed Frederick had announced his resignation as chancellor in 1990. Keith McFarland served as deputy chancellor, followed by Thomas Lindahl, who was appointed acting chancellor. Disappointed with the candidates produced by a search for a new chancellor, Hasselmo became convinced that major changes should be considered for the campus.[81] Charles Casey, then chairman of the Board of Regents, despite his local connections—he came from the first congressional district, which included Waseca—promised to support the closing, and he persuaded some reluctant regents to join him.

Hasselmo recalled the January day in 1991 when he went to Waseca to announce the closing:

> I had to go down to the Waseca campus and announce that I was recommending to the board that it be closed. There were two thousand protesters with barricades of farm equipment that Chuck Casey and I had to walk through. Chuck Casey—bless him—went down there with me to confront those angry constituencies. Boy! That was an act of courage.
>
> [A major] reason we felt that Waseca should be closed was that it kept having enrollment problems. We gave the campus an opportunity to come forward with a plan for a viable future and, after several months of negotiations and haggling, we finally decided that it wasn't a viable proposition and that we were expending some $5 million a year in Waseca that could well be spent more effectively elsewhere.[82]

In his remarks at Waseca, Hasselmo said, "My heart tells me not to do this. But Waseca as it now stands is not the way to deliver the kinds of educational programs that we have to deliver. We have to find other ways to serve the students who are here."[83] When Chancellor Thomas Lindahl left Waseca to become dean of the College of Agriculture at the University of Wisconsin in Platteville, Nan Wilhelmson, a faculty member and administrator in academic affairs and human resources, assumed the role of acting chancellor. The final class of four hundred students graduated in June 1992. In closing the Waseca campus, the university promised to provide continuing employment for all tenured faculty members and to try to place the other faculty and staff members in suitable positions.[84] A 1994 agreement with the Bureau of Prisons transformed the campus into a minimum-security prison; at full capacity (about 1,100 inmates), it would employ 250 people and have a payroll of more than $8 million annually.

Three people held the position of vice president for institutional relations under President Nils Hasselmo. Richard Heydinger, who had held the position under Kenneth Keller, was the first. Melvin George, an old friend of Hasselmo, came to the position on a short-term basis following his retirement as president of St. Olaf College in Northfield, Minnesota. Thomas Swain, an active alumnus and retired executive vice president of the St. Paul Companies, followed George.[85]

During these years a larger number of women assumed senior positions at the university, though some of them spent a relatively short time at Minnesota. In part the result of intense national competition to hire women, these departures were often for major positions elsewhere. They suggested, however, that Minnesota needed to ensure that it offered a supportive environment for women. Delores Cross served as associate vice president for minority affairs from 1988 to 1990, when she was named president of Chicago State University. Anne Petersen was associate vice president for research and dean of the Graduate School for three years before becoming deputy director of the National Science Foundation in 1994. In 1990, Surrell Brady came to the university as general counsel from a senior position in the U.S. Department of Justice but returned to Washington, D.C., after little more than a year. Anne Hopkins was vice president for arts, sciences, and engineering from 1990 to 1995, when she was recruited to become provost and executive vice president for academic affairs at Miami University of Ohio. Marvalene Hughes served as vice president for student affairs from 1990 to 1994, when she was appointed president of California State University in Stanislaus. Patricia Mullen continued as director of EEO.

During these years, three women served as acting vice presidents. Shirley Clark, a College of Education faculty member and assistant vice president for academic affairs from 1973 to 1980, was acting vice president for academic affairs in 1988–89. She became vice chancellor of academic affairs at the University of Oregon in 1990. Cherie Perlmutter, associate vice president for health sciences, served as acting vice president for health sciences from 1989 to 1992. Carol Campbell, who was acting vice president for finance and operations from 1988 to 1989, became vice president for finance and treasurer at Carleton College in 1990. JoAnne Jackson, chief financial officer for the Academic Health Center from 1994 to 1996, became senior vice president for finance and operations in 1996; she accepted a position as vice chancellor for financial affairs for the University of Alabama system in 1998.

Ettore Infante (1991–96) and Marvin Marshak (1996–97) served as the senior vice presidents for academic affairs. Robert "Andy" Anderson (1992–93), William Brody (1994–96), and Frank Cerra filled the senior positions in the Academic Health Center. Robert Erickson was vice president for finance 1991 to 1995. C. Eugene Allen was vice provost for professional studies, and W. Phillips Shively for arts, sciences, and engineering.[86]

## Balancing Access and Excellence

Jean B. Keffeler, chair of the Board of Regents between 1993 and 1995, recalled "great financial pressure and a need to clarify strategic direction."[87] Two decisions revealed that administrators were still grappling with the perplexing question of balancing access and excellence.

In September 1993, Hasselmo proposed a new approach to organizing undergraduate education on the Twin Cities campus by creating two entities: one to enroll full-time undergraduates and one to serve part-time and nontraditional students. Hasselmo and other administrators were concerned that counting both full-time and part-time students made graduation rates look extremely low. Under the new structure, full-time and part-time students would be considered separately, which would be fairer and would improve the university's standings compared to other institutions.

Although supportive of the plan, a Minneapolis *Star Tribune* editorial stated, "If there's a dark side to the Hasselmo proposal, it lies in the potential for [the part of the university serving nontraditional students] to have second-class status."[88] Protesters demonstrated against the plan for two points of entry to the university. One student, speaking for the demonstrators, said, "We are not radicals, but concerned students who know the effects this has."[89] By the end of fall quarter, the plan was dropped. The strong public reaction showed that the issues of access and excellence were still very much alive.

Three years later, the administration suggested that a citizens' committee should consider the status of the General College; the implication was that a study might lead to closing the college. This proposal was contested by those concerned about access to the university for underprepared students, who feared the plan would have a negative impact on students of color and those needing additional academic support.

The proposal raised the possibility that the college might be replaced by a community college that could be given space on the Twin Cities campus. Under its revised mission, as a part of the Commitment to Focus plan, General College had been required to eliminate its degree programs and serve as a point of entry for students who needed to improve their study skills before they entered one of the degree-granting colleges. As a result, the General College had taken on a developmental education mission, identifying ways to improve the teaching of underprepared students.

The proposal led to an impassioned public debate on the future of the General College. Friends of the college held a demonstration on the mall, a former dean of the College of Liberal Arts, Julia Davis, wrote a letter of support for the college, and Dean David Taylor challenged the logic of the administration's proposal. Taylor called the administration plan "ill conceived, tending toward elitism, harmful to students of color, and destined to save little money."[90] A number of regents, including Wendell Anderson, William Hogan, and Hyon Kim, expressed support for the General College and its role in providing access to the university. Hasselmo felt undercut when the regents voted nine to one to stop the proposal from moving forward. Speaking for the regents, board chair Thomas Reagan said, "The current process of evaluating the General College has been flawed and is not productive. It should be stopped."[91]

In retrospect, it appears that there was a misunderstanding between the regents and the administration. Shively believed he had the support to make major changes. He recalled that Regent Jean Keffeler had told President Hasselmo, "Mr. President, we want to have bold decisions from you. Bring us your tough decisions and we will provide you air cover." Hasselmo recalled a similar statement from Reagan: "Nils we want you to bring us the tough decisions you feel you need to make." Shively believed that these words indicated support from the regents for closing a college.[92] As the vote and public debate indicated, the regents apparently had not understood what Shively and Hasselmo had in mind. They tried to get the president to withdraw the General College plan, but he refused to do so.

Hasselmo later took "full responsibility for having brought this to the regents in a way that didn't work."[93] Shively also felt that they "did a lousy job of bringing it out."[94] One complicating factor was that the plan was made public prematurely, before any of the groups that would be affected by it had seen it. To the administration, it was a sound plan, not implemented well; to the regents, it represented not only a flawed process but also an unacceptable outcome. The regents' vote ensured that the General College would survive and that the university would carry out its mission in developmental education with backing from the governing body. Dean Taylor recalled that although the situation was painful at the time, the end result was positive.[95]

## New Facilities

The Hasselmo era began a period of construction on the Twin Cities campus, much of it made possible by private funds. These new buildings were a source of particular satisfaction to the president. A gift from the Donald Gabbert family made possible a new St. Paul campus building for the veterinary medicine–affiliated Raptor Center, a unit extremely popular with the public. Architecturally the most notable was the new University Art Museum, named for collector and donor Frederick R. Weisman, which opened in 1993. Hasselmo enjoyed telling the story of how the museum was built. The University Gallery, with its collection of American art by Marsden Hartley, Alfred Mauer, Georgia O'Keeffe and other painters, and pieces from structuralist Minnesota sculptor Charles Biederman, had for years been located on the second and third floors of Northrop Auditorium, in out-of-the way, cramped quarters:

> The new museum finally came to fruition through the wonderful sustained, concerted efforts of Jerry Shepherd [former vice president for academic affairs] and Lyndel King [director of the University Gallery] and through the generosity of Frederick Weisman, who fortuitously was reconnected with the University of Minnesota, which he had attended very early in his life.[96]

Weisman began collecting contemporary art during the 1940s; by the early 1990s he had more than a thousand works. On a visit to Minneapolis (where he had been born) he checked the telephone directory and found a William Weisman and called him up to see if they were related. They were not, but the two discovered a shared interest in contemporary art. Fred Weisman was then introduced to Lyndel King, director of the University Gallery. Subsequently, President Hasselmo invited Weisman to lunch at Eastcliff. Hasselmo recalled:

> At that luncheon I asked Frederick for $5 million for the art museum. He didn't blanch and said, "I'll think about it." Then I went out to Beverly Hills to his home and we signed off on a contract that amounted to about $4.5 million. That took us over the hump when it came to the museum.[97]

Hasselmo appointed a committee chaired by Penny Winton, who played a key role in the creation of the new museum. The committee recommended Frank Gehry as the principal architect. "I was the one," Hasselmo said, "who told Frank Gehry, 'Don't build another brick lump.'" The resulting museum was like no other building in Minnesota. As Hasselmo said, "Half the people like it and half hate it, which is quite appropriate for an art museum, I think. There's no lukewarm reaction to that art museum."[98] When the museum opened in November 1993, the *New York Times* said it had "five of the most gorgeous galleries on earth."[99] On the museum's fifth anniversary, the Minneapolis *Star Tribune*'s Mary Abbe wrote, "Its cheerful aura of intellectual confidence and cutting edge design brings twenty-first-century panache to the mostly nineteenth-century landscape."[100] Some thought the building, a mass of irregular angles clad in stainless steel panels, looked like a giant bird poised to fly down the Mississippi River. It received publicity in newspapers as far away as Hong Kong.

The museum has had a major impact on the campus. Many events— receptions, dinners, seminars, concerts, lectures, dances—are held at "the Fred," as it is informally known. The museum's signal design, central location, and exhibitions and programs increased the number of visitors from 30,000 a year to the old University Gallery to more than 150,000 a year in the new facility.[101]

Another new fine arts building, the 1,600-seat Ted Mann Concert Hall— made possible through the generosity of Ted Mann—was dedicated in 1993. Like Weisman, Mann was a Minnesota native who lived on the West Coast. A performance space had been part of the original plans for the new music building, Ferguson Hall, on the West Bank, but funding was not sufficient for its construction. For several years, operas and symphony concerts continued to be staged in the cramped auditorium in Scott Hall, the former music building, or in cavernous Northrop Auditorium. Karen Wolff, director of the School of Music, made the first contact with Mann. When Hasselmo became president, negotiations with Mann were already under way:

> He had already indicated that he was going to make a commitment. Ted Mann is a person who demands absolute perfection. He used to come to the campus every three months for discussions; we would meet with Ted and go through in detail exactly what was happening. He was very receptive when we said, "We can do it this way, but it will cost another $200,000. It really is the right way to do it." Ted invariably said, "We're going to do it the right way," and he came through with additional funding"[102]

A legislative appropriation was needed to supplement Mann's contributions; Hasselmo credited Judson "Sandy" Bemis with helping to secure it. Bemis, a lifelong supporter of the Minnesota Orchestra, had become an equally strong advocate for the new performance hall for the University. "He was there literally day and night with the legislative committee, and it got to be almost a joke that Sandy just wouldn't go home," Hasselmo said. The architects, the Minneapolis firm of Hammel Green and Abrahamson, produced an elegant building with excellent acoustics. Like the Weisman Museum, it overlooks the Mississippi River, but from the opposite bank. Large lobby windows allow concertgoers to enjoy river views. University groups and a number of outside organizations, including the St. Paul Chamber Orchestra, perform in the Ted Mann Concert Hall.[103]

Major buildings were also erected for the Medical School's basic sciences. The Basic Sciences and Biomedical Engineering Building, the largest project completed during Hasselmo's term as president, replaced the zoology and botany buildings, long familiar structures at the south end of the mall. The seven-story $75 million building, designed by the architectural firm BWBR, blended neoclassical and modern design. Faculty members from interdisciplinary programs of neuroscience, immunology, structural biology, cellular and molecular biology, and biomedical engineering were the chief occupants of the new building. Contemporary science at the end of the century demanded open modern laboratories enabling many scientists with varied backgrounds and training to interact.

A new building for the School of Management was constructed with significant private support. In 1986, Curtis L. Carlson earmarked $18 million of the $25 million he gave to Campaign Minnesota in 1986 to endow faculty chairs and professorships in the School of Management. In 1993, he made a gift of $10 million to be applied toward a new building for the school, which would later be named for him.[104] The new West Bank building, adjacent to the Humphrey Institute, was designed by Ellerbe Becket architects. Architecturally it was notable for its lofty atrium and its dual orientation toward the university and downtown Minneapolis. In addition to thirty-three computer-networked classrooms, a 250-seat auditorium, spaces where students could work on joint projects, and eleven career-placement interviewing rooms, it had conference rooms and dining facilities. New technology, estimated to cost more than $10 million in all, included a financial-markets laboratory enabling students to simulate transactions.[105] By 1994, Dean David Kidwell and the school's Board of Overseers, composed primarily of Minnesota CEOs, had raised $20 million from corporate donors, including the $10 million from Carlson. The legislature had appropriated $25 million to complete funding for the new building.

Carlson lived to see the building in use and the School of Management transformed. Shortly before his death in 1999, he gave another $10 million, most of which was to be used to create an endowment for the continuing advancement of the school's excellence. His cumulative gifts of $47 million had made him the university's most generous private donor. "Just as John Sargent Pillsbury is called the Father of the University," President Yudof commented, "Curt Carlson could be called the modern father of this institution. His devotion to the university, and to all that it has meant to this state, never wavered."[106]

A new steam plant to provide heating for the Minneapolis buildings was also urgently needed. The old steam plant was in poor condition. Shortly before he died, Gus Donhowe undertook a broad-based investigation of the options. Hasselmo and Donhowe were convinced that it was necessary to have a plant that could burn coal as an alternative fuel should gas become unavailable or overpriced. After considerable debate, a plan that allowed for alternative fuels was accepted. Construction was under way during the closing years of the decade.[107]

One of the achievements of the Hasselmo administration was better management of the University's request to the legislature for funds for building projects; partly through Donhowe's influence, it was carefully defined and prioritized.[108] Another change, implemented in 1997, strengthened the administrative authority of the deans by creating a more decentralized financial administration system called Incentives for Managed Growth (IMG). A steering committee chaired by Associate Vice Presidents Robert Kvavik and Richard Pfutzenreuter was formed to assess the need for new initiatives and to recommend ways in which they might be implemented. Under IMG, funding was tied more closely to enrollment than it had been— money was moved to where the students were. This meant that funding for the College of Liberal Arts, the Institute of Technology, and the Carlson School of Management was substantially increased. Through new revenue-sharing arrangements, the colleges received more of the income generated by the university's large continuing education enrollments. Another aspect of IMG, a controversial proposal to charge departments for physical facilities according to the amount of space they occupied, was not implemented. On balance, the new arrangements seemed to be a substantial improvement.

The university moved from quarters to semesters in the fall of 1999 to conform to the practice of other institutions of higher education. This change was handled by Peter Zetterberg, director of the Office of Planning and Analysis, and by Laura Coffin Koch, a General College faculty member. "Take Five," an advising initiative, encouraged students to take five courses a semester so that they would earn enough credits to graduate in four years. The transition to semesters required a major effort on the part of faculty members, who had to redesign their courses from quarters to semesters. The transition took place smoothly, without major difficulties.

## Improving the Undergraduate Experience

Undergraduate education had been a high priority in President Keller's Commitment to Focus plan and for Hasselmo while he was academic vice president in Arizona, where he had declared the Year of the Undergraduate: "We went all out to focus on undergraduate education, excellence in undergraduate teaching, and on the way the undergraduate experience could benefit from the environment of the research university." Hasselmo made it a priority at Minnesota, too:

> At Arizona and at the University of Minnesota, undergraduate education was an Achilles heel in the efforts to achieve true institutional excellence. It's almost a paradox that, in order to be a major leading research and graduate institution, you have to have quality undergraduate education. Otherwise you get surrounded by an aura of mediocrity.[109]

Ernest L. Boyer, president of the Carnegie Foundation for the Advancement of Teaching, offered a national perspective: "Colleges and universities," he wrote, "are focusing once again on undergraduates and the quality of undergraduate education.... Today I hear more talk about the curriculum, about teaching, and about the quality of campus life than I have heard for years."[110]

Curricular reform in the College of Liberal Arts had been addressed by the Chambers report. Hasselmo asked John Howe, another member of the history department, to chair a task force that would establish liberal education requirements for students in the other colleges—an issue that virtually every major university was then studying. The committee held hearings, talked with student advisers, prepared drafts, and succeeded in gaining the University Senate's approval of what was called the Differentiated Core Curriculum.[111] In addition to completing work in their major fields, students were now expected to grapple with a number of significant interdisciplinary themes, including environmental studies, citizenship and public ethics, cultural pluralism, and international perspectives. The committee hoped that advising, especially for freshmen, would be significantly strengthened, and it advocated the creation of small freshman seminars in which students could discuss their long-term liberal education goals. All of this would cost an estimated $16 million; since funding at that level could not be provided immediately, some projects were deferred. Freshman seminars, for instance, did not become a reality for a decade.[112]

Another part of the undergraduate initiative was new entrance requirements, suggested initially in Commitment to Focus and implemented in 1991. "We worked with high schools," Hasselmo said, "so that high schools provided the kinds of courses that we said would be required: four years of English, three years of mathematics and science, two years of foreign language, and a couple of years of social studies. In 1986, 17 percent of the admitted freshmen had fulfilled those requirements. Ten years later, over 80 percent had. It was a dramatic change in the preparation of the students."[113] There was a tremendous increase in the number of applications to honors programs.

Approximately $10 million reallocated from other uses was put into the undergraduate initiative. In one of its programs, the President's Forums on Teaching, Hasselmo personally invited about eighty faculty members to listen not to outside experts, but to their own colleagues talking about teaching. Special funding was made available to help reorganize or strengthen, sometimes through the use of new instructional technology, courses taken by a large number of undergraduates.

The Undergraduate Research Opportunity Program (UROP) provided grants allowing undergraduate students to carry out research projects under the supervision of a faculty member or assist scholars with their research. The Office of Special Learning Opportunities (OSLO) created internships. The Senate mandated student evaluation of courses, and resources were provided for processing 180,000 questionnaires covering 7,500 courses by the end of 1995.[114]

The undergraduate initiative significantly improved the student experience on the Twin Cities campus. Freshman applications in 1996 were up 20 percent from three years earlier. In 1986, 23 percent of class hours were taught by full professors; in 1995, that number had risen to 40 percent. In 1986, the mean class size was 32.6 students; in 1996, it had declined to 27.7. In 1996, 1,200 students participated in one-to-one mentoring programs, up from a handful of students a decade earlier. Graduation rates improved on all campuses. The five-year graduation rate for the class of 1986 was 30 percent; the 1991 entering class had a 41 percent rate.[115]

Residential life on the Twin Cities campus also changed considerably during the 1990s. Although only slightly more than half of the entering freshmen in 1987 lived in residence halls, 70 percent chose to do so in 1995. President Hasselmo noted that during the 1990s, the university built the first new residence halls in a quarter of a century:

> One was directly sponsored by the University: Roy Wilkins Hall, which is a beautiful dormitory over by Dinkytown [an East Bank business area near campus]. Then we had the good fortune of having a relationship with Jim Cargill, a businessman who has taken a keen interest in providing good residential facilities at the university. He built three privately financed, top-notch residential facilities in connection with the general residential complex down where Frontier and the other older halls are. That has made it possible for us to go from less than 50 percent of the incoming freshmen to over 70 percent of the incoming freshmen living on campus.[116]

Residential colleges, where students with shared academic interests lived and studied, had been under consideration since the 1980s and had been advocated by John Wallace, a philosophy faculty member with a special interest in undergraduate education. Hasselmo saw them as part of the undergraduate initiative. It was largely the enthusiasm of Marvin Marshak that brought these dreams to fruition. A number of Midwestern universities had established residential colleges following World War II; one of the most successful was the International College at Northwestern.

Among those who worked with Marshak to bring the Residential College Program into existence were Vice Provost Anne Hopkins, her assistant, Linda

Ellinger, and Professor Gayle Graham Yates of American studies. The program began in 1994 with 94 students housed in Territorial Hall; by 1998 it was serving 150 students in Territorial and 170 in Argyle House, one of the new dormitories. In addition to Yates and Marshak, faculty members from other fields were becoming involved.[117] There were weekly dinners with students and faculty, a program of weekly seminars in which faculty members and advanced students talked about their work, trips to museums and theater productions, and a party at Marshak's home (an event that became something of an institution).

Additional residential options, called Living Learning Communities, followed: the freshman Biology House program in Frontier Hall; special housing for honors students in Middlebrook Hall; the St. Paul Honors Housing community in Bailey Hall; the First-Year Experience Program offered in Frontier, Territorial, Sanford, and Bailey Halls. All of these programs offered students opportunities to meet socially and work with faculty members and students with similar interests. In fall 1999, a global studies house, a German house, and a Spanish house were added.[118]

Fraternities and sororities continued to provide a sense of community for students. The total number of fraternity and sorority members on the Twin Cities campus was nearly 4,000 in 1984, reached a low of just over 1,000 in 1994, and rose to over 1,400 in 1997.[119] During the late 1990s, there were twelve active sororities (down from a high of twenty-seven) and twenty-two fraternities, most of them located on or near "fraternity row" on the Minneapolis campus. There were also six houses on Cleveland Avenue adjacent to the campus in St. Paul. Although a number of sororities had abandoned their active chapters at Minnesota, several maintained alumnae groups. Some fraternities had been reactivated after a period of dormancy—Alpha Tau Omega was reestablished in 1998 after a three-year hiatus.[120]

In addition to operating the residence halls, the Office of Housing and Residential Life managed the campus rental properties at Pillsbury Court, the Como Student Community, and the Commonwealth Terrace Cooperative and maintained a list of off-campus housing and attempted to monitor its quality.

A 1991 study of the employment experiences of undergraduates on the Twin Cities campus[121] found that "undergraduates [were] heavily involved in paid work while attending the university: 83.3 percent worked during the academic year, and the average student spent 17.9 hours a week in paid employment. Most students who worked were employed outside the university, but just over a quarter of them, 27 percent, had campus jobs."[122] National statistics confirm that students at Minnesota were more likely to work than those at many comparable institutions. In 1997, the percentage of freshmen who held jobs while attending the University of Minnesota was 61 percent, compared to 49 percent at the University of Washington and only 23 percent at the University of Texas in Austin.[123]

## Maintaining Nationally Ranked Graduate Programs

Fifteen University of Minnesota graduate programs ranked among the National Research Council's top twenty in 1993. Eight of the programs (chemical engineering, mechanical engineering, aerospace engineering, civil engineering, mathematics, materials science, biomedical engineering, and electrical engineering) were in the Institute of Technology. Six programs (geography, psychology, economics, German, political science, and statistics) were in the College of Liberal Arts, and one (ecology, evolution, and behavior) was in the College of Biological Sciences. The rankings, based on a survey of faculty members and administrators, measured perceptions of the quality of the faculty in major graduate programs in the United States.[124]

Although its rankings were the most prestigious, the National Research Council (NRC) did not measure programs in professional schools in such fields as agriculture, education, health sciences, and law, and in fields such as American studies and speech communication, so that those noted here represent only a partial picture of nationally ranked Minnesota programs. Taken as a sampling of research at the university, these profiles illustrate varied approaches to building and leading programs and departments, show the rich variety of disciplines at the university, and document the ways in which research is put to use. Finally, these brief accounts suggest that, in addition to research, these outstanding departments were concerned about teaching at both the graduate and undergraduate levels; a number of them also sponsored outreach initiatives.

### Chemical Engineering and Materials Science

Chemical engineering was ranked first among all departments in the country by the National Research Council in 1982 and retained that ranking in 1993. Neal Amundson, known as "Chief," headed the department for a quarter century, from 1949 to 1974, and was the primary architect of the department's early success. He hired key faculty members including Rutherford Aris, Arnold G. Frederickson, L. E. Scriven, John S. Dahler, H. Ted

Davis, Kenneth H. Keller, and Lanny Schmidt. Like Amundson before them, three members of the faculty (Aris, Scriven, and Davis) were elected to the National Academy of Engineering and became Regents Professors. Schmidt was elected to the National Academy of Engineering. Reaction engineering, transport phenomena, fluid mechanics, and biomedical and biochemical engineering were areas of active research. Teaching remained a significant priority, encouraged by the practice begun under Amundson of undergraduate classes being taught by teams of senior and junior faculty sharing general lectures and small recitation sections. A student who was interviewed by an external review team in 1994 reported that "I never found a professor outside the department as good as professors inside it."[125]

After Amundson's twenty-five years as head of the department, Rutherford "Gus" Aris succeeded him in 1974 and held the position for four years.[126] Aris was followed by Kenneth Keller, who served as head for two years before he was appointed vice president for academic affairs in 1980; he was president of the university from 1985 to 1988. H. Ted Davis was department head from 1980 to 1995; soon thereafter, he became dean of the Institute of Technology. In 1995, Matthew Tirrell, another member of the National Academy of Engineering, became head, serving until 1999, when he accepted the position of dean of the College of Engineering at the University of California at Santa Barbara. Frank Bates, who came to the University of Minnesota from Bell Laboratories in 1989, became head in 1999.

At President Hasselmo's request, Ted Davis summarized what he saw as the key elements in the department's strengths: "hiring, mentoring, and retaining an intellectually diverse, first-class faculty, inculcating them with a spirit of congeniality, stimulating their intellectual exchange and collaboration, and engendering in them the belief that teaching and research are essential pieces of the same cloth."[127] Faculty member William Gerberich was philosophical about losing department heads to administrative positions, noting that a strong department does not want to hold back faculty members from significant opportunities and that changes create opportunities to bring in new faculty members who are drawn to the department by its strong reputation.[128]

In 1971, when the university closed its School of Mines and Metallurgy, faculty members with research interests in physical metallurgy joined the Department of Chemical Engineering, which got a new name: the Department of Chemical Engineering and Materials Science.[129] Materials science was ranked seventeenth in 1993. Among the research emphases were fracture mechanics, the study of reliability in materials, and, subsequently, thin films, a field of research that was to prove vital in a number of industrial applications, including the design of semiconductors and computer chips.

In 1988, the National Science Foundation provided funding to create the Center for Interfacial Engineering. Faculty members from chemical engineering and materials science, as well as from chemistry, played a role in developing the new center, which was headed by faculty member Fennell Evans. With an emphasis on coatings and surfaces, surfactants, polymers, thin films, and nonstructured and biomaterials, the center linked university faculty members with more than a hundred industrial fellows sent by more than sixty member companies.

John Weaver, who came to the department in 1982, initiated research in microelectronics. Understanding the structure and properties of metal and semiconductors was of central importance to the computer industry, particularly in the design of computer chips. In 1997, Weaver was named scientist of the year by *Research and Development* magazine; in 2000, he was named head of the Department of Materials Science at the University of Illinois. The addition of James Chelikowsky in 1988 and Christopher Palmstrøm, Daniel Frisbie, and Robert Cook in the 1990s expanded the department's effort in this area.

Chemical engineering and materials science continued its strong presence in research on polymeric materials, which had begun with the hiring of Christopher Macosko in 1971. When Matthew Tirrell, Frank Bates, and Timothy Lodge became a part of the department, a highly regarded interdisciplinary research group was formed to explore how variations in polymer synthesis and processing influenced hardness, elasticity, adhesion, and other material characteristics, producing information crucial to the production of a wide range of products. Michael Ward, who came from Dupont in 1991, brought expertise in organic crystal engineering, thus expanding the work of the department in the new area of "soft" materials. Robert Tranquillo, a researcher in artificial tissue, was hired in 1988.

In 1998, the National Science Foundation funded the new Materials Science Research Center, spearheaded by Professors Bates and Ward, for the study of polymers, artificial tissue, magnetic materials, and porous materials. Research in designer polymers explored many applications, including materials capable of delivering minute quantities of therapeutic drugs to specific parts of the body, thereby eliminating the unwanted side effects that sometimes occur when dosage is not precisely targeted. There was promise, also, that research in tissue engineering might eventually provide scientists with tools to create replacement tissue for burn victims and diseased organs. Research in magnetic materials, a bridge between the materials science program and other departments in the Institute of Technology, focused on novel structures important to hard disk technology and sensors.[130]

## Mechanical Engineering

Mechanical engineering was ranked eighth in the country by the National Research Council in 1995. It had become a department more than a century earlier, in 1889, and a bachelor's degree in the field had been offered as early as 1878. Early courses included Railway Design and Locomotive Construction.

The heat transfer laboratory rose to prominence when Ernst Eckert (later a Regents Professor) came to the department in 1951. He was joined in 1959 by Ephraim M. Sparrow and in 1961 by Richard J. Goldstein (later a Regents Professor). These three faculty members were elected to the National Academy of Engineering. For decades this laboratory was recognized as the world's preeminent center for heat transfer research. Warren Ibele was for many years a key figure in the field of thermodynamics, and heat transfer and gas property research; he was dean of the Graduate School from 1975 to 1983. The department's strength in heat transfer spawned several other prominent activities. Emil Pfender, who joined the department in 1964, founded the internationally recognized High Temperature and Plasma Technology Laboratory. In the 1950s, Kenneth T. Whitby established the Particle Technology Laboratory, also recognized internationally for its wide-ranging research. At the end of the century, this laboratory housed the activities of six faculty members; Regents Professor Benjamin Liu, also a member of the National Academy of Engineering, served as director of the laboratory for several decades and was known for his wisdom and leadership.

There are a number of highlights in mechanical engineering's past. James J. Ryan, informally known as "Crash" Ryan, became renowned as an automobile crash safety advocate and as inventor of the "black box" airplane flight recorder. He chaired the design division until his retirement in 1963. Perry Blackshear's pioneering research on blood cell fragility and artificial organs gained wide recognition. Thomas Murphy joined the department in 1946 to lead the engines research group, remaining one of the department's most beloved teachers until his death in 1994. Subbiah Ramalingam became the department's eighth member of the National Academy of Engineering in 1999, in recognition of his exceptional research on materials processing. Professor Edward Fletcher's innovative work in the use of solar energy led to a new field that remains an active area of research internationally.

The establishment of laboratories in which a number of faculty members with common interests conducted research was a key element in the success of the mechanical engineering department. It was also noteworthy that many of the most prominent faculty members continued to remain highly active as researchers and teachers well past the usual retirement age, following the example of Professor Eckert, who continued to publish at age ninety-five. Teaching was not sacrificed by this commitment to excellent research: at the end of the century, eight faculty members had won the Horace T. Morse–University of Minnesota Alumni Association Award for Outstanding Contributions to Undergraduate Education.[131]

## Aerospace Engineering and Mechanics

The early history of the Department of Aerospace Engineering and Mechanics laid the foundation for its strengths in research and teaching. It was ranked twelfth by the National Research Council in 1995. In 1929, two years after Charles Lindbergh flew across the Atlantic, Dean Ora M. Leland invited John D. Akerman, chief engineer at the Minneapolis-based Mohawk Aircraft Company, to form a new department at the university. Akerman was nationally recognized in the 1930s for his experiments with the tailless airplane, an aircraft that had an impact on the development of the stealth bomber in the 1980s. Another early faculty member, Jean Piccard, and his wife, Jeannette Piccard, had already earned international reputations in stratospheric ballooning when they came to the university in 1936. One of Jean Piccard's first projects at the university was to construct and launch from Memorial Stadium an unmanned hydrogen-filled transparent cellophane balloon for ascents ten to fourteen miles into the stratosphere. Jeannette Piccard, an active partner to her husband, became "the first licensed female balloonist and the first woman to ascend to the stratosphere."[132] In 1998, both Piccards were elected posthumously to the International Space Hall of Fame in Alamogordo, New Mexico.

The Rosemount Aeronautical Lab was established in 1946 as the department's primary research facility and for twenty years provided wind tunnel facilities for important research in aerodynamics, including hypersonics. One of the department's alumni, Donald "Deke" Slayton, was among the original seven *Mercury* astronauts.[133]

The Department of Aeronautical Engineering and the Department of Mechanics of Materials were merged in 1958 to form the Department of Aerospace Engineering and Mechanics. Benjamin Lazan, the first head of the combined departments, served until his death in 1965. From 1966 to

1992, the department was chaired by Patarasp "Pat" Sethna, who held a doctorate from Michigan and had worked as a senior engineer at the Bendix Aviation Laboratories in Detroit. The faculty included Regents Professor Daniel Joseph, a member of the National Academy of Sciences; four others were in the National Academy of Engineering. Sethna was followed by William Garrard, who encouraged the growth of experimentally and computationally based research. Fluid mechanics, control of aerospace vehicles, and mechanics of materials were strengths of the department.

The department emphasized fundamentals in both its undergraduate and its graduate programs. Students were trained in the engineering sciences and their application to aerospace vehicles, including aircraft, spacecraft, and launch vehicles. The curriculum included many unique topics such as wing theory, hypersonics, flight mechanics, dynamics and control of aerospace vehicles, spacecraft dynamics and controls, and the design of aerospace vehicles. Small in number of faculty, but with a large research program, aeronautical engineering and mechanics had "collegial relations among faculty and staff, high-quality research and teaching programs, and cross-disciplinary research efforts."[134]

## Civil Engineering

The National Research Council ranked civil engineering thirteenth among its peers. There had been a four-year degree program in civil engineering since 1888, with courses offered even earlier. Civil engineering became a department in 1910, bringing together structural engineering, road and sanitary engineering, and railway engineering. The St. Anthony Falls Hydraulic Laboratory opened in 1938, taking advantage of the falls for hydraulic research. The School of Mines, established in 1897, operated until 1970. The Department of Civil Engineering and Hydraulics (as it was then called) merged in 1970 with part of the former School of Mineral and Metallurgical Engineering to form the Department of Civil and Mineral Engineering, which administered, in addition to the hydraulic laboratory, the Mineral Resources Research Center.[135]

The civil engineering program was advanced by completion of the Civil Engineering Building in 1983; the department now had its own classrooms, offices, and research laboratories, including one of the country's best structural engineering laboratories. The new facility, designed by BRW Architects with the active involvement of department head Charles Fairhurst, was constructed almost entirely underground; it was recognized nationally as the Outstanding Civil Engineering Achievement of 1983. Among the features of the facility were solar lighting, earth sheltering, mined spaces over one hundred feet below grade, beamed sunlight, and a groundwater cooling system. Another benefit of the research and laboratory spaces was enhanced collaboration among faculty members: the new building brought together faculty members whose offices and laboratories had previously been located in several different buildings.[136]

A name change to Department of Civil Engineering occurred in 1994. Graduate programs included environmental engineering, geomechanics engineering, structural engineering, transportation engineering, and water resources engineering. Research contributions of the faculty included Charles Fairhurst's forty-year role in helping to introduce engineering science to the field of rock mechanics (drilling, mining, tunneling), Theodore Galambos's work on structural reliability, and Heinz Stefan's exploration of the impact of global warming on water quality. Galambos and Fairhurst were members of the National Academy of Engineering. In 1997, Catherine W. French, a structural engineer, became one of the first women to become a full professor in an Institute of Technology engineering department. Named associate head of the department in 1997, French researched structural responses to earthquakes and the application of high-strength materials to bridge girder systems. Steven L. Crouch, appointed associate dean of the Institute of Technology in 1997, was head of civil engineering from 1993 through 1997 and was instrumental in developing the department. His research, drawing on digital technology, related to the application of mathematical methods in areas such as pavement hydraulics, fracturing, blasting, and rock bursting in deep underground mines. Department head John Gulliver's research focused on the spreading of chemicals through the environment and their eventual impact on it.[137]

## Mathematics

The School of Mathematics, ranked fourteenth by the National Research Council, had been created in 1963, when two strong mathematics departments came together. The department in the Institute of Technology was led by Stefan Warschawski, who was recruited by Dean Athelstan Spilhaus. The College of Liberal Arts department was chaired by Robert Cameron. After the merger, the school traditionally held a preeminent position in analysis and applied mathematics.

The School of Mathematics faculty, notably Hans Weinberger and Willard Miller, were instrumental in establishing at Minnesota one of two national institutes devoted to the study of mathematics, the Institute for

Mathematics and Its Applications (IMA). Its founding director was Hans Weinberger, who was succeeded by Avner Friedman, a member of the National Academy of Sciences. At the end of the century, its director was Willard Miller. Mathematics was also recognized for research strengths in algebraic geometry, number theory, combinatorics, probability theory, and differential geometry.

The department head in 2000, Naresh Jain, a specialist in probability theory who joined the department in the 1960s, noted the key roles played by several retired faculty members, including Regents Professors James Serrin and Lawrence Markus and the Distinguished Institute of Technology Professor Hans Weinberger. He pointed out the major role played by Regents Professor Avner Friedman in the development of the IMA, in the establishment of the Minnesota Center for Industrial Mathematics, and in bringing new ideas to the applied mathematics program. Jain also cited the contributions of Nicolai Krylov, an eminent analyst and probabilist, holder of the Samuel G. Ordway Chair in Mathematics. Vladimir Sverak, a highly regarded applied mathematician, was named Distinguished McKnight University Professor in 2000. Jain observed that, in addition to its research and graduate and undergraduate teaching accomplishments, the department was proud of its longtime sponsorship of the University of Minnesota Talented Youth Mathematics Program, which offered advanced mathematics instruction to high school students.[138]

## Electrical Engineering

Electrical engineering, ranked eighteenth in 1993, had been among the university's strongest departments for many years, dating from the days of Henry Hartig and William G. Shepherd. It was renamed in 1998, becoming the Department of Electrical and Computer Engineering, reflecting a new degree in computer engineering. Mostafa Kaveh, head of the department since 1990, noted that Robert Collins, William Peria, and E. Bruce Lee had been important leaders in the department. Shepherd and Marshall Nathan were National Academy of Engineering members; Lee was elected an international member of the Polish Academy of Sciences.

Among the areas of specialization were biomedical engineering leading to products such as pacemakers, X-ray and ultrasound scanners; control systems used in computer disk drives, aircraft, space vehicles, and industrial robots; telecommunications; and signal processing for products such as cellular phones and speech recognizers. Electrical energy systems, another of the electrical engineering fields, related to the functioning of power stations and supplies, electric vehicles, and automotive electronics. Optics and magnetics had an impact on fiber-optic communications and magnetic and compact disc storage systems. Microelectronics and materials created products such as high-speed microchips and flat panel displays. Computer engineering, the department's second specialization, offered research and course work in computer networks leading to network switches, communication protocols, and network software; computer-aided design helping to design, simulate, and test complex digital and analog systems; and computer architecture and software leading to new microprocessor architectures, distributed computer systems, and operating systems. Kaveh noted that "electrical engineering is everywhere; its technologies define modern life."[139]

In addition to its reputation for research, the department had a major impact on Minnesota's economy: more than 350 high-technology companies had been founded by its graduates. Two of its best-known graduates were Seymour Cray (1949), a national leader in supercomputing and founder of Cray Research Inc., and Earl Bakken (1948), who founded the pacemaker/medical devices company Medtronic. Approximately 75 percent of the department's graduates remained in Minnesota after they received their degrees.[140]

## Biomedical Engineering

Biomedical engineering was ranked seventeenth in the 1993 National Research Council rankings. The university established a Ph.D. program in biomedical engineering in 1972 and an M.S. program in 1984, which contributed significantly to the growing medical device industry in the Twin Cities, known as Medical Alley. The graduate program gained national ranking during the 1980s, spearheaded by the multidisciplinary research of engineering professors Perry Blackshear and Kenneth Keller, and surgery professor Gene Bernstein, who collaborated on a number of projects related to heart replacement devices, other artificial internal organs, and blood-materials interactions more generally.

The Center for Biomedical Engineering, designed to increase collaborations between university scientists in medicine and those in engineering, was established in 1989 with a gift from the Medtronic Foundation and a legislative appropriation. Six years later, significant support from the Twin Cities medical technology community enabled the university to create the Biomedical Engineering Institute, linking education and research programs of the Institute of Technology and the Medical School. Faculty and graduate student researchers were involved in innovative uses of peptides, new approaches to characterizing and manipulating cell adhesion, development of miniature surgical instruments, and cardiovascular tissue engineering. In 2000, biomedical engineering was reorganized. A new undergraduate major in biomedical engineering joined the existing graduate offerings, and these degree programs formed a new department, biomedical engineering, in the Institute of Technology. The Biomedical Institute (involved in research and technology transfer) became part of the Medical School.

## Ecology, Evolution, and Behavior

Ecology, evolution, and behavior—a part of the College of Biological Science—was ranked fifteenth by the National Research Council. It had been formed as the Department of Ecology and Behavioral Biology in 1967. The first department head was Alan Brook, who was succeeded by Margaret Davis, head from 1967 to 1980. She was followed by Edward Cushing (1980–1986), Franklin H. Barnwell (1986–1993), Patrice A. Morrow (1994–1998), and Robert W. Sterner, who became head in 1998. The department was originally housed in the Bell Museum, moved to the bioscience complex in St. Paul in 1973, moved to the Zoology Building in Minneapolis in 1976, and finally moved to a new building in St. Paul in 1993. The department benefited from its interdisciplinary position and also from strengths in agriculture, natural resources, health sciences, and related biological fields.

Two faculty members, Regents Professors Margaret Davis and Eville Gorham, shared the distinction of election to the National Academy of Sciences. Davis's research was on paleoecology, the ecology of ancient organisms and plant forms; Gorham's was on the ecology of northern peatlands and their likely response to global warming and on the impact of acid rain on lakes and streams. David Tilman was internationally known for his research conducted at the Cedar Creek Natural History Area on the impact of biodiversity on grassland productivity and resistance to invasion. Distinguished McKnight Professors Craig Packer and Anne Pusey were recognized internationally for their work in animal behavior—Packer for studies of lions in Africa and Pusey for her work on chimpanzees. Evolutionary biologist James Curtsinger made significant contributions to the biology of aging, conducting studies using fruit flies as a model population. Margaret Davis offered a faculty perspective on the benefits of interdisciplinary contacts throughout the university: "You can find a course in almost any subject you think your students should be exposed to. I keep discovering new people and new programs and new laboratories and new assets, so my scientific horizon keeps widening as I learn more from all of these people."[141]

## Geography

Founded in 1925, Minnesota's Department of Geography was the third oldest in the country. Until World War II, the faculty was small and the intellectual emphasis was on economic and human geography. The appointment of John Borchert in 1949 marked the transition to the modern department. He was soon joined by John Webb and Fred Lukermann.[142] Dwight Brown, who came in the 1960s, described the department's growth:

> From 1954 to 1966, the geography department began to assemble a faculty with an interest in regional geography, included Philip Porter, Cotton Mather, Ward Barrett, Mei-Ling Hsu, Russell Adams, and John Rice, who all taught regional geography courses. That focus continued through the end of the century as one of the major areas of both teaching and research, despite the almost complete demise of regional geography in other major research university programs. The flavor of regional geography has changed throughout the years, with an increasing focus on development issues in Asia, Africa, and South America. To varying degrees, these same faculty members also sustained the curricular offerings in physical geography and provided the initial offerings of statistical methods applied to geographical analysis and cartography.[143]

The department continued to grow and chose faculty wisely. Those who came between 1966 and 1975 included Brown, Richard Skaggs, Roderick Squires, and Philip Gersmehl, who studied the physical environment and human-environment interactions John Fraser Hart and John Adams specialized in urban and regional geography; and Yi-Fu Tuan, in human geography.[144] Later appointments included scholars in economic geography (Eric Sheppard), population studies (Helga Leitner), medical geography (Connie Weil), urban studies (Judith Martin), and cartography (Robert McMaster). At all times, students were a vital part of the intellectual history of the department; they too brought varied interests and backgrounds. The demand for specialists in physical geography, including global environmental change, remained high. More than 60 percent of the Minnesota Ph.D.'s in this field went on to academic positions in doctoral-granting institutions; those in other areas more often found alternative employment. Interest in urban geography peaked in the 1970s; emphasis then shifted to quantitatively trained specialists in geographic information systems. The study of human and economic geography was influenced by the interest in postmodernism, Marxism, political ecology, and social justice common to many liberal arts disciplines.

Major research projects within the department included regional studies—the Minnesota Highway Research Project, the Lakeshore Development Study, the Minnesota State Land Use Project, and the application of remote sensing to land information systems in Minnesota—and international studies like the *South Asian Historical Atlas* produced under the direction of Joseph Schwartzberg and the interdisciplinary Water Resources Research Center directed by Dwight Brown. The ARGUS (Activities and Readings in Geography of the United States) program produced curricular materials, available on CD-ROM, for use in Russia and Japan; its emphasis on visual materials enabled students to link images to maps and written analysis. The Center for Urban and Regional Affairs (CURA), established in 1968 as a service initiative, became, as will be noted in the next chapter, one of the university's most respected outreach units, carrying out hundreds of university-based research projects each year. When CURA was founded, its mission to connect university-based research to community needs was influenced by the dramatic social changes of the late 1960s. Geographers Fred Lukermann and John Borchert established CURA in part to help address the "escalating problems of America's urban crisis."[145]

## Psychology

The Department of Psychology was founded in 1919 by Richard M. Elliott. Then only thirty-two years old, Elliott held a doctorate from Harvard and had taught briefly at Yale. Kenneth MacCorquodale, a later department chairman, described him in a talk given to new graduate students in 1975:

> Mr. Elliott came here in 1919. He remained as chairman for thirty-two years [until 1951], and during that time he left an imprint, gave the department a velocity, an impetus, and a definition that characterizes us still. . . . First of all, he was a patrician gentleman, a very proud man, and he was quite formal in his dealings and relations with other people. He was invariably courteous, including sometimes [to] people who were not very courteous to him. He was invariably kind. I never heard him make a harsh judgment about another person. . . . He had a good head—very bright, well educated, and extremely well read. He was not a stuffed shirt—he could begin to sound like that, I suppose. I have seen him absolutely infuriated but I never saw him lose his temper—that is a very desirable thing to be able to do.

(It's absolutely devastating to people one is dealing with if they have aroused his fury.) He was also extremely stubborn.[146]

One of Elliott's early decisions was that psychology should be regarded as a natural science department, which meant that it was better positioned to receive funding: "Everybody knows that natural science departments are more expensive to run than departments that just talk; they have to have laboratories." Then he demanded a separate building for the department, and he got it, not a new building but one previously used by the Medical School pathology department. In 1968, it was named for Elliott, who attended the ceremony. "It was a marvelous occasion," MacCorquodale recalled. "We expected a wispy old man to show up and sit down and look around. Far from it; when he was introduced, he sprang up and gave a long speech full of vigorous ideas, and very fresh." That building was demolished in 1969, by coincidence in the same week that Elliott died (he said it should have been torn down long before), and replaced by a "flossy, elegant, new building, so good, so functional," built largely through the efforts of John G. Darley, then department chair.

Elliott also was responsible for hiring behaviorist B. F. Skinner. When Skinner applied for a position in the department, the faculty voted not to employ him, but Elliott went to the dean and (again according to MacCorquodale) told him, "My department says don't hire this man and my department is wrong." Skinner, who came in 1936 and left in 1945, was responsible for teaching some of the people who later made the department great, including MacCorquodale and Paul Meehl, both later chairs. He also published his seminal book, *Behavor of Organisms,* before he left Minnesota to become chairman at Indiana.

For many years the Minnesota department was almost alone nationally in its emphasis on genetic factors in behavior. At a time when most American social scientists believed strongly in environmental influences, Donald Paterson was emphasizing hereditary factors in general intelligence and other basic capacities, such as mechanical ability. Studies of identical twins reared apart, conducted by Thomas Bouchard and his colleagues, yielded remarkable confirmation of Paterson's views. Several of Paterson's students, like Elliott's, stayed on to become prominent members of the department; these included Darley, Ralph Berdie, and Lloyd Lofquist.

The department also became known for the Minnesota Multiphasic Personality Inventory, or MMPI, developed by Starke R. Hathaway, a clinical psychologist, and J. C. McKinley, head of medicine, and published in 1942.

This soon became the most widely used and best validated personality assessment device in the country and still is the most widely used personality inventory in the world. The committee responsible for revising the test in 1989 included psychology faculty members James N. Butcher and Auke Tellegen. Several other personality tests were developed in later years, including Tellegen's Multidimensional Personality Questionnaire. A departmental self-study written in 1994 concluded that "the dominant impression is one of comparable growth and development in both the 'basic' and 'applied' areas from the very beginning. We think there has been an unusual amount of cross-fertilization between these two broad areas as their development has progressed." The success of this approach was demonstrated by the fact that in rankings made as early as 1956, "Minnesota shot up to the top, where it has remained ever since." Although Elliott ran the department for thirty-two years, his successors tended to have short terms in office. They included Meehl, Kenneth Clark, MacCorquodale, Darley, Lofquist, Bouchard, Gail Peterson, Mark Snyder, Eugene Borgida, and Matthew McGue. Along with Elliot, Regents Professor Paul Meehl was a major leader in developing the department. Other key faculty members included Regents Professor Ellen Berscheid, René Dawis, Marvin Dunnette, James Jenkins, and Norman Garmezy. William G. Iacono and Gordon E. Legge were named Distinguished McKnight Professors in 1999.

## *Economics*

The economics department, ranked tenth in 1995, was described by Craig Swan, who served as chair from 1992 to 1997:

> The modern history of the Department of Economics at Minnesota is closely linked to Walter Heller and Leonid Hurwicz. Heller came to Minnesota in 1946. He was successful in attracting Hurwicz in 1951. Although they worked in very different areas of economics and in very different ways, they had great respect for each other, set a tone of collegiality for the department, and collaborated to build one of the nation's leading departments.
>
> Heller's work was in the area of public finance and public economics. He is best known for his role as chairman of President Kennedy's Council of Economic Advisers. After he returned to Minnesota, he continued to be a leading participant in public debates over economic policy until his untimely death in 1987.
>
> Hurwicz's work on the foundations of choice theory and welfare theory, along with his seminal work in the area of economic mechanism theory,

have made him one of the nation's most distinguished economic theorists, as recognized by his election as president of the Econometric Society, the premier scientific society in the discipline, his selection as a distinguished fellow of the American Economic Association, his membership in the National Academy of Sciences, five honorary degrees, and his receipt of the National Medal of Science from President George Bush in 1990. He was named a Regents Professor in 1969, at a time when he was being heavily recruited by Harvard.[147]

Other members of the department who became Regents Professors between 1965, when the honor was established, and 2000 were Walter W. Heller, John S. Chipman, Edward C. Prescott, and, from agricultural and applied economics, Vernon W. Ruttan. Mathematical economics and econometrics were new and exciting aspects of the field in the 1950s. Developed chiefly at the University of Chicago and then at Yale, they expanded greatly with the coming of computers, though, as Edward Foster said, "the mathematical modeling side doesn't really require much in the way of computers. It's a pencil and paper business."[148] Foster, who joined the faculty in 1961, had worked on business cycle theory, a subject that went out of fashion but was later revived. The chief project of the economics department in those days was the Upper Midwest Economic Survey, financed in part by the Ford Foundation and directed by James Henderson.

Economics was a part of the business school in 1950; it was organized as a separate department in 1957 and in 1962 left the business school to join the College of Liberal Arts. Some observers believed that Walter Heller's hand lay behind this move, although he was in Washington, D.C., at the time, and that the decision was influenced by the fact that top-ranked economics departments were most frequently found in colleges of arts and sciences or liberal arts. Many of the faculty members hired by Heller and Hurwicz had long and distinguished careers at Minnesota. They included Ozwald Brownlee, Edward Coen, John Chipman, John Kareken, James Henderson, Herbert Mohring, Anne Krueger, N. James Simler, and Edward Foster. Craig Swan commented on approaches to adding faculty:

> The department has never attempted to cover the waterfront in terms of having individuals in every subfield. Job descriptions are not written for specific fields but rather to find the very best people regardless of field. The result has been to build a series of overlapping concentrations of strength. I would characterize the department as looking for strength in four broad areas: economic theory, macro- and monetary economics, econometrics,

and applied microeconomics. If one were to pull out a fifth area of strength it would be international economics–economic growth–economic development, although one could also situate much of this work within the original four areas.[149]

Tom Sargent, Neil Wallace, and Edward Prescott made Minnesota a leading participant in the "rational expectations" revolution in macroeconomics during the late 1970s and 1980s. Jim Simler served as chair for nearly a quarter of a century. His effective leadership enabled the department to sustain the position of national prominence achieved by Heller and Hurwicz. Department meetings were called only for urgent issues, such as hirings; other matters were generally left to Simler, Coen (a longtime director of undergraduate studies) and the director of graduate studies. Between 1957 and 1997, the department awarded 482 Ph.D. degrees—about one-tenth of all doctorates granted by College of Liberal Arts departments.

## German

German was ranked eleventh by the National Research Council. Dating back to 1867, students could take German, Latin, Greek, and French to meet graduation requirements. Master's degrees were awarded in 1910, and the first Ph.D. in 1919. Notable faculty members associated with the department were Konstantin Reichardt and Frederick Klaeber, although Klaeber was actually in the English department. During World War II, the department was heavily involved in teaching in the Army Specialized Training Program, preparing GIs for European assignments; the department offered a summer immersion program, Deutsches Haus. A sequel to that program was initiated in 1999, creating a German-speaking section of Sanford Hall, where students could speak German informally outside the classroom.

With a growing international interest and more readily available federal funding, the department became recognized for innovative seminars in East German literature, feminist literary theory, literature and film, cultural studies, and lexicography. In 1998, the department, with peers at Wisconsin, established the Center for German and European Studies, a Center of Excellence sponsored by the German Academic Exchange. The center's mandate was the formation of the next generation of scholars and scholarship related to Germany and Europe. The center consisted of two sites, one at the University of Minnesota, Twin Cities, the other at the University of Wisconsin, Madison. Graduate courses and symposia were offered jointly by faculty members from both institutions; students took them either in person or through distance education technologies. A broad and active faculty, among them Jack Zipes, Ruth-Ellen Joeres, Anatoly Liberman, Frank Hirschbach, Evelyn Firchow, Gerhard Weiss, and James Parente, contributed to the national ranking of the department.[150]

## Political Science

Political science was ranked thirteenth by the National Research Council in 1993. William Anderson, who was a towering figure in American political science, retired in 1957. The retirement of other faculty members and the departure of Herbert McClosky and Werner Levy, two rising stars among the younger full professors, caused concern about the department's future prospects. With the support of faculty members who had joined the department in the 1950s and early 1960s—Charles Backstrom, Harold Chase, Robert T. Holt, John Turner (later to become a Regents Professor), Edwin Fogelman, William Flanigan, Frank Sorauf (later a Regents Professor)—department chair Charles McLaughlin made plans for the future. Additional resources were crucial, and in 1963 John Turner prepared a report for academic vice president Jerry Shepherd documenting the precarious position in which the department found itself. Shepherd was alarmed and authorized the creation of eight positions.[151]

The process of rebuilding began. Among the new faculty members who later distinguished themselves as leading scholars were Roger Benjamin and Samuel Krislov. In addition to bringing in new talent, the department restructured its graduate program. Mary G. Dietz, Raymond D. Duvall, James Farr, John R. Freeman, W. Phillips Shively, Steven Smith, Virginia H. Gray, and John L. Sullivan (also made a Regents Professor) were added to the department in the 1970s and 1980s and soon had built impressive national reputations. Some sizable grants helped strengthen faculty research and financial support for graduate students. Gifts from faculty member Benjamin Lippincott to create a chair in political economy and from the Curtis Carlson family for a chair in American politics helped to strengthen the department. The careful planning and hard work paid off. Public law with Harold Chase, Samuel Krislov, and Frank Sorauf, and comparative politics with Roger Benjamin, Robert Holt, August H. Nimtz Jr., W. Phillips Shively, and John Turner were among the strongest in the country. With Benjamin Lippincott and Mulford Sibley from an earlier generation and Terrence W. Ball, Mary G. Dietz, and James Farr, and later Lisa J. Disch, political theory continued to maintain its outstanding reputation. In spite of turnover, Raymond D. Duvall, with support from

Martin W. Sampson, provided stability in foreign policy studies with Richard Price, Kathryn Sikkink, and Ethan B. Kapstein bringing expertise to this area in the 1990s. Kapstein held the Harold Stassen Chair. The cadre of scholars in the American government field remained small compared to other universities but its quality in the 1990s continued to be outstanding. Virginia H. Gray, Lawrence R. Jacobs, Wendy M. Rahn, Steven Smith, and John Sullivan were national leaders in their respective specialties. John R. Freeman, Diana E. Richards, W. Phillips Shively, and Sullivan made the department a world leader in innovative research methodologies. The high quality of the faculty as the twentieth century came to an end was illustrated by the recognition and awards received. Lawrence Jacobs, Richard Price, Diana Richards, David Samuels, and Kathryn Sikkink were made McKnight-Land Grant Professors, and John Freeman and Steven Smith were Distinguished McKnight Professors. Sikkink brought honor to the department by winning the prestigious Grawemeyer Award for Ideas Improving World Order. The department also emphasized undergraduate teaching and contributed leaders to university administrative positions. Over a thirty-year period, ending in 2000, sixteen political science faculty members won either the Motley Prize or the Morris-Alumni Award for excellence in undergraduate teaching. The faculty also recognized its obligations to serve the university. Harold Chase and Roger Benjamin both served terms as academic vice president; W. Phillips Shively was provost for the arts, sciences, and engineering; Frank Sorauf held the position of dean of the College of Liberal Arts; and Robert Holt served as dean of the Graduate School. All of them returned to active scholarship and teaching when their tours of administrative duty were over.[152]

## Statistics

Statistics was ranked thirteenth by the National Research Council. Seymour Geisser served as director from the establishment of the School of Statistics in 1971 through the end of the century. The school contained three units: applied statistics, theoretical statistics, and the Statistical Center. Key areas of faculty research expertise included Bayesian inference, graphical analysis, statistical computation, simultaneous analysis of multiple variables, economic game theory, survey sampling, design of experiments, prediction, and decision theory.

Bayesian inference, a probabilistic method for drawing on prior information and sample data drawn from a larger population, allowed researchers to make inferences about the characteristics of an entire population based on analysis of a subset of that population. For example, this methodology was used to analyze data generated by health sciences researchers to predict the probability of survival with respect to particular medical conditions and courses of treatment.

Graphical analysis made it possible to create a visual structure for large dimensional data sets identifying the interrelationships among many variables by appropriately reducing them to smaller but critically informative dimensions. Statistical computation techniques, using numerical approximation and Monte Carlo simulation, contributed to the analysis of data in such fields as weather forecasting and genetic pedigree analysis.

Faculty members' research had an impact on forensic genetics, AIDS research, biology, law, agriculture, geology, engineering, forestry, economics, and other social sciences. For agriculture, this research included the design and analysis of statistical information related to crop yields; for economics, modeling and appraising market strategies; for law, methods for evaluating employment discrimination; and in health-related fields, statistical information related to diagnostic testing and the creation of image-processing technology.[153]

It may be worth attempting to draw some conclusions from these nationally ranked departments. Many were formed by or enjoyed the continuing leadership of a long-serving head or chair. It also appears that in most cases members of the department got on well with each other or left each other alone to work without interference; by common consent, many matters were handled administratively, without taking faculty time for committees or frequent department meetings. A common theme and challenge facing each of the programs was to identify, recruit, and retain talented faculty members, who were often hired because of their intellectual promise rather than as specialists in narrowly defined fields.

There were several examples of interdepartmental collaboration within the Institute of Technology and the Medical School. Interdisciplinary centers, a number created with external funding, offered new means to advance research agendas. These fifteen programs illustrate the success of University of Minnesota faculty members in competing for research funds. In 1999, on a university-wide basis, sponsored research expenditures were just over $335 million.[154]

In addition to the obvious priority placed on research, it was notable that these programs paid attention to instruction and outreach. Equally important was the impact of graduates of these programs. In considerable numbers, they, like their counterparts in other departments, tended to stay in Minnesota and become contributing citizens—whether as employees, as the founders of companies, as researchers and teachers, or in other ways enhancing the intellectual capital of the state.

If there was one area of concern, it related to the National Research Council's aggregate ranking of institutions. Minnesota was ranked twentieth in 1993, a decline of four places from the previous ranking, in 1982.[155] While Robert Holt was dean of the Graduate School (1982 to 1991), he had been concerned by an earlier decline in rankings, between 1957 and 1983. Craig Swan, vice provost for undergraduate education, had voiced similar views about the rankings. Swan explained:

> I believe there is clear evidence that Minnesota has slipped. There is mixed evidence about how dramatic the change has been. Some may argue that, after all, the difference is not very big. Others may be relieved that the decline is not greater. I am concerned about this sort of complacency. Complacency about what has happened will only make future declines easier to accept. If we say that being pretty good rather than distinguished is good enough, that's where we will end up.[156]

Three years later, in his inaugural address, President Mark G. Yudof also commented on Minnesota's reduced standing in the NRC rankings and proposed specific actions: "targeted research initiatives, better facilities, better faculty salaries . . . a first-class undergraduate program, a commitment to access across all four campuses, and competitive graduate stipends."[157] Christine M. Maziar, who had become vice president for research and dean of the Graduate School in 1998, noted that one of the hoped-for benefits of university initiatives in molecular and cellular biology, as well as the broader reorganization of life science departments, would be increased recognition in the national rankings of research in the biological and life sciences carried out at Minnesota.[158]

An examination of the changes in ranking between 1982 and 1995 shows significant increases in the ranking of institutions such as San Diego, Johns Hopkins, and Duke, where significant new investments were made, illustrating the fact that Minnesota could not expect to hold its position, let alone advance it, without similar investments.[159] Investment in one of the most important economic resources of the state—the University of Minnesota—became the focus of public discussion in spring 2000.

In spite of legitimate concerns about Minnesota's overall ranking, it is important to keep the NRC rankings in perspective. Drawn from the opinions of scholars and administrators in the disciplines surveyed, the rankings were an indicator of current views, not necessarily an absolute measure of quality. There can be a lag time before improvements or declines in quality are recognized, and sometimes there is a halo effect whereby the overall reputation of an institution influences the ranking of a particular program.

Obviously, there are differences between public and private institutions. Ranked overall in the top twenty in 1995, Minnesota was among the top ten among the public institutions with high national ranking. As the most prestigious of the rankings, the National Research Council rankings have some influence on the allocation of local and national resources and on the university's capacity to continue to attract top students and faculty.

## Faculty Views of the University

Reflecting on interviews he conducted in the mid- to late 1990s, history professor Clarke Chambers concluded that the past fifty years in the history of the university fell into three contrasting periods. The first, the 1950s and 1960s, was an era of expansion and enthusiasm, often seen in retrospect as a golden age. A second phase began in the 1970s, when resources began to shrink and retrenchments set in: "The competition for funds in the 1970s became very acute. Inflation cut into the real worth of salaries for the professoriate and for supporting staff in every department. It was quite a changed environment." Planning and focusing efforts became important. A third era, he thought, saw the corporatization of the university, a national trend with both advantages and disadvantages: "One sees it in the acceleration of technology transfer, for example, in engineering, in the medical sciences, the health sciences, in management, and in computer science. There were spin-offs from research being done in these units, and a growing partnership with business or the corporate community. The University of Minnesota came to be seen as the engine that drove the economy of the state."[160]

For many faculty members, the 1990s presented new challenges as they sought to balance relationships in their own departments with scholarly contacts (made far easier through the Internet) with specialists at other institutions. In history, for instance, someone working on Tudor-Stuart England found it more helpful to work with scholars in England than with Minnesota colleagues whose chief interests lay elsewhere. Citing another challenge, historian John Howe noted that "higher education simply does not occupy nearly as high a priority in the public agenda as it did a decade ago."[161] Geography faculty member John Adams urged that the university rethink the way it recognized faculty accomplishments: "The way we honor people, the attention we give to things that we do. It's a Minnesota tradition that you just watch people. They can [pursue their work] for forty years and then you put them out to pasture. That's not good."[162] Leonard Kuhi, an astronomy faculty member and former vice president for academic affairs, with a perspective from his years at the University of California, came to a similar view, noting that Minnesotans were less aggressive about promoting strengths of colleagues, with the result that "the distinctions of Minnesota faculty are less recognized than they ought to be."[163] John Brandl, dean of the Humphrey Institute, believed that "the slow economic growth of America in the last twenty years contributed to a general frustration, not just in the academy but all over the country. The concerns of professors are the concerns of a lot of people in this society; they aren't peculiarly problems of the academy, except for the fact that the academy is just not held in as high regard as it once was." He thought the size of the university was a contributing factor: "It's hard to feel that one is part of a graspable community of fifty thousand people."[164]

After years of teaching philosophy to undergraduates, Marcia Eaton perceived a change in the character of students: "It is not that they are less bright . . . [it's that] they don't have the skills or the knowledge, the shared background, the facts that the students that I had in the early 1970s had."[165] On the other hand, historian Sara Evans believed that enhanced preparation requirements and improvements in undergraduate programs had a positive impact: "In the last decade or so, we've seen students who are in fact better prepared. That group at the top remains the same all the way through, but the difference is how wide the gap is from them to the students who are struggling. Like any large university, we have some students who are still learning to write and some who write brilliantly."[166] Looking back on his years as associate dean for undergraduate studies in the Institute of Technology, Russell Hobbie agreed: "Probably because of television, students cannot read as carefully or as long as they used to. The surrounding culture has created enormous pressures on young people."[167] Another scientist, Regents Professor Margaret Davis, recalled working with many "really outstanding graduate students. There are some stunningly bright undergraduate students here as well. The diversity of students in their academic preparation is rather wide and makes it difficult to teach courses, because you have to carry along students who aren't fully prepared."[168]

What Clarke Chambers identified as the melancholy of the professoriate had other aspects as well. Statistics showed that the number of faculty had decreased relative to the number of professional and administrative staff. Some faculty members believed that faculty governance was not as effective as it had been earlier; both the Senate and its Consultative Committee frequently felt that they were simply informed of actions that the administration had determined to take rather than given an opportunity to consider alternative strategies or suggest new approaches.[169] Committees continued to take up as much time as ever, despite some reforms in the 1980s, but there was a general feeling that relatively little faculty committee work was translated into action.[170]

A 1997 survey of faculty members indicated, however, that over 60 percent responded that they "agreed or strongly agreed" with the statement, "Overall, I am satisfied with my employment at the University."[171] One of the most thoughtful was Robert Bruininks, at that time dean of the College of Education and Human Development. He said in 1995, "We're dealing with some very dramatic changes in higher education. [The university] will continue to invest in very substantial restructuring of our academic priorities."[172] Bruininks was soon to find himself in a position from which he could lead the university in its ongoing efforts to maintain quality and community in the face of competing demands and constrained resources: he was named executive vice president and provost in 1997.

President Hasselmo described the problems arising from the Department of Surgery's handling of the product MALG (Minnesota Antilymphocyte Globulin) among the most troublesome of his presidency. MALG had been developed by Dr. John Najarian to provide resistance to organ rejection. Leonard Wilson, historian of the Medical School, explained that MALG "was an invaluable drug. For more than twenty years it was used to prevent the rejection of transplanted organs and save the lives of patients. At the time no other drug could take its place."[173] The apparently favorable outcomes and the demand from other academic transplant centers prompted an application to the Food and Drug Administration (FDA) in 1970 for approval of a plan to manufacture MALG for investigational purposes; it was to be made available for use with University of Minnesota transplant patients and patients at other transplant centers. As President Hasselmo recalled:

> It was August 1992 when a representative of the FDA came to my office and said, in no uncertain terms: "Mr. President, you have to look into the MALG program and its management because we cannot get satisfactory answers to the questions we are raising." Never was there evidence that the

FDA had tried to write to the dean of the Medical School to raise these questions when they didn't get answers from the Surgery Department, let alone to the vice president or the president.[174]

Investigations, lawsuits, and, ultimately, settlement of the MALG matter were to take six years, with a resolution occurring after Hasselmo left the presidency. These years included lawsuits against Dr. Najarian and his associates and a civil suit by the U.S. Department of Justice against the University of Minnesota. The National Institutes of Health (NIH) put the university on a restricted status, making the process of applying for grants far more cumbersome than it ordinarily was. The university's Institutional Review Board considered whether there were violations of patient safety and informed consent, and the faculty's Academic Misconduct Panel addressed whether there were violations of the university's policies on the conduct of scholarly research.

What follows is a very brief summary of the major events related to the matter. In October 1993, President Hasselmo issued a report prepared by the general counsel, with assistance from outside financial and legal experts, summarizing the principal findings about the administration of MALG. These included the sale of MALG products without commercial licensing; receipt of funds from the sale of MALG without FDA authorization; irregular transfers of MALG funds; operation of the MALG program in disregard of federal drug testing regulations; failure to disclose MALG revenues in annual filings to the NIH, and failure to notify the dean, the administration, or the regents of clinical and manufacturing problems raised by the FDA. In January 1994, Najarian reached an agreement with the FDA that he would be disqualified as a clinical investigator for new drugs.[175]

In April 1995, a federal grand jury issued twenty-two charges against Najarian. When the matter went to court ten months later, the judge dismissed all but six of the counts against Najarian, and the jury acquitted him on the remaining counts.

Meanwhile, within the university, two committees addressed Najarian's status as a clinical investigator and possible violations of the university's code for the conduct of scholarly research. On December 5, 1994, the University of Minnesota Institutional Review Board issued a report in which it withdrew Najarian's privileges to engage in human-subject research at the university. On February 13, 1995, the university informed Dr. Najarian that disciplinary measures would be imposed. istrative responsibilities) stemming from the report of the Academic Conduct Investigative Panel.

Soon thereafter, Najarian announced his resignation from the faculty. Although Najarian was no longer on the faculty, the university agreed to permit him to continue to see patients in the hospital.[176]

On December 20, 1996, the U.S. Department of Justice filed a civil suit against the university. The suit asked $100 million in damages, alleging grant mismanagement and the illegal sale of MALG. On the day the case was to go to trial, November 17, 1998, the university and the Justice Department reached a $32 million settlement; $20 million was paid directly to the government; $8 million, which the government owed to the university as part of another case, would be applied toward the MALG settlement; and the university would pay $4 million to faculty grant holders to replace money that the federal government otherwise would have provided. The funds for the university payment of the settlement and the considerable legal fees came from the proceeds of the sale of the University Hospital and Clinics.

The settlement brought to a close an extremely painful and difficult period and one about which there remained considerable disagreement. Supporters of Dr. Najarian, including patients, families of patients, colleagues, and some members of the community, looking primarily at the benefits that patients received from MALG, believed that both the federal government and the university had treated him unjustly. Conversely, the central administration, the Board of Regents, and others believed that the university's actions were necessary because the mismanagement of the program had compromised the integrity of the university. All agreed that the episode was tragic.

One of the outcomes of this difficult situation was the recognition that the university did not have the business systems to provide oversight by central management or to support faculty management of grants and contracts in an efficient and responsible way. Three years of work and an investment of $11 million made it possible for the university to ensure that a new grants management system would provide timely information to researchers, university officials, and funding agencies. By summer 2000, as a result of the new system, developed under the leadership of David Hamilton, professor of cell biology, most of the restrictions placed on the grants management process by the federal government were lifted, and it was hoped that all restrictions would be removed in 2001.[177]

Changes in the medical profession and in financing health care delivery came rapidly during the 1980s and 1990s. Demand for health care services continued to grow, but so did resistance—especially among employers—

to paying higher premiums for health care coverage. In Minnesota, where the concept of health maintenance organizations was developed, mergers and consolidations in a strong managed care market were considerably ahead of the rest of the nation. Large employers formed a coalition that awarded contracts for their employees' health care. Choice of physician and hospital became increasingly limited.

Medical schools, financed for decades in large measure by the revenues generated by faculty physicians, found that they needed new sources of revenue to cover the costs of teaching and research. Winston "Win" Wallin was one of the people the university turned to for advice on the fiscal and organizational issues related to the health sciences. In 1993, Wallin, who had retired as chief executive officer of Medtronic but was still its chair, agreed to serve as an unpaid special adviser to the president; he was instrumental in the restructuring of the health sciences into the Academic Health Center.

The new structure was designed to create more autonomy for the health sciences and to develop managerial and financial systems, such as the grants management system. Another change was the integration of the physicians' private practice plans into a single plan that could be more easily and efficiently administered. The private practice plans were individual contracts between the university and the physician–faculty member, designating the percentage of income brought in from patients that would be retained by the physician and the percentage that would flow to the university. The plans represented a significant benefit to the state and its taxpayers because the physicians were, in effect, paying a considerable portion of their own salaries. Over time, however, and without a centralized information system, the management and oversight of the individual plans was difficult. Integrating the separate plans into a single comprehensive plan offered administration and oversight while still making it possible for a physician to be paid an agreed-upon amount from private practice income.

One of the most helpful roles that Wallin played was to assist public policy makers understand the changes and complexities facing the health sciences. In an interview for this book, Wallin said:

> I believe that the state of Minnesota, the people ought to come to the conclusion that this [the Academic Health Center] is one of the very most important things in the state. . . . If there were no University of Minnesota, there would be no Medical Alley. Virtually all of the medical industry, wherever you go in the country, you find they are snuggled up against an academic health center.[178]

Soon after he was appointed provost for the Academic Health Center in 1994, Dr. William Brody identified the hospitals and financing medical education as one of the most urgent issues facing the university. The University Hospital, for decades the state's general hospital, admitted its patients mostly by referral; the largest percentage of admissions came from outside the metropolitan area or outside the state. With the growth of managed care and increased competition among health care insurers, there was new reluctance to cover costs associated with teaching and research, meaning fewer referrals to University Hospitals and Clinics. An added challenge for Minnesota was that, unlike a number of other university hospitals, it faced an extremely competitive marketplace, even for the most complex procedures such as cardiovascular surgery, cancer treatment, and some organ transplantation. The university found itself in competition with Twin Cities hospitals largely staffed by physicians trained in its own Medical School. Declining patient admissions and reduced reimbursement meant substantially reduced revenues (and patients) at University Hospitals. Equally important, these factors adversely affected medical education.

After considering a number of possible alternatives, Provost Brody recommended to the president and Board of Regents the sale of University Hospitals and Clinics and merger with Fairview Medical Center. The agreement took effect in 1997. President Hasselmo recalled how complex the transaction was: "You had to deal with two different personnel cultures, different unions, and you had to merge a public hospital with a nonprofit, community-based health care provider." He believed the results were satisfactory:

> Really, the key for us was not necessarily financial, although this was important—it was the patient flow, because without access to patients you can't run a good medical school. We could have closed the hospital and solved the financial problem. We just would not have had access to patient flow that would support education and research.[179]

## Tenure

Although tenure issues were discussed informally at national conventions of scholars in all disciplines, the discussion at Minnesota escalated into what one observer described as "arguably one of the fiercest battles over tenure in American higher education."[180] Outside consultants called in by Provost William Brody to advise on restructuring the Academic Health Center (AHC) believed—as did Brody—that the tenure code would make changes difficult. This led Brody to suggest reexamination of the tenure policy.

Speaking before a committee of the state legislature, Brody said that it would be difficult to implement changes in the health sciences without making changes in the tenure code. The legislature approved an AHC appropriation contingent upon changes in personnel policies, a thinly veiled wording for the tenure code. At the same time, Brody and the consultants were calling for radical changes in the AHC, including modification of tenure. This created an uproar among the AHC faculty.

Subsequently, Erwin Marquit, a physics faculty member, sent out a national e-mail message stating that the president and regents of the University of Minnesota were going to abolish tenure and suggesting that this would provoke similar action throughout the country. The *Washington Post* picked up the story, and angry messages began flooding the University, inflaming the situation further and making Minnesota the focal point of national attention.[181]

In early fall 1995, the regents initiated a review of tenure. As Hasselmo recalled, "I think one of the problems, from the very beginning, was that the issue got to the regents prematurely."[182] Hasselmo was pleased, after a series of misunderstandings with the faculty leadership that had caused a rift between him and the faculty, when the Faculty Senate in June 1996 (meeting a deadline set by the regents) proposed a set of recommendations that he could endorse. Hasselmo recommended that the regents adopt the Senate proposals; the board declined to do so and chose instead to take the matter under advisement, to the considerable consternation of the faculty, who believed that they had produced significant tenure code revisions under a very tight deadline. When the regents, who had engaged a national consultant to advise them, discussed the code in the fall, it was clear that they and the faculty were not of the same view. The University of Minnesota Foundation, the alumni association, the governor, and a number of legislators all urged that the tenure proposals prepared by the consultants for the regents not go forward.[183]

Faculty members were dismayed by a number of clauses in the code advocated by the regents' consultants. One section that particularly alarmed them allowed the regents to close "programs," which might be small parts of departments, dismissing the faculty involved. The regents' proposal appeared to reserve the right to lay off faculty members who were "not performing satisfactorily," perhaps without according them due process. The section that attracted the most attention indicated that faculty members could be disciplined for failure "to maintain a proper attitude of industry and cooperation with others within and without the university community."[184] This provision was unacceptably vague to a large number of faculty members; it suggested that tenured faculty members might be dismissed simply because they lacked collegiality. Five senior committee chairs described the changes in the tenure code proposed by the regents as "the most radical seen in fifty years."[185] Academic freedom was a major issue. Regents Professor Ellen Berscheid said, "Don't let anyone ever tell you that academic freedom is not an issue today. We face it every day in our work."[186] Earlier attempts to silence Mulford Sibley were frequently mentioned, as was the guarantee in the existing tenure code that faculty members could not be dismissed for political reasons.

Faculty leaders called for a union election on three campuses. Under the state's collective bargain regulations, no changes could be made in the terms and conditions of employment while an election was pending—and soon collected enough signatures to place all but one unit of the university (the Law School) under a "cease and desist" order.

The resulting situation was complex. By state law, the Academic Health Center and the Law School were to vote separately from the rest of the Twin Cities campus on whether or not to unionize; Crookston and Morris also were to vote separately. At this time, Law School dean E. Thomas Sullivan brought to the regents a draft tenure code for the Law School that came to be known as the Sullivan principles, or (since there were later modifications of it) Sullivan I. After Dean Sullivan presented his proposal at the October regents' meeting, the regents decided to forward both his draft and their own to the Faculty Senate for review.

The faculty, divided about whether they should even consider the Sullivan proposal (because it was only for the Law School), nonetheless debated it at a Senate meeting. On Halloween, Dean Sullivan released a revised draft of his proposed tenure revisions, with changes based on discussions at the Faculty Senate (Sullivan II). That same day, however, the Law School also filed signatures, thus preventing further discussion of revisions to any tenure code. That same day, Regent Jean Keffeler, perceived to be one of the principal supporters of the code the regents had developed with the consultants, announced that she would resign from the board effective December 1. Public opinion, mirrored in newspaper editorials, a statement from Governor Arne Carlson, and pressure from a number of significant constituencies, had shifted decisively away from the regents' proposal.

In early November, the state agency responsible for supervising union elections determined that the Law School had not filed a sufficient number of signatures. The regents met twenty-four hours later and, with little discussion, unanimously adopted Sullivan II for the Law School. The faculty saw this as a message from the regents because Sullivan II was perceived to be very close to the Faculty Senate tenure code presented to the regents the previous June. Later in November, the Morris campus and the Academic Health Center voted against collective bargaining; the vote at Crookston was tied, resulting in a failed vote.

The rest of the Twin Cities campus faculty debated the merits of collective bargaining for several months, and in February 1997 voted (by a margin of less than 1 percent) not to unionize. The Faculty Senate continued to review the provisions of Sullivan II and made a few recommendations for changes; the faculty and the board came to an agreement on Sullivan II in May 1997. According to Professor Sara Evans, chair of the "negotiating" committee the faculty had appointed to work with the regents, there was a sudden breakthrough: "Once it happened, it happened very fast."[187]

In May 1997, both the Faculty Senate and the Board of Regents accepted the revised code. Despite the initial opposition of the Board of Regents, faculty governance survived and President Hasselmo's stand was vindicated.[188] Regent William Hogan, a businessman and former member of the engineering faculty at the University of Kansas who had pressed for adoption of the Sullivan compromise, became chair of the board in June. Law professor Fred Morrison thought the regents viewed faculty members as employees rather than as independent professionals. It was, he thought, "this challenge of 'employee-ization' that was the crux of the Minnesota crisis." It had already affected members of the medical profession, whose work had come to be regulated by health maintenance organizations, and it was seen as a threat to scholars in other fields. There was a fear that "lean and mean" managers might resort to downsizing and layoffs, as in an industrial organization.[189]

Biochemistry professor Vic Bloomfield concluded:

> One of the things that's really weird about this is that we've come out very well. I think we have a tenure code that's a pretty good one, and some of the changes were in the right direction. We have the best Board of Regents that we've had since I've paid attention to that issue. We have sympathy towards the university, on the part of the public, that we haven't had in a long time. It has been very painful, and may well have been very destructive of faculty governance, but in terms of what we care about, it's ended up positive. Wars sometimes do, in strange ways.[190]

## The Hasselmo Years

A list of the activities of Nils Hasselmo and his wife, Pat, illustrates the diverse expectations for the president and his wife. He delivered 318 speeches between February 1989 and December 1996; quite varied in character, they included commencement addresses, presentations to the legislature, talks to Rotary Clubs, remarks at community visits throughout the state, and comments at receptions for alumni and friends of the university.[191] He visited communities in Greater Minnesota, making connections with extension educators and community leaders, and traveled internationally. He recalled in particular visits to Taiwan; to the People's Republic of China, where he signed three agreements on teaching and international education; and to Korea, where he and Regent Hyon Kim presented an honorary degree to President Kim Young Sam, who had attended the University of Minnesota. Hasselmo, like his predecessors, devoted a considerable amount of time to meeting potential donors, in Minnesota, throughout the country, and abroad.

The Hasselmos made it a point to be present at numerous University events. Pat Hasselmo recalled: "We tried hard to be very visible on the university scene in as many aspects of university life as we could. We would try always to go to some of the musical events, to some of the theatrical events, to touch the broad range of what was going on, although we were so scheduled with our own agenda of entertaining various groups and constituencies that it was really hard to do that."[192] They attended basketball games and always entertained groups of fans before home football games.

Like other Gopher fans, they were elated in March 1997 when the Gopher basketball team made it to the Final Four National Collegiate Athletic Association tournament after finishing the season at the top of the Big Ten for the first time in fifteen years. The team earned a perfect home court record for the first time in Coach Clem Haskins's eleven years at Minnesota. Although Kentucky defeated the Gophers 78–69, the journey to the Final Four was at the time a great triumph. Serious rules violations that were subsequently uncovered led to an internal inquiry and an NCAA investigation, casting a disturbing shadow over that victorious season, over the basketball program, and over the university itself.

In one of his final speeches, the May 1997 Graduate School commencement address, Hasselmo commented on some of the mementos he was packing as he prepared to vacate his office. One was a framed copy of the poem "Ithaca" by C. P. Cavafy—a gift from history professor Theofanis Stavrou. (As Stavrou noted: "The poet tells us we have a destination, an objective. But what really counts is the process, the intellectual journey.")[193] Hasselmo also had a picture of the new Basic Sciences and Biomedical Engineering building, just completed, considered to be among the finest facilities of its kind in the world; seals of universities in China, Korea, and Indonesia; memorabilia from trips to reconnect with 18,000 alumni in the Pacific Rim; an Indian pipe from Pipestone, Minnesota; the key to the city of Lindstrom, Minnesota; and memorabilia from visits to many other communities around the state.[194]

When Hasselmo retired, *St. Paul Pioneer Press* columnist Nancy Livingston suggested that he should be credited with three pivotal accomplishments: restoring the university's credibility with the legislature, improving the undergraduate experience, and "deflecting the most serious challenge to tenure faced by any major university."[195] A Minneapolis *Star Tribune* editorial noted that "there were times when his presidency seemed to be a case study in crisis administration": closing the Waseca campus, hospital financial problems, the steam plant, the regents' tenure code, the General College proposal, and the ALG matter.[196] Despite these daunting problems, the editorial noted, "better education is his legacy." Among his accomplishments, the editorial cited Minnesota's movement from the bottom of the Big Ten to third in admissions selectivity, doubling the number of undergraduate courses taught by full professors, and smaller classes. Other accomplishments linked to the Hasselmo years were more writing assignments, a network of alumni mentors to help ease students from the campus to the world of work, and substantial improvements in graduation rates.[197]

Hasselmo had intended to return to teaching in the Department of German, Scandinavian, and Dutch following a year's leave, but he was asked to be president of the Association of American Universities, headquartered in Washington, D.C. He assumed that office on July 1, 1998. In retrospect, he viewed his years at Minnesota with satisfaction:

> I consider myself, in spite of the trials and tribulations that I have gone through, extraordinarily fortunate to have come to the University of Minnesota and to have been allowed to be, for a brief period, the president of that magnificent University.[198]

# Chapter 5
# The University at
# the End of the Century

We must have a vision that is ecumenical and distinctly Minnesota, both national and international, neither parochial nor oblivious of the heritage of a great land-grant university.

—*Mark G. Yudof, inaugural address, October 1997*

A S THE CENTURY ENDED, the University of Minnesota celebrated its 150th anniversary. Festivities began in June 2000 with performances of Aaron Copland's opera The Tender Land at eight regional farms by students and faculty from the School of Music. Other events invluded a presidential lecture series, recognition at the State Fair, Homecoming, and the annual Martin Luther King concert; a celebration at the State Capitol; and the President's Anniversary Tribute at Northrup. The grand finale planned for June 2001 was a return to the Twin Cities campus of the Minnesota Orchestra as part of the University of Minnesota Alumni Association annual meeting.[1]

## President Mark G. Yudof

Mark G. Yudof became the university's fourteenth president in July 1997. His central strategy called for "clearly defined initiatives, plus quality, hands-on undergraduate education with reasonable access as the foundation for sustaining all programs at the university."[2] His first three years in office were helped by the considerable investment the university had made in undergraduate education, by a flourishing economy, and by broad acceptance of his key initiatives. He was also successful in bringing into rare accord the university community, legislators, and the public on the pivotal importance of a strong university to the future well-being of the state.

Yudof's appointment was the result of a search very nearly aborted as two other candidates withdrew, leaving him the sole candidate—an echo of 1985. Governor Arne Carlson doubted that the selection process should continue but agreed to meet Yudof. Reporter Greg Breining wrote about the selection process in *Minnesota Monthly*, a Minnesota Public Radio publication: "It must have been a hell of an interview, for Carlson proclaimed Yudof, 'the joy of the maroon and gold.' The governor was not alone in his praise of Yudof; the chorus of praise that greeted his candidacy was extraordinary." The Board of Regents vote for Yudof was unanimous.[3]

The new president, born in 1944, held a bachelor's degree and a law degree, both awarded with honors by the University of Pennsylvania. He spent most of his academic career at the University of Texas at Austin, where he joined the law faculty in 1971, was named dean of the Law School in 1984, and became executive vice president and provost in 1994. In that post, the second highest in the university, he had been active in improving undergraduate education by initiating improvements in advising, establishing awards for outstanding undergraduate teachers, and organizing a program of freshman seminars designed to give all entering freshmen the experience of a small class with intimate, challenging discussions. He had written widely on legal topics; among his highly respected books was *When Government Speaks: Politics, Law, and Government Expression in America*. When Mark and Judy Yudof came to Minnesota, their son, Seth, a graduate of the University of Pennsylvania, was living in Los Angeles and their daughter, Samara, was a sophomore at Southern Methodist University in Dallas.[4]

Judy Yudof was involved in community service work in both the secular and the Jewish community. In Texas, she served on numerous boards and commissions related to the delivery of health and human services. After arriving in the Twin Cities in 1997, she became an active member of the board of directors of the University Children's Foundation (supporting the Department of Pediatrics), the Weisman Art Museum Colleagues Advisory Board, the advisory board for the Tweed Museum of Art, the Friends of the Goldstein Gallery, and the Development Advisory Board of the College of Continuing Education. She also was honorary chair of the Twin Cities Jewish Coalition for Literacy and honorary chair of the Year 2000 Twin Cities International Citizens Awards. She served on the boards of several non-university organizations in the Twin Cities as well as serving as a national officer of the United Synagogue of Conservative Judaism. Her efforts in the restoration of Eastcliff, the president's official residence, were a labor of love. Eastcliff was placed on the National Register of Historic Places in June 2000. She observed, "I have been impressed with the high profile the University of Minnesota has within the state. The stewardship of the university is an awesome, daunting, and exciting responsibility. I am proud of my husband and delighted to be given the opportunity to play an active role in outreach to alumni and friends of the university."[5]

President Yudof was inaugurated in October 1997. In perfect autumn weather, the academic procession made its way along the west side of the mall from the plaza in front of Coffman Union to Northrop Auditorium. One of the major themes in his inaugural address was the importance of a research and land-grant university to economic development:

> Information and knowledge are the bellwethers of our economic future. The future of agronomy, manufacturing, computer software, finance, medical devices, publishing, mass media, retail trade—all areas of economic activity depend on the intellectual capital of the state.... Now more than at any time in the history of Minnesota, the fortunes of the state and its only land-grant research university are intertwined.... We will rise or fall together.[6]

Yudof was explicit in his views on the access-versus-excellence debate:

> Minnesotans expect us to be fair in providing access for their sons and daughters. If we do not provide reasonable access—including access for those who are underprepared and historically underrepresented in higher education and in the upper levels of our socioeconomic life—the taxpayers and state government will turn their backs on our graduate, research, and outreach functions.[7]

A year later, in his first State of the University address, he amplified his vision: "I want the University of Minnesota to offer the highest quality, most hands-on, most humane undergraduate education of any comparably sized public research university in America."[8] He had decided to abolish the three provost positions established by Hasselmo and return to a system similar to one in Texas and to the earlier administrative structure at Minnesota in which a single executive vice president and provost held the number two post. To this position he appointed Robert Bruininks, then dean of the College of Education and Human Development. Yudof noted that Bruininks was highly regarded by both faculty and administrators, and added, "I absolutely had to have someone who understood the university and understood Minnesota. I come in as a Philadelphia lawyer by way of Texas, a not entirely legitimate route."[9]

As his chief of staff, Yudof brought with him Tonya Moten Brown, a lawyer who had been assistant director of admissions for the Texas Law School, because "I needed someone who knew me and someone I knew and trusted."[10] Frank Cerra remained the top-ranking academic and administrator in the health sciences with the new title senior vice president. McKinley Boston served as vice president for student development and athletics. Christine Maziar, previously vice provost and professor of electrical and computer engineering at the University of Texas, became vice president for research and dean of the Graduate School. Mark Rotenberg continued as general counsel. In 1998, Sandra Gardebring, a former justice of the Minnesota Supreme Court, succeeded Tom Swain as vice president for institutional relations, thus completing Yudof's initial administrative appointments. In 1999, Mary Heltsley, who had been dean of the College of Human Ecology from 1987 to 1999, was named associate vice president for outreach.

In other changes, Yudof elevated human resources to a vice presidential level, appointing Carol Carrier to that position. He abolished the position of vice president for finance and operations and the office of the treasurer and created a new position, vice president for university services, held by Eric Kruse. Richard Pfutzenreuter chaired the financial management group and served as chief budget officer and, formally, as treasurer. In spring 1999, Tonya Moten Brown assumed oversight of the university's athletic programs and subsequently was named vice president and chief of staff. McKinley Boston continued to serve as vice president for student development through the 1999–2000 academic year.[11] In June 2000, the regents approved the appointment of Robert Jones, professor of agronomy and plant genetics, and associate provost for minority affairs, as interim vice president for student development, succeeding Boston.

As of fall 1998 the university had approximately 7,500 full- and part-time academic employees and just over 9,800 civil service and bargaining unit staff members. In addition, more than 13,000 students were employed by the university.[12] Despite its size, the university managed to avoid impersonality and indifference; observers agree that one factor was the efforts of university employees, both faculty and staff, to help students become accustomed to campus life.

Steven Rosenstone, dean of the College of Liberal Arts, had come to Minnesota in 1996 from the University of Michigan. He observed, "Early on, I was struck by the dedication of university staff members, by how much they care. I am very, very impressed and hope that won't be lost in the history of the university."[13] Stephanie Dilworth, a principal auditor who chaired the university's Civil Service Committee in 1999–2000, credited the loyalty among civil service staff members in some measure to the job security associated with a civil service position at the university, but also to the challenge and variety of university employment. "The university," she pointed out, "is a miniature city, and it is possible to move around to different positions without leaving it."[14]

## Preserving the Past/Nurturing the Future

One of President Yudof's early initiatives was Beautiful U Day, along with a commitment to restore historic buildings, deal with the effects of deferred maintenance, and enhance the beauty of the university's campuses. This encouraged students and faculty to be proud of the university's heritage, traditions, and environment.

In his appeal to the legislature for supporting funds, Yudof had pointed out that the university had a number of historic buildings—some of them more than a hundred years old—that needed renovation to make them safe, serviceable, and technologically up to date. He noted that "preserving the past is also about respecting the beauty, heritage, and design of this great university." His appeal was not simply retrospective; he argued that "the university must plan for tomorrow's economy, preparing our students for 21st-century jobs, improving the health of Minnesotans, creating and growing new technologies for transfer to private businesses."[15] This meant that he would seek funds for new construction as well as for renovation: "I have the goal of entering the new millennium with world-class programs, faculty, and campuses."[16]

To justify the university's legislative request, Yudof explained to legislators and the public the benefits to be expected from five interdisciplinary initiatives: in molecular and cellular biology, digital media, design, media studies, and agriculture. The total amount requested from the legislature in 1998 was $249 million for capital improvements and $41.5 million to recruit and support faculty and classroom improvements for the five initiatives along with funding for faculty and staff compensation.[17] By the end of the 1998 legislative session, in good measure due to the personal leadership of the president, a united front by the regents and the administration, and active lobbying by the alumni association volunteer network, the university had received $206 million in state and university bonding for these projects.

The largest dollar amount was $53.6 million for remodeling Walter Library for use by the Center for Digital Media. The new facility was designed to include "[computer] workstations and supercomputers ... [research and development] laboratories, conference rooms, distance learning classrooms, computerized study areas."[18] The second-largest project, also related to science and technology, was $35 million for University of Minnesota bonding for the Molecular and Cellular Biology Building; construction began in winter 2000 on a site vacated by the demolition of the Lyon Labs, built in 1952, and Owre (1930) and Millard (1912) Halls. Jackson Hall, also part of the medical complex, was preserved and remodeled to house the basic science departments of the Medical School.

The Ford and Murphy Hall renovations, also bonded for the university, came to $18 million covering renovation of these two adjoining buildings for journalism and communications as well as to house the Institute for New Media Studies. Nora Paul, an expert in Web-based research and journalism who had come to Minnesota from a faculty position at the Poynter Institute for Media Studies in St. Petersburg, Florida, was appointed director of Minnesota's Institute for New Media Studies in summer 2000. Albert R. Tims, director of the School of Journalism, and Steven Rosenstone, dean of the College of Liberal Arts, underscored the importance of media-related fields to Minnesota's economy. Rosenstone noted that "the opportunity is ripe to build a program in the intellectual and technological vanguard of journalism and communication."[19]

Other projects funded in 1998 included upgrades of selected Minneapolis buildings and infrastructure in the Northrop Mall area, funding (along with private dollars) for women's softball and soccer facilities, and an addition and remodeling of Amundson Hall and Mechanical Engineering. Private gifts led to establishment of the Barbara Barker Dance Center as part of the West Bank Arts Quarter.[20] An innovative redesign of the South Mall, known as the Riverbend Commons, based on Cass Gilbert's vision of opening to the Mississippi River, was launched during the 1999–2000 academic year. Yudof called this "the best site in America." This renovation included a new underground garage, state-of-the art dormitory rooms, and a complete renovation of Coffman Union to house student activities as well as the faculty-staff Campus Club. Students voted to help fund the Coffman Union renovation with student fees.[21]

At the end of the 2000 legislative session, the university received $35 million for the Molecular and Cellular Biology Building in addition to funds authorized two years earlier, making a total of $70 million. State funding of $18.5 million was approved for a new Art Building; the rest of the funds for the $41 million building were to be raised by the university. The 1998 and 2000 bonding years promised major changes in St. Paul as well: $6.9

million for remodeling Peters Hall to add new classroom and research areas; $4 million for the addition and remodeling of laboratories for Snyder and Gortner Halls; authorization of $10 million for the Microbial and Plant Genetics Building, to match a gift from Cargill. The new and upgraded St. Paul technical facilities and labs were central to the all-university priorities of molecular and genetic research. The Crookston campus received funding for remodeling and renovation of Knutsen and Owen Halls; a new Early Childhood Education Center was to replace a lab that had been built in the first decade of the twentieth century. Funding was authorized for completion of the final phase of the Morris science and mathematics building renovation; Duluth received funding for a new library, for a music performance lab, and for classroom renovation. Collectively, funding for Crookston, Duluth, and Morris campus projects and for the research and outreach centers totaled over $23 million in 1988 and 2000.[22]

New signs, fresh coats of paint and varnish, and new historical markers were added throughout the campuses. By fall 1999, so much construction was under way that students at the Twin Cities campus freshman convocation were issued hard hats. President Yudof gratefully observed that "we're the construction crane capital of the Upper Midwest."[23]

## Student Life

Yudof wanted to nurture on the larger Twin Cities and Duluth campuses the strong sense of community characteristic of the Crookston and Morris campuses. In the Twin Cities, he suggested restoration of the freshman convocation. In pageantry reminiscent of a presidential inauguration, geography faculty member John Adams carrying the university mace, followed by several regents, the president, senior administrators, and faculty members, filed down the main aisles of Northrop Auditorium to open the 1998 Freshman Convocation. Regent William Hogan II, chair of the board, welcomed the new freshmen, suggesting they be open to a range of ideas, to go to the library, and to make new friends.

Nikki Kubista, Minnesota Student Association president, encouraged participation in campus activities, noting that "students who get involved succeed more. The power to succeed is in your hands." Sara Evans, professor of history and chair of the Faculty Senate, told the students that she had been at the university for more than twenty years and had found it to be a "great place." She explained that she had become a historian "to get to know the shoulders you stand on." Being at Minnesota, she recalled,

"helped me be part of creating a new field of study—the history of women."
She suggested that "the capacity to make history will make this a better
world" and urged students to take advantage of their time at the university, which would offer them "more time to explore than ever again in
your lives."[24]

President Yudof welcomed the students and described what the university was doing to make their experience a good one: the convocation itself,
freshman seminars, the Academy of Distinguished Teachers encouraging
outstanding instruction, campus beautification efforts, more residence halls.
He urged the students to take risks and try new subjects. He described the
distinction of the faculty and its contributions to agriculture, health care,
and the arts. With the humor that was his trademark, he advised students:
"Seek out the deeply instilled meaning of life in pancakes," a favorite food
of Yudof's. Provost Robert Bruininks encouraged the students to plan their
course work so that they would be eligible to reconvene in Northrop in
spring 2002 for graduation ceremonies.[25]

In fall 1998, the four campuses enrolled nearly 52,000 students, 51 percent of them women and 49 percent men. There were close to 6,000 students of color, representing 11.5 percent of the student body, and almost
3,000 international students, from 130 different countries.[26] Students traveled frequently between Minneapolis and St. Paul, taking classes on both
campuses. Each year, approximately 1,200 students took advantage of university-sponsored study and travel opportunities in more than sixty countries. A generation serious about careers, the students appreciated mentor-
ship opportunities offered through their colleges and the University of
Minnesota Alumni Association. During the 1999–2000 academic year on
the Twin Cities campus, 1,500 students participated in freshman seminars—
a 245 percent increase over the previous years; 85 percent of the members
of the freshman class returned for their sophomore year.[27]

Campus organizations, conferences, celebrations, and awards reflected
increased diversity in the campus community. Nancy "Rusty" Barceló, appointed associate vice president for multicultural and academic affairs in
1996, was the most senior system administrator offering leadership in diversity and multicultural affairs. On the Twin Cities campus, one of her areas
of responsibility was overseeing the four multicultural centers: the African
American Learning Resource Center, the American Indian Learning Resource Center, the Asian/Pacific American Learning Resource Center, and
the Chicano/Latino Learning Resource Center. Each had strong programs
and active members.

President Kenneth Keller had initiated the President's Distinguished Faculty Mentor Program in 1986. Robert Jones, a faculty member in agronomy and plant genetics, served as the first director of the program, which paired faculty mentors with undergraduate students with similar academic interests; he headed the program through 1997. In 1994, Jones was named assistant vice president for multicultural and academic affairs. Among other duties, he assumed the directorship of the Multicultural Undergraduate Research Program, a summer research program for students of color interested in pursuing graduate studies created in 1987 by Patricia Jones-Whyte. President Mark Yudof appointed him vice provost for faculty and academic personnel in 1998.[28]

The Gay, Lesbian, Bisexual, Transgender (GLBT) Program Office served as the Twin Cities focal point for understanding GLBT experience, interests, and issues. Through a gift from Steven J. Schochet, the Steven J. Schochet Center for Gay, Lesbian, Bisexual, and Transgender Studies was established to "enhance the creation of knowledge about GLBT lives through academic study and interaction."[29] In March 2000, the Office for Multicultural and Academic Affairs served as national sponsor and host site for a national teleconference titled "Women's Lives, Women's Voices, Women's Solutions: Shaping a National Agenda for Women in Higher Education." The conference explored strategies for improving campus climates for women in a multicultural world.

Grants strengthened programs for people with disabilities. One grant allowed Disability Services to study ways to enhance international study for students with disabilities. A second supported development of service learning options for students with disabilities. A third grant, through a partnership with General College, was directed at creating a nationally replicable model "for more effectively teaching students with disabilities."[30] In addition to the learning resource centers and the Gay, Lesbian, Bisexual, Transgender Program Office, Barceló's multicultural and academic affairs portfolio included the Office for University Women, the Minnesota Women's Center, Disability Services, the Diversity Institute for Student Development and Educational Training, the multicultural Center for Academic Excellence, the Multicultural Undergraduate Research Program, the Office of University Women, and the President's Distinguished Faculty Mentor Program.

On January 19, 2000, multicultural and academic affairs and the university community celebrated the nineteenth annual Dr. Martin Luther King Jr. Memorial Concert. Initiated by the late Reginald T. Buckner, professor of music, the annual concert honored the life of Dr. King through the performing arts. Buckner, an outstanding musician, composer, and educator, was instrumental in establishing jazz studies at the university.[31] In 1997, the university created the Josie R. Johnson Human Rights and Social Justice Award as a way to recognize contributions to the cause of social justice. The award was named in honor of Josie Robinson Johnson, who had supported the establishment of the Afro-American and African studies department, served as senior fellow in the College of Education, served on the Board of Regents, and been associate vice president for academic affairs.

Skateboards and in-line skates became almost as common on campus as bicycles. A new online registration system, in spite of initial glitches, virtually eliminated the long registration lines of earlier decades. A wired generation comfortable with computers and other information technologies, students at the end of the century had almost as much computing power at their disposal in laptop computers as the Pentagon had during World War II.

A summa cum laude graduate of the College of Liberal Arts (CLA), Afro-American and African studies major Toja Okoh acknowledged that it required some persistence to navigate the Twin Cities campus successfully. She lived at Middlebrook Hall and remembered talks with friends at Espresso Royale in Dinkytown. Okoh got to know well—and appreciated the guidance she received from—faculty mentors John Wright and Victoria Coifman. Receiving a Donovan Scholarship, one of the first foundation-endowed scholarships created in the 1960s to honor CLA graduate and *Time* magazine executive Hedley Donovan, allowed Okoh to travel to Nigeria to do research on the dispersion of African peoples for her summa thesis. Okoh cited "red tapism" and "getting classes needed to graduate" as things she didn't like about the university, but she was emphatically positive about her overall experience: "Despite the hugeness, the U had all the opportunities one could ask."[32]

Caitlin Fashbaugh came to Minnesota, where her father had been a graduate student in the 1960s, from Michigan. She chose Minnesota, she reported, "because I wanted to go to a place that was egalitarian and just huge. I wanted to get lost for a while. . . . I wanted so much to meet people who were different from me." Still, she marveled at the many people she encountered as an usher at Northrop Auditorium, observing that their numbers "probably equaled the size of my hometown."[33]

Fashbaugh, like most of her peers, held part time-jobs throughout her undergraduate years.[34] Completing her degree in five years, Fashbaugh cleaned dormitory halls her first two years and had work-study jobs tutoring other students her last two. Balancing work with academics at the level expected of an honors student was not always easy: "I had a couple of dark years in the middle, my sophomore and junior years, where I lost contact with friends. But in the last two years, I started making a conscious effort to balance my academic, work, and social lives." A double major in English and Spanish, Fashbaugh recalled the support of English faculty members Michael Dennis Browne, Calvin Kendall, Toni McNaron, and Edward Griffin. Her summa project was a collection of poems that she had written during her five years at the university.

Kingsley Calvo-Jordan entered the university through the College of Continuing Education, taking extension classes to improve his grade-point average so that he could be admitted to CLA. He majored in international relations with a minor in art history. Calvo, who is Hispanic, came to Minnesota when he was two years old. He found that art history provided a valuable social and cultural context to balance the courses in history and political science that he took as part of his program in global studies. Asked his perspective of the university as a Hispanic student, he said that he found the university friendly, but quite homogeneous. He hoped that CLA would encourage more students to travel internationally to help broaden their perspective. Teachers he found helpful included historian David Kieft, with whom he took courses in diplomatic history, and global studies faculty member Russell L. Moses.[35]

Institute of Technology student Greg Lauer, a civil engineering major, characterized the honors program as "giving a small college feel to a big institution like the U of M." Lauer noted that the opportunity to do research as an undergraduate had been a factor in his applying to the university.[36]

General College student Kate Jurik greatly appreciated support from faculty member Jay Hatch, who worked with her to ensure that her cerebral palsy did not interfere with the biology laboratory class she was taking from him. Jurik observed that "what makes GC different is the willingness to experiment to find out what works, to help me learn more about myself and what accommodations I need." Both Jurik and Hatch were surprised at how few accommodations were required.[37]

Alyssa Hawkins, who had transferred to the College of Natural Resources from a smaller institution, wrote to Dean Alfred Sullivan when she received her bachelor of science degree in 1998:

> I had visions of getting lost in the system. . . . I can say that none of my fears were realized. I was welcomed by name, comfortable in small classes,

and encouraged to participate and even call my professors at home if I needed to. When I came, I never imagined examining soils profiles, assessing land-use plans, testing water quality. All the skills I have gained interest prospective employers and give me the tools to work confidently in the natural resources field.[38]

Not only were students actively involved on the campus, they also looked for opportunities abroad. Aaron Horne, a 1999 computer science graduate, participated in an international internship with a Japanese computer graphics company, and Aaron Reed, a mechanical engineering graduate, studied at Lancaster University in England. Among the first Institute of Technology students to combine study abroad with their regular studies, they were encouraged to do so in part in response to interest among employers for entry-level workers with international experience.[39]

Agriculture business major Adam Manwarren and Leah Becker, an agriculture major, participated in a College of Agricultural, Food, and Environmental Sciences visit to Russia. Manwarren, who rated his time at the university "fabulous," reported: "By the time I was a junior, I realized that if I graduated without international experience, I would have had an incomplete education."[40] Becker was impressed with the opportunities for women in agriculture.[41]

When Julie Schultz entered the Medical School in fall 1996, hers was the first entering class in which women outnumbered men. She, like a number of her classmates, was no stranger to the basic sciences and research. She had been introduced to research as an undergraduate through an internship at the University with Gregg Phillips. After her first year of medical school, Schultz was selected for a research year at the National Institutes of Health in Bethesda, Maryland, through a program funded by the Howard Hughes Medical Institute. As a medical student, Schultz was active in the Internal Medicine Interest Group and the Women in Medicine student group.[42]

Kristin Fallstrom, a student from the Duluth campus School of Medicine, won national recognition from the American Association of Family Practice for her research paper "Caring for Dying Patients and Their Families"; it was the third consecutive year that UMD students had taken home the group's top prize. In 1998, Duluth medical students Lisa Lyons and Sonja Redetzke won second place for their study "Recruitment and Retention of Rural Family Physicians." Faculty mentor James Boulger noted that he "expected the judges to be impressed with these students. I'd put them up against Harvard or Yale any day."[43]

Murisiku Raifu knew he wanted to become a doctor from the time he was eight years old, watching helplessly as his best friend in Ghana died of cholera. He sought to broaden his educational opportunities by coming to the United States. After earning a bachelor's degree at Amherst College in Massachusetts, Raifu was admitted to the University of Minnesota Medical School. During his second year, in fall 1999, he lived in the Phi Chi medical fraternity and was co-chair of the Student International Health Care Committee, which sponsored an annual forum on international health care. He also served as a mentor to university undergraduates with a future interest in medicine. Raifu gained perspective from the diverse students he encountered at the university; he smiled as he said, "And I thought *I* had a story."[44] Carolyn Porta, who completed a bachelor's degree in nursing, served on an American Red Cross intervention team in Rwanda before returning to the university to complete a dual master's program in nursing and public health. Extremely pleased with her training, Porta said, "the field of nursing is so huge you can do anything." For the future, she had her eye on the possibility of a Ph.D. in public health nursing.[45]

## Colleges and Campuses

President Yudof acknowledged in his inaugural address that the real work of the university took place on campuses, in colleges, centers, and departments:

> To the best of my recollection, no great scientific discovery, no insightful social science tracts, no novels have been produced in Morrill Hall [the administration building]. No classes are taught in Morrill Hall. No patients are made well in Morrill Hall. My point is that we must value delegating academic and other decisions to campuses, colleges, schools, departments, and faculties.... Without authority invested where the real work of this university is done, the light of excellence will only grow dimmer.[46]

Drawing on his experience as provost at Texas, Yudof encouraged the creation of written planning compacts as a way of clarifying overall direction and freeing deans and department heads to move forward toward agreed-upon goals. They represented "horizontal relationships between equals," not a top-down process; Yudof called them "dreams with a deadline" and "a kitchen table discussion of family priorities for the next year or two." The compacts, which were available to the public, clearly stated the vision, goals, and expected outcomes of the major schools and colleges of the university. Yudof intended them to be flexible, adjustable as circumstances required.[47]

## The College of Liberal Arts

The College of Liberal Arts (CLA) at the end of the century, as in 1950, was the largest college in the university. Fall 1950 enrollment was just over 6,000; by fall 1999, enrollment had more than doubled to over 16,000 students. Steven J. Rosenstone, a political scientist known for his research and writing on electoral politics, became dean in 1996.[48] Asked what he was proudest of in the College of Liberal Arts, Rosenstone replied, "Its excellence." He cited economics, geography, German, history, political science, psychology, and statistics—all in the top twenty programs in the country as evaluated by the National Research Council—as sources of pride. Dance had been selected in three years in the late 1990s to perform nationally in what Rosenstone described in an analogy to basketball as "the Final Four of dance." Rosenstone also pointed to the national recognition accorded Minnesota ceramic artists Mark Pharis, Curtis Hoard and retired Regents Professor Warren MacKenzie.[49]

International commitments included additional support for teaching and research related to Asia, particularly China, India, and Japan. Interdisciplinary initiatives connected CLA to health psychology, medical anthropology, and other fields. A new joint Ph.D. program in communication studies linked Minneapolis students and faculty with students and faculty at the Mayo Clinic.

The college committed continuing support for the West Bank Arts Quarter, a part of the campus that was enhanced in spring 1999 by completion of the Barbara Barker Dance Center, and made plans to create a humanities district in the historic knoll area on the East Bank. A number of CLA departments, once dispersed in different parts of the campus, moved to Nolte Center in spring 2000.

Afro-American and African Studies and American Indian Studies had thirtieth anniversaries in 1999; Chicano Studies had its twenty-fifth anniversary two years earlier. Women's Studies celebrated its twenty-fifth anniversary, and the Center for Advanced Feminist Studies, its fifteenth, in 1998. There was a new major in Global Studies, a bachelor of fine arts degree in Theatre offered in collaboration with the Guthrie Theatre, and new interdisciplinary minors in Information Technology and Law and Justice Studies developed with the Institute of Technology and the Law School. These degrees, along with volunteer and internship options, complemented the more generalist perspectives of existing programs.

Because CLA is the university's largest college, its welfare has always been central to the reputation of the university as a whole. More than a decade of attention to the undergraduate experience paid off: incoming students had met the recommended prerequisites; CLA offered smaller classes, additional freshman seminars, and improved advising; donors and friends of the college increased private support for scholarships, faculty positions, and new facilities. Dean Rosenstone observed that "part of our responsibility as a land-grant institution is to offer quality education to the people of Minnesota. We do that by ensuring that the best and the brightest come to the university, want to stay here, and take jobs here."[50]

## The Institute of Technology

In fall 1998, the Institute of Technology (IT) was organized around three major disciplines: engineering, mathematics, and the physical and computational sciences.[51] Fourteen interdisciplinary and interinstitutional centers were affiliated with the institute, which continued to have a strong research profile. As of 1999, twenty-five IT faculty members had been elected to the National Academy of Engineering and sixteen to the National Academy of Sciences.[52] Following Ettore Infante, Francis Kulacki was dean from 1993 to 1995. Regents Professor H. Ted Davis had been dean since 1995.[53]

In addition to maintaining its research strengths, improving undergraduate education had been a high priority since the early 1990s. Physics professor Marvin Marshak explained:

> There's been an overall change in higher education in the United States. Previously, with plentiful resources . . . universities became compartmentalized [between graduate and undergraduate education]. In the past few years, the resources aren't there any longer. . . . for a research institution to prosper, it will have to do all it can do to attract undergraduates. And to do that it must pay a lot of attention to the quality of undergraduate education.[54]

As part of this effort, IT divided entering students into groups of 80 to 100 and assigned each group a faculty adviser, a graduate student adviser, and an undergraduate peer adviser. The students in each group were assigned to at least two common classes and attended group social events. Rama Murthy, the Taylor Professor of Undergraduate Education, reported: "We found that one of the most important criteria for success in IT is camaraderie with other students and faculty."[55]

Professor Sally Gregory Kohlstedt of the history of science and technology program served as associate dean from 1989 to 1995, helping develop programs to encourage young women to enter IT and to support them after they enrolled. Under Susan Marino's direction, the IT organization Women in Technology developed summer computer camps to encourage elementary school girls to plan careers in science and engineering. Enrollment of women increased from less than 2 percent to 13 percent in the early 1980s, to 20 percent of undergraduates in fall 1996, and to 26 percent of freshmen admitted in fall 1997.[56]

IT's Academic Programs for Excellence in Engineering and Science, directed by Samuel Moore (originally established in 1979 as Project Technology Power), recruited minority students to IT. As a result of this and other initiatives, IT had become more diverse in terms of racial and ethnic makeup. Although still small in absolute numbers, African American, American Indian, Chicano, and Latino students increased by 50 percent between 1984 and fall 1997. The number of engineering degrees awarded had increased threefold since 1972.[57]

An important measure of IT productivity was the number of companies—in computers, medical technology, consulting, manufacture of instrumentation, and consulting/engineering/manufacturing—started by IT graduates: 1,003 in a count made in 1993.[58] The hard work and long odds involved in founding a company were described by Thomas G. Kamp, founder of Magnetic Data and Magnetic Peripherals: "Opportunity comes dressed in overalls. It is not just going to happen. Lots of people have brilliant ideas but never do anything with them. It takes a lot of work and is not easy. Be prepared to work at half pay and even no pay because of cash flow problems."[59]

## *The Carlson School of Management*

The Carlson School of Management ended the century having met self-established benchmarks related to undergraduate education, international programs, industry/research and learning centers, executive education, and new facilities. Dean David Kidwell's goal was a top-twenty national ranking. His key strategy was to create "a professional learning community that fosters interaction of students, alumni, management professionals, and scholars to share knowledge and insights to address current and emerging management problems."[60]

In 1996, the school accepted its first lower-division students—before that, undergraduates had entered at the upper-division level—and the change proved to be extremely popular, attracting some of the most talented undergraduates in the university. The school also sought to balance the needs of its undergraduate and graduate students. The School of Public Health master's degree program in health care administration moved to the Carlson School, reflecting a national shift to business schools training health care administrators.[61] Among the international initiatives completed or nearing completion was the executive M.B.A. degree program with Lingnan University in Guangzhou, China, similar to the Vienna and Warsaw executive M.B.A. programs begun earlier.[62]

## The College of Education and Human Development

In 1995 the College of Education was renamed the College of Education and Human Development, reflecting the college's wider involvement in a range of initiatives "to improve the well-being of our children, youth, families, and communities."[63] It had six departments and twenty research and service centers. The college was ranked tenth in the country, according to *U.S. News & World Report.*[64] It had come through a long period of strategic planning in which more than fifty individual teacher education and graduate programs had been consolidated, eliminated, or improved, positioning the college more strongly for investments in a few key areas. In 1997, Dean Robert Bruininks was chosen by President Yudof to be executive vice president and Twin Cities campus provost. Following Charles Hopkins's service as interim dean, Steven R. Yussen became the twelfth dean of the college in 1999.[65]

Among new initiatives in the late 1990s were the Comparative and International Development Program, the Postsecondary Education Policy Studies Center, and the Center for Developmental Neuroscience, merging the efforts of the Institute of Child Development, the Medical School, and the Graduate School. Other priorities included expanding policy research in pre–K-12 education, extending program delivery beyond the Twin Cities, maintaining initiatives to strengthen urban schools, and continuing programs in school leadership with Minnesota State College and University (MnSCU) partners.[66] In addition, there was a collegewide focus on literacy. With twenty retirements at the end of the century, the college was in a position to make a number of new hires.

## General College

In his inaugural address, referring to the General College, President Mark G. Yudof said: "The University of Minnesota has created the best balance between access and excellence that I have observed in any public university in the country."[67] Yudof confirmed the college's mission in developmental education, preparing students to transfer to other colleges of the university or to other postsecondary institutions. Speaking at the 1999 General College convocation, Dean David Taylor cited four major accomplishments: a curriculum with greater integrity and effectiveness, excellence in instruction, a significant increase in research, and record-level student satisfaction with student services.

General College received significant support and endorsement from alumnus Stanley S. Hubbard, CEO of Hubbard Broadcasting and founder of United States Satellite Broadcasting Company, who entered the university through the General College. When he gave a significant gift to the college, he said: "I know there are many students who, like myself, need the stepping stone that General College provides in order to succeed in their future studies and professional lives.... I don't know where I'd be if it weren't for General College."[68]

Based on its mission in general and developmental education and its commitments to multiculturalism, General College, along with the Institute of Technology and the College of Education and Human Development, played a key role in assisting K-12 outreach, especially in urban communities. Taylor was pleased with the changes in the college and its standing at the beginning of the new century: "We have once more become a national model for the delivery of developmental educational services and research into effective teaching practice." In June 2000, the college was named one of the country's top five programs for "best practices" in developmental education in a national study by the American Productivity and Quality Center in Houston.[69]

### The Law School

Under Robert Stein, who served as dean from 1980 to 1995, the Law School became successful in recruiting outstanding women faculty members. When Stein became dean, there were three women among the tenured faculty; when he left, there were eleven. In 1979, there were no racial minorities among the tenured faculty; in 1994, there were four.[70] The school's first significant international initiatives were 1980 links to Uppsala University in Sweden and to several law schools in China. The following year, a summer exchange program was established with University Jean Moulin in Lyon, France. A faculty exchange program was developed in 1987 with Christian Albrechts University in Kiel, West Germany.

Following Stein's departure to become executive director of the American Bar Association, Fred L. Morrison served as acting dean. E. Thomas

Sullivan, a specialist in antitrust law, became the school's eighth dean in 1995, coming to the position from the deanship of the University of Arizona Law School.

The Law School became actively engaged in 1997 in a number of all-university initiatives in law, biotechnology, and bioethics; in intellectual property; and in encouraging new international exchange programs.[71] Other initiatives included new joint Law School/Graduate School degree programs in areas such as health care and life sciences; science, technology, and environment policy; and molecular, cellular developmental biology, genetics, ecology, conservation biology, and pharmacology and the law. Formal ties had been established for a J.D./M.B.A with the Carlson School of Management and a J.D./M.P.A. with the Humphrey Institute of Public Affairs. The Law School had agreed to contribute expertise in "intellectual property protection" and "jurisdictional issues" related to Internet publication, digital technology, and multimedia.[72]

## *The College of Architecture and Landscape Architecture*

Throughout the 1990s, the College of Architecture and Landscape Architecture (CALA) offered two undergraduate degrees: the bachelor of environmental design and, with the College of Liberal Arts, the bachelor of arts in architecture. The college also offered professional and postprofessional degrees in architecture and landscape architecture. Harrison Fraker headed the college from 1984 to 1995. Thomas Fisher, previously editor of *Progressive Architecture* magazine, was named dean in 1996.

During the 1990s, the Design Center for American Urban Landscape, an urban design center in CALA, developed a national reputation for planning and design that helped municipalities deal with community urbanization as well as with social and demographic changes. Helping to define "sustainable development principles" was an important part of the work of the center, headed by William Morrish and Catherine Brown. A 1994 *New York Times* article said the center had "the most valuable thinkers in American urbanism today."[73] The college and Dean Fisher played a leading role in helping to shape an all-university initiative, funded in 1998 to promote the value of design, to educate the public and general student body about it, and to reestablish Minnesota as a national leader in this field.

After many years of operating with extremely cramped studio space, the college received funding in 1998 for an addition to be built adjacent to the existing building. The addition, designed by Steven Holl working with Vincent James and Ellerbe Beckett, was to include public gathering areas and an auditorium as well as a library and slide library, computer labs, student advising space, design studios, and faculty and staff offices.[74] Based on extensive surveys of Minnesota's architecture and landscape architecture communities, the college also planned a new continuing professional education curriculum.[75]

## Hubert H. Humphrey Institute of Public Affairs

In six decades, the Humphrey Institute and its predecessors, the Public Administration Training Center and the School of Public Affairs, granted nearly twelve hundred graduate degrees.[76] Harlan Cleveland served as dean from 1980 to 1986, when the institute's new home on the West Bank was dedicated. G. Edward Schuh was appointed dean in 1987 and made a Regents Professor in 1995. He was succeeded by John E. Brandl in 1998. Describing the culture of the institute, Brandl observed, "If there's one thing that distinguishes the Humphrey Institute, it's the belief that things can be changed. There's a forward-looking optimism here that binds us all together."[77]

Enrolling approximately 130 new students a year, the Humphrey Institute offered an executive master of public affairs degree as well as master's degree programs in public policy; Urban and Regional Planning; and Science, Technology, and Environmental Policy.[78] The institute played an influential role as a nonpartisan resource for individuals, communities, and organizations. More than a dozen research and outreach centers addressed a wide spectrum of issues affecting the public good, from welfare reform to the impact of diversity on philanthropy. In addition to its twenty-one faculty members and several dozen adjunct faculty, the institute had fourteen fellows and senior fellows. Students selected a concentration from seven areas: advanced policy analysis methods; economic and community development; foreign policy and international affairs; public and nonprofit leadership and management; science and technology policy; social policy; and women and public policy.

The institute collaborated with the Carlson School of Management to offer a program in Warsaw, Poland, and ran a midcareer degree program in Olsztyn, Poland. The institute's classroom, research, and outreach programs had an endowment exceeding $50 million.[79] Other institute responsibilities included the Policy Forum, established by former United States vice president Walter Mondale, and coordination of the Carlson Distinguished Lecture Series.

*University Libraries*

With five major facilities and eleven branch sites on the Twin Cities campus, University Libraries held more than 5.5 million volumes, supplemented by hundreds of electronic information resources, placing Minnesota among the top ten public research libraries in the nation.[80] The primary Twin Cities campus libraries were the O. Meredith Wilson Library, the Elmer L. Andersen Library, the Biomedical Library, the Law Library, and the Magrath Library in St. Paul, named in 1999 in honor of the university's eleventh president. Within the Biomedical Library, ranked among the top 10 percent of health sciences libraries, was the Owen Wangensteen Historical Library of Biology and Medicine, which contained more than 62,000 rare and out-of-print books, journals, and manuscripts dating from the medieval period to the early twentieth century.

Andersen Library, completed in 1999 and named in honor of former governor and regent Elmer L. Andersen, housed University Archives and a number of the university's special collections: the Kerlan and Hess Collections of children's literature; the papers of the Charles Babbage Institute for the History of Information Processing, the Immigration History Research Center, the Social Welfare History Archives, and the Kautz Family YMCA Archives; the Elmer L. and Eleanor R. Andersen personal collection, emphasizing the art of the book; the Archie Givens Collection of African American Literature; and the Sherlock Holmes Collection.[81] The library was designed to provide storage space for infrequently used volumes in the main library collection as well as similar materials from public and private libraries throughout the state and to house MINITEX, Minnesota's library resources sharing network.[82]

"It's a wonderful thing," university librarian Thomas Shaughnessy said of Andersen Library's combination of underground storage caverns and above-ground spaces. "I don't think another university has done anything like it." The library was named one of the Seven Wonders of the Engineering World in 1999, and Middleton Engineers and CNA Consulting Engineers were cited for the design and construction of the curved, prefabricated concrete walls that line the cavern. The architects were the Minnesota firm of Stageberg Beyer Sachs. Because much of it was underground, the facility could be conveniently located on the West Bank, a short distance from Wilson Library. Most universities had been forced to develop storage at distant sites; Harvard, for instance, kept rarely used library materials thirty miles from the campus.[83]

In 2000, the Law Library was the sixth-largest academic law library in the United States. It had exceptional basic collections in Anglo-American and comparative and international law. It also housed one of the premier legal rare book collections in the country.

Renovations were planned for the Architecture Library in 2001 and in 2002 for Walter Library, the latter to house the all-university Digital Technology Initiative and the Science and Engineering Library. Beyond the brick and mortar changes, the underlying software for the LUMINA system, serving as the point of electronic access to the libraries, was to be replaced in 2002 by a common system, MnLink, connecting academic, public, and K-12 library systems throughout Minnesota. Selected materials from the Archie Givens Collection of African American Literature and the James Ford Bell Map Collection had been put in digital form in 1998 and 1999— serving as initial tests of a long-term plan to digitize other library holdings.[84]

University librarian Thomas Shaughnessy noted that the libraries faced a number of key issues in the twenty-first century: the ongoing need to adapt to changes in scholarly communication resulting from the impact of new information technologies; the challenge of creating new services to accommodate different student learning styles; and finding ways to deal with extraordinary increases in the cost of scholarly books and periodicals. He noted also that, paradoxically, as library users became more Internet proficient, they expanded their use of learning resources and their need for staff assistance. He pledged that the libraries would seek to make the "fullest use of technology while preserving the best in paper and other more traditional formats and would continue to function as the university's intellectual crossroads and as a revitalized center for research and scholarship."[85]

## The Academic Health Center

As the century ended, both the legislature and private donors were supportive of the Academic Health Center. The legislature had approved $70 million for construction of the new molecular and cellular biology building. In January 2000, members of the family of noted surgeon C. Walton Lillehei announced a gift to establish the Lillehei Heart Institute, an interdisciplinary center bringing together faculty members involved in clinical as well as basic research on the prevention and treatment of heart disease.[86] Outreach continued to connect Academic Health Center programs and services to citizens throughout Minnesota. Senior Vice President Frank Cerra was optimistic that the Academic Health Center would remain "a leader as a producer of technology, new therapies, and new treatments."[87]

The molecular and cellular biology facility, under construction in the heart of the Academic Health Center on the site where Millard and Owre Halls once stood, was designed for interdisciplinary research, connecting biochemists, biologists, geneticists, and molecular scientists from the College of Biological Sciences and the Medical School. President Mark Yudof, who had helped create a similar center at the University of Texas, considered this one of the most significant initiatives of his administration: "We have simply got to get it right. The academic future of the university and the economic health of Minnesota are at stake." He noted that 70 percent of all research expenditures at the university were for biology, broadly defined.[88]

Cerra predicted that the molecular and cellular biology center would allow researchers to perform at the leading edge of scientific exploration, significantly increasing their understanding of the functioning of cells, thereby enhancing their capability to predict, prevent, and correct illnesses. Discoveries at Minnesota, and in other leading scientific centers, were expected to have a dramatic impact on a number of diseases. There was collaboration not only with the College of Biological Sciences faculty, but also with faculty members in child development, psychology, engineering, and philosophy.

## The Medical School

The Medical School was the largest of the units in the Academic Health Center in enrollment, faculty size, and research dollars, ranking nationally among the top ten public institutions in the receipt of National Institutes of Health grants. It had four deans in the 1990s; David Brown, Shelly Chou, Frank Cerra, and Alfred Michael. In his 2000 annual report on the state of the Medical School, Regents Professor and Dean Alfred Michael expressed optimism despite daunting challenges facing medical education: "We see ourselves once again poised as national and international leaders in medicine."[89] On another occasion, Michael stressed the important developments in the biological sciences: "There is no field of medicine untouched by the search that has come out of understanding DNA and cell biology."[90]

In June 1999, in recognition of his research on viral infections, Ashley Haase, chair of microbiology, was elected Regents Professor. Haase's work on viruses that lie dormant in the body before becoming active had major implications for the study of the AIDS virus and had helped in the university's being designated a national center for AIDS research. Commenting on medical research at the university at the end of the century compared to earlier decades, Haase observed that "the breakthroughs in the 1990s are more subtle: advances in cardiovascular disease, studies of viral infections, responses to new drug therapies do not have the same visibility as a new heart." If they were less visible, they were no less important; Haase had suggested that from a scientific point of view, molecular biology "was as exciting [in 2000] as physics was seventy-five years ago." Alongside the new emphases, he cited continuity with the Medical School of earlier generations: "The commitment to teamwork for which Minnesota is known continues as basic scientists and clinical researchers work to maintain the circular path of research linking the laboratory to the bedside."[91]

In 2000, Haase was named director of the Academic Health Center's new biomedical genomics center. Working in such areas as stem cell development, cancer genomics, and drug discovery, the center planned collaboration with the plant and microbial genomics group as well as with the Law School. One of the center's key objectives was to acquire and share technologies for functional genomics research. In recognition of the critical importance of information technology in carrying out microbial research, the Academic Health Center invested in biological computational expertise by developing the Center for Bioinformatics.[92]

Catherine Verfaillie, nationally recognized for her research in stem cell biology, came to the university in 1988. The pathbreaking research in this field, of which Verfaillie's research was a part, led to better understanding of cell development. Verfaillie reported that scientists were close to being able to identify stem cells that could regenerate diseased organs and correct abnormalities. About her experience at Minnesota, Verfaillie observed: "The biggest strength is the diversity of people. There is extreme collegiality. You can learn as much as you could possibly want to from peers. . . . There is support from people at all levels. . . . It's real." She also complimented the students, noting that she found her M.D. and Ph.D. students to be "extremely good."[93]

Christopher Pennell explored molecular solutions for a "magic bullet" that could target leukemic cells while missing healthy cells.[94] To encourage research on the brain, the U.S. Congress had designated the 1990s the Decade of the Brain. Faculty members from neurosurgery, neurology, physiology, laboratory medicine, and pathology joined together in 1999 to form the Department of Neuroscience to integrate their research. Department head Tim Ebner, an M.D. and Ph.D., pointed out that there were "more diseases of the brain than [of] any other system of the body. . . . We must understand it better. There's hardly anyone who hasn't been touched in some way by conditions like Alzheimer's, Parkinson's disease, strokes, epilepsy, and schizophrenia."[95] Karen Hsiao's research on Alzheimer's disease contributed significantly to a broader understanding of the disorder; her mouse model was considered one of the top ten medical advances of 1996. Researchers were under pressure from animal rights groups. In 1999, animal rights activists broke into two university research labs, released animals, tampered with research data, and destroyed equipment.[96] In 1999, a new procedure for detecting cancerous tumors was patented by Dr. Douglas Collins of the Mayo Clinic and his former adviser, Harry Hogenkamp of Minnesota's biochemistry department.

The nation's medical schools faced an issue that had been developing over many years: the funding of medical education. Medicare and other health insurers, stretched with growing demand, limited their payments to patient care and discontinued reimbursements for costs associated with training physicians. Minnesota legislators, aware that the state was contributing only about 11 percent of the cost of medical education and wanting to ensure that Minnesota would continue to be ranked among the nation's top medical schools, worked closely with administrators to address the funding shortfall. In 1999–2000, the legislature allocated to the university for medical education some of the funding received in the settlement of a lawsuit against tobacco companies and also replaced a portion of the Medicare dollars that had been provided for post-M.D. specialty training. Although the problem of providing funds for medical education was far from solved, university administrators were grateful for the legislative assistance. Continuing to address this question was one of the new century's top priorities.[97]

## Dentistry

The School of Dentistry continued to be among the country's leaders in dental education, with a model clinical education program. The school had long been regarded as a national leader in training outstanding clinicians. The Dental Clinics served more than 125,000 patients annually; they were a major source of dental care for indigent people. The school had trained 95 percent of Minnesota's dentists and was the only dental school in the northern states between Wisconsin and the West Coast. Richard Elzay served as dean from 1986 to 1996, Michael Till from 1996 through August 2000. Till, who had been head of pediatric dentistry for twenty years prior to becoming dean, was one of the developers of the well-known No Cavity

Clinic.[98] In August 2000, Peter Polverini, former head of the Department of Oral Medicine, Pathology, and Oncology at the University of Michigan, became the school's eleventh dean. Known for his research on blood vessel growth, Polverini was attracted to the position by the strengths of the Academic Health Center: "It has the potential to be one of the outstanding institutions in the world."[99]

The dental school was organized into four departments: diagnostic and surgical sciences, oral sciences, preventive sciences, and restorative sciences. Priorities at the end of the century included development of a new master of science degree program, continued participation in the university's Center for Biomaterials and Biomechanics, and outreach programs. The Virtual Dental Patient, a software program developed by researchers William Douglas and Ralph Delong, was designed to help predict in advance the probability of wear on dental enamel long before it actually occurred.[100]

Dean Till noted that dental research continued to evolve, including an emphasis on prevention and care as well as on treatment. Dentists were making continued improvement in the use of bonding materials. He reported that patient comfort had been dramatically improved: "We have come a long way from the days of belt-driven drills. Now there are ultra-high-speed drills that are far more comfortable for patients."[101] Dental researchers were joining with colleagues in other disciplines to carry out research at the molecular level. Dentistry faculty members Donald Simone and Patrick Mantyh, for example, developed "molecular missiles" to destroy nerve cells that create sensitivity to pain.[102] Dental hygiene, the second university-affiliated dental hygiene program in the United States, celebrated its seventy-fifth anniversary in 1995. Enrollment in the program had increased to over 100 students at the end of the century, when the program accepted only bachelor's degree candidates, having phased out its two-year program in 1990.[103]

## Nursing

School of Nursing dean Sandra Edwardson described the 1990s as a period of "cultural transition from an academic unit that emphasized teaching and public service much more than research to a unit that can balance all three roles, but places a greater emphasis on research and graduate education. . . . We are trying to integrate practice, research, and teaching more completely."[104] Edwardson acknowledged the leadership of Deans Irene Ramey (1975–79) and Ellen F. Fahey (1980–90) in guiding these changes. The

Katharine J. Densford Center for Nursing Leadership, established in 1998 and named in honor of the school's director from 1930 to 1959, was the first university-based center of nursing to be dedicated explicitly to nurse leadership. Gifts to the center came from individuals, corporations (3M, Medtronic), and the Fairview Health System Foundation.[105] Nursing alumna Kathryn Lillehei gave a $3 million endowment to help fund the director's salary.[106]

In 1999, the Academic Health Center became the first in the country to offer a graduate minor in complementary care.[107] The new degree program, offered as an interdisciplinary minor in complementary therapies and healing practices, was housed for its first three years in the School of Nursing. Subsequently a part of the Center for Spirituality and Healing, it was one of the most innovative Academic Health Center interdisciplinary programs. Mariah Snyder, head of the division of adults, gerontological nursing, and psychiatric/mental health nursing, was director of graduate studies for the program. Snyder explained that in addition to offering master's-level work, the program could serve doctoral students interested in research on complementary treatment and healing.[108] Mary Jo Kreitzer, Ph.D., and Gregory Plotnikoff, M.D., were key figures in the development of the center. Assistance from Bruce Dayton and Ruth Stricker, who made a lead gift, helped establish it.[109]

## The College of Pharmacy

As the development of new drugs continued at an unprecedented pace and as the post–World War II baby-boom generation entered their fifties, America saw dramatically escalating costs related to the development of new drugs and to inappropriate uses of medication; it was estimated that costs related to the inappropriate use of drugs, including hospitalization, additional medication, and further medical care, were as high as $76 billion a year.[110] Because pharmacists were often the most accessible health care professionals, they were in a position to advise both patients and physicians, and their role in health care broadened accordingly. Pharmacy faculty member Joseph Hanlon, holder of the VFW Endowed Chair in Pharmacotherapy for the Elderly, said, "If you put a smart pharmacist with smart doctors, you will be able to manage medication better and maybe keep some people out of the hospital or the emergency room." As part of his research on medication use by the elderly, he developed a medication appropriateness index to guide pharmacists and other health care professionals.[111]

Stephen Schondelmeyer's research focused on one of the most pressing public policy issues of the 1990s—the affordability of prescription drugs. Schondelmeyer highlighted the gap between availability and affordability: "We have great drugs available, but many people cannot afford [them]. It seems a vast irony that drugs are not being used because the people who need them can't afford them."[112] Other faculty members were researching drug delivery, new drugs for breast cancer, drug therapy for epilepsy in the elderly, opiate receptor activity, antiviral studies, and physical characterization of drugs for dosage formulation. Indicative of its national reputation, the College of Pharmacy continued to oversee the publication of two professional pharmacy journals, the *Journal of Medicinal Chemistry* and the *Journal of Pharmaceutical Sciences.*[113]

Pharmacy's 1992 centennial offered an opportunity to review past accomplishments: national leadership in curriculum development, close ties to the practicing pharmacy community, and the strong research record of its faculty.[114] In 1994, the college received a $13.5 million gift—at the time, the second-largest private gift to the university—from alumnus William Peters and his wife, Mildred, who had operated Lowry Hill Pharmacy in Minneapolis. The Peters gift was used to expand scholarships, enhance endowed chairs,[115] and establish the Peters Institute of Pharmaceutical Care to advance the practice of pharmaceutical care through publications, conferences, and research.[116]

Minnesota's doctor of pharmacy (Pharm.D.) curriculum, pioneered in the 1970s and the only entry-level professional degree beginning with the class of 1995, emphasized training generalist practitioners. Faculty members Linda Strand, Robert Cipolle, and Peter Morley had gained national and international recognition for their work on the development of principles of pharmaceutical care central to the curriculum. In the mid-1990s, a newly established Pharmaceutical Care Laboratory allowed students to develop skills appropriate to the different settings they might encounter when they entered practice. Marilyn Speedie, formerly chair of the Department of Pharmaceutical Sciences at the University of Maryland, was named dean in 1996. Speedie underscored the importance of patient care: "In a forty-year practice, facts will change, practice will evolve; focus on patient care will remain central."[117]

The College of Pharmacy remained at the forefront of change as the profession continued to evolve from a focus on dispensing drug products to a broader emphasis on patient care and use of medications. In addition to the entry-level Pharm.D. degree, the college offered practicing pharmacists an opportunity to acquire the degree using a Web-based curriculum, and also continued to offer master's and doctoral work in pharmaceutical disciplines. The national reputation of the college remained high as the century ended: it was ranked fifth among colleges of pharmacy by *U.S. News & World Report*. As the only college of pharmacy in Minnesota, where two-thirds of the practicing pharmacists were its graduates, the college continued to benefit from close working connections to the practice community.

## The School of Public Health

The School of Public Health observed its fiftieth anniversary in 1995 and celebrated its achievements: its faculty members were involved in landmark discoveries of the links between cholesterol and heart attacks, and between smoking and health problems, as well as programs that led to cleaner air and water, safer farms, and healthier people, particularly babies. Exemplifying the benefits of a healthy lifestyle and diet, researcher Ancel Keys celebrated his ninety-fifth birthday in 1999. His recommendations to eat vegetables and fish, minimize beef and pork, engage in moderate physical activity, and avoid smoking were revolutionary when he made them in the 1960s; in the 1990s, they were widely accepted.

In 1996, Edith Leyasmeyer was selected dean, a position she held through December 2000. Before joining the School of Public Health in 1980 as associate dean and executive officer, Leyasmeyer, who had earned a Ph.D. in hospital and health care administration from the University of Minnesota, had been director of the University Area Health Education Center and director of education for the Northlands Regional Medical Program. In addition, Leyasmeyer had served as acting or interim dean three times, for a total of nearly six years. The school remained among the top five state schools of public health in the country. New initiatives included dual degrees with the Law School and the School of Journalism, and delivery of courses to the University of Minnesota in Rochester.

Leyasmeyer noted: "Threats to public health are as formidable as ever. In this country, heart disease, cancer, and stroke are the major causes of death. Other afflictions, not even perceived as issues a few decades ago, pose ominous threats to society; [among them are] AIDS, violence, substance abuse, teen pregnancy, health problems of the elderly, and environmental pollution." The faculty was at the cutting edge of knowledge about these issues.[118] In 1996, Leonard M. Schuman, who had established the school's advanced program in epidemiology forty years earlier, was awarded the Sedgwick Memorial Medal of the American Public Health Association, its highest honor.[119] Mark P. Becker became dean in 2001. Before coming to Minnesota, he served as associate dean for Academic Affairs and professor of biostatistics at the University of Michigan School of Public Health.

## The College of Veterinary Medicine

The College of Veterinary Medicine, continuing to benefit from its affiliation with the Academic Health Center, was ranked eighth among colleges of Veterinary Medicine in the Gourman Report and eleventh by *U.S. News and World Report*.[120] David G. Thawley, chair of the Department of Large Animal Sciences and acting dean in 1988, became dean in 1990 and served for eight years. In 1998 Jeffrey Klausner, a faculty member in the Department of Small Animal Clinic Sciences, became acting dean and the following year was made dean. During the 1990s, the college undertook a major curriculum revision encompassing its doctor of veterinary medicine (D.V.M.), graduate degrees and continuing education and extension programs. The new curriculum strengthened the emphasis on lifelong learning, communication and information management skills, flexibility, and the integration of the basic and clinical sciences. Other initiatives were advances in technology that enhanced learning in all programs, restructuring graduate programs, and the introduction of new outreach programs. The 385 D.V.M. students in the fall of 2000 represented a fifteenfold increase over the first class enrolled in the fall of 1947.

The 1990s were also marked by an increase in service activities. The Veterinary Diagnostic Laboratory and the Teaching Hospital continued to expand their activities and case loads, serving both state and region. The Teaching Hospital saw over 35,000 small animals and 2,500 large animals annually, and the Diagnostic Clinic provided state-of-the-art diagnostic tests, often developed within the college. The Raptor Center remained one of the university's most popular and visible programs, nationally known for its expertise in the treatment of bald eagles, hawks, owls, and falcons. When the bald eagle was removed from the endangered species in 1999, Patrick Redig, director and cofounder of the center, was a key participant at the White House ceremony to recognize this change. Although the ten-thousandth admission was an injured eagle from Venezuela, most of the birds treated came from Minnesota and surrounding states. A number of injured birds of prey from outside Minnesota were flown in for treatment at the university by Northwest Airlines.[121]

Research in the College focused on molecular and cellular investigations as well as studies of whole animal health. Work in the advanced Genetic Analysis Center by faculty in the Department of Veterinary Pathobiology led to the landmark sequencing of the entire genome of the organism *Pasteurella multocida*, a common cause of disease among livestock. The Food Animal Biotechnology Center was created as a site for molecular biology and genome mapping research applied to food production. Other centers addressed companion animal and equine health, dairy health management and food quality, and veterinary clinical investigation of new medications and devices. College faculty and researchers developed new diagnostic tests for avian pneumovirus, crucial for the state's turkey industry, as well as a vaccine for porcine reproductive/respiratory syndrome directed at a virus that attacks unborn pigs.[122] College faculty identified a gene and developed a test for lethal white syndrome in paint horses. By 1998, animal research expenditures had increased more than 50 percent over the previous decade.

## The Graduate School

The Graduate School awarded its first Ph.D. in 1888; it was among the earliest programs granting doctorates in the United States. Since 1950, the program had grown in numbers and had become more balanced in terms of gender. In fall 1998, the Graduate School had just over 8,000 registrants; 48 percent were women. In 1950, there had been about half as many students, only 14 percent of them women. The number and variety of programs had also grown. In 1950, there were 90 graduate programs; in fall 1997, there were 167.[123] In 1950, sponsored research expenditures were just over $4 million; for fiscal year 1998–99, they were over $35 million.[124] In 1950–51, eight patents were issued; in fall 1997, there were sixty-six.[125]

In 1992, the responsibility for overseeing research was combined with the Graduate School deanship. Anne Petersen held the new position, vice president for research and dean of the Graduate School, from 1992 to 1994; she left the university when she was appointed deputy director of the National Science Foundation by President Clinton. Mark Brenner served as acting dean from 1994 to 1996, and as dean from 1996 to 1998. In 1998, President Yudof appointed Christine M. Maziar, professor of electrical and computer engineering and vice provost at the University of Texas, to the position. She was responsible for the university's research grant activity, approximating $350 million a year; for the nearly $5 million dollars in central funding for graduate student fellowships; and for overseeing the Supercomputer

Institute, Sponsored Projects Administration, Patents and Technology Transfer, the Office of Oversight Analysis and Reporting, University of Minnesota Press, the Hormel Institute, the Center for Urban and Regional Affairs, the Large Lake Observatory, Sea Grant, and the Center for Transportation Studies. Vice President Maziar and the Institute of Technology assumed responsibility for leading the university's new Digital Technology Initiative.

The Graduate School improved internal processes, implementing a new registration system, reviewing the Research Subjects Protection Program, improving the Grants Management Program, and reorganizing the Office of Research and Technology Transfer Administration into three separate functions: Sponsored Projects Administration, Patents and Technology Marketing, and the Office of Institutional Analysis Reporting.[126]

## The College of Biological Sciences

For the College of Biological Sciences (CBS), the 1990s were a time of extraordinary opportunity. Paul T. "Pete" Magee was dean from 1987 to 1995. Robert Elde, who became dean in 1995, strongly endorsed collaboration with the Academic Health Center, explaining that "work at the molecular and cellular level is the basis for curing disease, making our food supply safer, and generating crops that can feed a hungry world more sustainably and efficiently."[127] Graduate and undergraduate programs were offered in both Minneapolis and St. Paul, and the faculty was involved in the university's investments in molecular biology. Steve Gantt, head of plant biology, indicated that new staff members and resources would allow the department "to become a major player in genomics."[128] Larry Wackett, professor of biochemistry, molecular biology, and biophysics, and Michael Sadowsky, professor of soil, water, and climate, combined their expertise at the molecular and cellular level to study whether bacteria could be engineered to clean up contaminated soil. Their results, based on the study of an accidental spill of 250 gallons of atrazine, were positive.[129]

Another faculty researcher, Robert Herman, maintained a collection of more than 3,500 strains of the nematode worm *C. elegans,* which he supplied to researchers worldwide working to understand the genome of this model organism. In the same department, genetics, cell biology, and development, Professor Perry Hackett constructed a DNA sequence that could move itself from one vertebrate chromosome to another. Nicknamed "Sleeping Beauty," this gene was revived from one that ceased functioning 15 mil-

C. Peter Magrath, eleventh president of the university, confers an honorary doctor of laws degree on Minnesotan Chief Justice Warren Burger. Photograph by John Ryan.

Norman Borlaug examines sheaves of wheat. The impact of his work on global food production was recognized in 1970 when he received the Nobel Peace Prize. Photograph courtesy of the University of Minnesota Archives, Twin Cities.

Ronald Phillips, faculty member in agronomy and plant genetics, and subsequently Regents Professor and McKnight Presidential Chair in Genomics, gives a presentation in 1977 at the West Central Experiment Station in Morris. Photograph by Dave Hansen; courtesy of the University of Minnesota Agricultural Experiment Station.

Farmers gathered to hear University of Minnesota Extension agents and other specialists discuss ways of dealing with the severe crisis in agriculture in the 1980s. Photograph courtesy of the University of Minnesota Agricultural Experiment Station.

Attending a dinner in 1978 at which it was announced that the School of Public Affairs was to be renamed the Hubert H. Humphrey School of Public Affairs are business leader and university benefactor Curtis L. Carlson, Hubert Humphrey, university president C. Peter Magrath, attorney Julius Davis, and chair of the Board of Regents Wenda W. Moore. Photograph courtesy of the University of Minnesota Archives, Twin Cities.

The University of Minnesota actively renewed connections with China following President Nixon's reopening of relations with the People's Republic in 1972. This university delegation in 1979 was led by chair of the Board of Regents Wenda W. Moore. Photograph courtesy of the University of Minnesota China Center.

Testimony to a heightened consciousness about environmental concerns, Duluth students celebrated Earth Days in 1971. It would become an annual campus event. Photograph courtesy of the University of Minnesota Archives, Duluth.

A group of madrigal singers participates in the Elizabethan dinners held at the University of Minnesota Duluth from 1974 to 1987. Photograph courtesy of the University of Minnesota Archives, Duluth.

The Bulldogs raise coach Mike Sertich on their shoulders to celebrate Duluth's first Western Collegiate Hockey (WCHA) championship in 1984. Photograph provided by the *Duluth Herald Tribune*.

Mychal Thompson plays in a game in 1977 in which the Gophers defeated Air Force 66 to 50. Photograph courtesy of University of Minnesota Men's Intercollegiate Athletics, Twin Cities.

Minnesota amateur golfer Patty Berg was one of the first community leaders to work actively to increase athletic opportunities for women. Berg is shown here in 1977 making a fundraising film to support Women's Intercollegiate Athletics. To Berg's left is Ce Ce Cox, a Gopher runner; to her right is Gopher cross-country All-American Cathie Twomie and cross-country coach Mike Lawless. Photograph by Pam Smith; courtesy of the University of Minnesota Women's Intercollegiate Athletics, Twin Cities.

Kenneth H. Keller, twelfth president of the university. During his administration, Commitment to Focus articulated principles guiding university planning. Photograph by Tom Foley.

Nils Hasselmo, the university's thirteenth president, and student Derek Stevenson, participating in a College of Education mentoring program. Photograph by Tom Foley.

Donald Sargeant, chancellor at Crookston since 1985, meets with Soo-Yin Lim-Thompson, a faculty member in early childhood education at Crookston. Photograph courtesy of Media Services, University of Minnesota Crookston.

Attending the opening of the Duluth Campus Center in 1995 are (left to right) Lawrence Ianni (chancellor from 1987 to 1995); Gerry Heller, widow of Robert Heller (chancellor from 1976 to 1987); Kathryn A. Martin (chancellor since 1995); and Robert Carlson, faculty member in chemistry and former vice chancellor of academic administration and chair of the building committee. Photograph courtesy of the University of Minnesota Archives, Duluth.

David Johnson, chancellor of the University of Minnesota Morris from 1990 to 1998 and Samuel Schuman, chancellor in 2000. Photograph courtesy of University Relations, University of Minnesota Morris.

David Pui, Distinguished McKnight Professor in the Department of Mechanical Engineering (left); Christine Wendt, assistant professor in the Medical School; and Da-Ren Chen, assistant professor of mechanical engineering, with the "gene gun" they developed for inserting DNA into cells. Photograph by Jonathan Chapman, Institute of Technology Communications.

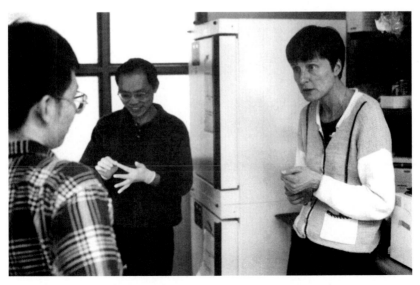

Catherine Verfaillie, director of the Stem Cell Institute, professor of medicine, and member of the university's bone-marrow transplant research group, with two post-doctoral researchers in her laboratory. She is nationally recognized for her research in stem cell biology. Photograph by Richard G. Anderson.

Robert J. Jones, professor of agronomy and plant genetics, demonstrates for student Starr Autman the impact of heat on kernel development in maize. Photograph by Tom Foley.

Political science faculty member Katherine Sikkink (left), winner in 2000 of the Grawemeyer Award for Ideas Improving World Order, discusses with student Janet al'Azar her project on "Democratization in Latin America." Photograph by John Noltner.

Students in the Native Americans in Medicine Program at Duluth. Begun in 1984, this is one of the most successful programs providing medical training for Native American students. Photograph courtesy of the University of Minnesota Archives, Duluth.

St. Paul resident Helen Chaseley is one of 25,000 people who listen each week to the University of Minnesota television program *Health Talk and You*. Hosted by Gregory Vercellotti, associate dean of the Medical School (shown on the television screen), the weekly one-hour program addresses a variety of medical and health topics. Photograph by Richard G. Anderson.

The victory of the men's Gopher hockey team over Northern Michigan in March 1993 was the second of two consecutive WCHA postseason tournament championships. Photograph courtesy of University of Minnesota Men's Intercollegiate Athletics, Twin Cities.

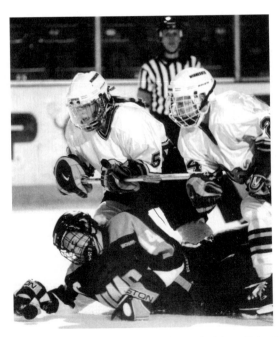

Women's hockey became a major sport in Duluth and the Twin Cities. Pictured is the December 3, 1999, game between the teams, won by the Duluth Bulldogs, 5 to 4. In 2000 the Gophers won the American Women's Collegiate Hockey Alliance tournament, becoming the first University of Minnesota women's team to win a national championship. The Bulldogs were semifinalists in the same tournament. Photograph courtesy of University of Minnesota Women's Intercollegiate Athletics, Twin Cities.

Craig Everett "Rett" Martin, College of Liberal Arts, from Fergus Falls; Mark Sier, Carlson School of Management, from Appleton, Wisconsin; and Laura Braith, University College, from Delano, on the Minneapolis campus mall following the fall 1999 freshman convocation. They were given hard hats in recognition of the extensive construction under way on the campus. Photograph by Tom Foley.

Jack Zipes, faculty member in German and children's literature, talks with students in front of Folwell Hall on the Minneapolis campus. Photograph by Mitch Kezar.

Mark G. Yudof, the university's fourteenth president, and his wife, Judy, accompanied by chair of the Board of Regents Patricia Spence, participate in inaugural ceremonies for Campaign Minnesota. Photograph by Tom Foley.

lion years ago and is part of a body of research expected to offer a better understanding of hereditary diseases.[130]

An example of field research was the work of faculty member Anne Pusey, professor of ecology, evolution, and behavior, who spent twenty-five years doing research on female chimps in Tanzania's Gombe Stream under the direction of Jane Goodall, world-renowned expert on chimpanzees. Pusey became the first scholar to "show the effect of rank" in the lives of female chimps. Pusey's efforts and the cooperation of Jane Goodall led to the university's becoming the repository for Goodall's papers and establishment of the Jane Goodall Institute's Center for Primate Studies, maintaining important data for future scholars.[131]

The college managed the Lake Itasca Forestry and Biological Station, and the Cedar Creek Natural History Area. Located two hundred miles north of the Twin Cities, in Itasca State Park, the Lake Itasca Station was situated at the meeting place of three plant regions of the United States. Students could enroll in six-week, dawn-to-dusk "boot camp" sessions in neuroscience and molecular biology as well as in traditional field research classes. The station offered well-equipped research labs in a field station. In 1999, the station celebrated its ninetieth anniversary with more than two hundred alumni and friends present. Originally a part of the College of Forestry, the station had been managed by the College of Biological Sciences since 1970. The Cedar Creek Natural History Area, located on the edge of the Twin Cities metropolitan area, was a world-renowned center for ecological and biodiversity research.[132]

CBS made major contributions to university-wide improvements in undergraduate residential life. In the late 1990s, the college created Biology House, a block of rooms in Frontier Hall for students interested in biology; Biology House students participated in a fall field trip to the Lake Itasca Station and visited the Raptor Center, the Bell Museum of Natural History, and the Science Museum in St. Paul.

## The College of Agricultural, Food, and Environmental Sciences

The College of Agricultural, Food, and Environmental Sciences (COAFES) ranked among the top ten agricultural science programs in the United States; a number of its departments ranked among the top five nationally.[133] A considerable number of faculty members who taught in the undergraduate programs were members of the university's Academy of Distinguished Teachers. Administrators of the college were Keith Wharton (interim dean, 1988–

90), Richard L. Jones (dean, 1991–95), Michael V. Martin (dean, 1995–98), Philip O. Larson (interim dean, 1998–99), and Charles Muscoplat, who became dean and director of the experiment station in 1999. Key priorities were adding faculty positions in soybean production, disease and pest management, plant genetics and breeding, and water management; expanding the role of the research and outreach centers, formerly known as experiment stations; and strengthening programs linked to the all-university initiatives in molecular and cellular biology, digital technology, and design.

The college was committed to expanding undergraduate partnerships such as those with Southwest State University, Fond Du Lac Tribal College, and the University Center in Rochester.[134] One of the major public policy issues facing COAFES, as well as other university units involved in molecular research, related to the genetic alteration of food; early in the new century, public concern about the safety of genetically altered food escalated.[135] COAFES was involved in long-range planning for future use of the 7,500 acres at the Rosemount Research Center south of the Twin Cities; a task force appointed by President Yudof and chaired by Thomas Fisher, dean of the College of Architecture and Landscape Architecture, recommended that an integrated plan be developed to address the complex agricultural, environmental, and ecological issues implicit in the future development of this extensive tract of land.

### The College of Human Ecology

Celebrating its centennial in 2000, the College of Human Ecology had three departments—Design, Housing, and Apparel; Family Social Science; and Food Science and Nutrition—and the School of Social Work. Surveys placed it second among its peers in undergraduate education. Joanne B. Eicher was named a Regents Professor in 1995. The college was closely linked to the all-university design initiative and had plans to continue offering the master of social work degree by distance education in Rochester. The college's alumni participation rate was among the highest in the university.

The college was led for nearly thirty years by two deans. Keith McFarland served from 1973 to 1987. Mary Heltsley became dean of the college in 1987, and in 1999 became associate provost of the Twin Cities campus, assuming responsibility for expanding the university's role in Rochester.[136] Daniel Detzner, associate dean for academic affairs and a family social science faculty member, was interim dean until Shirley Baugher, professor and chair of family and consumer services at the University of Nebraska-Lincoln—known for her scholarly work in cross-cultural and community issues—was appointed dean in 2000.[137]

## The College of Natural Resources

The College of Natural Resources continued to be ranked among the country's top colleges. Building on its original emphasis on the conservation and use of natural resources, particularly forests, the college expanded its curriculum to include "broader environmental and natural resource concerns of ecosystem management, sustainable development, and environmental quality."[138] Its departments were fisheries and wildlife; forest resources; and wood and paper science. The forestry program was ranked first in the Gourman report in two successive years; fisheries and wildlife ranked fifth, and natural resources management ranked seventh. The college also oversaw the James Ford Bell Museum of Natural History, the Cloquet Forestry Center, and programs at the North Central Experiment Station in Grand Rapids.

The college was actively involved in all-university molecular and cellular biology initiatives. A key priority was distance-delivered courses offered by the Department of Wood and Paper Science at Rainy River Community College, Itasca Community College, and the University of Minnesota, Duluth. The college planned private fund-raising for rebuilding the Bell Museum of Natural History and to expand its programming, particularly distance learning programs. Alfred Sullivan became dean in 1993 and held that position through the end of the century.

## *The Experiment Station*

Since World War II, experiment station faculty members in agronomy and plant genetics, entomology, soil science, plant pathology, and horticulture had carried out basic research on plants, often at the molecular level, building on the accomplishments of E. C. Stakman, H. H. Flor, J. J. Christensen, and, more recently, of Regents Professor Ronald Phillips. Researchers explored tillage and crop rotation, disease resistance and nutritional make-up of grains and grasses, ornamental flowers and shrubs, and fruits. Their counterparts in animal science, dairy science, and poultry science carried out research in areas such as breeding, maintenance, health, and nutritional management of swine, sheep, beef and dairy cattle, and poultry. Agricultural engineering ensured that the Minnesota economy benefited from the dramatic changes affecting equipment and technology, and agricultural economists contributed to a greater understanding of the impact of the local and global economy on Minnesota business and agriculture. Researchers from food science and nutrition were leaders in studies of food safety, community nutrition, quality milk and dairy products, and cereal chemistry and technology.

A few indicators since 1945 illustrated the approximate extent of this impact on yields per acre: wheat increased from 17 to 42 bushels, corn from 33 to approximately 133 bushels, and soybeans from 18 to 40 bushels. Crops new to Minnesota developed in part through experiment station research included sunflowers, soybeans, and sugar beets. At the end of the century, Minnesota agriculture accounted for $8.5 billion in total receipts and $2.3 billion generated through agricultural exports, representing approximately 20 percent of state revenues. Commercial horticulture added $2.3 billion in revenues. Minnesota ranked seventh in the country in total cash receipts from agriculture.[139]

Faculty members in the College of Forestry carried out basic research on growth patterns, disease resistance, and regeneration. They helped develop a new industry in fiberboard and particles drawn from pine and spruce, and played a role in new issues that developed as forests were considered from the multiple perspectives of industry, recreation, and ecology. Faculty members in home economics (in 1990 renamed Human Ecology) concentrated on how people are affected by their social, physical, and biological environments. They conducted research on nutrition, at-risk behaviors among adolescents, and stress and tension in family business. Food science and nutrition, administered jointly by the College of Agricultural, Food, and Environmental Sciences and the College of Human Ecology, was a leader in research in areas such as cheese production, food safety, and quality in dairy products.[140]

## The University of Minnesota, Crookston

When the state experienced revenue problems in 1991, the university considered closing the technical college at Crookston as well as the campus at Waseca. Both campuses were asked to submit proposals encompassing dramatic changes; it was clear that bold action would be required if Crookston were to survive. In effect, Chancellor Donald Sargeant and his colleagues received a "change or close" ultimatum. They proposed a plan to increase enrollment by three hundred full-time-equivalent students a year, to lower the cost of instruction per student. They also proposed adding baccalaureate degrees, which was approved by state higher education authorities in 1993.

Perhaps the most interesting innovation involved computers. In summer 1992, UMC surveyed more than a thousand individuals to ascertain the skills and abilities needed by baccalaureate graduates. Employers, high school students, parents, alumni, and counselors indicated that skills in communications and human relations as well as computer literacy were increasingly important. In particular, the survey noted that employers found college curricula lacking in courses on computer technology; employers believed the gap between the computer competencies they hoped to find in employees and what they were actually finding was widening. Crookston seized the initiative to become one of the first colleges in the world to provide all faculty and students with notebook computers. Campus facilities were "wired" to provide connectivity at every classroom seat, dorm room, and gathering place; computer-based technology was integrated into the total teaching and learning environment. Becoming a "laptop university" offering career-oriented baccalaureate degrees provided the basis for a dramatic turnaround. By fall 1999, enrollment had reached nearly 2,500, and *U.S. News & World Report* had acknowledged Crookston's leadership.[141]

As a polytechnic baccalaureate institution, Crookston offered degrees in agriculture, business, communications, environmental sciences, human resource development, and technical studies that emphasized both applied theory and specialized skills. New degrees initiated at the end of the century included a B.S. degree in golf facilities and turf systems management; a natural resources law enforcement option offered through partnership with Bemidji State University; and a B.S. degree in hotel, restaurant, and institutional management instituted with Southwest State University in Marshall. The B.S. degree in sports management initiated in 1998 proved to be extremely popular, as did the program in equine industries management.[142]

Donald Sargeant, in his fifteenth year as chancellor and his thirtieth year as a faculty member, commented on the investment in computer technology: "The primary benefit is that students will acquire the technological savvy they will need for jobs in the twenty-first century."[143]

Along with experiment station and extension service staff members, UMC faculty and staff were aggressive in responding to changes affecting the area and continuing agricultural research. The campus was a leader in regional and community involvement addressing critical needs in economic development. Barbara Muesing, director of outreach programs at the campus, reported:

> Because the Crookston campus sits in the middle of the farm crisis, there is every reason to think that our school would be in a similar state of crisis. But we are not. The reason is that our campus community embraces change as a way of life and of doing business. Consequently, we provide an effective bridge for dozens of farm men and women who are forced to leave their farming operations and change careers.[144]

Two families demonstrated how education could help make the transition from farming to alternative careers that would allow them to remain in northwestern Minnesota. Carolyn and Dan Weber stopped farming when the farm economy worsened and Dan, at age thirty-eight, had a stress-related heart attack. They auctioned off their farm equipment but decided to stay on the homestead near Crookston and both enrolled at UMC. Carolyn decided to enter graduate school, describing her academic career as "from GED [general equivalency diploma] to Ph.D." Lane and Diane Loeslie of Marshall County left farming in the early 1990s to enroll at UMC. Nervous at first about returning to school after many years, both completed degrees and assumed professional positions.[145]

## The University of Minnesota, Duluth

The Duluth campus fared well during the 1990s, recognized for its contributions as a comprehensive regional university with a Sea Grant designation, making the campus eligible to receive research funding for study of the Great Lakes, and land-grant affiliation. UMD was regularly ranked among the top Midwestern regional universities by *U.S. News & World Report*.[146] With enrollments throughout the decade of approximately 7,500 students, UMD offered eleven bachelor's degrees in seventy majors. In addition to the two-year School of Medicine program, UMD had graduate programs in eighteen fields. With more than fifty buildings, including the Tweed Museum of Art, the Marshall W. Alworth Planetarium, and the Marshall Performing Arts Center, UMD occupied 244 acres overlooking Lake Superior.

Lawrence Ianni served as chancellor from 1987 to 1995; his last year coincided with the celebration of the campus's 100th anniversary. A specialist on the life of novelist Sinclair Lewis, Ianni had been provost and vice president for academic affairs at San Francisco State University. The 1998 UMD graduating class of 1,503 students was one of the largest in the school's history. Of the close to 8,000 students enrolled in fall 1998, approximately

25 percent came from St. Louis and Cook Counties; 40 percent from the Twin Cities area; 21 percent from other parts of Minnesota; 10 percent from Wisconsin and North and South Dakota; and 3 percent from elsewhere, including international students. The School of Medicine tied for second place out of 125 institutions offering programs in rural medicine—60 percent of its graduates practiced in communities of fewer than 50,000 people—and the school received an award from the American Academy of Family Physicians. About 100 UMD undergraduates were involved in research projects, many in science and engineering—an area in which UMD was a national leader.

Matti Kaups, professor of geography and ethnohistory, was knighted by the government of Finland in 1999 in recognition of his efforts to preserve Finnish culture. George "Rip" Rapp was named a Regents Professor in 1995; he was the first faculty member from one of the outstate campuses to receive the university's highest faculty honor. A specialist in geoarchaeology, Rapp had taken part in a number of archaeological expeditions, including one to the site of Homer's Troy. In 1994, Kenneth Foxworth, the African American student adviser, raised more than $100,000 to benefit minority and disabled students in his 154-mile "Run for Excellence" from St. Paul to Duluth. Ruth Myers, a co-director of the American Indian programs in the School of Medicine, received an honorary doctorate in 1994. In 1998, Lester Drewes, chair of the Department of Biochemistry and Molecular Biology, received a $1.2 million National Institutes of Health grant that allowed him to study the endothelial cells that create a barrier between the bloodstream and the brain; it was hoped that this work might make it possible to create more effective drugs to treat strokes and other neurological disorders.

A refitted research vessel, the *Blue Heron,* provided a floating laboratory on Lake Superior for the study of water currents, salinity, clarity, and chlorophyll concentrations. The largest university-owned research ship on the Great Lakes, it was operated through the university by the Large Lakes Observatory in cooperation with the Center for Freshwater Research and Policy, established in 1998.

In intercollegiate athletics, Jay Guidinger became the first person to be named the Northern Sun Intercollegiate Conference (NSIC) Player of the Year on three occasions; he ended his Bulldogs basketball career as the school's all-time leader in points, rebounds, and blocked shots. Dina Kangas was named NAIA (National Association of Intercollegiate Athletics) All-American three times and scored more points during her four years than anyone in the history of Minnesota collegiate basketball, man or woman. Karen Stromme, women's basketball head coach since 1984, was named Coach of the Year in the Northern Sun Intercollegiate Conference in 1995, having garnered seven NSIC titles and appearances in national tournaments. Dale Race, head coach of the men's basketball team, was selected NSIC Coach of the Year six times, while his teams appeared in eight national tournaments. A new field house, dedicated in 1993, was named in honor of the late Ward Wells, head of UMD's physical education department for many years and a strong advocate for physical education as part of a liberal arts program. The 1999–2000 season, its first at Division I level of competition, was extraordinarily successful; the team finished fourth in the American Women's College Hockey Alliance. The Duluth Bulldogs won the WCHA regular season and also the WCHA playoff with a 2–0 victory over the Gophers.[147]

UMD celebrated its 100th anniversary in 1995 with festivities in the Marshall Performing Arts Center and banners on the campus. After a fire set by an arsonist in 1993, it became necessary to demolish Old Main, the original building on the lower campus, constructed at the turn of the century; its arches remain to mark the site. The new Campus Center, dedicated in 1995, provided classroom and office space as well as a gathering place for faculty and students.

Lawrence Ianni was succeeded as chancellor by Kathryn A. Martin, formerly dean of the College of Fine and Applied Arts at the University of Illinois; she was the first woman chancellor in the University of Minnesota system.[148] One of Martin's highest priorities was private fund-raising. A $28 million capital campaign was launched in fall 1999. Chancellor Martin and campaign chair Mitchell J. Sill announced receipt of $15 million, including $10 million, the largest single gift to the campus, from the Swenson Family Foundation for scholarships and undergraduate chemistry research programs and a pledge of $7.5 million toward a new laboratory science building.[149]

Martin called the new state-of-the-art library, completed in fall 2000, "one of the most technologically advanced libraries in the state and perhaps the nation, serving students, faculty, business, and industry in a new century." The four-story building's copper-domed rotunda gave it a distinct architectural presence. With extensive electronic and print collections, an interactive television classroom, three digital media instruction classrooms, a multimedia laboratory, and group study areas with network connections, the library enhanced its role as a major information resource both for the campus and for researchers throughout northern Minnesota.[150]

In its 1999 planning compact, UMD confirmed its role as a comprehensive, public university with Sea Grant designation and obligations to the university's land-grant mission. The compact noted that the campus "was an inclusive, diverse community, with special emphasis on American Indian Education."[151] Dr. Gerald Hill, associate to the dean of the School of Medicine and former director of the University of Minnesota Center of American Indian and Minority Health, received the American Indian Physician of the Year Award.[152]

Students enjoyed the school's location near Lake Superior, hiking trails, a ski run, and, somewhat further away, the Boundary Waters Canoe Area. As one student said, "We're in the third biggest city in Minnesota and you can still walk a mile and be in the woods." Students also appreciated the accessibility of the faculty. As one student said, "All my professors are really good and I have always been able to talk to them whenever I needed to."[153]

Milan Bajmoczi, a native of the Slovak Republic, was a member of the class of 1998; his education was initially supported by money saved by his father, an engineer. Bajmoczi earned a 3.99 grade point average and graduated summa cum laude. His father said that "he had to have a chance in this world, because we, in our life, didn't have that. He's the new generation." His parents, two aunts, and an uncle came from Eastern Europe to see him receive his biochemistry degree. Bajmoczi was accepted into an M.D. and Ph.D. program at Harvard; as his first year at Harvard drew to a close, Bajmoczi said he was pleased with the preparation he had received at UMD and was convinced that many of his classmates in biochemistry "would also be competitive at Harvard."[154]

The campus continued to be organized into six collegiate units. The three largest were the Colleges of Liberal Arts, Science and Engineering, and Education and Human Service Professions, followed by the School of Business and Economics, the School of Medicine, and the School of Fine Arts. The campus also was home to the Natural Resources Research Institute. Senior administrators on the campus, included Vincent Magnuson, vice chancellor for academic administration; Bruce Gildseth, vice chancellor for academic support and student life; and Gregory Fox, vice chancellor for finance and operations. The deans were Linda Krug, liberal arts; Sabra Anderson, and later James Richl, science and engineering; Paul Deputy, education and human services professions; Kjell Knudsen, business and economics; Richard Ziegler, medicine; and W. Robert Bucker, fine arts.

The campus supported twenty freshmen seminars and more than a hundred students in the Undergraduate Research Opportunity Program. The colleges introduced four new technology majors: the bachelor of science in information systems and technology, the bachelor of business administration in management information, the master of fine arts in graphic design, and the bachelor of fine arts with an emphasis in art and technology. A new master's degree in engineering management was approved in 1999. Freshwater research was strengthened by the research and service contributions of faculty members connected to the Large Lakes Observatory program. To encourage student research, the College of Science and Engineering continued its longtime sponsorship of the Chemistry Undergraduate Research Program and the Mathematics Summer Undergraduate Research Program.[155] Campus sponsored-research expenditures were above $10 million annually.[156]

Outreach initiatives included the UMD Center for Economic Development's move to the Duluth Technology Village, a community initiative to attract high-technology business, as a source for software programmers and for Technology Village staff and faculty. The College of Education and Human Service Professions collaborated with area educators in a laboratory school initiative. A third major goal at the end of the century was increasing the UMD presence on the Iron Range by implementing "2+2" agreements—whereby students completed two years of study at a community college and spent their final two years at UMD—with six northeastern Minnesota community colleges.[157] University College, in 2000 renamed Continuing Education, offered both credit and noncredit courses, including such programs as the University for Seniors—a participant-led, Elderhostel-affiliated program—and sponsored summer Elderhostel programs on the Gunflint Trail, on campus, and at the International Wolf Center in Ely. University College also offered College in the Schools, college-level courses in area high schools in a number of subjects.[158] UMD hosted the Split Rock Arts Program, summer workshops offered under the auspices of the College of Continuing Education.[159]

## University of Minnesota, Morris

The Morris campus could point to significant achievements as it completed its fourth decade. The faculty numbered 120, and 28 of its members had received the Horace T. Morse–Alumni Association Award for Outstanding Contributions to Undergraduate Education. Chemist Joseph Latterell had received both the Morse award and an award for undergraduate academic advising. Eight faculty members had been inducted into the university's

Academy of Distinguished Teachers. Although teaching loads were heavy and research facilities for scientists were limited, the Morris faculty had amassed very creditable publication records.

A new program aimed at attracting high-ability students proved very successful; coupled with national publicity that called Morris a "gem" among liberal arts colleges, this produced an enrollment of 2,021 in 1990. Since a student body of this size strained facilities and courses, tight controls were placed on new admissions, with the goal of admitting 500 students a year (660 were admitted in 1987) and stabilizing total enrollment at 1,850. In 1999, the student body numbered 1,859.[160]

An active program of recruiting minority students had by the fall of 1998 produced a minority enrollment of 15 percent, one of the highest in the University system.[161] Since its founding years, UMM had increasingly attracted students from a broad geographic area; the college had a number of international students as well as students from other states. During the 1990s, almost a third of the students came from the seven-county Twin Cities metropolitan area, primarily from the suburbs rather than from Minneapolis or St. Paul proper. Morris boasted one of the highest retention rates in the system: more than 80 percent of the freshmen returned for their sophomore year, and nearly half (47 percent) were still there as seniors. About a quarter graduated within four years.[162]

In 1990, Jack Imholte ended his twenty-one years as chief administrative officer—first called provost, then, after 1985, chancellor. Former students began to return with faculty or administrative appointments: Gary McGrath, who had been student body president in 1968, became vice chancellor for student affairs; Thomas McRoberts, student body vice president in 1967, was named associate director of the Morris unit of University College; Michael Korth, a 1978 graduate, returned as a physics faculty member and became chair of the Division of Science and Mathematics. James Carlson, professor of music and director of the Morris jazz bands, had come to UMM as a high school student in 1960 to play in the band; he later enrolled, graduating in 1965.

Imholte was succeeded by David Johnson, professor of sociology. "Chancellor Dave," as students called him, came from a background of administration and teaching in both public and private colleges; he had most recently been dean of Gustavus Adolphus College. His goals included expanding international and domestic exchange programs and internships and study-abroad opportunities for students as well as encouraging students to consider graduate programs that would prepare them for careers in higher education.

One of Johnson's most important achievements was to restart the long-range campus building program. In 1995, the firm of Hammel, Green, and Abrahamson completed a master plan for the Morris campus that reinforced the need for additional facilities. In 1997, with the state's finances again on firm ground, Johnson pressed forward with a bold request for a multi-million-dollar building program. Assisted by Lowell Rasmussen, head of UMM's physical plant and master planning who had come from the Waseca campus, supported by the central administration, and aided by intense lobbying—by the campus, community, parents, and alumni—Johnson obtained appropriations for the long-overdue third phase of the science complex. A cooperative campus-community regional fitness center and an addition to the heating plant also were approved.

Johnson hired Cathleen Brannen as UMM's first woman chief financial officer in 1993. Two years later, when Bettina Blake retired as vice chancellor and dean, Samuel Schuman, formerly chancellor of the University of North Carolina at Asheville, succeeded her.

Kjersti Hanneman graduated with high distinction in 1999. She had first come to the campus in 1990 as an eighth-grader to participate in a summer program, the Henjum Creative Institute for Learning. Exposed to photography, dance, music, and Chinese language through the institute, she put Morris on her list when it came time to apply for college. Affordability made it a necessary choice. Two weeks into her freshman year in fall 1995, she reported, "I knew I would stay."

Hanneman worked her way up the ladder on the newspaper, becoming editor-in-chief her senior year, when the major campus issue was whether the college should award athletic scholarships; both faculty and students were divided, providing much news for the paper to cover. A double major in history and women's studies, Hanneman wrote a major paper on resistance to apartheid in South Africa, using interlibrary loans and sources she found on the Internet. She was first introduced to a feminist perspective by women's studies head Miriam Frenier in an introductory world history course informally known as "Sludge to 1500." Fascinated by women's history, she became a history major, was selected to represent history students in a weekly meeting of history faculty members, and became a teaching assistant.

Seeking a breather before applying to graduate school, Hanneman spent the following year as a community programs consultant in the Center for

Small Towns, a regional think tank and service provider located on the Morris campus. Thinking over her time at Morris, she said:

> Morris was fun, dazzling. There was so much really great learning experience. It allowed me to learn about myself, my boundaries and abilities. There was a lot of academic learning, street learning through my editorship, and service learning through my internship.[163]

As a small, residential liberal arts college that is part of a large public university system, Morris has always been unique, or nearly so. "There really isn't another animal like us," Jack Imholte said. "There is one in Maryland [St. Mary's of Maryland] and possibly New College in Florida. We had kind of a charmed existence within the university, or perhaps within American higher education."[164]

Bettina Blake, the former vice chancellor for academic affairs and one of the organizers of a national consortium, the Council of Public Liberal Arts Colleges, summarized UMM's commitment to the liberal arts:

> We are passionate about our work; we really believe in the power of liberal education to transform people; we care about our students as individuals and we try to make sure that they are getting a genuine undergraduate education—"the real stuff"—at our institution. Our efforts are focused not on personal or institutional aggrandizement but on our students, on freeing and empowering them to be fully themselves as human beings of intelligence, compassion, and sound judgment.[165]

In announcing Samuel Schuman's appointment as the fourth chancellor at Morris, President Yudof said, "Sam has performed brilliantly as interim chancellor. He combines leadership, vision, and devotion to the liberal arts that will serve the campus well in the future."[166]

## University of Minnesota, Rochester

University ties to the Mayo Clinic went back to 1915, when the Mayo Foundation for Medical Education and Research became a part of the University of Minnesota Graduate School. As Mayo Clinic historian Victor Johnson noted:

> The clinic and the University became pioneers in the distinctly American system of advanced education of physicians for specialty practice, sponsored eventually by the American Medical Association, the American College of Physicians and other official agencies. . . . Until the Mayo Foundation was

established, graduate school education in clinical medical fields leading to an M.S. or a Ph.D. did not exist. One might earn an advanced degree in physiology, biochemistry, or anatomy, but nowhere was there systematic training in clinical medicine or surgery leading to an academic degree beyond the M.D. That phase of medical education originated entirely with William and Charles Mayo and the University of Minnesota.[167]

The university, as a result of a legislative appropriation, had established a physical presence in Rochester in 1966. Subsequently, credit and non-credit offerings were coordinated through Continuing Education and Extension.[168] IBM had long been a site for televised Institute of Technology courses. Master's degree options were available in nursing, education, computer and information sciences, electrical and mechanical engineering, and social work.[169] After 1977, Continuing Education and Extension as well as the Olmsted County extension office were located in the Friedell Building in downtown Rochester. In 1992, Continuing Education and Extension moved to the new campus on the eastern side of Rochester to join with Rochester Community College, Riverland Technical College, and Winona State University–Rochester to form the University Center Rochester.

Carol E. Lund, who served as the university's Continuing Education and Extension director from 1986 to 1998, and K. S. P. "Pat" Kumar, associate dean of the Institute of Technology and coordinator of the institute's Rochester programs, anchored the university's presence in Rochester. Lund observed that expanding the university's role in Rochester was based on advocacy by state senator Nancy Braatas, her successor, Senator Sheila M. Kiscaden, and Representative David Bishop. Lund credited such community volunteers in Rochester as realtor Marilyn Stewart, retired IBM manager Don Sudor, and former Mayo faculty member Joseph Gibilisco with further long-term efforts to enhance higher education in Rochester. Early meetings were favored; administrators became accustomed to driving two hours from the Twin Cities in time for seven o'clock breakfast meetings. It was, Lund recalled, a kind of "breakfast magic."[170]

In 1999, Mary Heltsley, associate vice president for outreach, became interim provost, helping to guide further expansion of the university presence in Rochester and to collaborate on joint program planning with partners in the University Center. *Partnerships for the 21st Century: Academic Plan for Rochester* spelled out in a report to the Minnesota Legislature the mission and roles of the participating institutions, emphasizing the lower-division instruction of Rochester Community and Technical College, upper-division and professional instruction by Winona State University–Rochester, and professional, upper-division, graduate, professional degree, and technology transfer offered by the University of Minnesota.[171] In 2000, the regents approved the appointment of David L. Carl, dean of the School of Graduate and Professional Studies at Cameron University in Lawton, Oklahoma, as provost of the University of Minnesota, Rochester.

## Outreach

In his inaugural address, President Yudof said, "It is imperative that we continue to embrace our land-grant roots if we are to thrive."[172] Institutionalized through the two largest formally constituted outreach units, the University of Minnesota Extension Service and the College of Continuing Education, service to the state was also central to the mission of the Center for Urban and Regional Affairs. Beyond these units with an explicit outreach mission were numerous outreach activities by campuses, colleges, and departments. Each year hundreds of initiatives linked the university to the state, stemming from virtually every disciplinary area.

Registrations in courses offered through the College of Continuing Education and in short courses and conferences offered by the University of Minnesota Extension Service were one and a half times to twice the number of students enrolled in traditional undergraduate and graduate programs.[173] Other examples of outreach include 25,000 viewers of *Health Talk and You*, 100,000 patient visits in the Dental Clinics, 215,000 visitors to the Landscape Arboretum, 90,000 people attending concerts, plays, and dance programs on the campuses, and 500,000 people visiting the university museums—the Bell Museum of Natural History, the Goldstein Gallery, the Tweed, and the Weisman.

University students and faculty members participated in internships, research projects, and community service initiatives. The World Wide Web, one of the newest forms of outreach, provided information about the university and its colleges and campuses at any hour of the day or night, anywhere in the world. The Twin Cities campus home page had 39,000 "hits" on Friday, April 28, 2000.[174] That figure does not include departmental Web pages. Although it is difficult to document precisely, it appears that university outreach programs reached between one-quarter and one-half of the state's 4 million people each year.[175]

Thomas Scott, director of the Center for Urban and Regional Affairs since 1978, was well aware of the strengths and durability of University of

Minnesota outreach and service. Noting the deep roots of the university's commitment, he cited three elements of that commitment: the strategic advantage of the university's having both an urban and a statewide presence; the land-grant commitment to statewide service; and the strong belief, dating from the eras of Presidents Vincent and Coffman, that outreach is also a vital part of the mission of a research university.[176]

## The University of Minnesota Extension Service (UMES)

Continued agricultural research and outreach was vital to ensuring rural Minnesota's quality of life, President Yudof believed. The extension service played an ongoing role in helping Minnesota families adjust to changes in agriculture and placed a priority on reaching new audiences, including those in urban areas. Its new name, the University of Minnesota Extension Service, reflected a broader mission: to deliver "research-based education to people of all ages throughout the state." Extension agents, whose title was changed to extension educators, assumed expanded roles in linking the university to Minnesota citizens.

The four people who served as dean and director of the University of Minnesota Extension Service during the 1990s—Patrick Borich, Gail Skinner-West, Katherine Fennelly, and Charles Casey—adapted the organization for the changing needs of the state.[177] In 1999–2000, the organization had a staff of just over a thousand people, reaching throughout the state and into every county. Although there was no formal ranking system for extension services, Minnesota was generally regarded as having one of the most innovative programs in the country. Each of the county extension offices offered Internet access. A twenty-four-hour telephone service provided answers to questions related to families, farms and gardens, and the environment. Among the best known of hundreds of initiatives were the 4-H Youth Development, Master Gardener, and agricultural programs, as well as nutrition education. While retaining traditional elements, UMES served new audiences by reaching persons of color and immigrant communties from Southeast Asia, and adding to programs in Greater Minnesota and in the inner city and suburbs.[178]

As the century ended, the Minnesota farm economy was again in crisis, and again the extension response was both rapid and innovative. Among its priorities were raising awareness of farming conditions and making a coordinated response through Rural Response Teams by bringing together integrated provider networks in and around twenty-five communities. Through UMES leadership of a rural-response team, state and local agencies and organizations worked together in twenty-five communities to raise awareness of the dire conditions and to activate assistance and support. The rural-response initiative received the U.S. Department of Agriculture award for superior service from agriculture secretary Daniel Glickman in June 2000.

Other initiatives included the Rural Response Web site to reach out to audiences in Minnesota, with information and expertise drawn from extension experts in other states. Citizen forums jointly sponsored with public television station KTCA, the Minneapolis *Star Tribune,* and Minnesota Public Radio provided a forum for public discussion of the complex economic and social issues facing the state's rural communities and agriculture. The extension service was providing training for extension educators in the use of its popular financial management software, FINPACK.

## The College of Continuing Education

The College of Continuing Education (CCE), the university's other formally constituted outreach unit, went through several significant changes during the 1990s. A 1997 merger with University College gave Continuing Education the opportunity to grant its own degrees for the first time. A redesign of university revenue sharing related to continuing education offerings created added incentives for colleges and departments to offer continuing education courses. In 1998, longtime dean Harold A. Miller, a national leader in continuing education, retired. During his twenty-seven years as dean, offerings and registrations had grown from approximately 32,000 registrations in 1972 to over 47,000 students in credit classes in 1998.[179]

Consistently one of the largest and most comprehensive continuing education programs in the United States, CCE functioned as an "expansion joint" for the university, offering access to the university for nontraditional, working, part-time students. CCE linked faculty who wished to teach with people who wanted to take courses. At the end of the century, the college offered five applied bachelor's degrees through partnerships with area community colleges, an interdisciplinary master of liberal studies degree, and two bachelor's degrees in the Inter-College Program and the Program for Individualized Learning.[180] It also included extension classes, the summer session program, independent and distance learning, media resources, Compleat and Practical Scholar, the Split Rock arts program, Elderhostel and the Elder Learning Institute, and neighborhood programs.

Interim Dean Gail Skinner-West led a systematic strategic planning effort to strengthen work-related, noncredit, and personal enrichment programs.

CCE also worked closely with other colleges of the university to plan credit courses for part-time students. One of the college's more successful initiatives during the 1990s was establishment of the Technical Education Center in Edina, with courses in high-demand subjects such as UNIX and C/C II. In 1999, the regents approved a new name for the college, the College of Continuing Education. Closer to its earlier name (Continuing Education and Extension), the new name was descriptive of its focus on lifelong learning.[181]

## The Center for Urban and Regional Affairs

A response to the urban crisis of the 1960s, the Center for Urban Affairs (CURA) was founded to involve university students and faculty members in working on problems facing Minnesota via three key operating principles: focus on initiatives that cut across new disciplines, select initiatives that link University of Minnesota resources to community needs, and spin off activities once they can stand alone.

While a number of colleges and universities had similar initiatives, few of them lasted for more than a decade. CURA's success was based on the clarity of its mission and on stable and committed leadership by two directors, John Borchert (1968–76) and Thomas Scott (1976–).

With a permanent staff of fewer than twenty people, half the number it had a decade earlier, CURA in 1998–99 maintained approximately three hundred studies and projects annually, along with a regular series of publications documenting findings and work in progress. The projects, typically involving applied research by university faculty and students, encompassed these program areas: communities and neighborhoods; economic development and employment; education; environment and energy; housing; human services; land use; and population. CURA initiatives involved faculty and students from the Twin Cities, Crookston, Morris, and Duluth campuses.[182]

## The University of Minnesota Press

The University of Minnesota Press participated in the university's outreach mission by publishing scholarly books that disseminated research in a number of academic disciplines and books on Minnesota and the region that provided information on culture, history, and natural history. As the university celebrated its sesquicentennial in the 2000–2001 academic year, the press observed its seventy-fifth anniversary, having been authorized by the Board of Regents in 1925. The press has had five directors: Margaret S. Harding, who was hired as a part-time editorial assistant in 1927, became an editor, and, in 1941, was appointed director; Helen Clapesattle, 1952–56; John Ervin, 1957–87; Lisa Freeman, 1990–97; and Douglas Armato, who joined the press in 1998.

The financial stringencies of the 1970s led to a decision to increase the number of books it published and to publish books that would reach wider scholarly audiences as well as a broader general audience while maintaining a commitment to the highest academic standards. The press met these goals by publishing in a broader range of academic disciplines—areas of concentration included race and ethnic studies, Scandinavian studies, urban studies, cinema studies, women's studies, art and architecture, literature, sociology, and political science—and reviving its regional publishing program, which now encompassed horticulture, natural history, nature writing, and cooking. At the end of the century, the press had over 500 books in print and published 110 books annually, having more than doubled the number published each year in the early 1980s.

A number of books served as hallmarks of the press's history. Regional publications included *The Birds of Minnesota* by physician turned ornithologist Thomas S. Roberts, published in 1932 and winner of the Brewster Medal of the American Ornithologists' Union, which became a collector's item; *Minnesota: A History of the State* by Theodore C. Blegen, dean of the Graduate School, winner of the American Association for State and Local History award, published in 1963; *Minnesota's Natural Heritage* by John R. Tester, a guide to the ecology of the state published in 1995 and winner of a Minnesota Book Award; and the reissue of a number of works by Sigurd Olson, including *Reflections from the North Country*, articulating the wilderness philosophy he developed while working as an outspoken advocate for the conservation of America's natural heritage. The Tester and Olson books were published in the Fesler/Lampert series, established to support publications of significance to the people of Minnesota.

Notable books in the medical sciences ranged from *The History of Surgery* by Owen Wangensteen, long-serving chief of surgery at the University, and *A History of Infectious Diseases* by Wesley Spink, a member of the Department of Medicine, both published in the 1970s, to the popular *The Doctors Mayo*, the story of the Mayo Clinic and its founders, by Helen Clapesattle, second director of the press, one of the best-selling books on the press's list. Publication in English translation of two plays by Bertolt

Brecht, *The Caucasian Chalk Circle* and *The Good Woman of Setzuan,* in 2000 continued the tradition of the press's publishing in theater arts.

A publishing milestone was the Theory and History of Literature series edited by Wlad Godzich, who left the Minnesota faculty for the University of Geneva, and Jochen Schulte-Sasse, professor of cultural studies and comparative literature at Minnesota; arguably, the series changed the intellectual landscape of the humanities in the late twentieth century. Designed to bring poststructuralist continental theory to the United States in translation, and moving beyond that to include American critics doing theoretical work inspired or informed by the European models, the series, composed of eighty-eight volumes published from 1981 to 1997, included such authors as Jean-François Lyotard, Paul de Man, Hélène Cixous, Catherine Clément, and Theodor Adorno.

Publication of a very different sort is represented by the Minnesota Multiphasic Personality Inventory and its successors. Beginning as a modest questionnaire developed by Minnesota professors Starke R. Hathaway, a clinical psychologist, and J. C. McKinley, head of medicine, and published by the press in 1942 as the Minnesota Multiphasic Personality Schedule, it has become the most widely used test of personality in the world. It serves as the cornerstone of the press's test publishing program, which now includes a revision of the original MMPI, the MMPI-2, a version for adolescents, the MMPI-A, and several other tests of clinical and normal personality.

## College and Departmental Outreach

Outreach initiatives often came directly from colleges and departments. The Consortium on Children, Youth, and Families, another university-wide group with an outreach mission, addressed such varied issues as parenting, family violence, nutrition, poverty, and community family support. The Design Center for the American Urban Landscape, headed by William Morrish, had a national reputation both for design and for interaction with communities. The Center for the Studies of Small Towns and the Center for Rural Design addressed issues related to Greater Minnesota. Cultural outreach included the activities of the university's several museums—the Tweed Museum in Duluth, the Goldstein Gallery in St. Paul, the Weisman and Bell museums in Minneapolis. There were concerts and performances at Northrop Auditorium and the Ted Mann Concert Hall, and drama at the Rarig Center.

In describing College of Liberal Arts outreach initiatives, Dean Steven Rosenstone pointed to high school students taking college courses through the Post Secondary Education Options Act, high school students involved in summer honors classes, and dozens of K-12 relationships offered in the arts, social sciences, and language departments. CLA faculty, along with faculty in other colleges, had helped design the advanced "College in the Schools" courses for high school teachers. After completing the program, they returned to their respective schools and offered courses that made their students eligible for advanced placement in courses at the university and at some other colleges. Approximately a thousand students a year participated in a variety of internships and service-learning opportunities. The Minnesota Historical Society and the Department of History continued to sponsor Minnesota History Day, a statewide essay contest for students in grades six to twelve. At the end of the century, there were more than 30,000 entries.[183]

The Institute of Technology's Talented Youth Mathematics Program, directed by Harvey Keynes and known by a nursery rhyme–like acronym. UMTYMP (pronounced *umpty-ump*) was established in 1978. Participating students, typically in the sixth or seventh grade, were selected on the basis of a competitive examination; in 1999, 169 students, 40 percent of them girls, were selected from 1,500 applicants for the weekly classes. UNITE (University-Industry Television for Education) offered about fifty courses a quarter at a number of corporate sites; students participated via television in live courses transmitted from the university. In 1999, fifteen of these courses were offered through "streaming video," making them accessible any place and at any time. Through UNITE, students could earn master's degrees in fields such as computer and information sciences, computer engineering, electrical engineering, and mechanical engineering.[184]

General College continued its sponsorship of the African American Read-In—part of a broader campaign by the National Council of Teachers of English to draw a million participants to a "read-in." In 2000, plans were under way for the Givens Foundation for African American Literature to join with the college as a local sponsor for the campaign. In 1999, approximately 4,500 Minnesotans participated in the reading campaign.[185] College of Biological Sciences outreach included workshops for K-12 teachers, summer research programs for high school students, and a zoology day camp for young children.[186]

The Academic Health Center had a number of outreach programs. Since 1971, the Medical School's Rural Physicians Associates Program had placed more than 850 third-year medical students in 100 Minnesota communities for nine-month residencies; almost two-thirds of them ended up practicing in rural areas. School of Nursing partnerships helped nurses in rural areas get training to become nurse-midwives, physician assistants, or nurse practitioners. The School of Dentistry's Summer Migradent program sent students to provide care for migrant farm workers and their families. The dental school also offered a clinic in the Wilder Senior Center and the St. Paul Mission Gospel Center. The School of Public Health and the College of Agricultural, Food, and Environmental Sciences worked jointly on a training program to improve health in migrant labor camps in southern Minnesota.[187] In 1999, veterinary medicine activated a Web site where veterinarians and others could find answers to their questions about animals.[188]

The Telemedicine Network connected Academic Health Center physicians and physicians at Fairview-University Hospitals with Greater Minnesota. *Health Talk and You,* a live television show, was hosted originally by Regents Professor of Pediatrics Dr. Paul Quie and subsequently by Medical School associate dean Greg Vercellotti.

Beyond outreach to the state and region, Minnesota continued to build international connections. The University of Minnesota Alumni Association had seven international chapters, five of them in Asia. Between 1979 and 2000, nine senior delegations from the University of Minnesota visited China, including two visits by President Nils Hasselmo and two by President Mark Yudof. Agricultural connections to Morocco continued, and new ones were added in Senegal and Malawi. Faculty and student programs took place on every continent. At the end of the century, C. Eugene Allen, most recently provost for professional studies (1995–97), became executive director of the Office of International Programs, overseeing study abroad, International Student and Scholar Services, the Center for Advanced Research on Language Acquisition (CARLA), and the China Center. In the College of Agricultural, Food, and Environmental Sciences, Richard Swanson served as director of International Agricultural Programs.

The Institute for Global Studies helped coordinate the extensive language and area studies programs offered through the College of Liberal Arts. The Carlson School of Management opened an office of international programs and offered an emphasis in international business; faculty members were involved in international degree programs developed in cooperation with partner institutions in Austria, China, and Poland. The College of Education and Human Development instituted a program in comparative and international developmental education that drew students from all over the world and offered a graduate-level minor in international education.

International students continued to come to the university in increasing numbers and, similarly, more students than ever from the university studied or traveled abroad. In fall 1999, there were more than 3,000 students from 130 countries at the university, more than six times the number enrolled in 1950. Active on many fronts, a number of international students participated in the Minnesota International Student Association. In addition, the university hosted well over a thousand visiting scholars and researchers. Approximately a thousand University of Minnesota students went abroad for study and travel through university-sponsored study-travel programs, and other students took advantage of other opportunities to go beyond the boundaries of the United States. The university consistently ranked in the top twenty in the nation in its total population of international students, and in the top ten in the number of visiting scholars and staff.[189]

## Gopher Athletics and Recreational Sports

Mark Dienhart became director of men's athletics in 1995. Jim Wacker coached the Gophers for five seasons, from 1992 through 1996. Glen Mason, who became head coach in 1997, lived up to the nickname, "Mr. Fixit" (he had repaired the fortunes of several teams): the Gophers posted an 8–3 record in the 1999 season and were invited to their first postseason tournament since 1967—the Sun Bowl in El Paso, Texas, where the Gophers were defeated 24–20 by the Oregon Ducks.[190] In June 2000, Coach Mason signed a seven-year contract with the university that made him the third-highest-paid coach in the Big Ten.

Doug Woog coached the Gopher hockey team for fourteen seasons (his record was 389–187–40) before transferring to a fund-raising role following the 1998–99 season. Coach Don Lucia, who came to Minnesota in 1999 after six seasons at Colorado College, addressing an issue faced by earlier Gopher hockey coaches, indicated that, although he thought that a "majority of the recruits would come from Minnesota," he was willing to consider players from other states—a significant change in Gopher hockey.[191]

The basketball team under Coach Clem Haskins won the 1993 National Invitational Tournament championship and the 1997 Big Ten championship, and made it to the Final Four in the 1997 National Collegiate Athletic Association (NCAA) postseason tournament. In 1998, the team won the NIT championship. The following year problems were uncovered in the basketball program, which reversed many of these successes.

In March 1999, the University commissioned an investigation into allegations of academic fraud. It took eight months, involved 150 people, produced 2,500 pages of information, and revealed that three individuals had set up a system involving fraudulent course papers and examinations in order to keep basketball players eligible to play. It was the most serious athletic scandal that had occurred at the university and one of the most serious among major universities. As many as eighteen basketball players were involved and had competed while ineligible. In the course of the investigation, Coach Haskins resigned. Given the findings of the investigation, President Yudof restructured reporting relationships for athletics and brought in new leadership. Tonya Moten Brown, Yudof's chief of staff, was made a vice president and assumed responsibility for oversight of intercollegiate athletics. Tom Moe, previously managing partner and at the time the chairman of the Dorsey and Whitney law firm, was appointed director of men's athletics. Dan Monson, formerly coach at Gonzaga University, became the basketball coach. Yudof set up a system of checks and balances to ensure that abuses would not recur.[192]

On October 24, 2000, drawing on the University's self-investigation, the NCAA issued its infractions report. The NCAA acknowledged the penalties the university had imposed upon itself, among them, a one-year absence from postseason play, elimination of four scholarships, and return to the NCAA of 90 percent of the revenues from postseason play between 1993 and 1999, the years in which ineligible players had competed. The NCAA added other sanctions, including public reprimand and censure, four years of probation, loss of an additional scholarship, and forfeiture of season records from 1993 to 1999. President Yudof said, "We are deeply ashamed, but relieved.... We will not forget the serious lessons learned from this difficult experience.... We need both people and systems that put academic integrity first. We have both in place now and we pledge again to merit the trust that the people of Minnesota have put in us."[193]

While football, basketball, and hockey dominated headlines, men's intercollegiate athletics had other accomplished teams: baseball, cross-country, golf, gymnastics, swimming and diving, track and field, and wrestling. These sports were notable for their successful records and the stability of leadership; head coaches John Anderson in baseball, Roy Griak in cross-country and track, Fred Roethlisberger in gymnastics, and Wally Johnson in wrestling collectively had coached more than eighty years.[194]

Federal regulations mandating gender equity in athletics had led to major improvements in women's programs. No intercollegiate athletic opportunities existed for women in 1950, although there was a strong intramural program. The creation of the women's intercollegiate athletics program in

1975 signaled a period of change that lasted through the century. Chris Voelz became director of women's athletics in 1988, replacing Merrily Dean Baker, who had taken a position with the NCAA. When Voelz arrived, the budget was $2.8 million and only one of the teams ranked in the NCAA top twenty. There were 187 athletes competing in basketball, cross-country, golf, gymnastics, softball, swimming, tennis, track and field, and volleyball. Soccer was added in 1993, ice hockey in 1997, and rowing in 1999.[195]

Women's soccer and hockey, expected to attract large numbers of fans, got new stadiums: the Elizabeth Lyle Robbie Women's Soccer Stadium near the campus in St. Paul, and the Jane Sage Cowles Softball Stadium on the campus in Minneapolis. The first women's intercollegiate ice hockey game was played on November 2, 1997, before a crowd of 6,854 fans. In spring 2000, within three years of becoming an intercollegiate sport, the women's hockey team won the American Women's Hockey Alliance title; it was the first University of Minnesota women's team to win a national championship. A clear indication of the talent in Minnesota was that the Gophers' semifinal opponents, whom they defeated 3–2, were the UMD women's team.

The women were good students as well as good athletes: for twenty-five successive terms, the grade point average of the athletes exceeded 3.0.[196] Four exceptional players of the 1990s were basketball player Carol Ann Shudlick, selected as a Wade Trophy winner, a national award for the country's outstanding basketball player; national champion gymnast Marie Roethlisberger; swimmer Gretchen Hegener, holder of an American record for the breaststroke; and hockey goalee Erica Killewald.

By the end of the decade, approximately 60 percent of the Twin Cities campus student body participated in some form of recreational sports.[197] The University Recreation Center, which opened in 1993, offered sixteen handball and racquetball courts; five squash courts; two fitness centers equipped with aerobic and weight-lifting equipment; two full gyms for basketball, volleyball, and badminton; new locker rooms; lounge spaces; and a health food delicatessen. Remodeling of the St Paul gymnasium in 1995 meant that both campuses could offer recreational opportunities in swimming, basketball and handball, and exercise equipment use.[198]

## Philanthropy and Alumni Relations

Continued momentum in private support in the 1990s was made possible by effective collaboration between University of Minnesota Foundation professionals and volunteer board members. With strong alumni and community support for the university, gifts increased from $47 million in 1990 to $85 million in 1996, and to $135 million in 1999. During these same years, due to a rising stock market and the acumen of financial advisers, the combined university endowment grew from $955 million to $1.5 billion.[199] Board chairs in the 1990s were Marvin Borman, Duane R. Kullberg, James R. Campbell, and Luella G. Goldberg. Douglas Leatherdale, chief executive officer of the St. Paul Companies, served as board chair at the beginning of the twenty-first century. Gerald B. Fischer, an executive with First Bank System in Minneapolis, became president of the University of Minnesota Foundation in 1990, leading university fund-raising during a decade in which private support increased 187 percent.

In the late 1990s, a second major university-wide fund-raising campaign was announced.[200] Alumnus Russell Bennett, who had graduated from the the Law School in 1952 and had been co-chair of the 1986 campaign, agreed to serve as convening chair and campaign spokesperson. The theme, "A Defining Moment," reflected awareness that the new millennium represented a time of opportunity for the university and the state. President Yudof expressed the key Campaign Minnesota themes:

> We live in an era of ideas and innovation, a time when Minnesota's intellectual capital is clearly its most vital resource. Campaign Minnesota will raise $1.3 billion to cultivate this resource and enable the University to recruit, retain, and develop top faculty, attract students with promise and help them succeed, and invest in Minnesota's future. There has never been a more exciting moment in the history of higher education and scientific research.
>
> Every institution has its defining moments—points in time when talented individuals, working cooperatively, can influence the course of events for generations to come. I believe this is one such time for the University of Minnesota.[201]

Of the $1.3 billion campaign goal, approximately $540 million was earmarked for endowments to support faculty, students, and strategic priorities; $760 million for research, outreach, and new facilities. Hundreds of volunteers from all of the campuses and colleges were part of the campaign.

The University of Minnesota Foundation continued to attract major community leaders to chair the board; Donald F. Wright, previously president and chief executive officer of the *Los Angeles Times Mirror*, became the second foundation board chair of the twenty-first century. The first major commitment during the exploratory phase of the new campaign was a 1998 gift of $10 million from entrepreneur Richard "Pinky" McNamara, chief executive officer of Activar, a Minneapolis-based holding company. McNamara, a College of Liberal Arts student in the 1950s who had received a football scholarship, arranged for his gift to be given to several university units: the College of Liberal Arts, intercollegiate athletics, and the alumni association for its new Twin Cities alumni and visitor center.[202]

Prior to alumnus and benefactor Curt Carlson's death in 1999, he had committed an additional $10 million to the university, $8 million for the Carlson School of Management and $2 million for a heritage gallery in the new alumni and visitor center; the gift was announced on July 9, which would have been Carlson's eighty-fifth birthday.[203] Next, Warren Staley, president of Cargill, a privately held global agribusiness company, announced a gift of $10 million for a new microbial and plant genomics facility in St. Paul. It was the largest gift the company had ever made. According to Staley, the study of the molecular and cellular structure of plants and animal life was "essential to meet[ing] society's growing needs for better food as well an improved environment."[204] Matching funds were provided by the legislature.

An unrestricted McKnight Foundation gift of $15 million was to be used to create fifteen new endowed faculty chairs, to be assigned at the president's discretion to attract or retain faculty members in fields of critical importance to the university. President Yudof commented on the value of flexibility: "Normally, a chair comes in restricted to engineering or law or business. I'm not aware of any program in the country where a president or a provost can sit down and say, 'Nanotechnology or human ecology looks (like) where the action is.' ... That really makes it a godsend."[205] In October 2000, Hubbard Broadcasting announced a $10 million contribution to the School of Journalism and Mass Communication.

Sally Anderson, senior vice president of Kopp Investment Advisors, served as chair of the Minnesota Medical Foundation Board of trustees. Brad Choate had become its president and chief executive officer in 1996, coming to the position from Pennsylvania State University, where he had been associate vice president of development and university relations. In December 1999, the Minnesota Medical Foundation had been in existence for sixty years. Nadine Smith, M.D., James Reagan, Bob Griffin, Paul Birkeland, and Barbara Forster served as chairs of the Medical Foundation Board during the 1990s.[206] Judith F. Shank became chair in 2000.

At the beginning of the new century, Brad Choate reported news of a major gift to the Medical School and the School of Nursing. The family of C. Walton Lillehei gave $16 million in 2000: $13 million to the Medical School to establish the Lillehei Heart Institute and $3 million to the School of Nursing to create an endowed chair to support a director for the Katharine J. Densford Center for Nursing Leadership. World-renowned as a faculty member, a pioneer in open-heart surgery, and as an early innovator in biomedical technology, C. Walton Lillehei earned all his degrees from the University of Minnesota and was a world-renowned faculty member who performed the first successful open-heart surgery and encouraged Earl Bakken in the development of the first battery-powered heart pacemaker. Katherine Lillehei was a student in the School of Nursing during the 1940s and made her gift to recognize Katharine Densford's strong example as a leader.

Private giving had reached levels unimagined by those who had laid the groundwork for private support for the university in earlier decades. The university ranked sixth among public universities in private support in 1998. When Campaign Minnesota was announced, $628 million, nearly half of the $1.3 billion goal, was already in hand. In 1999, the combined university endowment was $1.5 billion. As important as the dollars, these successes signified that private donors had become active partners in supporting the university, offering resources crucial to maintaining the excellence of the institution and the competitive position of the state.

## Reaching Out to Alumni

In June 2000, the University of Minnesota Alumni Association (UMAA) had 43,000 members, more than ever before and three times more than in 1950. There were sixty alumni chapters, in Minnesota and throughout the country, and eleven international affiliates: four in China and one each in Korea, Taiwan, Singapore, Indonesia, Japan, Morocco, and Iceland.

The UMAA coordinated alumni mentor programs linking students with alumni; was the key sponsor of the Alumni Legislative Network, dedicated to generating support for the university among lawmakers (approximately 3,000 people served as advocates for the university in 1999); hosted forums for potential candidates; was an active partner in orientation and the New Student Convocation; encouraged staff, faculty, and students to wear school colors on "Maroon and Gold Fridays"; and created professional networks among alumni through its Career Connection program. *Minnesota,* the UMAA magazine, published six times a year, had a circulation of 40,000. Margaret Carlson had been executive director since 1985, continuing the tradition of strong leaders. As the new millennium began, she was the second-longest-serving alumni director in the Big Ten and had one of the longest tenures among women alumni directors in major American universities.

The UMAA was the major institutional backer of awards to recognize outstanding teaching. Long a supporter of the Morse-Alumni Award, UMAA continued its support of that award for undergraduate instruction and extended it to include graduate instruction for the first time in 1999. Winners of both the Morse-Alumni Award (for undergraduate teaching) and the Graduate and Professional Teaching Award became members of a new body—the Academy of Distinguished Teachers. Members of the academy were honored as role models for exceptional teaching. Regents Professor Margaret Davis commented at the time she was given this recognition: "I believe graduate students should know about my own self-doubt as a young scientist. . . . They need to know I didn't just walk into a professorship at Minnesota, but encountered obstacles to professional success as they will." Chemistry professor Thomas Hoye cited the importance of teaching: "If I had never published a paper, the world might not be worse off; if I had never trained a student, it would be." John S. Wright, associate professor of English and Afro-American and African studies, commented on the importance of humor: "Humor is one of the homelier virtues I increasingly find essential to the learning process. . . . I find the customary classroom pieties much more tenable when leavened with appropriate doses of mother wit and laughter."[207]

In addition to the ongoing initiatives of the alumni association, volunteers and staff members spent considerable time planning and raising funds for a new Twin Cities campus alumni and visitor center, which had been their number-one goal since 1994. "It is no exaggeration to say that this is a dream come true," Carlson declared. Carlson received the President's Award for Outstanding Service in recognition of her advocacy for the center.[208]

## The McNamara Alumni Center, University of Minnesota Gateway

The McNamara Alumni Center, University of Minnesota Gateway—named to acknowledge the generosity of Richard "Pinky" McNamara—opened in fall 1999. The new building, designed by internationally renowned architect Antoine Predock, was intended as a place to welcome visitors to the campus. The ninety-foot-tall Memorial Hall has as its focal point the processional arch from Memorial Stadium, where the Gophers played football between 1924 and 1981. Saving the arch at the time the stadium was demolished was due in considerable measure to the generosity and far-sightedness of members of the Class of '42. Weighing sixty-eight tons and containing more than seven thousand bricks and ninety-two pieces of stone, the arch originally was erected as a memorial to University of Minnesota alumni who died during World War I.

The main floor of the McNamara Alumni Center was devoted to public spaces. The A. I. Johnson Great Hall, with a fireplace suggesting the warmth of a Minnesota cabin, provided an attractive site for gatherings of up to a hundred people. Gateway Café became a popular lunchtime meeting place for the university community and visitors. Goldy's at Gateway offered T-shirts, caps, buttons, banners, and other university memorabilia. The Curtis L. and Arleen M. Carlson Heritage Gallery, designed by Vincent Cuilla Associates, displayed photographs, interactive displays, and live video contact with the university's other campuses. An illustrated chronological time line allowed visitors to follow major events in the history of the university, from the granting of its charter by Minnesota's Territorial Legislature in 1851 through the twentieth century and into the twenty-first century. One of the most striking features of the gallery was its wall of books, more than five thousand of them, about the university or written by alumni, students, or faculty members.

In addition to the public spaces, the McNamara Alumni Center provided offices for the University of Minnesota Foundation, the University of Minnesota Alumni Association, and the Minnesota Medical Foundation—the three owners and principal tenants of the new facility. Three alumni leaders, Fred Friswold, Larry Laukka, and Dale Olseth, spearheaded the drive to create the new center. Friswold noted that the project, based on a unique public-private partnership, supported through private gifts, was not always an easy task and spanned the administrations of three university presidents before it was accomplished. The $45 million McNamara Alumni Center leased meeting rooms and offices to the Board of Regents as well as to university groups such as the Children, Youth, and Family Consortium, Office of the General Counsel, the Elder Learning Institute, the Minnesota 4-H Foundation, and the University of Minnesota Retirees Association. One of the benefits of the new facility was bringing together a number of outreach units in one location.

The McNamara Center represented only the third time—the first two were the building of Northrop Auditorium and Memorial Stadium—that alumni had collaborated on a major all-university project. Speaking in compelling, straightforward terms about his gift to the university, Pinky McNamara may have expressed the feelings of many alumni: "If I lived five lifetimes, I couldn't repay the university for what it has meant in my life and career."[209]

# Epilogue

THIS HISTORY BEGAN IN 1945, when the university consisted of the extension offices and eight branch experiment stations, a campus in Minneapolis and one in St. Paul. Over the next five decades, the university expanded to include campuses at Crookston, Duluth, and Morris as well as a presence, along with other postsecondary systems, at the University Center Rochester. With agriculture, engineering, and health science fields added to liberal arts programs and professional fields such as architecture, education, and law, the University of Minnesota continued to have one of the most comprehensive curricula in the United States.

The university grew from just under 12,000 students in 1945 to over 58,000 at the end of the century. It also became more diverse and cosmopolitan. In 1950, women were just over 25 percent of the student body; by the fall of 1998, they accounted for 51 percent of the systemwide enrollments. Students of color increased from 5 percent of enrollments in 1972, the first year they were counted, to 11 percent of the student body in the fall of 1998. International students increased from over 500 students in 1945 to almost 3,000 students in 1998. Faculty and staff also became more diverse.

Through its outreach and service programs, the university consistently maintained extensive statewide and town-gown connections: in the arts, education, health care, and social services; in government; and in business and professional enterprises. As the century ended, at least a quarter of the state's 4.7 million citizens came into contact with the university each year through its programs and services.[1]

Minnesotans attended concerts and plays, athletic events, lectures, and convocations. They were treated in university-affiliated dental clinics and brought their pets to the university's veterinary clinic or hospital. They attended workshops and field days at the experiment stations, and they participated in numerous programs offered through the University of Minnesota Extension Service.[2] They took classes offered through the College of Continuing Education and came into contact with one of three hundred research or service projects carried out by the Center for Research and Urban Affairs or offered by a college, department, or center. Beyond face-to-face and telephone contacts, the university's extensive presence on the World Wide Web created a new form of citizen connection in the mid-1990s. During 1998–99, there were approximately 200,000 hits each week on the university's Web site.[3]

Minnesota benefited from university-based accomplishments and innovations: the release of more than eighty crop varieties, the development of taconite, the invention of the flight recorder, the eradication of poultry and livestock diseases, the invention of the first heart pacemaker, the ongoing success of one of the world's leading organ transplant programs.[4] Alumni had founded more than fifteen hundred high-technology companies employing more than 100,000 people and adding more than $30 billion to the economy. In all more than 3,000 companies had been founded by alumni.[5]

Research at Minnesota and other major universities became more important following World War II, spurred by the discoveries growing out of the war effort and by the relative ease of obtaining federal funding. By the year 2000, sponsored research expenditures had risen to more than $376 million annually; between 1990 and 1998, 332 patents were issued.[6]

Voluntary support had become an increasingly important source of support for the university. In 1998, Minnesota ranked sixth in voluntary support among all public universities. By late 2000, Campaign Minnesota had raised $945 million, 73 percent of its goal of $1.3 billion to be used for new endowments, research grants, facilities, and programs.[7]

Although there was much to be proud of as the new century began, one area of concern was Minnesota's position among its research peers. As other states were investing more in their universities, Minnesota's national competitive advantage suffered. In 1950, 41 percent of university funds had come from the state; by 1998, state support had fallen to 35 percent.[8] Although the university remained among the top twenty research universities in National Research Council rankings, its overall ranking had declined from sixteenth to twentieth and had fallen among public universities in expenditures for research and development from fifth to thirteenth.[9] Another concern was Minnesota's position as twenty-sixth among public and private universities in faculty salaries.[10]

A six-day Minneapolis *Star Tribune* series in April 2000 noted that the university had declined from 7 percent to 5 percent of the state's budget and, if inflation were taken into account, "it had not received a raise since

1987." Observing that Minnesota was not keeping up with other states in support of new company formation, the paper cautioned that "if Minnesota is to regain a leading place in the knowledge economy, it cannot neglect its greatest intellectual asset." It recommended that state policy makers consider increases in faculty salaries, the creation of a state research fund, and a center near the Twin Cities campus where small businesses could be started.[11] These views were most welcome to friends of the university.

The university transformed the lives of many of the students, faculty members, and administrators interviewed for this history. We have seen that to a number of people, the university had a meaning that went beyond breadth and scale, teaching and research. Minneapolis *Star Tribune* columnist Jim Klobuchar wrote that the university "was what the union was to the working person and something very close to what the church was to the penitent. It was shelter and lodge and discovery. It was a mark of citizenship. It was everybody's college."[12] Known simply as "the U," the university had left a strong imprint on the citizens of Minnesota. Efforts by administrators to make changes in the university ran into intense public opposition, if the suggested changes were viewed as limiting access.

It seems appropriate to give the final word on the culture and impact of the university to a voice familiar to many of our readers, that of writer and commentator Garrison Keillor, host of Minnesota Public Radio's "Prairie Home Companion." Keillor, a University alumnus, made these remarks in 1999 as part of the launch of Campaign Minnesota:

> The most beautiful reason for the University of Minnesota is to enlarge the thinking of ordinary people and to give them a chance to dream.... My dream was to be a writer, you had your dream, they all had theirs!... They came here from small towns, from blue-collar families and families like mine which had very little money, families in which you were always keenly aware of what everything cost.
>
> They came to this campus and they dreamed of a larger life and then they scattered to the four corners of the world and most of them we'll never see again. Wherever I go, in London or Europe, all around the country, people come up to me and say, "I went to the University of Minnesota too."
>
> They are out there in the foreign service, they are in government agencies, they are in large corporations, in small startups, they are teachers, they are researchers, they are writers, and they are all living a life that they dreamed of as they walked down the mall and over the foot bridges.

*Epilogue*

They are all over the world making a difference and leading their lives....
To give people who have not great means the chance to have the best edu-
cation, if only they have the imagination to want it. This is the idea of
America!

## APPENDIX A

# University of Minnesota Enrollments

# Fall Quarter Enrollments for Selected Years

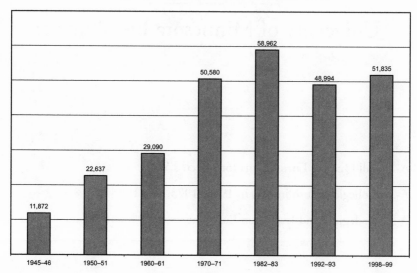

Sources: *Biennial Report* 1944–46, 1950–52, 1960–62; Office of Institutional Research and Reporting, University of Minnesota, 1970–71, 1982–83, 1992–93, 1998–99

# Collegiate Enrollments in 1950, 1973, and 1998

| College or School | Fall 1950[1] | | | Fall 1973[2] | | | Fall 1998[2] | | |
|---|---|---|---|---|---|---|---|---|---|
| | Men | Women | Total | Men | Women | Total | Men | Women | Total |
| Agriculture, Forestry, and Home Economics | 1,127 | 559 | 1,686 | | | | | | |
| Agricultural, Food, & Environmental Sciences | | | | 1,013 | 295 | 1,308 | 422 | 493 | 915 |
| Architecture & Landscape Architecture | | | | | | | 15 | 13 | 28 |
| Biological Sciences | | | | 336 | 130 | 466 | 333 | 511 | 844 |
| Dental Hygiene | | 91 | 91 | 3 | 163 | 166 | 5 | 98 | 103 |
| Dentistry | 340 | 6 | 346 | 489 | 24 | 513 | 230 | 128 | 358 |
| Education & Human Development | 1,041 | 1,309 | 2,350 | 894 | 1,639 | 2,533 | 633 | 1,188 | 1,821 |
| General College | 1,087 | 351 | 1,438 | 1,488 | 1,017 | 2,505 | 868 | 770 | 1,638 |
| Graduate School[3] | 3,196 | 536 | 3,732 | 5,260 | 2,226 | 7,486 | 4,311 | 3,890 | 8,201 |
| Human Ecology (Home Economics) | | | | 40 | 1,213 | 1,253 | 168 | 771 | 939 |
| Law | 485 | 16 | 501 | 598 | 109 | 707 | 434 | 364 | 798 |
| Liberal Arts | 3,939 | 2,065 | 6,004 | 8,569 | 7,588 | 16,157 | 5,916 | 8,316 | 14,232 |
| Management | 838 | 39 | 877 | 1,179 | 147 | 1,326 | 826 | 733 | 1,629 |
| Medicine | 551 | 34 | 585 | 972 | 143 | 1,115 | 896 | 733 | 1,629 |
| Medical Technology | 7 | 88 | 95 | 10 | 119 | 129 | 24 | 49 | 73 |
| Mortuary Science[4] | | | | 80 | 4 | 84 | 33 | 28 | 61 |
| Natural Resources (Forestry) | | | | 477 | 47 | 524 | 319 | 237 | 556 |
| Nursing | 2 | 188 | 190 | 20 | 361 | 381 | 33 | 190 | 223 |
| Occupational Therapy | 4 | 50 | 54 | 4 | 58 | 62 | 1 | 18 | 19 |
| Pharmacy | 390 | 25 | 415 | 272 | 108 | 380 | 118 | 252 | 370 |
| Physical Therapy | 15 | 11 | 26 | 13 | 45 | 58 | 1 | | 1 |
| Public Health | 95 | 184 | 279 | 162 | 91 | 253 | 44 | 185 | 229 |
| Technology | 2,423 | 18 | 2,441 | 3,423 | 239 | 3,662 | 3,575 | 891 | 4,466 |
| University College | 47 | 14 | 61 | 157 | 153 | 310 | 93 | 153 | 246 |
| Veterinary Medicine | 164 | 4 | 168 | 220 | 50 | 270 | 76 | 221 | 297 |
| Duluth | 1,165 | 513 | 1,678 | 2,997 | 2,463 | 5,460 | 3,941 | 3,890 | 7,831 |
| Morris | | | | 985 | 671 | 1,656 | 774 | 1,143 | 1,917 |
| Crookston | | | | 580 | 185 | 765 | 1,111 | 1,381 | 2,492 |
| Waseca | | | | 231 | 175 | 406 | | | |
| | 16,916 | 6,101 | 23,017 | | | | | | |
| Duplicates | (274) | (106) | (380) | | | | | | |
| System Total | 16,642 | 5,995 | 22,637 | 30,472 | 19,463 | 49,935 | 25,200 | 26,635 | 51,835 |
| Gender Percentage (%) | 73.52 | 26.48 | | 61.02 | 38.98 | | 48.62 | 51.38 | |

[1]Per table 11A, Collegiate Enrollment Report by Quarter, 1950–51
[2]Per official registration statistics
[3]Graduate School totals in 1998 included 198 architecture and landscape architecture students and 200 students in the Humphrey Institute of Public Affairs.
[4]Mortuary Science included in Medicine in 1950–51

Table compiled by Institutional Research and Reporting, April 2000

## Collegiate and Extension Enrollments in 1950, 1973, and 1998

| | Fall 1950 | Fall 1973 | Fall 1998 |
|---|---|---|---|
| Extension Enrollment | | | |
| General extension and Center for Continuation Study credit and noncredit registrations (Continuing Education & Extension in 1972, University College in 1996–99, College of Continuing Education after 1999). | 23,901[a] | 32,381[b] | 47,912[c] |
| Minnesota Extension Service Agricultural Short Courses and other Extension Enrollments | 18,549[a] | 31,836[b] | 32,651[d] |
| | 42,450 | 64,217 | 80,563 |
| Collegiate Enrollments | 22,637 | 49,935 | 51,835 |
| Total Enrollments* | 65,087 | 114,152 | 132,398 |

[a]Biennial Report of the President 1950–52, pp. 11, 209
[b]Biennial Report of the President 1972–74, pp. 146–47
[c]University College Annual Report 1998–99, p. 8
[d]Minnesota Extension Service

Note: These figures do not include the considerable number of other contacts made through the University of Minnesota Extension Service (estimated at 700,000 at the end of the century), noncredit courses, attendance at Northrop Auditorium, and listeners to Radio K and Radio KUMD, offered through the College of Continuing Education, or the extensive outreach of other colleges and departments in the university.

Table compiled by Institutional Research and Reporting, April 2000

## APPENDIX B

# Graduate Program Rankings

# University of Minnesota Graduate Programs Ranked Nationally among the Top 20 from the 1993 National Research Council Rankings

| Department | Faculty Quality | College |
|---|---|---|
| Chemical Engineering | 1 | IT |
| Geography | 3 | CLA |
| Psychology | 7 | CLA |
| Mechanical Engineering | 8 | IT |
| Economics | 10 | CLA |
| German | 11 | CLA |
| Aerospace Engineering | 12 | IT |
| Political Science | 13 | CLA |
| Statistics | 13 | CLA |
| Civil Engineering | 13 | IT |
| Mathematics | 14 | IT |
| Ecology, Evolution, and Behavior | 15 | CBS |
| Materials Science | 17 | IT |
| Biomedical Engineering | 17.5 | IT |
| Electrical Engineering | 18 | IT |

Source: Rankings compiled by the Office of Planning and Analysis and Office of the Senior Vice President for Academic Affairs, *1996 Accreditation Self-Study of the Twin Cities Campus: A Land-Grant University for the Twenty-first Century* (Minneapolis: University of Minnesota, 1996), pp. 254 and 256. Note: This NCR ranking was made on the basis of departments scoring 3.5 and above on faculty quality as perceived by faculty members participating in the evaluations.

IT = Institute of Technology
CLA = College of Liberal Arts
CBS = College of Biological Sciences

## Rankings of Universities Based on the Sum of Their Rating Scores for Programs with Rankings above 3.5 for Faculty Quality in the 1993 National Research Council Study

| University | 1993 Rank | Change from 1982 | No. of Programs Ranked above 3.0 in Faculty Quality |
|---|---|---|---|
| University of California, Berkeley | 1 | 0 | 36 |
| Stanford University | 2 | 0 | 34 |
| Cornell University | 3 | +5 | 32 |
| University of Michigan | 4 | +2 | 31 |
| Harvard University | 5 | 0 | 27 |
| Princeton University | 6 | −3 | 28 |
| University of Chicago | 7 | +2 | 27 |
| University of California, Los Angeles | 8 | −4 | 27 |
| University of Pennsylvania | 9 | +5 | 27 |
| Massachusetts Institute of Technology | 10 | +3 | 23 |
| Yale University | 11 | −4 | 24 |
| University of Wisconsin, Madison | 12 | 0 | 26 |
| Columbia University | 13 | −3 | 25 |
| University of Texas, Austin | 14 | +1 | 25 |
| University of California, San Diego | 15 | +14 | 21 |
| University of Washington | 16 | +3 | 20 |
| California Institute of Technology | 17 | +1 | 18 |
| Johns Hopkins University | 18 | +5 | 19 |
| University of Illinois, Urbana-Champaign | 19 | −8 | 18 |
| University of Minnesota | 20 | −4 | 18 |
| Northwestern University | 21 | −1 | 18 |
| Duke University | 22 | +13 | 17 |
| University of North Carolina, Chapel Hill | 23 | −6 | 16 |
| New York University | 24 | +2 | 13 |
| Brown University | 25 | −4 | 12 |

Source: Office of Planning and Analysis and Office of the Senior Vice President for Academic Affairs, *1996 Accreditation Self-Study of the Twin Cities Campus: A Land-Grant University for the Twenty-first Century*, p. 253.

Note: Minnesota ranked twentieth among the top 25 institutions, tenth among the public universities, and was among four Big Ten institutions in the top 20 (Michigan 4th, Wisconsin 12th, Illinois 19th, and Minnesota 20th).

# University Campuses, Research and Outreach Centers, and Other Research Sites

# University of Minnesota Campuses, Research and Outreach Centers (ROCs), and Other Research Sites, September 2000

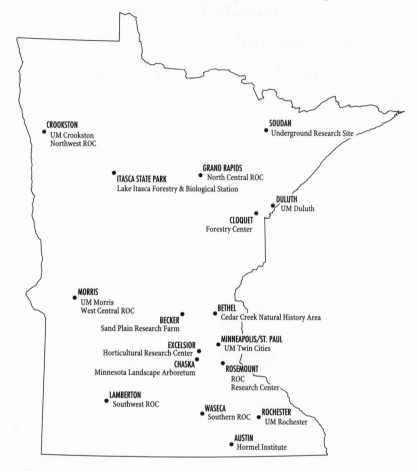

CROOKSTON
• UM Crookston
Northwest ROC

SOUDAN
• Underground Research Site

GRAND RAPIDS
• North Central ROC

ITASCA STATE PARK
Lake Itasca Forestry & Biological Station

DULUTH
• UM Duluth

CLOQUET
• Forestry Center

MORRIS
• UM Morris
West Central ROC

BETHEL
• Cedar Creek Natural History Area

BECKER
Sand Plain Research Farm

EXCELSIOR
Horticultural Research Center

MINNEAPOLIS/ST. PAUL
• UM Twin Cities

CHASKA
Minnesota Landscape Arboretum

ROSEMOUNT
ROC
Research Center

LAMBERTON
• Southwest ROC

WASECA
• Southern ROC

ROCHESTER
• UM Rochester

AUSTIN
• Hormel Institute

The Research and Outreach Centers are affiliated with the Agricultural Experiment Station and the College of Agricultural, Food, and Environmental Sciences.

The University of Minnesota Extension Service has offices throughout the state in all counties and makes more than 700,000 contacts statewide annually.

The University of Minnesota Rochester is a partner in the University Center Rochester with Rochester Community and Technical College and Winona State University–Rochester.

The College of Continuing Education offers classes at various sites throughout the Twin Cities metropolitan area.

# University of Minnesota Fund Sources and Expenditures for Selected Years

# University of Minnesota
# Comparison of Sources of Funds
(exculdes University Hospital)

F.Y. 1999

Current $(000)
1,742,318

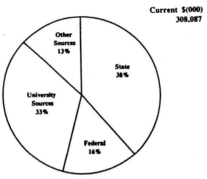

F.Y. 1974

Current $(000)
308,087

F.Y. 1950

Current $(000)
37,057

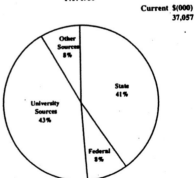

Source: Annual Financial Report
Office of Institutional Reseach & Reporting
April 2000

# Expenditures for Fiscal Years 1950, 1974, and 1999

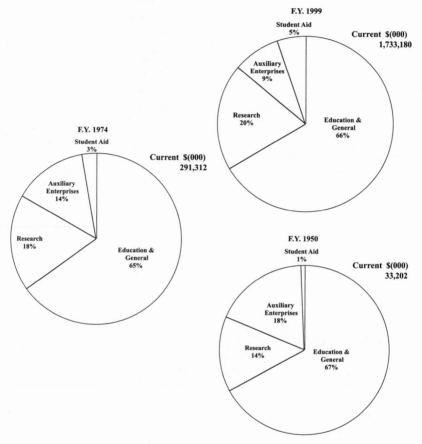

**F.Y. 1999**

Student Aid
5%

Auxiliary
Enterprises
9%

Research
20%

Education &
General
66%

Current $(000)
1,733,180

**F.Y. 1974**

Student Aid
3%

Auxiliary
Enterprises
14%

Research
18%

Education &
General
65%

Current $(000)
291,312

**F.Y. 1950**

Student Aid
1%

Auxiliary
Enterprises
18%

Research
14%

Education &
General
67%

Current $(000)
33,202

Source: Annual Financial Report, Office of Institutional Research and Reporting, April 2000
Note: Excludes University Hospital

# Presidents and Chairs of the Board of Regents

## Presidents of the University of Minnesota

| | |
|---|---|
| James L. Morrill | 1945–1960 |
| O. Meredith Wilson | 1960–1967 |
| Malcolm Moos | 1968–1974 |
| C. Peter Magrath | 1974–1984 |
| Kenneth H. Keller | 1985–1988 |
| Nils Hasselmo | 1989–1997 |
| Mark G. Yudof | 1997– |

## Chairs of the Board of Regents

| | |
|---|---|
| Fred B. Snyder | 1914–1951 |
| Raymond Quinlivan | 1951–1963 |
| Charles Mayo | 1963–1967 |
| Lester Malkerson | 1967–1971 |
| Elmer L. Andersen | 1971–1975 |
| Neil C. Sherburne | 1975–1977 |
| Wenda W. Moore | 1977–1983 |
| Lauris Krenik | 1983–1985 |
| Charles F. McGuiggan | 1985–1987 |
| David M. Lebedoff | 1987–1989 |
| Charles H. Casey | 1989–1991 |
| Elton R. Kuderer | 1991–1993 |
| Jean B. Keffeler | 1993–1995 |
| Thomas R. Reagan | 1995–1997 |
| William E. Hogan II | 1997–1999 |
| Patricia A. Spence | 1999– |

# Notes

Many of the publications here were published by the university itself and are available in the University Archives. Generally speaking, they are either all-university or Twin Cities campus publications, except where noted otherwise.

The *Minnesota Daily* was the Twin Cities campus student newspaper. *Brief, Report, Kiosk, Update, M,* and *Facts* were published by the central administration for various audiences. Alumni publications during the years covered by this volume included *Voice of the Alumni, Minnesota Alumnus, Alumni News,* and *Minnesota* magazine. In addition, many departments, colleges, and campuses published newsletters or magazines for their alumni and friends: *ITEMS,* later *Inventing Tomorrow* (Institute of Technology); *CLA Today* (College of Liberal Arts); *Management Review* (Carlson School of Management); *CALA Works* (College of Architecture and Landscape Architecture); *Frontiers* (College of Biological Sciences); *The Lyceum* and *The Link* (College of Education and Human Development); *The Cutting Edge* (Department of Surgery). The University of Minnesota Foundation published *Legacy* and other materials for donors.

Biennial reports from the university to the Minnesota Legislature, cited frequently for the years from 1945 to 1974, were discontinued in 1974.

At the end of the century, at the urging of President Mark Yudof, the major units of the university created "compacts" spelling out their visions, goals, and expected results; a number of them are cited here.

## Acknowledgments

1. Minnesota Commission on Higher Education, *Higher Education in Minnesota* (Minneapolis: University of Minnesota Press, 1950), pp. 320–21.
2. Warren Ibele interview with Clarke Chambers, May 1995, p. 27.

## Introduction

1. Eric Sevareid, "Ivory Tower," *Lincoln Mercury Times,* January 4, 1954.
2. James Gray, *The University of Minnesota 1851–1951* (Minneapolis: University of Minnesota Press, 1951), p. 44.
3. Quoted in Gray, *University of Minnesota,* p. 270.
4. University of Minnesota news release, April 12, 1962.
5. Quoted in Gray, *University of Minnesota,* p. 32.

## 1. The University at the End of World War II, 1945–1959

1. Richard Rhodes, *The Making of the Atomic Bomb* (New York: Simon & Schuster, 1986), pp. 144–46 and illustration p. 24 (Lawrence's cyclotron).

2. Stephane Groueff, *Manhattan Project: The Untold Story of the Making of the Atomic Bomb* (New York: Little, Brown, 1967), p. 214.

3. Rhodes, *Making of the Atomic Bomb,* p. 332 and illustration p. 46 (Nier with his mass spectrograph).

4. *Minnesota Daily,* March 30, 1946.

5. *Minnesota Daily,* April 2, 1948.

6. Robert C. Brastad, "Interview with I. M. Kolthoff," reprinted from *Journal of Chemical Education* 50 (October 1973): p. 663.

7. Of the 843 employees granted leave for service in the war effort, 363 were academic employees, 342 were medical fellows, 24 were nurses from University Hospitals, and 114 were civil service employees. In 1944–45, the university had a full-time-equivalent staff of just over 4,000, almost equally divided between civil service (2,144) and academic employees (2,035). *Biennial Report of the President and the Board of Regents of the University of Minnesota to the Legislature of the State of Minnesota, 1944–1946,* December 31, 1946, pp. 10, 86.

8. They were Wallace Armstrong, Ancel Keys, Raymond Beiter, Gerald T. Evans, James J. Ryan, Owen W. Wangensteen, Maurice Visscher, W. M. Lauer, R. T. Arnold, William G. Clark, N. Logan, H. M. Tsuchiya, Milton Levine, and E. A. Strackosch. *Minnesota Daily,* August 1, 1946.

9. *Minnesota Daily,* April 2, 1948.

10. Leonard G. Wilson, *Medical Revolution in Minnesota: A History of the University of Minnesota Medical School* (St. Paul: Midewiwin Press, 1989), pp. 416–24.

11. James Gray, *Education for Nursing: A History of the University of Minnesota School* (Minneapolis: University of Minnesota Press, 1960), pp. 139–44, quote p. 144.

12. Office of Planning and Analysis, University of Minnesota, 1998.

13. *Biennial Report, 1944–1946,* p. 49. The schools were the Central School of Agriculture in St. Paul, the Northwest School of Agriculture in Crookston, the West Central School of Agriculture in Morris, and the North Central School of Agriculture in Grand Rapids. Enrollments in 1945–46 in the four schools totaled 1,815 students: 1,163 men and 652 women. A fifth school, the Southern School of Agriculture, was to open in Waseca in 1953; see *Waseca Herald,* June 19, 1953.

14. *Biennial Report, 1944–1946,* pp. 50–51. General Extension registrations in 1945–46 were 21,678: 10,654 in General Extension evening classes and 11,024 in correspondence study. The Center for Continuation Study (named Nolte Center in honor of extension director Julius Nolte) enrollment in 1945–46 was 3,441. Its offerings included a banker conference and an institute for county highway engineers, both annual events; an institute for probation and parole workers; a mining symposium; and courses in techniques of home building and tuberculosis control. In 1945–46, 6,882 people were enrolled in agricultural schools and short courses.

15. *Biennial Report of the President and the Board of Regents of the University of Minnesota to the Legislature of the State of Minnesota, 1960–1962,* June 30, 1962, pp. 270–71, provided amounts and sources of research funding from 1946–47 through 1961–62.

16. "Minnesota's Eighth President," *Minnesota Alumnus,* April 1946.

17. Quoted in a tribute to Morrill written shortly after his death by Russell I. Thackery in *NASULGC (National Association of State Universities and Land-Grant Colleges) Circular Letter,* August 28, 1979, pp. 23–24.

18. *The Crisis of Mankind: The Urgent Educational Tasks of the University in Our Time* (Minneapolis: University of Minnesota Press, 1947).

19. Ibid., p. 107.

20. *Minnesota Daily,* April 26, 1945. Quigley was an authority on both pre- and postwar China and Japan; see *Political Science* (winter 1969): pp. 1960–61.

21. University of Minnesota News Service, April 13, 1963.

22. *Biennial Report 1944–1946,* p. 150, and *Biennial Report of the President and the Board of Regents of the University of Minnesota to the Legislature of the State of Minnesota, 1950–1952,* December 31, 1952, pp. 208, 212.

23. Al Sandvik, "The Legacy of the G.I. Bill," *Minnesota,* March/April 1999, pp. 30–32; John Lundquist, "University of Minnesota Era Ends: Time Runs Out This Month for G.I. Bill," *Minneapolis Star,* February 11, 1965. A second bill established the Veterans Vocational Rehabilitation program for veterans with disabilities.

24. Information about the G.I. Bill from Clarke Chambers's interviews with persons referred to in the text.

25. David Berg interview with Clarke Chambers, November 1994, p. 59.

26. Enrollment in the fall of 1946 was 20,359 men and 7,623 women; see *Biennial Report, 1946–1948,* June 30, 1948, pp. 150, 208. The veterans numbered 18,929. Enrollment figures for 1947–48 showed that 99 percent of the General College students were from Minnesota; 54 percent of the Graduate School students were from outside Minnesota. Minnesota Commission on Higher Education, *Higher Education in Minnesota* (Minneapolis: University of Minnesota Press, 1950), p. 356.

27. In keeping with the university's long tradition of research on student life, the veterans' experience was documented carefully; an exit interview was scheduled with each of them. James D. Kline, "Specialized Counseling for Veterans at the University of Minnesota," *Educational Outlook* 22 (1947): 3–4.

28. *Minnesota Alumnus* 45 (1945): 71.

29. "The Problem of Student Housing in Relation to the Future of the University," typed statement by J. L. Morrill, October 31, 1945, University Archives.

30. Gladys M. Peterson, "University Village Housing 1948–1950," *Hennepin History* (summer 1996): pp. 31–32, and letter to alumni association editor Shelly Fling, March 1999. James Peterson had a long career in geological exploration; he published more than 150 papers and was awarded the University of Minnesota Outstanding Achievement Award in 1996.

31. John Borchert interview with Clarke Chambers, October 1984, p. 16.

32. "Student Housing Bureau Residence Study 1957–58," University Archives; "Memorandum on Off-Campus Housing," E. G. Williamson to Malcolm Willey, May 18, 1955, University Archives.

33. Margaret N. Space and Maybelle G. McCulloch, "History of Off-Campus Housing at the University of Minnesota," November 1982, p. 16, University Archives.

34. "Handbook for Residents of Pioneer and Centennial Halls," about 1950, University Archives.

35. "Discipline at Sanford Hall Residence for Women, University of Minnesota," a Plan B paper for Psychology 233 by Nancy Jane Hickman, 1949, p. 23, University Archives.

36. "Handbook for Residents of Pioneer and Centennial Halls."

37. J. Trout Lowen, "Temporary Buildings Have Historic Past," *Minnesota Daily,* August 25, 1987, p. 10.

38. Vernon Heath interview with Ann Pflaum, August 1999, pp. 3–6.

39. Sandvik, "Legacy of the G.I. Bill," p. 32.

40. Personal communication from Anne Truax to Ann Pflaum, July 1999.

41. Arvonne Fraser interview with Ann Pflaum, August 20, 1999 (based on written notes of the interview).

42. Ibid.

43. Judy Lebedoff interview with Ann Pflaum, July 1998, p. 4.

44. Personal communication from Emily Anne Mayer Staples Tuttle to Ann Pflaum, July 27, 1998.

45. Walter F. Mondale interview with Ann Pflaum, September 1999, p. 1; see Betty Wilson, "A Life of the Party" (a profile of Orville Freeman), *Minnesota,* March/April 1999, pp. 16–21.

46. Harvey Mackay interview with Ann Pflaum, June 1999, p. 4. Mackay was a member of Phi Epsilon Pi fraternity.

47. Betty Ann Whitman interviews with Ann Pflaum, July and August 1999, p. 2.

48. Jim Peterson, "The Problem Parents of the Greeks," *Minnesota Daily,* Ivory Tower Edition, November 2, 1953, pp. 4–5.

49. The authors wish to thank Conrad Jones for his information on Kappa Alpha Psi and on the experiences of black students at the University of Minnesota. See interview with Ann Pflaum, July 1999, pp. 7–9.

50. Tinglum's view of student subgroups corresponds with the characterization of "three distinct student subcultures: college men and women, outsiders, and rebels" by Helen Lefkowitz Horowitz in *Campus Life: Undergraduate Cultures from the End of the Eighteenth Century to the Present* (Chicago: University of Chicago Press, 1987), p. xii.

51. He later became an attorney. Sverre Tinglum interview with Ann Pflaum, July 1999.

52. "The Once and Future Dinkytown," *Kiosk,* April 1998. Schmidt, who later worked in counseling at the university, did not graduate until 1970, but her views were typical of those held earlier.

53. Jim Klobuchar, "'U' Doesn't Have to Be What It Was 40 Years Ago," Minneapolis *Star Tribune,* September 7, 1993, 3B.

54. Kathy Kildow, ed., *University Centennial Gopher,* University Student Publications, 1951.

55. Dave Burrington, "Quiet Life of the St. Paul Campus," *Minnesota Daily,* Ivory Tower Edition, November 2, 1953, pp. 4–5.

56. Russell Bennett interview with Clarke Chambers, October 1995, p. 4.

57. Curtis L. Carlson, who attended the university in the 1930s, also valued his fraternity experiences: "I took great pleasure . . . in the social life that revolved around my fraternity. I made many close friendships there that have stood the test of time. That fraternity activity, by the way, was instructive as it was fun. It taught me how to

deal with my peers, how to initiate and develop close, working relationships.... To this day I look favorably on any job candidate who has been an officer of a fraternity, sorority, or other such social organization.... Finally, it was at the University that I met the...young woman (Arleen Martin) who would eventually become my wife." Curtis L. Carlson, *Good as Gold: The Story of the Carlson Companies* (Minneapolis: Carlson Companies, 1994), p. 14.

58. Joint interview of Roger Page, Carol Pazandak, and William Beyer with Clarke Chambers, November 1994, p. 4.

59. Roger Page interview with Clarke Chambers, August 1984, p. 19.

60. "A Letter to the SLA Faculty," Department of General Studies, February 1956.

61. The authors are indebted to Arthur Naftalin, Philip Siegelman, and Hyman Berman for background on this department.

62. Jonathan Lebedoff interview with Ann Pflaum, July 1998, p. 2, and quote from Philip Siegelman from a eulogy given in honor of Ralph Ross, April 11, 2000; enrollment information from the General Studies Letter to the SLA Faculty, 1956, p. 5.

63. Roger Page interview with Clarke Chambers, August 1984, p. 19.

64. *Biennial Report, 1950–1952,* December 31, 1952, pp. 194–97.

65. Theofanis Stavrou interview with Clarke Chambers, June 1998, pp. 35–36, and Robert Holt interview with Clarke Chambers, September 1992, pp. 2–3.

66. Douglas Wallace interview with Clarke Chambers, October 1994, p. 3.

67. David Halberstam, *The Fifties* (New York: Villard, 1993), p. x.

68. Wallace interview with Chambers, p. 10.

69. Holmer later left the university to teach at Yale; after his retirement he returned to live in Minnesota.

70. Wallace interview with Chambers, pp. 3–4.

71. Maynard Reynolds interview with Clarke Chambers, July 1994, pp. 2–3.

72. *University of Minnesota Football, 1998,* Men's Intercollegiate Athletics, 1998, p. 21.

73. *Gopher Goal Post,* October 7, 1950, p. 30.

74. Wendell Anderson interview with Ann Pflaum, June 1999, p. 4.

75. The *Minnesota Daily* described the resignation in an extra edition, only the third in its history—the first had reported the fire that destroyed the original Old Main building in 1904, while the second dealt with the repeal of compulsory military drill in 1934. See *Minnesota Voice of the Alumni,* December 1950, p. 3.

76. Otis Dypwick, "Bernie Bierman," *Gopher Goal Post,* October 7, 1950, p. 12.

77. Ross Bernstein, *Fifty Heroes/Fifty Years: A Celebration of Minnesota Sports* (Minneapolis: Ross Bernstein, 1997), pp. 20–21.

78. Ibid.

79. *Minneapolis Sunday Tribune,* November 14, 1954.

80. Tracy Bauman, "A Time to Give," *Minnesota,* November/December 1998, pp. 30–32.

81. Bernstein, *Fifty Heroes,* pp. 24–25.

82. *University of Minnesota Baseball,* Men's Intercollegiate Athletics, 1998, p. 81.

83. Harvay Mackay interview with Ann Pflaum, February 1999, p. 2.

84. Steve Perlstein, ed., *Gopher Glory: 100 Years of University of Minnesota Basketball* (Minneapolis: Layers Publishing, 1995), pp. 34–37.

85. *Biennial Report 1950–1952,* pp. 185–86.

86. N. James Simler interview with Clarke Chambers, August 1984, pp. 2–4.

87. Craig Swan interview with Clarke Chambers, October 1994, p. 9.

88. Edward Foster interview with Clarke Chambers, October 1994, p. 5, and personal communication to Ann Pflaum, April 17, 2000.

89. "Orbis Novus Terrarum: Centro Relocata," Department of Geography self-study, 1974, pp. 53–56; *Minnesota Daily,* February 10, 1983; *Report,* April 1993.

90. "Orbis Novus Terrarum," p. 8.

91. Clarke Chambers interviews with John Borchert, October 1984, p. 19, and Richard Skaggs, September 1994, pp. 8–9.

92. "Orbis Novus Terrarum," Part B, Appendix.

93. Leo Marx, "United States Studies: Notes for a Myth of Origins," *American Studies after Fifty Years,* a conference at the University of Minnesota, October 20–23, 1994, p. 2. The authors are grateful to Professor Gayle Graham Yates for making available manuscripts from the conference.

94. "History of American Studies," 1987 American Studies Program Review, pp. 70–73.

95. Marx, "United States Studies," p. 2.

96. Ibid., pp. 1–2.

97. Ibid, p. 4.

98. Personal communication from Sverre Tinglum to Ann Pflaum, July 15, 1999.

99. James Gray, *The University of Minnesota 1851–1951* (Minneapolis: University of Minnesota Press, 1951), pp. 127–28, 200–201, 255, 428–29, 459.

100. James Shannon interview with Clarke Chambers, December 1995, pp. 1–5. Warren was at Minnesota from 1942 to 1951. See Joseph Blotner, *Robert Penn Warren: A Biography* (New York: Random House, 1997), for an account of Warren's years in Minnesota.

101. Department of Psychology Program Review: Self-Study Report, 1986, vol. 1, pp. 79–83.

102. Ibid., p. 89.

103. A. M. Tinker, "Progress in Psychology at Minnesota: 1890–1953," Department of Psychology, 1953, p. 3.

104. Neal Amundson interview with Clarke Chambers, July 1995, p. 10.

105. Ibid., p. 11.

106. Ibid., pp. 5–11. Scriven was also named a Regents Professor.

107. William G. Shepherd interview with Clarke Chambers, September 1984, p. 11.

108. J. Arthur Myers, "Owen W. Wangensteen," *Journal-Lancet* (Minneapolis) 87 (1967): 218.

109. Wilson, *Medical Revolution in Minnesota,* pp. 486–87.

110. J. Bradley Aust in *The Cutting Edge,* surgery department newsletter, April 1991, p. 3.

111. Myers, "Owen W. Wangensteen," p. 222.

112. Aust, *Cutting Edge,* p. 2.

113. Myers, "Owen W. Wangensteen," pp. 220, 227.

114. Aust, *Cutting Edge,* p. 5.

115. Personal communication from Keith McFarland to Stanford Lehmberg and Ann Pflaum, February 19, 1998.

116. Noel D. Vietmeyer, "Norman E. Borlaug," *Science Year: The 1984 World Book Science Annual* (Chicago: World Book, 1983), p. 340; J. J. Christensen, "The Ninety-Eighth President of the AAAS," *Scientific Monthly* 68 (1949): 31–34; C. M. Christensen, *E. C. Stakman: Statesman of Science* (St. Paul: American Phytopathological Society, 1984), pp. 80–130.

117. Willard C. Cochrane, *Agricultural Economics at the University of Minnesota, 1886–1979,* Agricultural Experiment Station, Miscellaneous Publication No. 21, 1983, p. 27.

118. Ibid., pp. 32, 40.

119. Ibid., pp. 27–42.

120. Sherwood O. Berg interview with Ann Pflaum, August 1999, pp. 6–7.

121. Philip Raup interview with Clarke Chambers, August 1984, p. 26.

122. Vernon Ruttan interview with Clarke Chambers, April 1995, pp. 18–19.

123. Amundson interview with Chambers, pp. 19–20.

124. James L. Morrill, *Gopher Chats,* March 1, 1946.

125. Quoted in article by Wendell Weed, *Minneapolis Star,* October 11, 1956.

126. Ivan Frantz Jr. interview with Clarke Chambers, May 1995, p. 35. Other faculty members corroborate this memory.

127. Quoted in John T. Flanagan, *Theodore C. Blegen: A Memoir* (Northfield, Minn.: Norwegian American Historical Association, 1977), p. 162.

128. Personal communication from Peg Wipperman to Ann Pflaum, February 21, 2000.

129. *Minnesota Daily,* Ivory Tower, March 30, 1959, p. 12.

130. E. W. Ziebarth interview with Clarke Chambers, August 1984, p. 40.

131. Presidents Vincent, Burton, Coffman, Ford, and Coffey had also used this as their official residence. For an account of the Pillsbury home, see *The Minnesota Alumnus* 45 (1946): 247.

132. Quoted in Gary Elliott Engstrand, "Faculty Control of Athletics: A Case Study of the University of Minnesota," Ph.D. dissertation, University of Minnesota, 1995, pp. 419–20.

133. "Biographical Sketch of Malcolm M. Willey," 1966, University Archives.

134. Ziebarth interview with Chambers, p. 26.

135. David Berg interview with Clarke Chambers, p. 15.

136. Ziebarth interview with Chambers, p. 28.

137. Letter from Richard Caldecott to Ann Pflaum and Stanford Lehmberg, January 1998.

138. David Berg interview with Clarke Chambers, pp. 15–16; Margaret "Peg" Wipperman, personal communication to Ann Pflaum, July 1, 2000.

139. Ziebarth interview with Chambers, pp. 23–26.

140. Letter from James Mullin to Stanford Lehmberg, September 1999.

141. Ibid.

142. Dorlesa Barmettler Ewing, "Edmund Griffith Williamson: The Pursuit of Arete," M.A. thesis, California State College at Hayward, August 1966, pp. 48–52; E. G. Williamson autobiography in William H. Van Hoose and John J. Peitrofesa, *Counseling and Guidance in the Twentieth Century: Reflections and Reformulations* (New York: Houghton Mifflin, 1970), p. 370. Sverre Tinglum recalled that the office of the dean of students maintained lists of approved off-campus housing for students. He remembered

that his roommate Bob Brunsell, who was editor of the *Daily,* had privately challenged Williamson's control over their lives. In this case, it was Williamson who ducked. Williamson was, Tinglum guessed, "smart enough not to get into a fight with the editor of the *Minnesota Daily.*" Personal communication to Ann Pflaum, July 15, 1999.

143. Terese Lewis, "McDiarmid Linked SLA's Rich Past to CLA's Bright Future," *CLA Today,* 125th anniversary edition, September 1994, p. 6.

144. Sonar had been developed by Paul Bonar of the University of Texas at Austin.

145. William G. Shepherd interview with Clarke Chambers, September 1984, pp. 13–14; Warren Ibele interview with Clarke Chambers, May 1995, p. 16; Andrew Donohue, "Peers Remember Visionary Dean," *Minnesota Daily,* April 1, 1998, pp. 1, 12; Allie Shah, "Athelstan Spilhaus, 86, Futurist, Marine Scientist, Former Dean at U of M," Minneapolis *Star Tribune,* April 1, 1998. In addition to its engineering departments, the Institute of Technology housed a strong Department of the History of Science and Technology.

146. *Biennial Report, 1950–1952,* pp. 208–9; *Biennial Report, 1960–1962,* pp. 123, 207–8.

147. *Minneapolis Star,* "Man Who Made Taconite Profitable Dies," December 5, 1973; for additional information, see E. W. Davis, *Pioneering with Taconite* (St. Paul: Minnesota Historical Society), 1964.

148. *Minneapolis Star,* November 9, 1956.

149. Robert Beck, *Beyond Pedagogy: A History of the University of Minnesota College of Education* (St. Paul: North Central Publishing Company, 1980), p. 175. Beck, professor of educational policy studies and administration, was named a Regents Professor in 1976.

150. Ibid., pp. 171–80.

151. *Biennial Report, 1950–1952,* p. 169.

152. Denny Shapiro, "The Loophole Effect: A Short History of University College, 1930–1972," University of Minnesota, 1973, p. 10.

153. N. W. Moen, ed., "A Documentary History of the College," *General College Newsletter,* February 1967, pp. 10 and 13.

154. *Biennial Report, 1950–1952,* pp. 208–9; *Biennial Report, 1960–1962,* pp. 207–8. All enrollment figures are for fall quarter.

155. Norman Moen, "General College: The Open Door through Fifty Years, 1932–1982," *General College Newsletter* 30 (1983): 7–10.

156. Pirsig's son Robert, author of the best-selling book *Zen and the Art of Motorcycle Maintenance* (1975), became a hero of the 1960s generation.

157. Robert A. Stein, *In Pursuit of Excellence: A History of the University of Minnesota Law School* (St. Paul: Mason Publishing, 1980), pp. 123–264.

158. Ibid.

159. "University's School of Architecture Trains Students in Art, Science, and Business," *Greater Minneapolis,* June 1952, pp. 10–11.

160. Frederick Koeper, "A Master of Modernism," *Architecture Minnesota,* July/August 1984, pp. 38–49.

161. *Biennial Report, 1950–1952,* pp. 117–18; Whitney Young biography file, University Archives.

162. School of Journalism and Mass Communication, *Campaign Minnesota,* 1999, pp. 4–7; Paul Dienhart, "What's Happening to the J School," *Update,* September 1989,

pp. 1–3. For the influence of Charnley and Hage, see Kate Stanley interview with Ann Pflaum, July 1999.

163. *Biennial Report, 1950–1952*, pp. 208–9; *Biennial Report, 1960–1962*, pp. 207–8; *Management Review*, fall 1994, pp. 4–5.

164. Flanagan, *Theodore C. Blegen*, pp. 55–59; *The Minnesotan*, May 1960, p. 15, copy in Morrill biographical file, University Archives.

165. *Biennial Report, 1960–1962*, p. 271.

166. Flanagan, *Theodore C. Blegen*, p. 95.

167. "University of Minnesota Library," *Report of the President 1946–1948*, pp. 142–43.

168. Institute of Agriculture, *Faculty Newsletter*, fall 1950, pp. 19 and 22, reported enrollment of 1,761 students. *Biennial Report, 1950–1952*, p. 208, cited enrollment of 1,668 students. The difference is probably related to counting graduate students.

169. Gray, *University of Minnesota*, p. 402.

170. Roland H. Abraham, *Helping People Help Themselves: Agricultural Extension in Minnesota, 1879–1979*, Minnesota Extension Service, 1986, pp. 143, 173–74.

171. Ralph E. Miller, *The History of the School of Agriculture, 1851–1960*, Institute of Agriculture, Forestry, and Home Economics, 1979, pp. 79, 130–31; eulogy by the Rev. Edwin C. Johnson, St. Anthony Park Congregational Church, August 8, 1961, University Archives.

172. Richard Skok (Kaufert's successor as dean), letter to Stanford Lehmberg and Ann Pflaum, March 20, 1998.

173. Martin Bronfenbrenner, *Academic Encounter: The American University in Japan and Korea* (Glencoe, Ill.: Free Press, 1961), pp. 170–86, described the challenges and complexities of international institution building.

174. H. H. H. Kernkamp, "The College of Veterinary Medicine, Its Origin and Development," *Minnesota Veterinarian* 5 (1965): 6.

175. *The College of Veterinary Medicine, 1947–1997: 50th Anniversary*, College of Veterinary Medicine, p. 5.

176. *1996 Accreditation Self-Study of the Twin Cities Campus: A Land-Grant University for the Twenty-first Century*, p. 123; *Minnesota Daily*, November 10, 1976.

177. *Journey Home: College of Human Ecology 1894–1996—A Celebration and Evolution of Home Economics at the University of Minnesota*, College of Human Ecology, 1996, p. 45.

178. Harriet and Vetta Goldstein, *Art in Everyday Life* (New York: Macmillan, 1925), p. 1.

179. Esther Warner Dendel, *Beauty and the Human Spirit: The Legacy of Harriet and Vetta Goldstein*, University of Minnesota, 1993, p. 32. The book was published in connection with the hundredth exhibition of the Goldstein Gallery.

180. Keith McFarland et al., *College of Human Ecology 1894–1996: A Celebration and Evolution of Home Economics at the University of Minnesota*, University of Minnesota Board of Regents, 1998, p. 19.

181. *Minnesota Magazine: The Voice of Alumni*, October 1949, p. 23.

182. Shelley Chou interview with Ann Pflaum, July 1999, p. 13.

183. Winston Wallin interview with Clarke Chambers, October 1995, pp. 4–5.

184. Wilson, *Medical Revolution in Minnesota*, pp. 503–23; G. Wayne Miller, articles on Lillehei in Minneapolis *Star Tribune*, February 14–17, 1999; *St. Paul Pioneer*

*Press,* July 9, 1999. Lillehei, who earned all his degrees from Minnesota, went to the New York Cornell Medical Center in 1967 and returned to the university as a professor of surgery in 1975. His lifetime contributions to surgery were monumental. Considered the "father of open heart surgery," he contributed to the design of four prosthetic heart valves as well as introducing the use of the bubble oxygenator and the wearable pacemaker. As an educator he trained more than a thousand cardiac surgeons, wrote more than seven hundred scholarly articles in medical journals, and was recognized for ongoing contributions in biomedical engineering. He died July 5, 1999.

185. *Celebrating 50 Years: Medtronic 1999 Annual Report* (Minneapolis: Medtronic, 1999), p. 2; for an account of the twentieth anniversary of St. Jude Medical, see Ronald A. Matricia, "A Milestone for St. Jude."

186. Wilson, *Medical Revolution in Minnesota,* pp. 483–85, 492, 503–4, 509–20.

187. Diehl quoted in Wilson, *Medical Revolution in Minnesota,* p. 443.

188. Ibid., p. 454.

189. *Biennial Report, 1950–1952,* p. 6.

190. Robert J. Gorlin, "Living History—Biography: From Oral Pathology to Craniofacial Genetics," *American Journal of Medical Genetics* 46 (1993): 317–34, and interview with Ann Pflaum, February 1999, pp. 5–6.

191. Mellor R. Holland, *A History of the University of Minnesota School of Dentistry,* School of Dentistry, 1993, pp. 101–5.

192. For the fiftieth anniversary, see Brenda H. Canedy, ed., *Remembering Things Past: A Heritage of Excellence: University of Minnesota School of Nursing Diamond Jubilee, 1909 to 1984,* University of Minnesota Biomedical Graphic Communications, 1983, p. 172; video on Katharine Densford created by the School of Nursing.

193. Gray, *Education for Nursing,* pp. 95, 150–71; *From the 40th Milestone: A Publication in Honor of the 40th Anniversary of the School of Nursing,* School of Nursing, 1949.

194. *Nursing Alumni News,* December 1978, pp. 1–2; Gray, *Education for Nursing,* pp. 139–41; *From the 40th Milestone.*

195. Wulling had exceptionally broad interests. He embarked on a medical education, then diverted to pharmacy but continued to take numerous medical courses throughout his lifetime. After coming to Minnesota in 1892, he completed a law degree. Within the university, he helped establish graduate work in medicinal chemistry comparable to that in other sciences. *College of Pharmacy Review,* February 1911, pp. 2–4. During World War I, the college contributed to the war effort by maintaining, on the future site of Northrop Auditorium, a large garden devoted to producing digitalis. See "A Century of Challenge and Change," *College of Pharmacy Review,* spring 1992, pp. 1–8.

196. *College of Pharmacy Review,* 1977, pp. 8–9.

197. *Pharmacy Record: The Newsletter of the College of Pharmacy,* spring 1992, p. 5.

198. University News Service, February 13, 1951.

199. *Pharmacy Record,* spring 1992, p. 4.

200. *50 Years: A Legacy and a Vision: University of Minnesota School of Public Health,* School of Public Health, 1994, pp. 4–9.

201. The original K rations packets contained dried sausage, candy, peanut butter, and a few crackers. A later version also included cheese, two cigarettes, matches, and

toilet paper. Tom Majeski, "U Public Health School Celebrates 50 Years," *St. Paul Pioneer Press,* January 27, 1995.

202. Ancel Keys, "Notes from a Medical Journal," *Lancet,* 1951, p. 3.

203. *Time,* January 13, 1961, p. 50.

204. Ann Pflaum, "Administrative History," Continuing Education and Extension Self-Study," April 1992, vols. 1 and 12, part 4, pp. 19–40.

205. Alan Brown tape, November 16, 1984. Brown had been director of the Continuation Center.

206. *Biennial Report, 1950–1952,* pp. 170–74.

207. Richard Cisek interview with Clarke Chambers, September 1995, pp. 8–9.

208. Philip Davies, "University of Minnesota Alumni Association." The authors are grateful to Tom Garrison of the alumni association for sending this to us. The exact membership number in 1950 was 12,752. *Biennial Report, 1950–1952,* pp. 189–90, and *Biennial Report, 1960–1962,* pp. 187–88.

209. Ken Moran and Neil Storch, *UMD Comes of Age: The First One Hundred Years* (Virginia Beach, Va.: Donning, 1996), p. 41. We are indebted to the authors of this useful history of UMD for advice and perspective. See also Julian Hoshal, "A Chronology of UMD Events," University of Minnesota News Service, 1984. A number of audiotaped interviews were made by Jackie Moran, Neil Storch, and Jim Vileta. We consulted interviews with Raymond C. Gibson, Wendell P. Glick, Charles Nichol, George "Rip" Rapp, Lawrence Ianni, Gerald Heaney, Albert Tezla, and John E. King. We thank library and archives staff members who made materials available during our visits to Duluth.

210. Moran and Storch, *UMD Comes of Age,* p. 63.

211. Ibid., p. 57. He later served as director of the United States educational mission in Peru and then, from 1955 to 1976, as professor of higher education at the University of Indiana.

212. Alice Tweed and her husband, George, were major donors to UMD. In 1941, they gave the university the former Cotton mansion, which served as home to their collection of nineteenth-century French paintings until 1958, when the collection moved to the new Humanities building. It became known as the Tweed Art Gallery; the Alice Tweed Tuohy Addition was completed in 1965. Alice Tweed's second husband was Dr. Edward L. Tuohy, a co-founder of the Duluth Clinic. Alice Tweed Tuohy was the first woman to receive the University of Minnesota Regents Award, made in October 1960. See Moran and Storch, *UMD Comes of Age,* pp. 77, 80, 137.

213. *Biennial Report, 1950–1952,* p. 208.

214. Elmer L. Andersen interview with Clarke Chambers, October 1995, p. 6.

215. James Mullin to Stanford Lehmberg, September 1999. Mullin reported that his father had other interests besides the university. Among them were the state court system, judges' salaries, state parks, and social welfare legislation. Mullin was the author of fair employment practice statutes.

216. Elmer L. Andersen interview with Clarke Chambers, p. 6. Stanford Lehmberg is grateful to Mullin's son Jim for comments that confirm Andersen's views.

217. Mullin to Lehmberg.

218. Wendell Weed, *Minneapolis Star,* October 11, 1956.

219. Andersen interview with Chambers, p. 7. James Mullin reported to Stanford Lehmberg that his father resigned from the legislature in 1957, accepting the presidency

of Minnegasco (earlier he had been its general counsel). He received the first Regents Award and continued to support the university until his death in 1982.

220. Ellen W. Schrecker, *No Ivory Tower: McCarthyism and the Universities* (New York: Oxford University Press, 1986), p. 21. The university had an earlier instance of academic freedom clashing with prevailing views when William A. Shaper was dismissed from the faculty in 1917 for his allegedly pro-German views and for his opposition to the entry of the United States into World War I. Professor Shaper's sentiments seem mild today. While he supported victory for the Allies, he indicated, when he was called before the regents, that he did not think that "the Hohenzollerns should be wiped out root and branch." He also found it difficult to condemn his own relatives in Germany. Twenty years later, the Board of Regents recognized the injustice of Shaper's dismissal and offered him an apology and a financial settlement, which he gave to the political science department to support research. See Gray, *University of Minnesota*, pp. 247, 386–88, and *A History of the Department of Political Science, 1872–1994*, issued by the department in 1995, p. 11.

221. As Robert Oppenheimer once testified, Frank had so many other interests, including music and art, that "he couldn't have been a very hard-working communist." See Peter Goodrich, *J. Robert Oppenheimer, Shatterer of Worlds* (New York: Fromm, 1985), especially pp. 238, 287.

222. A year later, seventy-five AAUP members requested that the university reexamine the decision. Gary Paul Hendrickson's doctoral dissertation, "Minnesota in the McCarthy Period, 1946 to 1954" (University of Minnesota, December 1981), explored a number of the academic freedom cases.

223. "President Morrill Clarifies Wiggins Dismissal," *Minnesota Chats*, 32 (1952): 3–4; Gary Paul Hendrickson, "Minnesota in the McCarthy Period, 1946 to 1954," p. 28.

224. *Biennial Report, 1950–1952*, p. 16.

225. *Minnesota Alumnus*, October 1949, pp. 32–34; copy in Morrill biographical file, University Archives. An account of the Williamsburg address is found in *Minnesota Alumnus*, October 1949, pp. 2–35.

226. Ibid., pp. 19 and 34.

227. Reported in a review of Morrill's presidency in *The Minnesotan*, May 1960, p. 7.

228. Schrecker, *No Ivory Tower*, p. 340. Malcolm Willey saw Morrill's record on academic freedom positively, citing this as an area of accomplishment. The AAUP gave a dinner in his honor prior to his retirement. *Minnesotan*, p. 7.

229. *Minnesotan*, p. 7.

230. Research expenditures in 1945–46 were $1.1 million (cited in correspondence to President J. L. Morrill, January 8, 1952). In 1960, expenditures had risen to $15 million.

231. *Biennial Report, 1944–1946*, p. 48 (11,872), and *Biennial Report, 1960–1962*, p. 207 (29,090).

232. Noncollegiate enrollment in 1960–61 was 26,323 for the General Extension Division, including correspondence registrations; 18,229 in schools and agricultural short courses; and 9,914 in programs of the Center for Continuation Study. *Biennial Report, 1960–1962*, pp. 210–14.

233. A complete self-study is located in the University Archives. References are taken from a mimeographed guide to its recommendations published in August 1957.

234. Richard Rainboldt, *Gopher Glory* (Wayzata, Minn.: Ralph Turtinen, 1972), p. 169.

235. Ibid., p. 173.

## 2. Years of Growth and Years of Protest, 1960–1974

1. *Biennial Report of the President and the Board of Regents of the University of Minnesota to the Legislature of the State of Minnesota, 1960–1962*, June 30, 1962, p. 269.

2. *Time* magazine, March 20, 1961, pp. 52, 57.

3. Official Rose Bowl program, Pasadena, California, January 2, 1961, p. 12.

4. Richard Rainboldt, *Gopher Glory* (Wayzata, Minn.: Ralph Turtinen, 1972), p. 172.

5. *Alumni News,* December 1960, p. 21.

6. *Gopher Goal Post,* September 30, 1961, p. 28, and *Alumni News,* December 1962, p. 28.

7. *Gopher Goal Post,* p. 28, and *Alumni News,* p. 18.

8. Sandy Stephens interview with Ann Pflaum, May 1999, p. 4. Stevens died June 5, 2000.

9. *University of Minnesota Football,* Men's Intercollegiate Athletics, 1998, p. 225.

10. The authors are indebted to Marian Wilson for pointing out that she and her husband attended the Rose Bowl for three consecutive seasons. She said things became pretty "routine" by the third trip. Marian Wilson interview with Ann Pflaum, February 2000.

11. O. Meredith Wilson, interview with Clarke Chambers, September 1983, p. 11.

12. O. M. Wilson biography file, University Archives; *Minnesota Daily,* January 15, 1960.

13. Barbara Flanagan, "Wilson Family Settles in New St. Paul Home," *Minneapolis Tribune,* March 12, 1961.

14. Marian Wilson interview with Ann Pflaum, February 2000, pp. 1, 2, 7.

15. "Wilson to Get $27,000 Salary," *Willmar Daily Tribune,* January 15, 1960, p. 1.

16. Text of O. Meredith Wilson's inaugural address, *Minneapolis Tribune,* February 24, 1961, p. 18.

17. E. W. Ziebarth interview with Clarke Chambers, August 1984, p. 1.

18. O. Meredith Wilson interview with Clarke Chambers, pp. 31–32.

19. *Minneapolis Tribune,* September 24, 1967, p. 2C. The September editorial quoted from July 18, 1967, editorial.

20. *Biennial Report of the President and the Board of Regents of the University of Minnesota to the Legislature of the State of Minnesota, 1962–1964,* June 30, 1964, p. 1.

21. Wilson interview with Chambers, pp. 6–7.

22. Warren Ibele interview with Clarke Chambers, May 1995, p. 19.

23. Neal Amundson interview with Clarke Chambers, July 1995, p. 14.

24. Wilson interview with Chambers, p. 10.

25. Ibid., p. 8.

26. Ibid., p. 9.

27. *Biennial Report of the President and the Board of Regents of the University of Minnesota to the Legislature of the State of Minnesota, 1972–74,* June 30, 1974, pp. 31–33 and for enrollment, p. 145.

28. *Biennial Report of the President and the Board of Regents of the University of Minnesota to the Legislature of the State of Minnesota, 1970–1972,* June 30, 1972, p. 212. Research dollars in 1960–61 were $10,870,117; in 1969–70 they were $29,411,049.

29. *Biennial Report of the President and the Board of Regents of the University of Minnesota to the Legislature of the State of Minnesota, 1964–1966,* June 30, 1966, p. 271.

30. Ibid., and *Biennial Report of the President and the Board of Regents of the University of Minnesota to the Legislature of the State of Minnesota, 1966–68,* June 30, 1968, p. 115–17.

31. Matthews Hollinshead, "Rank and File," *Minnesota* 85, no. 7 (1986): 8.

32. "Fat of the Land," *Time,* January 13, 1961, pp. 48–52, and "The Pragmatic Professor," *Time,* March 3, 1961, pp. 18–22. Heller was on leave to chair the Council of Economic Advisers.

33. Ibele interview with Chambers, pp. 19–20.

34. Wilson interview with Chambers, p. 12.

35. Not everyone agreed with this view. Serge Chermayeff, professor of architecture at Harvard, proposed that the university go east, moving the football stadium and practice fields and building on that site; the Minneapolis City Planning Commission was interested in studying this suggestion. *Minneapolis Star,* January 24, 1958.

36. Wilson interview with Chambers, pp. 11–12.

37. Robert Venable Turner, *Campus: An American Planning Tradition* (Cambridge, Mass: MIT Press, and New York: Architectural History Foundation, 1984), p. 251.

38. Ibid., p. 250.

39. *Minnesota Daily,* March 18, 1961. Lehmberg occasionally taught seminars in these rooms. They were indeed good for large classes, but the West Bank buildings have always lacked good spaces for small seminars and discussion groups. Different Minnesota architectural firms were responsible for the three buildings: they were Magney, Setter, Leach, & Lindstrom (classroom building); Thorshov & Cerney (social sciences); and Hammel & Green (business administration). General architectural coordination was provided by Pietro Belluschi and Lawrence B. Anderson of Cambridge, Massachusetts, together with Winston Close.

40. *History of the Department of Political Science,* p. 39.

41. Wilson interview with Chambers, p. 14.

42. Rents had been raised drastically because of the severe financial troubles affecting CRA.

43. Wilson interview with Chambers, pp. 13–15.

44. Gerhard Weiss interview with Clarke Chambers, August 1994, pp. 22–23. Among the libraries the committee inspected were Purdue, Brandeis, and Notre Dame. David Harris Willson loved to tell the story of scholars in England who mistakenly assumed the library was named to honor him.

45. We are indebted to Craig Swan for the observation on the functionality of the library.

46. "Mixing Up Books with People," *Alumni News,* December 1968, p. 31.

47. John Parker interview with Clarke Chambers, December 1994, p. 6.

48. *Kerlan Collection Newsletter,* spring 1999, p. 1–2.

49. For a description of the J. O. Christianson Award, see brochure for the conference "Exploring Our Global Community: People, Food, and Agriculture," July 6–11, 1999, p. 7.

50. "The New Undergraduate," *Alumni News,* December 1961, p. 6.

51. Linda Brekke Mona interview with Ann Pflaum, October 4, 1999, pp. 5ff.

52. *College of Veterinary Medicine, 50ᵗʰ Anniversary,* 1947, p. 5.

53. Ibid., p. 2.

54. There were three extension service directors from the 1960s through the late 1970s: Skuli Rutford (1954 to 1963), Luther Pickrel (1964 to 1967), and Roland Abraham (acting director from 1967 to 1968, director 1968 to 1979).

55. For a comprehensive history of the extension service, see Roland H. Abraham's *People Helping Themselves: Agricultural Extension in Minnesota 1879–1979,* Minnesota Extension Service, 1986, especially pp. 195–211.

56. For the fall 1960 enrollments, see *Biennial Report, 1960–62,* p. 207, and for fall 1974, *North Central Accreditation, Self-Evaluation,* University of Minnesota, January 12, 1974, Section D, pp. 20–21. There were 1,790 students in 1960 and 3,558 in 1974.

57. In 1960, enrollments in medicine, nursing, dentistry, and public health were 1,519; by 1974, they had risen to 2,927. Students in allied health fields of physical therapy, occupational therapy, dental hygiene, and mortuary science grew from 257 in 1960 to 558 in 1974. *Biennial Report, 1960–62,* p. 207, and, for fall 1974, *North Central Accreditation,* Section D, pp. 20–21.

58. N. L. Gault interview with Ann Pflaum, January 1999, p. 33.

59. Shelley Chou interview with Ann Pflaum, July 1999, p. 15.

60. Leonard Wilson, *Medical Revolution in Minnesota: A History of the University of Minnesota Medical School* (St. Paul: Midewiwin Press, 1989), pp. 529–44.

61. Mellor R. Holland, *A History of the School of Dentistry: 1888–1988,* School of Dentistry, 1993, p. 132.

62. Ibid., p. 129

63. Lawrence Weaver interview with Ann Pflaum, February 1999, pp. 1–4.

64. "The Relationship between the College of Pharmacy and University Hospitals," a report by the Pharmacy Review Committee, fall 1973.

65. Isabel Harris interview with Ann Pflaum, February 1999, pp. 10–11; University of Minnesota news release, March 22, 1966.

66. *50 Years: A Legacy and a Vision: University of Minnesota School of Public Health,* School of Public Health, 1994, pp. 11–15.

67. Ibid., p. 11.

68. Ibid., pp. 11–15.

69. Personal communication from Thomas Kottke to Ann Pflaum, November 24, 1999.

70. Ibid.

71. Judy Larson Mogelson interview with Ann Pflaum, October 1999; Holland, *History of the School of Dentistry,* pp. 678–79; Charles Netz, *History of the University of Minnesota College of Pharmacy 1892–1970,* College of Pharmacy, 1971, pp. 165–66.

72. Wilson interview with Chambers, p. 17.

73. Elmer L. Andersen interview with Clarke Chambers, October 1995, pp. 6–7.

74. D. J. Leary interview with Clarke Chambers, October 1995, pp. 12–13.

75. Ibid., p. 13.

76. George Robb interview with Clarke Chambers, August 1995, p. 8. Wenberg had been in the army and studied at the university under the G.I. Bill. He had done some graduate work but, according to Robb, was largely self-educated. "He had done a little travel, a lot of reading, and a lot of talking to people. One of the real tragedies of Stan Wenberg's career was that more people on the faculty didn't realize just how intelligent and thoughtful an educator he was" (p. 15).

77. For an excellent overview of the board and the regent selection process, see Peter J. Kizilos, "Regent Selection in Review," *Minnesota,* January/February 1995, pp. 16–20.

78. Personal communication from Barbara M. Muesing to Ann Pflaum, June 1999.

79. Women members of the Board of Regents between 1950 and 2000 were Marjorie Howard, Loanne R. Thrane, Josie R. Johnson, Wenda W. Moore, Kathryn Vander Kooi, Mary T. Schertler, M. Elizabeth Craig, Jean B. Keffeler, Mary J. Page, Ann J. Wynia, Julie Blehyl, Hyon T. Kim, Jessica J. Phillips, Patricia A. Spence, and Maureen Reed. Information provided by the Board of Regents office.

80. Board chairs from 1950 to 2000 are listed (with their dates of service) in Appendix E.

81. William E. Hogan interview with Ann Pflaum, July 1999, p. 3.

82. Elmer L. Andersen, quoted in *Isanti County News,* June 13, 1996.

83. Wenda W. Moore interview with Ann Pflaum, October 1999, pp. 1–4.

84. Jean B. Keffeler interview with Ann Pflaum, July 25, 1999, p. 6.

85. Quoted in Ken Moran and Neal Storch, *UMD Comes of Age: The First One Hundred Years* (Virginia Beach, Va.: Dunning, 1996), p. 162.

86. Robert Bergland interview with Ann Pflaum, April 1999, p. 13.

87. David M. Lebedoff interview with Ann Pflaum, August 1999, p. 13.

88. Patricia A. Spence interview with Ann Pflaum, September 1999, p. 2.

89. Regents Professors file, University Archives.

90. Personal communication from Sheldon Goldstein to Ann Pflaum, 1999.

91. Dave Winfield with Tom Parker, *Winfield: A Player's Life* (New York: Norton, 1988), p. 75.

92. Steve Perlstein, ed., *Gopher Glory: 100 Years of Gopher Basketball* (Minneapolis: Layers Publishing, 1995), pp. 76–77.

93. Winfield with Parker, *A Player's Life,* p. 75.

94. Ross Bernstein, *Fifty Years/Fifty Heroes: A Celebration of Minnesota Sports* (Minneapolis: Ross Bernstein, 1997), pp. 22–23.

95. *Hockey, 1998–1999,* Men's Intercollegiate Athletics, 1998, p. 110.

96. *Golf, 1998–99,* Men's Intercollegiate Athletics, 1998, pp. 12, 39.

97. *Baseball, 1998,* Men's Intercollegiate Athletics, 1998, pp. 64, 76. Coach Dick Siebert, one of the "winningest" baseball coaches, led the baseball teams between 1948 and 1978.

98. *University of Minnesota Baseball Media Guide,* 1998, p. 76, and Bernstein, *Fifty Years Fifty Heroes,* pp. 26–27.

99. Bernstein, *Fifty Years Fifty Heroes,* pp. 26–27, and *University of Minnesota Base-ball Media Guide,* 1998, p. 70.

100. *Prelude: The Early History of Campus Sports* and *1997 Annual Report,* Department of Recreational Sports, 1997, p. 15.

101. *University of Minnesota Alumni News,* May 1969, pp. 12–13.

102. *Biennial Report, 1960–1962,* p. 188, and *Biennial Report, 1972–1974,* p. 130.

103. Personal communication from Robert Odegard to Ann Pflaum, June 22, 1999; and "Building a Great University: the Contributions of the University of Minnesota Board of Trustees, 1962–1998," University of Minnesota Foundation.

104. Bernard Ridder, "Pathway to Philanthropy Interview," University of Minnesota Foundation, September 25, 1992.

105. Ibid. Board chairs between 1962 and 1975 were Henry C. Mackall, Carlyle E. Anderson, Arthur H. Motley, Bernard H. Ridder Jr., Donald C. Dayton, and Curtis L. Carlson.

106. Donald Dayton, "Pathway to Philanthropy Interview," University of Minnesota Foundation, September 25, 1992.

107. Robert Odegard interview with Clarke Chambers, July 1994, pp. 1–4, and communication to Ann Pflaum, June 1999.

108. Dan Berglund, "Director Receives Award for U Fund Raising," *Minnesota Daily,* February 16, 2000, pp. 1, 8.

109. Following Platou and Wangensteen, presidents of the MMF Board of Trustees through 1988 were Wesley W. Spink, Vernon D. Smith, Karl W. Anderson, Malvin Herz, Herman Drill, Arnold Lazarow, Corrin Hodgson, John Frost, John Alden, Lewis Lehr, Donn Mosser, Reuben Berman, Anthony Bechik, John B. Coleman, and Terrance Hanold. Eivind Hoff remained as executive secretary at the foundation through 1985. He was succeeded by David Teslow, who served as executive director until 1996, when Brad Choate became president and chief executive officer. For an account of the early history of the foundation, see "The Minnesota Medical Foundation: Fifty Years of Support," insert in *University of Minnesota Medical Bulletin,* fall 1988.

110. Wilson interview with Chambers, p. 21.

111. Ibid.

112. Ibid.

113. Ibid., p. 22.

114. Ibid., p. 35.

115. Ibid.

116. Ibid., p. 34.

117. Ibid., p. 35.

118. On Ph.D. oral examinations, Sibley would sometimes ask a series of seemingly reasonable questions that led students to an obviously untenable conclusion. He would then smile, say "thank you," and sit back.

119. William G. Shepherd interview with Clarke Chambers, September 1984, p. 20.

120. "Wilson Ends 'Tranquil' 7-Year Administration," *Minnesota Daily Extra,* July 3, 1967, p. 1.

121. John Lundquist, *Minneapolis Star,* June 23, 1967.

122. Personal communication from Zev Aelony to Ann Pflaum, November 1999.

123. Maureen Smith, "Mulford Q. Sibley," summer 1982, p. 11.

124. Tuition at Morris was far lower than tuition at private liberal arts colleges in Minnesota and elsewhere.

125. T. H. Fenske, "West Central: Fifty-Three Years," in *The Moccasin Golden Finale* (WCSA Yearbook, 1963), pp. 45–52; James Gray, *The University of Minnesota, 1851–1951* (Minneapolis: University of Minnesota Press, 1951), p. 407.

126. Report of the Legislative Commission on Agricultural Schools Submitted to the Legislature of the State of Minnesota, January 1959, p. 14.

127. Anderson died in May 1999; he had been awarded the UMM Alumni Association Distinguished Services Award for his long support of the Morris campus.

128. Gary L. McGrath, "The Establishment and Early Development of the University of Minnesota, Morris" (Ed.D. dissertation, Indiana University, 1974), pp. 24–25.

129. The development of the Duluth and Morris campuses of the University of Minnesota was in keeping with a general trend toward multicampus systems in American universities. By 1971, 40 percent of all college students attended schools that were part of multicampus institutions. See Clark Kerr's foreword to Eugene C. Lee and Frank M. Bowen, *The Multicampus University* (New York: McGraw-Hill, 1971), reprinted in Clark Kerr, *The Great Transformation in Higher Education, 1960–1980* (New York: State University of New York Press, 1991), pp. 251–58.

130. Report of the Legislative Commission on Agricultural Schools, p. 24. The report (p. 10) noted that there were twenty-nine public and private postsecondary institutions in the eastern half of the state and only four in the western.

131. Ibid., p. 10. The agricultural schools were located at Crookston and Morris as well as at Grand Rapids, Waseca, and St. Paul.

132. Middlebrook to Morrill, May 28, 1959, quoted in McGrath, "The Establishment and Early Development of the University of Minnesota, Morris," p. 43. Stanley Wenberg was also instrumental in promoting the cause of Morris.

133. Minutes of the University of Minnesota Board of Regents, October 31, 1959, pp. 569–70.

134. *Minneapolis Tribune,* November 6, 1959, p. 11, quoted in McGrath, "The Establishment and Early Development of the University of Minnesota, Morris," p. 57.

135. McGrath, "The Establishment and Early Development of the University of Minnesota, Morris," pp. 36–46.

136. Elizabeth Blake, Steven Granger, and Gary McGrath, "The Morris Campus," March 1999, pp. 2–3; this background paper was prepared for the authors by senior administrators on the Morris campus.

137. Ibid., pp. 1–3.

138. John Q. Imholte interview with Clarke Chambers, August 1984, pp. 4–5.

139. Stephen Granger, *Historic Buildings of the West Central School of Agriculture Converted to Use by the University of Minnesota, Morris in 1960,* Morris Plant Services, 1998.

140. Stephen Granger, "A Tribute to Rodney Briggs," speech at the memorial service for Briggs, October 21, 1995.

141. We are grateful to Gary McGrath for information about athletics at Morris.

142. McGrath, "The Establishment and Early Development of the University of Minnesota, Morris," p. 119.

143. Imholte interview with Chambers, p. 9.

144. The Morris account rests heavily on Blake, Granger, and McGrath, "The Morris Campus."

145. Ruth Anne Stymiest, *Cycle: A Chronicle of the Northwest School of Agriculture and Experiment Station, 1895–1968,* Crookston Office of Alumni and Development, 1988, p. 24. More than 5,400 students graduated from the School of Agriculture during its sixty-three years of operation.

146. Bernard Youngquist interview with Clarke Chambers, July 1994, pp. 9–10.

147. *Crookston Daily Times,* September 10, 1981.

148. Barbara Weiler, "Founding Provost Built College on Contacts," *Red River Scene,* December 3, 1984, p. 3.

149. Barbara Weiler, "Crookston Gym Named for Coach Lysaker," *Report,* November 1982.

150. *The Commentator,* University of Minnesota Technical Institute, December 14, 1996.

151. R. E. Hodgson, "The Southeast Experiment Station," *Farm Home and Science* 6 (1949), 8–9.

152. *Corn Tassel '52–'73,* vol. 21, pp. 36, 39, 51.

153. *Report,* November 15, 1971, p. 2.

154. *Biennial Report, 1960–1962,* p. 207; *Biennial Report, 1972–1974,* p. 146.

155. University of Minnesota News Service, November 7, 1951. Remarks on the designing of the Duluth campus by university architect Winston Close.

156. *Duluth News Tribune,* April 30, 1972.

157. Moran and Storch, *UMD Comes of Age,* p. 79.

158. Ibid., p. 90.

159. Ibid., p. 128.

160. Ibid., p. 98.

161. Ibid., pp. 80, 101, 105.

162. Ibid., p. 127.

163. Ibid., pp. 112, 152, 184.

164. Ibid., pp. 95–144.

165. Personal communication from James Boulger to Ann Pflaum, February 1999.

166. *Duluth News Tribune,* Sunday, April 30, 1971, p. 12; *Biennial Report, 1970–72,* p. 125, for fall 1971 undergraduate and graduate enrollment. The report indicated that although these enrollments were far higher than the 1951 projections, there were in fact slight decreases during the 1970–72 biennium owing to "the national economic changes, the draft, and growth of junior and vocational-technical schools in the region."

167. University of Minnesota typed information on President Wilson at the time he announced his resignation (no date, but from the context, it was July 1967). Wilson files, University Archives.

168. Wilson files, University Archives.

169. *Minnesota Daily Extra,* July 3, 1967, p. 1.

170. Personal communication from Tracy Moos to Ann Pflaum, December 1999, and from Grant Moos, July 2000.

171. Beth Kent, "President Moos to Give Major Talk at 'Communiversity Conference,'" University of Minnesota News Service, September 20, 1967; on CURA, see *CURA after 25 Years,* Center for Urban and Regional Affairs, 1996, p. 103.

172. On the "multiversity," see Malcolm Moos, "The Future of Higher Education: The Multiversity," December 11, 1969, pp. 3–5.

173. Brian Anderson, "Man behind the Big M: Malcolm Moos," *Minneapolis Tribune,* May 5, 1968, p. 7; for the David Berg quote, see his interview with Clarke Chambers, November 1994, p. 14.

174. For information on the Kappel Professorship, see *The Minnesotan,* December 1967, pp. 8–9, and on national fund-raising, see Maureen Smith, "Reflections on a Presidency: Moos Looks Forward, Back," in *Report,* September 1973, p. 1.

175. For a summary of administrative appointments and officers under President Moos, see Smith, "Reflections on a Presidency," p. 1.

176. Malcolm Moos, "The Student in an Open Society," convocation address, September 28, 1967, p. 6.

177. E. W. Ziebarth interview with Clarke Chambers, August 1984, p. 47.

178. "The Embattled University," *Daedalus,* winter 1970, p. v.

179. Gary Reichard, "Hubert H. Humphrey," *Minnesota History,* summer 1998, pp. 62–63.

180. Matthew Stark interview with Ann Pflaum, July 1999, p. 19.

181. Walter F. Mondale interview with Ann Pflaum, September 1999, pp. 4–5.

182. Marv Davidov interview with Clarke Chambers, September 1995, p. 18.

183. Stark interview with Ann Pflaum, p. 19, confirmed in personal communication from Jim Johnson to Ann Pflaum, March 2000.

184. Ibid.

185. Mogelson interview with Ann Pflaum, July 1999, p. 5.

186. Ibid., p. 3.

187. John Wright interview with Clarke Chambers, August 1994, p. 7.

188. Ibid., p. 8.

189. Ibid., p. 9.

190. Office of the President, University of Minnesota, "The Events of January 13–15, 1969" (undated, but presumably written soon after the events took place).

191. Josie R. Johnson interview with Clarke Chambers, January 1995, p. 16.

192. Shepherd interview with Chambers, p. 34.

193. Fred Lukermann interview with Clarke Chambers, September 1984, p. 23.

194. "Former University Proxy Praises Handling of Morrill Incident," *Waseca Journal,* May 14, 1969, p. 7.

195. Press conference of Malcolm Moos, May 4, 1970, Malcolm Moos biography file, University Archives.

196. "Transforming Lives for 75 Years," *Management Review,* fall 1994.

197. Sherwood O. Berg interview with Ann Pflaum, August 1999, p. 13.

198. Darwin Hendel, "Seven Days in May: University of Minnesota Students Respond to United States Involvement in Cambodia," July 8, 1970, *Research Bulletin,* Office of Student Affairs, pp. 3–4.

199. Ibid., pp. 4–5 and Table 1.

200. Davidov interview with Chambers, September 1995, pp. 28–30.

201. Ibid., pp. 32.

202. Lukermann interview with Chambers, p. 36.

203. Johnson interview with Chambers, p. 16.

204. Wright interview with Chambers, p. 9.

205. Lukermann interview with Chambers, pp. 38–39.

206. Cooperman interview with Chambers, pp. 31–33.

207. Lukermann interview with Chambers, p. 25.

208. Edith Mucke interview with Clarke Chambers, August 1984, pp. 1–2.

209. Ibid., pp. 9–10.

210. Betty Friedan, *The Feminine Mystique* (New York: Bantam Doubleday Dell, 1984), p. 373.

211. Sara Evans interview with Ann Pflaum, July 25, 1999, p. 1.

212. Donald L. Opitz, *Three Generations in the Life of the Minnesota Women's Center*, University of Minnesota, 1999, pp. 8–10.

213. Brian Anderson, "Women on University Faculty Organize Fight for Rights," *Minneapolis Tribune*, March 14, 1971, p. 15A.

214. Ibid.

215. *Biennial Report, 1960–62*, p. 161, and Josef Mestenhauser interview with Clarke Chambers, August 1994, pp. 5–8; Barbara Stuhler personal communication to Ann Pflaum, August 2000.

216. Theofanis Stavrou interview with Clarke Chambers, June 1998, pp. 35–36.

217. *Biennial Report, 1964–1966*, pp. 231–37.

218. *Biennial Report, 1972–1974*, pp. 30–31, 66–67; information provided to the authors by Richard Swanson, assistant dean and director, International Programs, August 2000.

219. William Wright interview with Clarke Chambers, September 1994, pp. 17–19.

220. See Noel D. Vietmeyer, "Norman E. Borlaug," in *Science Year 1984 World Book Annual, 1983*, pp. 340–51, and the University of Minnesota Archives, which is the repository of the Borlaug papers.

221. Stavrou interview with Chambers, pp. 35–36.

222. See Richard Gibson, "Pressure from Within, Without, Brought Moos Decision to Quit," *Minneapolis Star*, August 10, 1973, 1A–6A.

223. Shepherd interview with Chambers, p. 39. Shepherd had disagreed with Moos over the decision to create a vice presidency for the health sciences, which Shepherd thought would unnecessarily divide the university, and he had discovered that Moos had tried to prevent him from testifying before the legislature, which Shepherd believed undermined both his personal credibility and the authority of the academic vice president.

224. Ron Zellar, "A Crisis in Academia Not Leadership, Moos Says," *Minnesota Daily*, April 20, 1973, pp. 1, 25.

225. See *Minnesota Daily*, February 17, 1972, p. 1A, for amount of Moos's spending.

226. It is not entirely fair to criticize Moos for his absence; he had been a hands-on president and on several occasions had personally talked with students in earlier demonstrations, effectively calming troubled waters. For a positive assessment of Moos,

see Neal Pierce, *The Great Plains States of America: People, Politics, and Power in the Nine Great Plains States* (New York: Norton, 1973).

227. Tom Nelson, "Riots at U in 72: 'Out of Control'" *Minnesota Daily,* May 12, 1992, p. 1—a retrospective look twenty years later.

228. Ibid.

229. Ibid.

230. Ibid.

231. Gibson, "Pressure from Within, Without."

232. For a helpful account of the twists and turns as the suit evolved into a class action suit and became a landmark in academic employment litigation, see George R. LaNoue and Barbara A. Lee, *Academics in Court: The Consequences of Faculty Discrimination in Litigation* (Ann Arbor: University of Michigan Press, 1987), pp. 177–220.

233. Elmer L. Andersen interview with Clarke Chambers, October 1995, p. 14.

234. Lester Malkerson's observations are found in Bill Huntzicker, "Moos Looks Back on Years at U," University of Minnesota News Service, June 21, 1974, p. 2. Lyle A. French's and Robert Odegard's reflections were made in personal communications to Ann Pflaum, August 2000. Malcolm Moos's recollections are from a guest editorial in the *Rochester Post Bulletin* by Malcolm Moos, May 8, 1976, p. 7.

235. *Minnesota Daily,* "The Resignation of Malcolm Moos," August 10, 1973, p. 6.

## 3. Planning in a Time of Austerity, 1974–1984

1. "Minnesota: A State That Works," *Time,* August 13, 1974, pp. 24–35. The quote about the university is on p. 34.

2. Paul Dienhart, "Re-shaping the University," *Update,* September 1984, p. 4.

3. Joseph F. Kauffman, "The College Presidency: Yesterday and Today," *Change,* May/June 1982, p. 17.

4. See page 1 of the October 16 and 17 and November 5, 1974, *Minnesota Daily* for Terry Brown's articles on anti-Semitism in the search process.

5. Quote from Senator Coleman in Terry Brown, "Lee: Religion Had No Effect on Final Presidential Choice," *Minnesota Daily,* October 16, 1974, p. 1.

6. Minnesota Legislature, Senate Committee on Education, Subcommittee to Examine the University of Minnesota Presidential Selection Process, January 13, 1975, recommendations, pp. 27–30.

7. C. Peter Magrath interview with Ann Pflaum, December 1998, p. 6.

8. "New U President Scores as Lobbyist," *Minneapolis Star,* April 13, 1974, p. 1A.

9. Magrath interview with Pflaum, December 1998, p. 3.

10. Mitchell Pearlstein interview with Clarke Chambers, July 1994, pp. 7–8.

11. *Minnesota Daily,* October 15, 1974, p. 5.

12. Quoted in Terry Brown, "Magrath Affirms U's Position on Lettuce, Chile, Athletic Issues," *Minnesota Daily,* February 7, 1975, p. 11.

13. Arthur Levine, *When Dreams and Heroes Died: A Portrait of Today's College Student* (San Francisco: Carnegie Council on Policy Studies in Higher Education in conjunction with Jossey Bass, 1980), pp. xi–xii.

14. Quoted in Gregor W. Pinney, "Magrath's Goal of Excellence Remains Elusive," *Minneapolis Tribune,* October 1, 1978, p. 7A.

15. Kate Stanley interview with Ann Pflaum, July 1999, p. 5.
16. Ibid., 18–19.
17. Magrath interview with Pflaum, December 1998, p. 8.
18. Stanley interview with Pflaum, p. 10.
19. C. Peter Magrath inauguration speech, November 26, 1974, pp. 1–2.
20. Other key members of the senior administrative group were Jeanne Lupton and Mitchell Pearlstein, assistants to the president. Albert J. Linck was associate vice president for academic affairs and George Robb assistant vice president for institutional planning. David J. Berg, as head of Management Planning and Information, provided crucially important information for colleges and the central administration. James Brinkerhoff was vice president for finance from 1971 to 1980; Frederick Bohen held that position from 1980 to 1983 and David Lilly from 1983 to 1988.
21. Pearlstein interview with Chambers, pp. 7–8.
22. Joan Clodius and Diane Skomars Magrath, *The President's Spouse: Volunteer or Volunteered* (Washington, D.C.: National Association of State Universities and Land-Grant Colleges, 1984).
23. "New U President Scores as Lobbyist," p. 1A.
24. Magrath interview with Pflaum, December 1998, p. 7.
25. George Robb interview with Clarke Chambers, August 1995, p. 24.
26. Charles Backstrom interview with Clarke Chambers, April 1995, pp. 13–15. Although Backstrom himself credited Moos with preventing the kind of violence that other institutions experienced, he believed that legislators did not share this assessment and tended to believe that Moos had allowed the situation at the university to get out of control.
27. *Minnesota Daily*, October 23, 1973, p. 6.
28. *Minnesota Daily*, October 22, 1973, p. 8.
29. Terry Brown, "Faculty Estimation of Magrath after 8 Months," *Minnesota Daily*, May 1, 1975, p. 1.
30. Magrath to Members of the University Community, February 23, 1976, University Archives.
31. Magrath to Members of the University Community, September 29, 1976, University Archives.
32. Magrath to Members of the University Community, February 5, 1979, University Archives.
33. Magrath to Members of the University Community, February 23, 1976, University Archives.
34. Eventually the Law School rejected collective bargaining and the faculty at UMD voted to unionize, thus losing their representation on the University Senate.
35. Magrath to Members of the University Community, October 3, 1978, University Archives.
36. The non–Western studies requirement had long been advocated by history professor Edward Farmer. "When Clarke Chambers was chairing a commission to reexamine the undergraduate curriculum requirements," Farmer said, "I got out my old priorities memos from the early 1970s and dusted them off and fired off a proposal that we ought to have a non-Western requirement in our curriculum. When it hit the Chambers Committee, they thought maybe that sounded like a good idea, so they enacted

something like that. The dean named me to chair a committee to choose courses that would meet the requirement." Farmer interview with Clarke Chambers, January 1994, p. 20. Chambers commented that "the group had heard things like this from other places too."

37. Interim Report of the CLA Committee on Undergraduate Education, May 1979, and Report of the CLA Committee on Undergraduate Education, January 1980, University Archives. In a paper written about 1987, Roger Benjamin, then associate dean of the college, placed the Chambers report in a national context, noting that similar studies had been undertaken at Harvard (the Rossovsky report), Stanford, and Michigan. "The goals had been similar—to cut back on the proliferation of courses, reaffirm the importance of the core liberal arts, and raise the standards." Benjamin, "From Growth to Change: The Role of the University in Postindustrial Society," CLA Dean's Office, p. 25, University Archives. Chambers himself was enthusiastic about the committee and its report: "It was a small committee and the best committee I have ever worked with. We worked very hard for six or seven months. Then we did our final report in 1980 and saw it through the College Assembly. I'm really very proud of it." Clarke Chambers interviewed by Karen Strauss, March 1996, p. 24.

38. *Report,* April 1, 1977, p. 8.

39. Among the influential members of the committee were Edith Mucke, director of Continuing Education for Women, and Anne Truax, head of the Women's Center.

40. Janet Spector interview with Clarke Chambers, April 1998, pp. 18ff.

41. Anne Truax interview with Clarke Chambers, July 1994, p. 21.

42. *Celebrating 15 Years,* Center for Advanced Feminist Studies, 1998, pp. 6–8; 17–18.

43. Spector interview with Chambers, p. 19.

44. Barbara Kundson interview with Clarke Chambers, September 1994, p. 22.

45. Marcia Eaton interview with Clarke Chambers, April 1995, pp. 10–12.

46. Roger Page interview with Clarke Chambers, August 1984, p. 69.

47. *Self-Study Report: The Humphrey Institute,* 1995, p. 4.

48. "Today's College of Liberal Arts Is Aristotle, Computers, and Dakota," *Alumni News,* January 1975, pp. 22–28.

49. Edward M. Griffin interview with Clarke Chambers, December 1994, p. 54.

50. Information provided to the authors by Roland Delattre, Jean O'Brien, David Noble, and Gayle Graham Yates.

51. Margery Sabin, "Evolution and Revolution: Change in the Literary Humanities, 1968–1995," in Alvin Kernan, *What's Happened to the Humanities* (Princeton, N.J.: Princeton University Press, 1997), p. 86.

52. Toni McNaron interview with Clarke Chambers, August 1984, p. 15.

53. Department of Classical and Near Eastern Studies, "Self-Study Report," 1990; "Classical and Near Eastern Studies," *CLA Today,* September 1994, p. 19; and William Malandra, personal communication to Ann Pflaum, July 2000.

54. The authors thank David Good, chair of the department, for information about the status of hiring at the end of the century.

55. Richard Cisek interview with Clarke Chambers, September 1995, p. 25.

56. The authors thank Jeffrey Kimpton for information on the school.

57. Enrollment information from *The Lyceum,* June 1977, p. 14, and, for the department structure, Robert H. Beck, *Beyond Pedagogy: A History of the University of*

*Minnesota College of Education* (St. Paul: North Central Publishing Company, 1980), p. 242.

58. Robert Bruininks, interview with Clarke Chambers, May and June 1995, p. 27.

59. Ibid.

60. Paul Dienhart, "The Making of a Super Department," *Minnesota,* July/August 1986, p. 20.

61. Personal communication from Richard Weinberg to Ann Pflaum, July 13, 2000.

62. *Pre-Kindergarten through Grade 12 Inventory of University Programs,* Center for Applied Research and Educational Improvement (CAREI), May 1993, p. iv.

63. Margaret Davis interview with Ann Pflaum, October 1999, p. 7.

64. "CBS Celebrating 30 Years," College of Biological Sciences, 1995, p. 6.

65. Information provided to the authors by Donald G. Truhlar and Michael Olesen, August 2000.

66. "A Brief History of the University Library," University of Minnesota, 1999, pp. 1–2; for more information on the personnel issues related to the libraries, see *Minnesota Daily,* July 15, 1987, pp. 1ff.

67. University News Service, June 14, 1974, and John Oslund, "Agriculture VP to Mellow Directness in New Post," *Minnesota Daily,* August 19, 1974.

68. Pat Kaszuba, "Hueg Resigns Top Position at University of Minnesota St. Paul Campus," University of Minnesota News Service, July 5, 1983, p. 2.

69. Materials on the Institute Agronomique et Veterinaire Hassan II provided by the Office of International Agriculture Programs, University of Minnesota, fall 1999.

70. Richard Skok, "Forestry Education in the United States," in Peter McDonald and James Lassoie, *The Literature of Forestry and Agroforestry* (Ithaca, N.Y.: Cornell University Press, 1996), pp. 168–97. During the 1970s and 1980s, there was a debate in the legislature about the possibility of moving the College of Forestry to Duluth. Dean Skok argued effectively that the college was serving the entire state from St. Paul; the legislature established the Natural Resources Research Institute at UMD in 1983.

71. *Journey Home: The College of Human Ecology 1894–1996,* University of Minnesota, 1996, pp. 46–47.

72. Maureen Smith, "Women in Vet Med Find Bias Fading" and "Woman in Veterinary School Isn't Just One of the Guys," *Report,* May 15, 1975, pp. 1–3, and Charlene Follett, Darwin Hendel, and Wendy Anberg Klohs, "Women and Men in the College of Veterinary Medicine: Their Comments about Student Services," Measurement Services, University of Minnesota, September 2, 1975.

73. *The College of Veterinary Medicine 50th Anniversary,* College of Veterinary Medicine, 1997, p. 13.

74. See Appendix C for a map showing the campuses, experiment station sites, and other outreach facilities.

75. Patrick Borich interview with Ann Pflaum, August 1999, pp. 14–15.

76. Ibid., p. 4.

77. Lyle A. French interview with Ann Pflaum, February 1999, p. 5.

78. Mellor R. Holland, *History of the University of Minnesota Dental School 1888–1988,* School of Dentistry, 1993, p. 129.

79. *College of Pharmacy Record,* June 1981, p. 1.

80. Magrath interview with Pflaum, p. 10.

81. Leonard G. Wilson, *Medical Revolution in Minnesota: A History of the University of Minnesota Medical School* (St. Paul: Midewiwin Press, 1989), p. 561.

82. Chuck Benda, "Transplants: A New Catch 22?" *Minnesota,* April 1983, p. 7.

83. Laura Willers, "Lyle French Resigns as Vice President," *Health Sciences,* fall 1981, p. 9.

84. Paul Quie interview with Clarke Chambers, November 1994, pp. 26–30.

85. Frank Clancy, "Ethics on Line," *University of Minnesota Medical School Bulletin,* Minnesota Medical Foundation, fall 1999, pp. 22–23.

86. *Biennial Report of the President and the Board of Regents of the University of Minnesota to the Legislature of the State of Minnesota, 1972–1974,* June 30, 1974, p. 163, and information provided by Gayla Marty, Office of International Programs, June 28, 2000.

87. *Building Bridges: University Alumni in China,* University of Minnesota China Center, 1998, p. 49.

88. Background information on Dr. Tang provided by the China Center, March 2000.

89. Background information on Dr. Tsiang provided by the China Center, March 2000.

90. Joe Soucheray, "Terry Ganley Gains All-American Swim Status but Few Know It," *Minneapolis Tribune,* March 28, 1974, pp. 1C and 3C. The article added that "Miss Ganley works half days, carries a full course load, and still has enough energy left each day for what Miss Freeman calls excellent displays of powerful sprinting."

91. Mary C. O'Brien and Cynthia Kommers, eds., *The Gold Book: Women's Athletics 1975–1985,* Gold Club–Women's Athletic Alumni, 1986, p. 15.

92. Quoted in Alexandra Epstein, "Equal or Equitable: The Effects of Title IX on Women's Athletics at the University of Minnesota, 1972–1982," history department senior paper, 1995, p. 9.

93. *Minnesota Daily* editorial, May 23, 1974, p. 6, and George Regis, "Women's Athletic Director Voices Support for ICSA Complaint," *Minnesota Daily,* May 22, 1974, p. 22.

94. Dick Gordon, "U Plans No Women's Sports Scholarships," *Minneapolis Star,* November 14, 1974, p. 1D.

95. Epstein, "Equal or Equitable," p. 16.

96. Ann Pflaum and Gary Engstrand served as staff members for the Title IX self-study. Engstrand concentrated on intercollegiate athletics, Pflaum on all other aspects of gender equity.

97. O'Brien and Kommers, *Gold Book,* p. 84, and Cindy Dickson, "New U Women's Athletic Director Wants Fair Access to Sports Coffers," *Minnesota Daily,* June 30, 1976.

98. Personal communication from Women's Intercollegiate Athletics to Ann Pflaum, 1999.

99. Personal communication from Chris Voelz to Ann Pflaum, January 25, 1999. One of the groups that supported Women's Intercollegiate Athletics and raised scholarship funds for athletes was the Patty Berg Advisory Committee, established in 1975 and named in honor of Minnesota's finest golfer. Gladys Brooks, a university alumna

and former member of the Minneapolis City Council, chaired the Patty Berg committee for several years.

100. *Biennial Report, 1972–1974,* pp. 131–33.

101. Ross Bernstein, *Frozen Memories: Celebrating a Century of Minnesota Hockey*
(Minneapolis: Nodin Press, 1999), pp. 129–31.

102. Ibid., p. 127.

103. Men's Intercollegiate Athletics, *Golden Gopher Hockey 1999–2000,* University
of Minnesota, 1999, pp. 154–58.

104. For a discussion of the Ohio State incident, see chapter 2.

105. *Media Guide: Basketball 1998–99,* Men's Intercollegiate Athletics, 1998, pp. 175–76.

106. Ibid., p. 133. Because of subsequent NCAA penalties, Thompson became the
highest scorer.

107. For additional background, see Terry Brown, "U Expects NCAA Penalties Soon
on Alleged Violations," *Minnesota Daily,* January 5, 1976.

108. Tony Bianco, "Magrath Fighting Mad over Unjust Ruling," *Minnesota Daily,*
October 25, 1976, p. 1.

109. Magrath to Members of the University Community, January 24, 1977.

110. Personal communication from William Donohue to Ann Pflaum, March 27,
2000.

111. Tony Bianco, "Alumni, Corporations, Targets of Escalated U Fundraising Program," *Minnesota Daily,* November 11, 1976, p. 4.

112. Personal communication from Linda Berg to Ann Pflaum, April 12, 2000.

113. *Building a Great University: The Contributions of the University of Minnesota
Board of Trustees, 1962–1998,* University of Minnesota Foundation, pp. 3–5.

114. "The Minnesota Medical Foundation: 50 Years of Support," *University of Minnesota Medical School Bulletin,* fall 1988. Among the M.D.'s who served as president
were Donn G. Moser, Reuben Berman, Anthony Bechik, and John Coleman; Terrance
Hanold of Pillsbury and Lewis W. Lehr of 3M also were president.

115. Based on research carried out for the UMAA by Phil Davies (edited by Tom
Garrison) June 1999.

116. Ken Moran and Neil Storch, *UMD Comes of Age: The First One Hundred
Years* (Virginia Beach, Va.: Donning, 1996), pp. 145–46.

117. University of Minnesota Fall Quarter Student Headcount, *Institutional Research and Reporting.* In fall 1999, enrollment exceeded 8,500.

118. *Brief,* March 1976, noted that 40 percent of UMD students came from outside the Arrowhead Region. It had been 13 percent in 1965 and 28 percent in 1971. In
1976, 22 percent of the student body came from the Twin Cities.

119. New programs are documented in editions of *Brief:* bachelor of arts in early
child care and development and a minor in Indian studies, May 14, 1975; master of industrial safety, May 14, 1975; bachelor of fine arts, June 17, 1975; the women's studies
program, July 29, 1981; continuing education programs, November 24, 1976.

120. Moran and Storch, *UMD Comes of Age,* pp. 163, 165.

121. A complex of three new residence buildings was named Goldfine Hall in honor
of Regent Goldfine in 1989. Moran and Storch, *UMD Comes of Age,* pp. 145–46, 150,
182, 195.

122. Ibid., pp. 151, 154–55.

123. Ibid., p. 151 for the following gifts: Alworth Institute for International Studies and Saxe, p. 158; the Jack Rowe Chair in Engineering, the gift of Minnesota Power, p. 174; Glensheen, p. 211.

124. Ibid., pp. 149–50 for international programs.

125. Personal communication from Neil Storch to Ann Pflaum, February 5, 1999.

126. Moran and Storch, *UMD Comes of Age,* pp. 161–63.

127. Personal communication from Michael Heck and Karen Heck to Ann Pflaum, February 20, 1999.

128. Personal communication from Mary Vomacka to Ann Pflaum, February 12, 1999.

129. Moran and Storch, *UMD Comes of Age,* p. 169.

130. Background on the College of Science and Engineering courtesy of personal communication from Dean Sabra Anderson, December 1998.

131. Steve Granger, Elizabeth Blake, and Gary McGrath, "The Morris Campus," a paper prepared as background for this history, 1999, p. 5.

132. Ibid., p. 10.

133. Enrollment from the Office of Planning and Analysis, University of Minnesota, fall 1998.

134. John Q. Imholte interview with Clarke Chambers, August 1984, pp. 13–18.

135. *Self-Study Report of the University of Minnesota, Morris, Prepared for the North Central Association of Colleges and Schools,* 1990, p. 149.

136. Kathy Kuntz, "Student Participation at UMM: The Debates and the Debaters," July 20, 1988, University Archives.

137. Granger, Blake, and McGrath, "The Morris Campus," p. 7.

138. Ibid.

139. Elizabeth S. Blake, "Imagining Morris: Reflections on Two Decades at the University of Minnesota, Morris," a presentation to the University of Minnesota Retirees Association, Twin Cities campus, September 22, 1998. Blake recalled that one of those impressed with the college and its potential was higher education faculty member Marvin Peterson from the University of Michigan. Peterson had come to know Morris firsthand as a consultant.

140. University of Minnesota Technical College Crookston, information brochure, 1976.

141. E. C. Miller, with Bernie Youngquist, *Gleanings: 100 Years at the Northwest Experiment Station,* Crookston Office of External Relations, 1995, pp. 23–32.

142. "Background Information on the Agriculture Industry in Minnesota and the University of Minnesota Technical College Waseca," unpublished paper, 1973, p. 1, and Pat Wappelm, "Senate Unit Advises End to Waseca Campus," *Minnesota Daily,* April 1, 1973, pp. 12ff.

143. W. Clough Cullen, "History of the Animal Health Technology Program at the University of Minnesota Technical College-Waseca," unpublished paper, 1998.

144. *Ram Page,* University of Minnesota, Waseca, May 29, 1975, p. 1.

145. *Ram Page,* May 29, 1975, p. 1.

146. Office of Planning and Analysis, University of Minnesota, fall headcount figures.

147. Text of Magrath remarks was published in the *Minnesota Daily,* October 27, 1981, pp. i, 11.

148. *Report,* October 1982, pp. 1, 4.

149. John Howe quoted in Paul Dienhart, "Re-shaping the University," *Update,* summer 1984, p. 4.

150. Bruce Erickson quoted in Dienhart, "Re-shaping the University," p. 4.

151. See the discussion in chapter 2.

152. George R. LaNoue and Barbara A. Lee, *Academics in Court: The Consequences of Faculty Discrimination Litigation* (Ann Arbor: University of Michigan Press, 1987), pp. 214–15.

153. Magrath interview with Pflaum, p. 9.

154. Julie Clausen, "University, Community Leaders Evaluate Magrath's Performance," *Minnesota Daily,* May 24, 1984, p. 5.

155. Nils Hasselmo interview with Clark Chambers, March 1998, p. 34. When Chambers commented that "faster and more prophetic leadership by late Moos or early Magrath might have lessened the burden," Hasselmo said, "If true, there certainly was an opportunity that wasn't seized. How often that happens in history."

156. University of Minnesota Office of Equal Opportunity and Affirmative Action, Academic Non-Student Employment for the University of Minnesota 1980 and 1999.

157. Doug Iverson, "Magrath Says Work Complete: Regents Will Look for Fresh Ideas," *Minnesota Daily,* June 20, 1984, pp. 1, 5.

158. C. Peter Magrath, "Farewell Address to the Board of Regents," October 12, 1984, p. 3.

159. Ibid., p. 9.

160. Personal communication from Jeanne T. Lupton to Ann Pflaum, February 12, 2000.

161. Julie Clausen, "University, Community Leaders Evaluate Magrath's Performance," p. 1.

## 4. Finding Focus, 1985–1997

1. Raymond Bacchetti, remarks to the University of Minnesota Planning Council, 1981.

2. Regent David Lebedoff, who was named chair of the regents' search committee, thought that this was a mistake and that a number of the regents were not actually in favor of the restriction but voted for it in order to avoid division and dissent. David Lebedoff interview with Ann Pflaum, August 1998, pp. 13–14.

3. Kenneth Keller interview with Clarke Chambers, December 1997, pp. 12–13. Chambers conducted two long interviews with Keller, the first on October 23 and November 6, 1995, the second on December 1 and 3, 1997.

4. Keller interview with Chambers, December 1997, p. 14.

5. Lebedoff interview with Pflaum, pp. 14–15.

6. Keller interview with Chambers, December 1997, pp. 17–22.

7. Kenneth Keller, "A Commitment to Focus," Report of Interim President Kenneth Keller, February 8, 1985. By 1991, students entering the university were expected to have four years of English, two years of social studies, three years of mathematics,

three years of science, and two years of a second language. These standards were put into effect and were met.

8. Keller interview with Chambers, December 1997, pp. 17–22.

9. Lebedoff interview with Pflaum, p. 16.

10. Keller interview with Chambers, December 1997, pp. 17–22.

11. John Howe interview with Clarke Chambers, July 1994, pp. 24–25.

12. Coor later became president of Arizona State University.

13. Keller interview with Chambers, December 1997, pp. 27–28. Lebedoff's comment was, "I knew that there were regents who opposed his selection. I thought that once he was selected, they would come to strongly support him and work to support him, as I think a regent should. That did not occur and believing that it would was a serious misjudgment on my part. It was also a great unfairness to Ken Keller." Lebedoff interview with Pflaum, p. 17.

14. Timothy Delmont, a staff member in Management Planning and Information Services (MPIS), was impressed with how thoroughly Keller read the planning documents submitted by colleges and departments: "Keller benefited greatly from that mountain of reports. He read everything!" Timothy Delmont interview with Clarke Chambers, November 1994, p. 13.

15. Edward Farmer interview with Clarke Chambers, January 1994, p. 4.

16. John Kostouros, "The Keller Chronicles," *Minnesota,* April/May 1993, p. 38. This view is consistent with Keller's own, expressed in his second interview with Clarke Chambers, December 1997, p. 29.

17. Kostouros, "The Keller Chronicles," p. 38.

18. Keller interview with Chambers, December 1997, p. 24. Fred Lukermann, dean of the College of Liberal Arts, and Roger Benjamin, vice president for academic affairs, also made presentations about Commitment to Focus. Personal communication to Ann Pflaum, July 9, 2000.

19. D. J. Leary interview with Clarke Chambers, October 1995, pp. 21–23.

20. Ibid.

21. Personal communication from Hyman Berman to Ann Pflaum, December 1999.

22. David Berg praised the chairmen of the legislative higher education committees, Lyndon Carlson in the House of Representatives and Gene Waldorf in the Senate: "To their credit they never reneged on it in any way. They haven't fully performed what they had hoped to, but they've made every effort." David Berg interview with Clarke Chambers, November 1994, p. 23. "University of Minnesota Planning Report 1984–85," January 1985, pp. 24–26, and Kenneth H. Keller, "A Commitment to Focus," February 8, 1985, p. 8.

23. The committee's report, which ran 144 pages, was circulated with the title "Plan for Focus: Report of the Advisory Task Force on Planning, June 1987"; it is in the University Archives. Political science faculty member Robert Kvavik, subsequently associate vice president in the office of the executive vice president and provost, thought that the requirement to balance the budget was a major flaw in the committee's charge. Forcing the committee to decide where the funds should come from caused the group to come up with "a choice that could not easily be defended. As a consequence, the

president and everyone else were boxed in with not much room for maneuver." Personal communication from Kvavik to Lehmberg, December 28, 1998.

24. Edward Foster interview with Clarke Chambers, October 1994, pp. 20–21.

25. Personal communication from David Lebedoff to Ann Pflaum, March 14, 2000.

26. David Lilly interview with Clarke Chambers, October 1994, p. 19. Lebedoff believed that Benjamin had sent copies of the report to members of the faculty before discussing it with the regents; he thought that references to dentistry and veterinary medicine might have been reconsidered and deleted before the report was made public. Lebedoff interview with Pflaum, p. 19.

27. Keller interview with Chambers, October 1995, p. 35.

28. As Richard Elzay, dean of the School of Dentistry, pointed out, the dental school was one of the highest ranked among the fifty-eight such institutions in the country. "We're already in the top five," he said. "Why throw away your stars?" He also pointed out that the school's clinics provided dental care to 8,000 patients a year, many of whom had no dental insurance and would not have been treated elsewhere. Robert H. Dunlop, dean of the college of Veterinary Medicine, said that "the report's criticisms of the College were false. I'm furious about the negligence and triviality. . . . So much of what is in that report is just plain garbage." Quotations from Mellor R. Holland, *A History of the University of Minnesota School of Dentistry: 1888–1988,* School of Dentistry, 1993, p. 201.

29. Always a small program with fewer than a hundred students, mortuary science enrolled sixty-one in fall 1998. Regent Lebedoff reported in a communication to Ann Pflaum in July 1987 that he had as large a volume of mail from advocates of mortuary science as from supporters of the dental school or veterinary medicine.

30. Howe interview with Chambers, p. 41.

31. Keller interview with Chambers, December 1997, pp. 39–41.

32. Russell Bennett interview with Clarke Chambers, October 1995, pp. 23ff.

33. "The Minnesota Campaign: Progress Report," University of Minnesota Foundation, August 1991, pp. 1–2.

34. Bennett interview with Chambers, pp. 23ff.

35. Keller interview with Chambers, December 1997, p. 46.

36. Robert Odegard confirmed the involvement of Keller (and later President Nils Hasselmo) in fund-raising. "When you really boil it down," he said, "the president is the chief development officer of the university. I think he spends maybe 15 to 20 percent of his time gathering resources from both the public and the private sides. Not a week goes by, scarcely a day, when [the president doesn't] pay some attention to philanthropic efforts." Robert Odegard interview with Clarke Chambers, July 1994, p. 12.

37. Keller interview with Chambers, December 1997, pp. 45–46.

38. Ibid.

39. Bennett interview with Chambers, p. 30.

40. *Update,* December 1989, p. 10. Donors of the chair were the Edelstein-Keller family; they were not related to university president Kenneth Keller.

41. Elmer L. Andersen interview with Clarke Chambers, October 1995, pp. 12–13.

42. A committee established while Magrath was president to examine the need

for renovation met once or twice, but when Magrath left for Missouri, the renovation of Eastcliff was put on hold until a new president could be appointed.

43. Bennett interview with Chambers, p. 25.

44. Keller interview with Chambers, December 1997, p. 85.

45. Ibid., pp. 70–71.

46. This list of events leading up to Keller's resignation is from the Minneapolis *Star Tribune,* December 1, 1988. Owning its own telephone system was actually more cost effective. Eastcliff overruns were exaggerated; they included regular maintenance as well as a second phase approved after the original estimate.

47. George Robb interview with Clarke Chambers, August 1995, p. 35.

48. Richard Sauer interview with Clarke Chambers, July 1995, p. 28.

49. Lebedoff interview with Pflaum, pp. 18–20. A number of additional interviews conducted by Clarke Chambers contain perceptive comments on Keller's administration, among them interviews with David Berg, Timothy Delmont, and Ann Pflaum.

50. Keller interview with Chambers, December 1997, pp. 89–90.

51. Ibid.

52. In another part of his interview, Keller commented further on several regents. He noted that he and Lebedoff, although both were Democrats, had supported different presidential candidates in 1968: Keller had worked for McCarthy, Lebedoff for Humphrey. Still, their personal relationship had been good. "What was less understood by people who thought of me as the eastern transplant to Minnesota, associated with Twin Cities elitists of one sort or another, was that the people on the Board [with] whom I was most close were actually Lauris Krenik and Vern Long, the farm regents whom I thought of as wonderful people, who understood what I was trying to do, who were not close to me politically because I was a DFLer on the other side of things, but who understood and appreciated the notion of making the university excellent because that served people best. Chuck Casey was the other person I was very, very close to. All the non–Twin Cities regents were the ones I was close to. The other person who's worth saying something about is Wenda Moore. I think Wenda was the only person to vote against me as president. But Wenda saw, in what was happening at the end, a kind of populist uprising and discriminatory action against me that she was offended by. She actually was very supportive of me at the end and did not want me to leave office. She said, "You started the job and you ought to finish it." Keller interview with Chambers, December 1997, p. 94.

53. Ibid., pp. 91–92. Keller noted that "there were some things that happened that raised the issue of whether there was any anti-Semitism at work. . . . I need to state for the record that I never felt it."

54. Ibid., pp. 96–100.

55. Interview by Doug Grow in the Minneapolis *Star Tribune,* March 20, 1988, p. 1B.

56. Minneapolis *Star Tribune,* March 29, 1988, p. 3B.

57. Delores Lutz and Don Eggen, "Sauer Plans to Rebuild Trust," *Minnesota Daily,* March 28, 1977, pp. 1, 15.

58. Richard Sauer interview with Clarke Chambers, July 1995, pp. 35–37.

59. Sauer was particularly appreciative of the assistance he received on these speeches from George Robb. Sauer interview with Chambers, pp. 35–37.

60. Richard Sauer, "1988 in Review," in "Access to Excellence: A Minnesota Partnership," University Legislative Request for 1989–1991, pp. 2–3.

61. Sauer interview with Chambers, p. 52.

62. Some faculty members put forward the name of Walter Mondale, who had recently completed his term as vice president of the United States.

63. Hasselmo interview with Clarke Chambers, p. 59.

64. Sauer interview with Chambers, p. 43.

65. Hasselmo interview with Chambers, pp. 56–60.

66. Ibid., p. 6.

67. Ibid., p. 8.

68. Ibid., p. 14.

69. Ibid., pp. 24, 47–48.

70. Hasselmo was later to get approval for the president to make appointments without a search under certain circumstances. Hasselmo interview with Chambers, p. 64.

71. Ibid., p. 26.

72. Jean B. Keffeler interview with Ann Pflaum, July 1999, p. 4.

73. *Update*, December 1989, p. 10.

74. Ibid., p. 66.

75. Ibid., p. 67.

76. "It was a bureaucratic culture that was very hard to break—good people trying to do a good job but within a system that simply had not ever rewarded initiative but had punished mistakes." Hasselmo interview with Chambers, pp. 67–69.

77. Ibid., p. 58.

78. Ibid., p. 60. The university had the advantage of a good market and, as Hasselmo admitted, good luck.

79. Nils Hasselmo, "Access to Excellence: The University of Minnesota in the 1990s: Presidential Inaugural Address," University Archives.

80. Hasselmo, "Restructuring and Reallocation," 1991, pp. 5–6, University Archives.

81. Robert Ingrassia, "Hasselmo Rejects Four Finalists for U-Waseca," *Minnesota Daily*, October 18, 1990, p. 4.

82. Hasselmo interview with Chambers, pp. 61, 65. Associate Vice President Robert Kvavik pointed out that the real savings at Waseca would come from not having to put additional resources into repairs and maintenance of the campus.

83. Howard Sinker, "Hasselmo Greeted with Protest," Minneapolis *Star Tribune*, January 11, 1991, p. 1A.

84. Thirteen faculty members transferred to the Twin Cities campus, six to Duluth, and one to Crookston. Personal communication from Kathryn Hanna to Ann Pflaum, March 27, 2000. See also Lanier Holt, "Closing Scatters Waseca Faculty," *Minnesota Daily*, October 5, 1992, p. 3.

85. On Melvin George, see *Minnesota*, July/August 1994, p. 49.

86. Professional studies included architecture, education, law, and management but not the professional fields in the Academic Health Center.

87. Keffeler interview with Pflaum, p. 7.

88. "The Hasselmo Blueprint: A Sensible Split," Minneapolis *Star Tribune*, September 5, 1993, p. 28A.

89. Karine Michael, "Protesters Petition to Stop U2000," *Minnesota Daily,* November 11, 1993, p. 1.

90. See Minneapolis *Star Tribune,* March 27, 1996, p. B5, for an account of Dean Taylor's statement, and the *Minnesota Daily,* April 5, 1996, p. 1, for a statement by Julia Davis.

91. Jessica Burke, "Regents Strike Down Proposal to Close GC," *Minnesota Daily,* April 15, 1996, p. 1A.

92. W. Phillips Shively interview with Clarke Chambers, August 1997, p. 27.

93. Hasselmo interview with Chambers, p. 120.

94. Shively interview with Chambers, p. 28.

95. Personal communication from Dean David Taylor to Ann Pflaum, March 10, 2000.

96. Shepherd, although by profession an electrical engineer, had a long-standing interest in art. Lyndel King, director of the University Gallery, became the first director of the Weisman Art Museum.

97. Hasselmo interview with Chambers, p. 78.

98. Ibid., pp. 77–79, 86–87. Gehry had built something similar in Paris, and his Guggenheim Museum in Bilbao, Spain, also clad in metal plates, opened in 1998. In the fall of that year, President Bill Clinton presented the National Medal of the Arts to Gehry in a ceremony at the White House; a few months later, Gehry received the American Institute of Architects Gold Medal in recognition of his work, including the Weisman Art Museum.

99. Herbert Muschamp in The *New York Times,* November 22, 1993, p. 44.

100. Mary Abbe, Minneapolis *Star Tribune,* December 20, 1998, p. F1.

101. Information provided by Lyndel King, director of the Weisman Museum, to the authors, September 1999.

102. Hasselmo interview with Chambers, pp. 82–85.

103. Ibid.

104. Curtis L. Carlson, "Contributions to the University of Minnesota," press release from the University of Minnesota Foundation, 1999.

105. Genevieve MacLeod, "New Business School Facility Starts Construction," *Minnesota Daily,* June 28, 1995, p. 1A.

106. *Brief,* July 14, 1999.

107. Another project under way in the late 1990s was the long-sought addition to the Architecture Building, which included a new architecture and landscape architecture library. Architects for this space were Steven Holl Architects of New York, Vincent James Associates, and Ellerbe Becket, the latter two Minneapolis firms.

108. This point was emphasized by associate vice president Robert Kvavik in several conversations with Stanford Lehmberg in fall 1999.

109. Hasselmo interview with Chambers, p. 50.

110. Ernest L. Boyer, *Campus Life: In Search of Community* (Princeton: Carnegie Foundation for the Advancement of Teaching, 1990), pp. xii–xiii.

111. Senate approval did not come without debate. One faculty member, who saw the requirements as unwarranted interference in academic matters, described them as "Stalinist mind control." Howe interview with Chambers, pp. 44–48.

112. Ibid., pp. 49–50. Howe doubted that the recommendations regarding advising would ever be fully implemented because they expected faculty members to act as advisers. Many were reluctant to do so, and the professional advisers did not think that professors could be trusted to be familiar with graduation requirements. Hasselmo credited Robert Kvavik and Wayne Siegler with effective work in implementing the undergraduate initiative.

113. Hasselmo interview with Chambers, pp. 52–53.

114. The uniform questionnaire was drawn up by the Senate Committee on Educational Policy, chaired at that time by Stanford Lehmberg.

115. "That Was Then, This Is Now: Progress at the University of Minnesota, 1986 to 1996," Office of the Vice President for Institutional Relations, 1997.

116. Hasselmo interview with Chambers, p. 94. The residential facilities were built and operated by Dinniken Properties.

117. They were Amy Alving (aerospace engineering), Gail Peterson (psychology), Chris Paola (geology), Clarence Morgan (art), and Gordon Duke (business).

118. Some of this had been going on before establishment of the residential programs. In 1990–91 University Housing Services offered 555 educational and 1,193 social or recreational programs. Charles W. Lawrence, "Housing Services Annual Report 1990–91," University Archives, p. 5.

119. *Minnesota Daily,* February 10, 1998, p. 1. The same story chronicled a decline in the number of articles in the *Daily* mentioning Greeks: there were 150 in 1948, 70 in 1963, and 13 in 1997.

120. *Minnesota Daily,* February 17, 1998, p. 3.

121. Darwin D. Hendel and Jeanne Solberg, "Employment Experiences of University of Minnesota Twin Cities Campus Undergraduates," June 1991, University Archives, pp. 1–7. The 109-page study contains a great deal of additional information.

122. In 1996, 5,818 students were employed by the university in academic positions, primarily as teaching or research assistants; 5,216 students worked in civil service jobs and 325 worked in the hospitals. "A Land-Grant University for the 21st Century," p. 18.

123. *Brief,* March 25, 1998.

124. Appendix Tables B-1 and B-2 summarize the 1993 National Research Council rankings of the fifteen Minnesota programs ranked among the top twenty nationally. The rankings were made in 1993 and published in 1995. Table B-1 shows the fifteen Minnesota departments; Table B-2 shows the change in overall rankings between 1993 and 1982. These summaries are from *1996 Accreditation Self-Study: A Land-Grant University for the 21ˢᵗ Century,* University of Minnesota, 1996, pp. 253–54.

125. External Review Committee Report on Chemical Engineering, May 27 and 28, 1994, p. 4.

126. The chemical engineering building was renamed Amundson Hall in 1979 in recognition of Neal Amundson's contributions.

127. H. Ted Davis, "The Making of a Fine Department," speech delivered at Eastcliff, February 21, 1995, p. 4.

128. Personal communication from William Gerberich to Ann Pflaum, May 19, 2000.

129. Faculty members with an interest in the recovering aspect of mining joined civil engineering.

130. Frank Bates, William Gerberich, H. Ted Davis, and Theodore Zorn provided background information on chemical engineering and materials science. Ann Pflaum attended an informative lecture on the history of the department given on October 16, 1999, by L. E. Scriven.

131. See D. A. Frohib, University of Minnesota, Department of Mechanical Engineering, August 1999, and information provided by Peter McMurray, department head.

132. Paul Sorenson, "Looking Back," *AEM Update 1998–99,* Department of Aeronautical Engineering and Mechanics, 1998, p. 10. In 1974, Jeanette Piccard became one of the first women in the United States ordained as an Episcopal priest.

133. The authors thank Donna Rosenthal for providing background information for this history of aerospace engineering and mechanics.

134. William L. Garrard, personal communication to Stanford Lehmberg and Ann Pflaum, May 17, 2000.

135. *The Department of Civil and Mineral Engineering: Self-Survey Report,* November 1984, p. 2.

136. "The Outstanding Civil Engineering Achievement of 1983," *Civil Engineering,* June 1983, pp. 33–37.

137. *Alumni Bridge: A Newsletter for Friends and Alumni,* Department of Civil Engineering, December 1999, p. 3. An overview of some faculty research projects is found in "CE Bridge," May 1998, pp. 2–3.

138. Personal communication from Naresh Jain to authors, May 19, 2000.

139. Quote from M. Kaveh, "Inside EE," *EE Signals,* Department of Electrical Engineering, winter 1995, p. 2. The source for the description of the department specializations is an undated brochure, *Technologies Enabling the Information Age,* Department of Electrical and Computer Engineering.

140. A special issue of the Institute of Technology magazine *ITEMS,* summer 1991, listed more than 400 companies founded by IT graduates, with a large representation of electrical engineering graduates. Information on electrical and computer engineering graduates remaining in Minnesota was provided by department head Mostafa Kaveh, May 19, 2000.

141. Margaret Davis interview with Ann Pflaum, October 1999, p. 6.

142. Borchert was later named a Regents Professor, while Lukermann served as dean of the College of Liberal Arts.

143. Information from a short history of the department written for Stanford Lehmberg.

144. Tuan later moved to the University of Wisconsin; his elegant writings on human geography were widely admired.

145. Department of Geography information provided to Stanford Lehmberg; *CURA after 25 Years,* Center for Urban and Regional Affairs, 1996, p. 2.

146. Department of Psychology information provided to Stanford Lehmberg by Professor Gail Peterson, March 1998.

147. Drawn from a brief history of the Department of Economics prepared by Craig Swan for Stanford Lehmberg in spring 1998.

148. Edward Foster interview with Clarke Chambers, October 1994, p. 2–5.

149. Information by Craig Swan to Lehmberg, spring 1998.

150. *CLA Today—Special Edition,* College of Liberal Arts, September 1994, pp. 24–25. For more recent background, the authors thank Gerhard Weiss, an emeritus faculty member serving in 1999–2000 as interim director of the Center for Austrian Studies.

151. John Turner interview with Clark Chambers, April 1984, pp. 22–23, and personal communication from Robert T. Holt to Ann Pflaum, June 4, 2000.

152. *A History of the Department of Political Science,* published by the department in 1994, with an addendum, 1994–98.

153. The authors thank Seymour Geisser for providing information on the School of Statistics. For information about the department in the early 1990s, see *CLA Today—Special Edition,* p. 39.

154. Personal communication from Christine Maziar, vice president for research and dean of the Graduate School, to Ann Pflaum, December 2000.

155. *1996 Accreditation Self-Study: A Land-Grant University for the 21ˢᵗ Century,* p. 253.

156. Robert Holt interview with Clarke Chambers, September 1994, p. 48, and Craig Swan correspondence with Stanford Lehmberg, spring 1998.

157. Mark G. Yudof, inaugural address, October 17, 1997, p. 19.

158. Personal communication from Christine Maziar to Ann Pflaum, May 29, 2000.

159. Table B-2 illustrates this ranking.

160. Views differed on corporate influence in American higher education. For a somewhat critical view, see David F. Noble (of the University of Toronto, not Minnesota's David Noble), "Digital Diploma Mills: The Automation of Higher Education," *Monthly Review* 49 (1998): 38–52. For an example of a more positive influence, see the writings of University of Minnesota faculty member John Bryson, *Strategic Planning for Public and Nonprofit Organizations* (San Francisco: Jossey-Bass, 1988).

161. Howe interview with Chambers, pp. 53–54.

162. John Adams interview with Clarke Chambers, August 1994, p. 53.

163. Personal communication from Leonard Kuhi to Ann Pflaum, November 1999.

164. John Brandl interview with Clarke Chambers, October 1994, p. 28. Brandl pointed out that the sense of community at the university was more diffuse than that at smaller institutions.

165. Marcia Eaton interview with Clarke Chambers, April 1995, pp. 29–31.

166. Sara Evans interview with Ann Pflaum, July 1999, p. 8.

167. Russell Hobbie interview with Clarke Chambers, September 1994, p. 18.

168. Margaret Davis interview with Ann Pflaum, October 1999, p. 11.

169. In contrast, Nils Hasselmo believed that faculty governance at Minnesota remained remarkably strong in comparison to the situation at other universities. As president of the Association of American Universities, he was in a position to know. Hasselmo to Lehmberg, February 1999.

170. Barbara Knudson interview with Clarke Chambers, September 1994, p. 33.

171. Darwin D. Hendel, "The 1997 Faculty and Staff Climate Survey," Office of Institutional Research and Reporting, June 1999, p. 11. The combined figure was 62.1 percent.

172. Robert Bruininks interview with Clarke Chambers, May 1995, pp. 49–50.

173. Leonard G. Wilson, Minneapolis *Star Tribune,* November 25, 1998, p. A19.

174. Hasselmo interview with Chambers, pp. 112–13.

175. University of Minnesota, President's Investigative Report on the MALG Program, October 18, 1993, p. i.

176. Dr. Najarian did not appear before the Academic Misconduct Panel, which issued a report on February 3, 1995. Executive Summary, Public Documents Released February 21, 1995, Office of the General Counsel, February 21, 1995.

177. *Research Review,* University of Minnesota, Special Issue, February 2000, p. 1.

178. Winston Wallin interview with Clarke Chambers, October 1995, pp. 6, 22.

179. Hasselmo interview with Chambers, pp. 116–17.

180. Gary Elliot Engstrand, "Tenure Wars: The Battles and the Lessons," *American Behavioral Scientist,* February 1998, p. 607. We are grateful to Gary Engstrand, a longtime staff member of the University of Minnesota Faculty Consultative Committee, for reviewing this summary of the tenure issue and for making available both this article and a longer, unpublished manuscript, "It Is from Small Missteps That Great Tragedies Grow." Fred L. Morrison, a member of the law faculty and an expert on tenure codes who was personally involved in the dispute, published "Tenure Wars: An Account of the Controversy at Minnesota," *Journal of Legal Education* 47 (1997): 369–91. We are grateful to Engstrand and Morrison for providing copies of their work and granting permission to quote from it. Another account of the controversy, "Tenure Under Attack," appeared in *Footnotes* (a publication of the American Association of University Professors), fall 1997, pp. 1–7.

181. Engstrand, "Tenure Wars," p. 611.

182. Hasselmo interview with Chambers, p. 105.

183. Engstrand, "Tenure Wars," p. 617.

184. The phrase was borrowed and adapted from a tenure code at Michigan; the authority it granted had never been used there. Engstrand, "Tenure Wars," p. 616.

185. Quoted in Engstrand, "Tenure Wars," p. 616.

186. Quoted in Maggi Aitkens, "The Trials and Tribulations of Tenure," *Minnesota,* July/August, 1996, p. 45. Berscheid recounted being "attacked by a U.S. senator, a member of the Senate Appropriations Committee for the National Science Foundation" for her research on interpersonal relations. Because of tenure, she noted, "I knew my job was secure."

187. Engstrand, "Small Missteps," p. 789.

188. Mario Bognanno, chief of staff to the president, praised Hasselmo: "It took courage to say, 'Here's the way it is on tenure; please don't issue the Morris version of a tenure code.'" Mario Bognanno interview with Clarke Chambers, August 1997, p. 40.

189. Morrison, "Tenure Wars," pp. 384–91.

190. Engstrand, "Small Missteps," p. 809. Bloomfield followed Virginia Gray as chair of the Faculty Consultative Committee. Gray had also been active in the tenure discussions.

191. "President's Speech List," kindly provided by George Robb, who helped prepare a number of the addresses.

192. Patricia Hasselmo interview with Clarke Chambers, March 1998, pp. 17–18.

193. Theofanis Stavrou interview with Clarke Chambers, June 1998, pp. 60–61.

194. Hasselmo, Graduate School Commencement Address, May 17, 1997, University Archives, pp. 5–7.

195. Nancy Livingston, "U's Class Act Calls It a Career," *St. Paul Pioneer Press,* June 22, 1997, p. 6A.

196. Minneapolis *Star Tribune,* June 30, 1997, p. A10.

197. Ibid.

198. Hasselmo interview with Chambers, p. 157.

## 5. The University at the End of the Century

1. The University Sesquicentennial Planning Committee was co-chaired by Regents Professor Ellen Berscheid and Professor Robert Jones, interim vice president for student development. Susan Eastman served as principal staff member. Dean David Taylor of the General College served as chair of the history subcommittee.

2. Personal communication from Mark G. Yudof to Ann Pflaum, April 18, 2000.

3. Greg Breining, "The New U," *Minnesota Monthly,* October 1999, p. 102.

4. Background material on President Yudof was provided by the president's office, fall 1999.

5. Personal communication from Judy Yudof to Ann Pflaum, August 2000.

6. Mark G. Yudof, "The University of Minnesota: Historic Traditions, Academic Values, and 21st Century Challenges," inaugural address, October 17, 1997, pp. 7–8.

7. Ibid.

8. Mark G. Yudof, *State of the University,* October 15, 1998, p. 7.

9. *Kiosk,* June 1997, p. 4.

10. Personal communication from Mark G. Yudof to Ann Pflaum, April 18, 2000.

11. As a result of the allegations of academic misconduct in the men's basketball program, President Yudof had transferred oversight of athletics to Tonya Moten Brown in November 1999. McKinley Boston retained responsibility for student development.

12. *Facts,* 1999, p. 3.

13. Personal communication from Steven Rosenstone to Ann Pflaum, December 29, 1999.

14. Personal communication from Stephanie Dilworth to Ann Pflaum, May 4, 2000.

15. "Preserving the Past/Nurturing the Future," University of Minnesota 1998 Capital Request Brochure.

16. Ibid.

17. Ibid.

18. Phil Davies, "Walter Library," *Minnesota,* September/October 1998, pp. 20–21.

19. Steven J. Rosenstone, "A New School for the 21st Century: The School of Journalism and Communication," January 23, 1998, pp. 1–2.

20. *Legacy,* University of Minnesota Foundation, summer 1999, p. 6.

21. Maureen Smith, "Boom Times," *M,* fall 1999, pp. 1–3.

22. The authors thank Orlyn Miller, University of Minnesota Office of Planning and Programming, Facilities Management, for a summary of the bonding projects, November 2000.

23. Smith, "Boom Times," pp. 1–3.

24. The account of the September 23, 1998, convocation is based on notes made by Ann Pflaum.

25. Notes made by Ann Pflaum.

26. Fall Term University of Minnesota Students of Color Enrollment by Campus, 1989–1999, Office of the Executive Vice President and Provost, March 7, 2000. Appendix A provides enrollments by college in 1950, 1973, and 1998. Exact enrollments for the fall of 1998 are found in University of Minnesota *Facts,* 1999. The numbers were 51,834 systemwide collegiate enrollments, 5,977 students of color, and 2,966 international students.

27. *Fact Sheet,* Office of International Programs, March 1999.

28. Information from Robert Jones to Ann Pflaum, May 8, 2000.

29. Personal communication from Barbara Stedjie Chapin to Ann Pflaum, March 10, 2000. Enrollment from *Facts,* 1999.

30. Barbara S. Chapin to Ann Pflaum, March 10, 2000.

31. Ibid.

32. Personal communication from Toja Okoh to Ann Pflaum, February 1999.

33. Personal communication from Caitlin Fashbaugh to Ann Pflaum, October 1999.

34. Darwin D. Hendel and Jeanne Solberg, *Employment Experiences of University of Minnesota Twin Cities Undergraduates,* June 1991, pp. 1–7. In 1997, a follow-up study showed that 61 percent of freshmen had jobs compared to 49 percent at the University of Washington and 23 percent at the University of Texas at Austin. *Brief,* March 25, 1998.

35. Personal communication from Kingsley Calvo-Jordan to Ann Pflaum, August 2000.

36. Margaret Kaeter, "Cutting Edge," *Inventing Tomorrow,* spring 1996, p. 7.

37. "Defining Herself: Kate Jurik," *GC News,* General College, June 1998, pp. 1, 3.

38. Alyssa Hawkins letter to Dean Alfred Sullivan, College of Natural Resources, June 26, 1998.

39. Judy Woodward, "Going Global," *Inventing Tomorrow,* fall 1999, pp. 22–24.

40. Personal communication from Adam Manwarren to Ann Pflaum, January 2000.

41. Personal communication from Leah Becker to Ann Pflaum, January 6, 2000.

42. Personal communication from Julie Schultz to Ann Pflaum, December 1999.

43. "Extra Credit Homework," *Pictures of Health,* Academic Health Center, winter 1998, p. 9.

44. Personal communication from Murisiku Raifu to Ann Pflaum, January 6, 2000.

45. Kate Tyler, "Carolyn Porta: No Limits," *Network,* spring/summer 1999, pp. 22–23.

46. Yudof, inaugural address, p. 13.

47. Personal communication from Mark G. Yudof to Ann Pflaum, April 10, 2000.

48. The following served as deans or acting deans of CLA during the 1990s: Craig Swan (acting, 1989–91), Julia M. Davis (1991–96), Robert T. Holt (acting, 1996), Steven Rosenstone (1996–).

49. Hugh Davis Graham and Nancy Diamond, *The Rise of American Research Universities* (Baltimore: Johns Hopkins University Press, 1997), pp. 147, 167, placed Minnesota thirteenth among public universities in per-capita publications and funding for research and development between 1986 and 1990. The National Research Council's 1993 report noted CLA departments in the top twenty programs.

50. Steven Rosenstone telephone conversation with Ann Pflaum, December 29, 1999.

51. Engineering departments in 1999 were aerospace engineering and mechanics; chemical engineering and materials science; civil engineering; electrical and computer engineering; mechanical engineering; biomedical engineering; and the Center for Interfacial Engineering. Mathematics was represented by the School of Mathematics and the Institute for Mathematics and Its Application. The physical and computational sciences included astronomy, chemistry, computer sciences and engineering, geology, geophysics, the School of Physics and Astronomy, and the Institute for Theoretical Physics. Other IT units included the Army High Performance Research Center (an inter-university program addressing high-performance computation), the Babbage Institute for the History of Information Processing, the St. Anthony Falls Laboratory, the History of Science and Technology, the Microtechnology Laboratory, and UNITE (University-Industry Television for Education—offering courses via television to area corporations).

52. See Maggi Aitkens, "The Crowning Glory," *Inventing Tomorrow*, Institute of Technology, spring 1996, and p. 13 for listings of IT faculty members elected to the National Academy of Science and the National Academy of Engineering.

53. Acting deans of the Institute of Technology during the 1990s were Gordon Beavers (1991) and Willard Miller (1995).

54. Kaeter, "Cutting Edge," p. 5.

55. Ibid., pp. 5–7.

56. Jacqueline Couillard, "A History of Women in the Institute of Technology: The Technolog Looks Back," *Inventing Tomorrow*, spring 1997, p. 11.

57. Andrew Tellijohn and Paul Sorenson, "Developing Diversity: IT's Programs for Minorities Broaden Its Scope," *Inventing Tomorrow*, fall 1997, pp. 10–11.

58. Among the well-known entrepreneurs from IT were Earl Bakken, EE '48 (Medtronic); Seymour Cray, EE '49 (Cray Research); Frank Donaldson Sr., ME '12 (Donaldson Company); Frank Warner, AE '48, and Robert Keppel, AE '56 (Rosemount Engineering); J. L. Frame, AE '43, Robert Holdahl, AE '43, and James Holdhausen, CE '52 (Fluidyne Engineering). Special issue, "The IT 400," *ITEMS*, summer 1991, pp. 10 ff.

59. Ibid.

60. "The Carlson School of Management" in *A Land-Grant University for the 21ˢᵗ Century*, University of Minnesota Accreditation Self-Study, 1996, p. 162, and *Campaign Minnesota*, University of Minnesota Foundation, 1999.

61. *Brief,* February 15, 1997.

62. *Compact, 1999–2000,* Tab # 10, Carlson School of Management, pp. 2–3.

63. Robert Bruininks, "College Expands Name to Reflect Broad Mission," *The Link*, College of Education, spring 1995, p. 3.

64. *U.S. News & World Report* in 1999 ranked counseling and student personnel psychology, the Institute of Child Development, and school psychology first among national peers; special education and vocational and technical education were each ranked third. This information was provided by James Hearn, chair of educational policy and administration.

65. "University of Minnesota Compact Process, 1999–2000," Office of the Executive Vice President and Provost, Tab # 14, figure 5.

66. "University of Minnesota Compact Process, 1999–2000," Tab #14, pp. 3–4.

67. Yudof, inaugural address, p. 19.

68. "Alumni Profile: Stanley S. Hubbard," *General College Newsletter,* winter 1999, p. 2.

69. David V. Taylor, Dean's Column, *General College Newsletter,* fall 1999 p. 1.

70. Edward S. Adams, "In Pursuit of Excellence: A History of the University of Minnesota Law School, Part VII: The Stein Years—A Time of Advancement and Prosperity," *Minnesota Law Review,* June 1998, p. 1543.

71. *Compact, 1999–2000,* Tab # 23, Law School, pp. 1–2.

72. *Compact, 1999–2000,* p. 2.

73. Herbert Muschamp, "Two for the Roads: A Vision of Urban Design, *New York Times,* Architecture Review, February 13, 1994. Catherine Brown died of cancer in April 1998, at the age of forty-seven.

74. *CALA WORKS: The Journal of the College of Architecture and Landscape Architecture,* summer 1998, pp. 4–5, and fall 1998, pp. 4–5.

75. *CALA WORKS,* 1999, p. 35.

76. *Hubert H. Humphrey Institute Self-Study Report,* April 1995, p. 1.

77. *Hubert H. Humphrey Institute of Public Affairs Bulletin 1998–2000,* October 1998, p. 1.

78. According to the Office of Institutional Research and Reporting, enrollment numbers for the Humphrey Institute are not broken out separately, but are included in Graduate School totals. In fall 1998, there were 200 students enrolled in HHH programs.

79. *Hubert H. Humphrey Institute Self-Study Report,* p. 1.

80. *University of Minnesota Compact Process 1999–2000,* Tab #25.

81. "The Gift of Knowledge," *Legacy,* University of Minnesota Foundation, September 1999, p. 8.

82. Such a facility had been needed for many years. Among those who had long advocated for this, in addition to the university librarian, were library staff members Karen Nelson Hoyle and Andrea Hinding as well as faculty members Rudolph Vecoli and Clarke Chambers.

83. For the Shaughnessy quote and other information, see Minneapolis *Star Tribune,* August 2, 1998. University officials praised the ingenuity and superb craftsmanship that McCrossan brought to the project. See *Friends of the Library Newsletter,* fall 1998, p. 7.

84. *University of Minnesota Compact Process, 1999–2000,* Tab #25.

85. Thomas Shaughnessy, background paper presented to the authors, and personal communication to Ann Pflaum, July 2000.

86. The Lillehei gift is also discussed later in this chapter under "Philanthropy and Alumni Relations."

87. Frank Cerra interview with Ann Pflaum, August 1999, pp. 9, 17.

88. Maureen Smith, "Aiming at the Top in Biology," *Kiosk,* January 1998, p. 1.

89. In 1999, a floor of the University Cancer Center was named in Brown's honor. Chou served as deputy vice president and dean. Cerra became senior vice president of the Academic Health Center. Alfred Michael, "State of the Medical School," *AHC Community News,* April 2000, p. 4.

90. Alfred Michael interview with Ann Pflaum, March 1999, p. 2.

91. Personal communication from Ashley Haase to Ann Pflaum, March 27, 2000.

92. Peggy Rinard, "AHC Creates Biomedical Genomics Center," *AHC Community News,* March 2000, pp. 1, 3.

93. Personal communication from Catherine Verfaillie to Ann Pflaum, March 31, 2000.

94. *Medical Bulletin,* University of Minnesota Medical Foundation, spring 1999, p. 16.

95. *Medical Bulletin,* summer 1999, pp. 2–3.

96. Mark Engebretson, "Animal Research," *Pictures of Health,* Academic Health Center, summer 1999, pp. 5–6. Neuroscientist Walter Low and his research team lost months of research time on work on Parkinson's disease and on a vaccine for the treatment of brain tumors.

97. *AHC Community News,* March 2000, pp. 2, 4.

98. *Brief,* March 24, 1999.

99. Justin Costley, "New Dentistry Dean Has Vision for Future of U," *Minnesota Daily,* May 1, 2000, p. 8.

100. *Pictures of Health,* p. 9

101. Michael Till meeting with Ann Pflaum and Bonnie McCallum, March 22, 1999.

102. *Pictures of Health,* winter 1998, p. 1.

103. *Compact, 1999–2000,* Tab #13, Dentistry, p. 6.

104. "Four Deans and Administrators Share Their Thoughts on Education," *Minnesota,* May/June 1993, pp. 24–25.

105. *Minnesota Daily,* July 11, 1997.

106. *AHC Community News,* February 2000.

107. Frank Clancy, "Holistic Health Goes Mainstream," *Pictures of Health,* spring 1999, p. 10. Other Academic Health Center firsts included a successful pediatric bone marrow transplant, a kidney biopsy in a child, pediatric open-heart surgery, the development of safe neonatal and pediatric homodialysis, the development of successful pediatric renal transplant strategies, the development of charcoal hemoperfusion for poisonings, the use of an incubator to transport infants on planes, and a cystic fibrosis vest. *Medical Bulletin,* fall 1999, p. 10.

108. Clancy, "Holistic Health Goes Mainstream," p. 10.

109. "Achieving Wellness through Body, Mind, and Spirit," *Legacy,* summer 1999, p. 3.

110. Robert J. Cipolle, Linda M. Strand, and Peter C. Morley, *Pharmaceutical Care Practice* (New York: McGraw Hill, 1998), p. 6.

111. Jack Hayes, "Joe Pharmacist," *Pictures of Health,* spring 1999, p. 12. Hanlon was appointed to the VFW Chair of Pharmacotherapy for the Elderly in 1998.

112. Frank Clancy, "Drug Money," *Pictures of Health,* summer 1999, p. 8.

113. Background on the research agenda of faculty in a personal communication from Dean Marilyn Speedie to Ann Pflaum, September 1999.

114. *Pharmacy Record: The Newsletter of the College of Pharmacy, University of Minnesota,* spring 1992, offered a concise overview of the accomplishments of the college over 100 years.

115. Gordon Slovut, "Generous Couple Bequeaths Record $13.5 Million to University of Minnesota," Minneapolis *Star Tribune,* February 25, 1994, pp. 1A, 20A.

116. Among the institute's projects was a study of the developing practice of pharmaceutical care drawing on 13,000 patient encounters; another was a text for practitioners by Robert J. Cipolle, Linda M. Strand, and Peter C. Morley, *Pharmaceutical Care Practice,* cited earlier. The center also hosted meetings for international pharmacists.

117. Personal communication from Marilyn Speedie to Ann Pflaum, September 1999. Gilbert Banker was dean from 1985 to 1992. Robert J. Cipolle and Larry Weaver served as acting deans between 1992 and 1996.

118. Edith Leyasmeyer, *University of Minnesota School of Public Health Bulletin,* 1996, p. 3. Other deans were Robert Kane and Stephen Joseph.

119. "A Land-Grant University for the 21st Century," pp. 121–22; *The Nation's Health,* a publication of the APHA, August 1996; "School of Public Health Report on Outreach," 1997.

120. *Compact, 1999–2000,* Tab #34, Veterinary Medicine, p. 1.

121. "A Raptor to Remember," *Pictures of Health,* winter 1998, p. 10.

122. *Compact,* pp. 1 and 21.

123. *Biennial Report of the President and the Board of Regents of the University of Minnesota to the Legislature of the State of Minnesota, 1950–52,* December 30, 1952, p. 208, reported a total of 3,732 (536 women; 3,196 men), and page 155 reports the number of programs; *Facts 1999,* pp. 5–6, reported graduate enrollments of 8,201 (4,311 men and 3,890 women). For program numbers in the 1990s, see *Compact, 1999–2000,* Tab # 32, Graduate School, pp. 1–2.

124. Office of Sponsored Projects, Fall 1999, and for 1950 see letter, Office of the Comptroller, November 15, 1951, from C. S. Plank to E. C. Jackson. The total for 1950–51 was $4,058,615 (62 percent from federal sources, 14 percent from state sources, 20 percent from gifts, and 4 percent from endowments).

125. *The Biennial Report, 1950–52,* p. 270, and for the 1997 patents, "Levels and Trends in Sponsored Programs" (February 1998), University of Minnesota Office of Research and Technology Transfer Administration, p. 43. Within the eight patent applications for 1950–51 was Serial No. 218,712 to Alfred O. C. Nier, mass spectrometer apparatus. Nier had continued to refine the instrument that had led to his major discovery isolating uranium 235. The mass spectrometer that he constructed for his 1940 experiments weighed more than two tons; its great-grandchild, constructed by the physics department as part of a research project related to the NASA Mars flight in 1975, weighed eight pounds and was eight inches high and six inches deep. See Lesley Swanson, "The Mass Spectrometer," *Science and Technology,* University of Minnesota, fall 1970, pp. 3–4.

126. *Compact, 1999–2000,* Tab #32, Graduate School, pp. 6–7.

127. "Funding Success Is Boast for Biology," *CBS Alumni News,* spring 1998, pp.

1, 3; summer 1999, pp. 4–6. Following Richard Caldecott, Doug⌐
Harrison Tordoff (1986–87) were interim deans.

128. *Kiosk,* November 1998; *Brief,* October 7 and 15, 1997.

129. Deane Morrison, "Mighty Microbes," *Frontiers,* College ⌐
fall 1999, pp. 4–6.

130. Deane Morrison and Nancy Rose, "A Can of Worms," *F⌐*
10–11, and for the "Sleeping Beauty gene," information provided
assistant dean of the College of Biological Sciences, July 17, 2000.

131. Deane Morrison, "Gold from Gombe," *Frontiers,* spring 1⌐
was also known for her research, in collaboration with Craig Packer, ⌐
ber in the Department of Ecology, Evolution, and Behavior, on lion⌐

132. Geoff Gordon, "Minnesota's Wildest Classroom," *Frontiers,*
4–6.

133. *1996 Accreditation Self-Study of the Twin Cities Campus: A ⌐
versity for the Twenty-first Century,* Office of Planning and Analysis: O⌐
Vice President for Academic Affairs, April 1996, pp. 143–50. (Herea⌐
*Accreditation.*)

134. *Compact, 1999–2000,* Tab # 5, COAFES, pp. 1–5.

135. Minneapolis *Star Tribune,* April 30, 2000, p. 1A described con⌐
netically modified corn in Japan.

136. *Journey Home: College of Human Ecology 1894–1996,* University⌐
1996, p. 47; *1996 Accreditation,* pp. 156–57; and *Compact, 1999–2000,* Ta⌐
Ecology, p. 1.

137. Information provided by the College of Human Ecology dean⌐
2000.

138. *1996 Accreditation,* pp. 164–65, and *Compact, 1999–2000,* Tab #29⌐
sources, pp. 1–8.

139. Personal communication from Alan Hunter, associate dean, curric⌐
dent affairs, and Morse Alumni Distinguished Professor of Animal Science, J⌐

140. Mary K. Hoff, "Gene by Gene," *Pictures of Health,* spring/summer⌐

141. Herbert Wray, "High Tech Teaching," *U.S. News & World Repor⌐*
*leges, 1999,* August 31, 1998, p. 65.

142. *Compact, 1999–2000,* Tab #1, University of Minnesota, Crookston, ⌐

143. Wray, "High Tech Teaching," p. 65.

144. Personal communication from Barbara Muesing to Ann Pflaum, June⌐

145. Ibid.

146. Information provided by the UMD Office of University Relations, M⌐

147. Information provided by UMD Sports Information, May 2000.

148. Ken Moran and Neil T. Storch, *UMD Comes of Age: The First One ⌐*
*Years* (Virginia Beach, Va.: Donning, 1996), pp. 182–207, 211; "The New UMD ⌐
UMD fact sheet, 1998; *Duluth News Tribune,* August 8, 1997, July 27, 1998, M⌐
1999; *Research Review,* Office of Research and Technology Transfer, October 199⌐
sonal communication from Milan Bajmoczi to Ann Pflaum, March 7, 1999.

149. Susan Beasy Lotto, *UMD News,* October 8, 1999.

150. Information on enrollment from Gail Kehoe, Office of Institutional Res⌐
June 2000, and information on the library from Basil Sozansky, UMD librarian.

151. *Compact, 1999–2000,* Tab# 2, University of Minnesota Duluth, p. 1.

152. Chad Hamilton, "Dr. Gerald Hill Named 1999 American Indian Physician the Year," *UMD News,* October 20, 1999.

153. *Lake Effect: University of Minnesota Duluth,* no date, p. 3.

154. Personal communication from Milan Bajmoczi to Ann Pflaum, March 7, 1999.

155. UMD College of Science and Engineering, December 17, 1997, from Janny 'alker, assistant to the dean, to Ann Pflaum.

156. *Compact, 1999–2000,* Tab # 2, University of Minnesota Duluth, p. 2.

157. *Compact, 1999–2000,* Tab # 2, p. 8.

158. College in the Schools programs in Minnesota offered college-level enrichment o high school teachers, making available the possibility of advanced credit for high chool students who completed these courses. In 1998–99, courses were offered in omposition, computer science, economics, English literature, French, history, humani- ies, physics, Spanish, and theater. *University of Minnesota, 1998–99 Credit and Non- Credit Bulletin,* University College Duluth, Continuing and Professional Education, p. 68.

159. Personal communication from Louis Poirier, director of University College, University of Minnesota, Duluth, and Andrea Gilats, director of the Split Rock Arts Program, to Ann Pflaum, December 1999.

160. *Institutional Data Book, 1996–97,* University of Minnesota, Morris, p. 17.

161. Elizabeth Blake, Steven Granger, and Gary McGrath, "The Morris Campus," March 1999, p. 6.

162. *Institutional Data Book, 1997–98,* University of Minnesota, Morris.

163. Personal communication from Kjersti Hanneman to Ann Pflaum, January 6, 1999.

164. John Q. Imholte interview with Clarke Chambers, August 1984, p. 41.

165. Elizabeth S. Blake, "The Public Liberal Arts Colleges: Commonweal and Commonwealth," address at the annual meeting of the Council of Public Liberal Arts Colleges, Keene State College, Keene, New Hampshire, June 21, 1993, p. 3; copy kindly provided by Professor Blake.

166. Massy Dylla and Mike Nelson, "Samuel Schuman named Chancellor UMM," University of Minnesota News Service, February 21, 2000.

167. Victor Johnson, *Mayo Clinic: Its Growth and Progress* (Bloomington, Minn.: Voyageur Press, 1984), p. 10.

168. *1996 Accreditation,* p. 313.

169. *University College Report of Activities 1997–98,* University College was the co- ordinator for the university's presence in Rochester until July 1999, when that role was assumed by Associate Vice President Mary Heltsley.

170. Personal communication from Carol Lund to Ann Pflaum, November 1999.

171. *Partnerships for the 21st Century: Academic Plan for Rochester,* 2000.

172. Yudof, inaugural address, p. 13.

173. Appendix A documents enrollment in 1950, 1973, and 1998. In 1950, colle- giate enrollment was just over 22,000 and registration in Continuing Education and Minnesota Extension courses was 42,450; in 1973, collegiate enrollment was 46,000 and the UMES/CCE enrollment was 64,000; and in 1998, collegiate enrollment was over 51,000 and the two outreach units enrolled just over 80,000 students.

174. Information on the university home page "hits" from Tony Mommsen, Office of Institutional Relations, to Ann Pflaum, May 5, 2000.

175. "Campaign Minnesota: A Defining Moment" listed a number of annual outreach contacts: 700,000 through the University of Minnesota Extension Service; 150,000 visitors to the Weisman Art Museum; 100,000 patients through the Dental Clinics; 215,000 visitors to the Minnesota Landscape Arboretum; 90,000 people attending dance, music, and theater programs; 1 million youth and adults in Bell Museum classes, courses, and outreach programs.

176. Telephone communication from Thomas Scott to Ann Pflaum, May 2000.

177. Patrick Borich was dean and director of the University of Minnesota Extension Service from 1983 to 1995, Gail Skinner-West was interim director from 1995 to 1996, Katherine Fennelly was dean and director from 1996 to 1999, and former regent Charles Casey was interim dean in 1999.

178. Scott Joseph Peters, "Extension Work as Public Work: Reconsidering Cooperative Extension's Civic Mission" (Ph.D. dissertation, University of Minnesota, 1998), pp. 228–35.

179. *Biennial Report of the President and the Board of Regents of the University of Minnesota to the Legislature of the State of Minnesota, 1972–1974,* June 30, 1974, p. 147 showed CEE registrations for 1972–73 of 37,510; University College Report of Activities 1997–98 showed credit and noncredit registrations in 1997–98, Miller's last year as dean, of 137,923.

180. University College, College of Continuing Education, *Annual Report,* 1998–99, p. 9.

181. Information provided to the authors by Gail Skinner-West and Gerald Klement, interim dean and administrative officer of the College of Continuing Education, December 1999.

182. *CURA after 25 Years,* Center for Urban and Regional Affairs, University of Minnesota, 1996, p. 31. This publication provides an excellent overview of CURA's contributions to the state. Readers are also referred to the CURA *Reporter,* a publication documenting specific initiatives and findings.

183. The National History Day program for secondary school students was inaugurated by the history department while Stanford Lehmberg was chair in the 1980s. It encouraged thousands of students to undertake historical research projects and sent hundreds of them to national competitions, where a number received honors. See Minneapolis *Star Tribune,* April 26, 2000, p. E1.

184. Andrew Tellijohn, "Tuning in to Education," *Inventing Tomorrow,* summer 1998, p. 17.

185. "Givens Foundation Sponsors Read-In," *General College Newsletter,* winter 1999, p. 3.

186. *College of Biological Sciences Bulletin 1997–1999,* p. 49.

187. Jack Hayes and Peggy Rinard, "Country Clinicians," *Pictures of Health,* fall 1998, p. 9.

188. *Pictures of Health,* winter 1999, p. 4.

189. In fall 1999, there were 3,248 international students at the University of Minnesota. Institutional Research and Reporting, January 10, 2000, p. 14, and Mary Shafer, "Global U," *M,* winter 1999, p. 2.

190. Chris Coughlin Smith, "Grid Expectations," *Minnesota,* July/August 1999, p. 42, and Patrick Hayes and David LaVigue, "Mason Signs Seven-Year $7 Million Contract," *Minnesota Daily,* June 19, 2000, p. 7.

191. *Minnesota Hockey 1999–2000,* Men's Intercollegiate Athletics, 1999, p. 69.

192. Background information provided by the office of Vice President Tonya Moten Brown.

193. President Mark Yudof, press conference, October 24, 2000.

194. Media guides published by Men's Intercollegiate Athletics provide useful background on the histories of the teams with brief biographies of the players and coaches. Media guides were published each year for the ten intercollegiate sports: baseball, basketball, cross-country, football, golf, gymnastics, swimming, tennis, track and field, and wrestling.

195. *1998–99 Minnesota Women's Golf,* 1998, Women's Intercollegiate Athletics, p. 31, and Pam Schmid and Sheila Mulrooney Eldred, "Chris Voelz: Agent of Change," Minneapolis *Star Tribune,* May 2, 1999, pp. C1, C8.

196. Personal communication, Becky Bohm to Ann Pflaum, fall 2000.

197. Personal communication, James Turman to Ann Pflaum, fall 2000.

198. Ibid.

199. Gerald B. Fischer, "1999 Fund-Raising Highlights," Report to the Board of Regents, November 12, 1999, pp. 4, 16.

200. Dale R. Olseth, Russell M. Bennett, Marvin Borman, Duane R. Kullberg, James R. Campbell, Luella Goldberg, and Douglas W. Leatherdale, chairs of the foundation trustees from 1985 through the 1990s, laid the groundwork for Campaign Minnesota.

201. *Campaign Minnesota: A Defining Moment,* University of Minnesota Foundation, 1999, p. 1.

202. Tracy Bauman, "A Time to Give," *Minnesota,* November/December 1999, pp. 30–32.

203. Robert Franklin, "Carlson's Love for 'U' Lives on in $10 Million," Minneapolis *Star Tribune,* July 9, 1999, p. 1A.

204. Martha Douglas, "U of M Receives $10 Million from Cargill for Microbial and Plant Genetics Building," University of Minnesota News Service, September 7, 1999.

205. *M,* fall 1999, p. 3.

206. Mary Jane Smetanka, "McKnight Gives U $15 Million," Minneapolis *Star Tribune,* December 17, 1999, p. A29.

207. Excerpts from statements by teaching award winners, *Minnesota,* July–August 1999, pp. 51–52.

208. *M,* fall 1999, p. 14.

209. McNamara, quote, in Gerald Fischer, "1998 Fundraising Highlights," report to the Board of Regents, November 12, 1998, p. 31.

## Epilogue

1. *Facts,* March 2000, p. 1.

2. Figures for interaction with the public in 1998–99 included 700,000 contacts through the University of Minnesota Extension Service, 100,000 visitors to the Weisman

Art Museum, 100,000 patient visits in the Dental Clinics, 215,000 visitors to the Landscape Arboretum (University of Minnesota Foundation, *A Defining Moment,* June 4, 1999, p. 7).

3. The university's Web address in spring 2000 was http://www.umn.edu.

4. This list is from *Facts,* March 2000, p. 1.

5. *Facts,* March 2000, p. 2, and see University of Minnesota Foundation, *A Defining Moment.*

6. Office of the Vice President for Research, "Discovering Our Pride," August 2000, p. 3.

7. University of Minnesota Foundation, November 2000.

8. Information provided by the Office of Reseach Planning and Analyis, University of Minnesota, April 2000.

9. Among programs listed among the top ten in the 1993 National Research Council ranking were chemical engineering, geography, psychology, mechanical engineering, economics, forestry (natural resources), applied mathematics, management information systems, pharmacy, public health, education (educational psychology, special education, vocational/technical education, and counseling/personnel services), and health services administration. (The National Research Council did not rank agricultural programs or professional schools.)

10. Mark G. Yudof, Campaign Case Statement, June 4, 1999, p. 5.

11. Minneapolis *Star Tribune,* April 9, 2000, pp. A23–24.

12. Jim Klobuchar, "U Doesn't Have to Be What It Was 40 Years Ago," Minneapolis *Star Tribune,* September 7, 1993, p. 3B.

# Index

AAAC. *See* Afro-American Action Committee

Aalto, Alvar, 45

AAUP. *See* American Association of University Professors

Abbe, Mary, 216

Abraham, Roland, 83

Academic freedom, 97–98, 350n.220

Academic Health Center (AHC), 248–50, 252, 276–77, 307–8

Academy of Distinguished Teachers, 262

Acosta, Roberto, 137

Activism, 69, 114–27

Activities and Readings in Geography of the United States. *See* ARGUS program

Adams, Carl, 186

Adams, John, 233, 243–44, 261

Adams, Russell, 233

Administration: postwar, 37–47

Admission requirements: humanities program, 20

Adorno, Theodor, 306

Advanced Genetic Analysis Center, 284

Aelony, Zev, 99, 115

Aerospace engineering and mechanics, 227–29

African American Learning Resource Center, Twin Cities campus, 262

African American Studies, Department of, 20, 116–18, 123–24, 142, 147, 264, 268

Afro-American Action Committee (AAAC), 116, 118

Agricultural and Applied Economics, Department of, 27, 35–37

Agricultural Experiment Station. *See* Minnesota Experiment Station

Agricultural Extension Service. *See* University of Minnesota Extension Service

Agricultural, Food, and Environmental Sciences, College of (COAFES), 287–88

Agriculture, College/Department/ School of, xvi, 48–49; alumni society, 60; Crookston campus, 104

Agriculture, Forestry, and Home Economics, Institute of, 6, 27, 35, 47, 49, 82, 128, 161

Ag-Royal Days, 15

AHC. *See* Academic Health Center

AIDS research, 277

Akerman, John D., 227

Aldous, Joan, 126

Allen, C. Eugene, 162, 213, 308

Allen, Harold, 18

Alpha Tau Omega fraternity, 222

Al's Breakfast, Minneapolis, 14

**Stanford Lehmberg,** professor emeritus of history, was a member of the history department at the University of Minnesota from 1969 until his retirement in 1999; he served as department chairman during the 1980s. A historian of early modern England, he is the author of two biographies, two volumes on Parliament under Henry VIII, and two studies of English cathedrals. Twice a Guggenheim Fellow, he holds both the Ph.D. and the Litt.D. from Cambridge University and is a Fellow of the Royal Historical Society and the Society of Antiquaries of London.

**Ann M. Pflaum** earned the Ph.D. in history from the University of Minnesota; she also holds degrees from Smith College and Harvard University. She served on the staffs of several University of Minnesota presidents and vice presidents from 1976 through 1988, and from 1988 to 2000 she was associate dean of the College of Continuing Education. She was appointed the university's sesquicentennial historian in 2000.